The Philosophy of the Enlightenment

THE PHILOSOPHY
OF THE
ENLIGHTENMENT

By Ernst Cassirer

TRANSLATED BY FRITZ C. A. KOELLN AND
JAMES P. PETTEGROVE

BEACON PRESS · BOSTON

This is a translation of *Die Philosophie der Aufklärung*, the German edition of which was published by J. C. B. Mohr in Tübingen in 1932. All the translator's notes have been provided by Mr. Pettegrove, and unless otherwise specified, all French and Latin sources quoted have been translated by him. He is indebted to Dr. Walter H. Freeman for valuable assistance in translating the Latin.

First Beacon Paperback edition published 1955
Reprinted by arrangement with Princeton University Press

PREFACE

THE present book aims to be both more and less than a monograph on the philosophy of the Enlightenment. It is much less, for the primary task of such a monograph would be to offer the reader a wealth of detail and to trace the genesis and development of all the special problems of this philosophy. The form and intention of the "Outline of the Philosophical Sciences" (*Grundriss der philosophischen Wissenschaften*) do not permit such a treatment. Within the limits of the general plan of this series it was not possible to survey exhaustively the entire complex of problems with which the philosophy of the Enlightenment was concerned. An extensive treatment had to be sacrificed to the need for a purely intensive treatment. The Enlightenment had, therefore, to be approached in its characteristic depth rather than in its breadth, and to be presented in the light of the unity of its conceptual origin and of its underlying principle rather than of the totality of its historical manifestations and results. Under the circumstances, it seemed less desirable to give a merely narrative account of the growth and vicissitudes of the philosophy of the Enlightenment than to set forth, as it were, the dramatic action of its thinking. The peculiar charm and real systematic value of the philosophy of this age lie in its development, in the intellectual energy which spurs it on, and in the enthusiasm with which it attacks all its various problems. Looked at in this manner many aspects of the philosophy of the Enlightenment assume a unity which, if they were treated solely from the viewpoint of their results, would appear as irreconcilable contradictions or as a mere eclectic mixture of heterogeneous thought elements. The tensions and solutions, the doubts and decisions, the skepticism and unshakable conviction of this philosophy must be seen and interpreted from one central position if its real historical meaning is to be made clear.

Such an interpretation is the aim of this book. It places the philosophy of the Enlightenment against the background of another and broader historical and philosophical theme not enlarged upon here, but merely indicated in its general outlines.

Preface

For the movement to be described is not self-contained, but looks before and after beyond its own confines. It forms but a part and a special phase of that whole intellectual development through which modern philosophic thought gained its characteristic self-confidence and self-consciousness. In former works, especially *Individual and Cosmos in the Philosophy of the Renaissance* (1927) and *The Platonic Renaissance in England* (1932), I have tried to present and evaluate other phases of this great movement. The present account of the philosophy of the Enlightenment resembles those works both in matter and in method. It employs, too, the same approach to the philosophy of history, an approach whose aim is not to record and describe bare results, but rather to elucidate the inner formative forces. Such a presentation of philosophical doctrines and systems endeavors as it were to give a "phenomenology of the philosophic spirit"; it is an attempt to show how this spirit, struggling with purely objective problems, achieves clarity and depth in its understanding of its own nature and destiny, and of its own fundamental character and mission. I no longer dare to hope, much less to promise, that I shall still produce a comprehensive survey of all my preliminary studies. For the time being these studies may be considered as mere building stones of whose fragmentary character I am fully aware. But I hope they will be utilized in the construction of a larger whole when the time is ripe for such an edifice.

The philosophy of the Enlightenment offers especially favorable conditions for a treatment such as I have outlined. For the permanent results of this philosophy do not lie in teachings which it develops and tries to formulate into a body of dogma. Far more than the men of the epoch were aware, their teachings were dependent on the preceding centuries. Enlightenment philosophy simply fell heir to the heritage of those centuries; it ordered, sifted, developed, and clarified this heritage rather than contributed and gave currency to new and original ideas. Yet in spite of this dependence with respect to content, the Enlightenment produced a completely original form of philosophic thought. Even when it reworks prevailing ideas, when it merely continues to build on a foundation laid by the seven-

Preface

teenth century—as is the case with its cosmology—everything takes on new meaning and appears in a new perspective. For nothing less than the universal process of philosophizing is now seen in a new light. In England and France, the Enlightenment begins by breaking down the older form of philosophic knowledge, the metaphysical systems. It has lost faith in the "spirit of systems"; it sees in this spirit not so much the strength of, as an obstacle to, philosophic reason. But in renouncing, and even in directly opposing, the "spirit of systems" (*esprit de système*), the philosophy of the Enlightenment by no means gives up the "systematic spirit" (*esprit systématique*); it aims rather to further this spirit in another and more effective manner. Instead of confining philosophy within the limits of a systematic doctrinal structure, instead of tying it to definite immutable axioms and deductions from them, the Enlightenment wants philosophy to move freely and in this immanent activity to discover the fundamental form of reality, the form of all natural and spiritual being. Philosophy, according to this interpretation, is no special field of knowledge situated beside or above the principles of natural science, of law and government, etc., but rather the all-comprehensive medium in which such principles are formulated, developed, and founded. Philosophy is no longer to be separated from science, history, jurisprudence, and politics; it is rather to be the atmosphere in which they can exist and be effective. Philosophy is no longer the isolated substance of the intellect; it presents the totality of intellect in its true function, in the specific character of its investigations and inquiries, its methods and essential cognitive process. Accordingly, all those philosophical concepts and problems, which the eighteenth century simply took over from the past, move into new positions and undergo a characteristic change of meaning. They are transformed from fixed and finished forms into active forces, from bare results into imperatives. This is the really productive significance of the thought of the Enlightenment. It is revealed not so much in any particular thought content as in the use the Enlightenment makes of philosophic thought, and the position and task it assigns to such thought. If the eighteenth century proudly calls itself a "philosophical century," this claim is justified in so far as philosophy now comes into its own again and takes on its original, truly "classical" meaning. Philosophy is no longer limited to the realm of mere thought; it demands and finds access to that deeper order of things whence all intellectual activity, like thought itself, springs, and in which such activity—according to the fundamental conviction of the philosophy of the Enlightenment— must seek its basis. Thus we miss the real meaning of the philosophy of the Enlightenment if we regard it and dispose of it merely as a "philosophy of reflection." No less a thinker than Hegel first pursued this line of criticism, and by the authority of his name established it once and for all. But even in Hegel we find a tendency to correct himself, for the judgment of Hegel as historian and philosopher of history is by no means in complete agreement with the verdict which Hegel the metaphysician passes on the Enlightenment. In the *Phenomenology of the Spirit*, he draws a richer and deeper picture of the period of the Enlightenment than he usually sketches for purely polemical purposes. Actually the fundamental tendency and the main endeavor of the philosophy of the Enlightenment are not to observe life and to portray it in terms of reflective thought. This philosophy believes rather in an original spontaneity of thought; it attributes to thought not merely an imitative function but the power and the task of shaping life itself. Thought consists not only in analyzing and dissecting, but in actually bringing about that order of things which it conceives as necessary, so that by this act of fulfillment it may demonstrate its own reality and truth.

We gain no access to the deeper strata of the philosophy of the Enlightenment if, like most historians of the period, we merely consider this philosophy lengthwise, that is, if we just string its various intellectual formulations along the thread of time and study them chronologically. Such an approach is always unsatisfactory from the viewpoint of method, but its shortcomings never appear so clearly as in the treatment of eighteenth century philosophy. With the seventeenth century one can still hope to characterize the sum total of its philosophical content and development by tracing this development

Preface

from system to system, from Descartes to Malebranche, from Spinoza to Leibniz, and from Bacon and Hobbes to Locke. But this approach to philosophy fails us on the threshold of the eighteenth century. For the system as such has now lost its power to synthesize and represent the various elements of philosophy. Even Christian Wolff, who tried his hardest to retain the philosophical system because he looked upon it as containing the real truth of philosophy, sought in vain to reduce the totality of the philosophical problems of the time to a system. The thought of the Enlightenment again and again breaks through the rigid barriers of system and tries, especially among its greatest and most original minds, to escape this strict systematic discipline. The true nature of Enlightenment thinking cannot be seen in its purest and clearest form where it is formulated into particular doctrines, axioms, and theorems; but rather where it is in process, where it is doubting and seeking, tearing down and building up. All this constantly fluctuating activity cannot be resolved into a mere summation of individual teachings. The real philosophy of the Enlightenment is not simply the sum total of what its leading thinkers—Voltaire and Montesquieu, Hume or Condillac, d'Alembert or Diderot, Wolff or Lambert—thought and taught. It cannot be presented in a summation of the views of these men, nor in the temporal sequence of their views; for it consists less in certain individual doctrines than in the form and manner of intellectual activity in general. The fundamental intellectual forces with which we are here concerned can be grasped only in action and in the constantly evolving process of thought; only in process can the pulsation of the inner intellectual life of the Enlightenment be felt. The philosophy of the Enlightenment belongs to those masterpieces of intellectual fabric in which

> "One treadle sets a thousand threads in motion,
> The shuttles shoot to and fro,
> Unperceived the threads flow."[1]

Historical consideration and reconstruction of the period of the

---

[1] "Wo Ein Tritt tausend Fäden regt,
Die Schifflein herüber hinüber schiessen,
Die Fäden ungesehen fliessen. . . ."—Goethe, *Faust*, Part I, lines 1924-26.

Preface

Enlightenment must look upon the elucidation of these "unperceived" threads as its supreme task. The present book has tried to accomplish this task, not by endeavoring to give a history of individual thinkers and their teachings but by means of a history of the ideas of the epoch of the Enlightenment. It has aimed not only to set forth these teachings in their abstract theoretical form but also in their immediate operation. In order to do this, an abundance of detail had to be omitted; yet none of those essential forces could be neglected which shaped the picture of the philosophy of the Enlightenment, and which determined its basic view of nature, history, society, religion, and art. Pursuing this path, one sees that the philosophy of the Enlightenment, which is still usually treated as an eclectic mixture of the most diverse thought elements, is in fact dominated by a few great fundamental ideas expressed with strict consistency and in exact arrangement. Every historical account of the Enlightenment must begin with these ideas, for only so can it discover the sure key to the labyrinth of individual dogmas and doctrines.

A sytematic critique of the philosophy of the Enlightenment could not be undertaken within the scope of this book. I had to adopt for this study the Spinozist motto: "Smile not, lament not, nor condemn; but understand" (*non ridere, non lugere, neque detestari, sed intelligere*). The epoch of the Enlightenment has seldom been blessed with such a mode of presentation. It is customary to consider it a major shortcoming of this epoch that it lacked understanding of the historically distant and foreign, and that in naive overconfidence it set up its own standards as the absolute, and only valid and possible, norm for the evaluation of historical events. But if the Enlightenment cannot be acquitted of this fault, one must admit that it has suffered for it even beyond its deserts. For that very pride in "knowing better," of which this period has been accused, has been pointed out over and over again; and from it a multitude of prejudices have emerged which to this day are an obstacle to an impartial study and appraisal of Enlightenment philosophy. The following account, which has no polemical intentions, has nowhere ventured to criticize these prejudices and to "rescue" the En-

Preface

lightenment from them. The aim of this book was simply to develop and to explain historically and systematically the content and point of view of the philosophy of the Enlightenment. Such an explanation is the first and indispensable step toward a revision of the verdict of the Romantic Movement on the Enlightenment. This verdict is still accepted by many without criticism, and the slogan of the "shallow Enlightenment" is still in vogue. A major objective of this study would be achieved if it succeeded in silencing that slogan. Needless to say, following Kant's achievement and the intellectual revolution accomplished by Kant's *Critique of Pure Reason*, it is no longer possible to return to the questions and answers of the philosophy of the Enlightenment. But whenever that "History of Pure Reason" is written which Kant sketched in the last section of his *Critique of Pure Reason*, it will have to recall especially the period which discovered and passionately defended the autonomy of reason, and which firmly established this concept in all fields of knowledge. No account of the history of philosophy can be oriented to history alone. The consideration of the philosophic past must always be accompanied by philosophical reorientation and self-criticism. More than ever before, it seems to me, the time is again ripe for applying such self-criticism to the present age, for holding up to it that bright clear mirror fashioned by the Enlightenment. Much that seems to us today the result of "progress" will to be sure lose its luster when seen in this mirror; and much that we boast of will look strange and distorted in this perspective. But we should be guilty of hasty judgment and dangerous self-deception if we were simply to ascribe these distortions to opaque spots in the mirror, rather than to look elsewhere for their source. The slogan: *Sapere aude* (dare to know), which Kant called the "motto of the Enlightenment," also holds for our own historical relation to that period. Instead of assuming a derogatory air, we must take courage and measure our powers against those of the age of the Enlightenment, and thus find a proper adjustment. The age which venerated reason and science as man's highest faculty cannot and must not be lost even for us. We must find a way not only to see that age in its own shape but to release again

Preface

those original forces which brought forth and molded this shape.

I cannot end this preface without mentioning my indebtedness to Professor Fritz Medicus, on whose original suggestion this book was written and who assisted with the proofreading of the original edition. My thanks are also due to Miss Alix Heilbrunner for the authors' index in the original edition.

ERNST CASSIRER

Hamburg
October 1932

CONTENTS

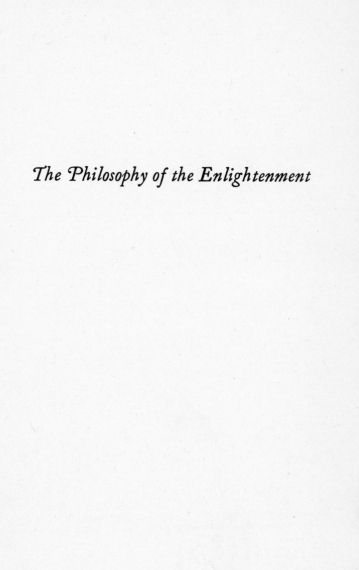

The Philosophy of the Enlightenment

CHAPTER I

The Mind of the Enlightenment

D'ALEMBERT begins his essay on the *Elements of Philosophy* with a general portrait of the mind of the mid-eighteenth century. He prefaces his portrait with the observation that in the intellectual life of the last three hundred years the mid-century mark has consistently been an important turning-point. The Renaissance commences in the middle of the fifteenth century; the Reformation reaches its climax in the middle of the sixteenth century; and in the middle of the seventeenth century the Cartesian philosophy triumphantly alters the entire world picture. Can an analogous movement be observed in the eighteenth century? If so, how can its direction and general tendency be characterized? Pursuing this thought further, d'Alembert writes:

"If one examines carefully the mid-point of the century in which we live, the events which excite us or at any rate occupy our minds, our customs, our achievements, and even our diversions, it is difficult not to see that in some respects a very remarkable change in our ideas is taking place, a change whose rapidity seems to promise an even greater transformation to come. Time alone will tell what will be the goal, the nature, and the limits of this revolution whose shortcomings and merits will be better known to posterity than to us. . . . Our century is called, accordingly, the century of philosophy par excellence. . . . If one considers without bias the present state of our knowledge, one cannot deny that philosophy among us has shown progress. Natural science from day to day accumulates new riches. Geometry, by extending its limits, has borne its torch into the regions of physical science which lay nearest at hand. The true system of the world has been recognized, developed, and perfected. . . . In short, from the earth to Saturn, from the history of the heavens to that of insects, natural philosophy has been revolutionized; and nearly all other fields of knowledge have assumed new forms. . . .

"The study of nature seems in itself to be cold and dull because the satisfaction derived from it consists in a uniform, continued, and uninterrupted feeling, and its pleasures, to be intense, must be intermittent and spasmodic. . . . Nevertheless, the discovery and application of a new method of philosophizing, the kind of enthusiasm which accompanies discoveries, a certain exaltation of ideas which the spectacle of the universe produces in us—all these causes have brought about a lively fermentation of minds. Spreading through nature in all directions like a river which has burst its dams, this fermentation has swept with a sort of violence everything along with it which stood in its way. . . . Thus, from the principles of the secular sciences to the foundations of religious revelation, from metaphysics to matters of taste, from music to morals, from the scholastic disputes of theologians to matters of trade, from the laws of princes to those of peoples, from natural law to the arbitrary laws of nations . . . everything has been discussed and analyzed, or at least mentioned. The fruit or sequel of this general effervescence of minds has been to cast new light on some matters and new shadows on others, just as the effect of the ebb and flow of the tides is to leave some things on the shore and to wash others away."[1]

These are the words of one of the most important scholars of the age and of one of its intellectual spokesmen. Hence they represent a direct expression of the nature and trend of contemporary intellectual life. The age of d'Alembert feels itself impelled by a mighty movement, but it refuses to abandon itself to this force. It wants to know the whence and whither, the origin and the goal, of its impulsion. For this age, knowledge of its own activity, intellectual self-examination, and foresight are the proper function and essential task of thought. Thought not only seeks new, hitherto unknown goals but it wants to know where it is going and to determine for itself the direction of its journey. It encounters the world with fresh joy and the courage of discovery, daily expecting new revelations. Yet its thirst for knowledge and intellectual curiosity are directed not only toward the external world; the thought of this age is even more

[1] D'Alembert, "Éléments de Philosophie," in *Mélanges de Littérature, d'Histoire, et de Philosophie*, nouvelle édition, six volumes, Amsterdam, 1759, vol. IV, pp. 3-6.

passionately impelled by that other question of the nature and potentiality of thought itself. Time and again thought returns to its point of departure from its various journeys of exploration intended to broaden the horizon of objective reality. Pope gave brief and pregnant expression to this deep-seated feeling of the age in the line: "The proper study of mankind is man." The age senses that a new force is at work within it; but it is even more fascinated by the activity of this force than by the creations brought forth by that activity. It rejoices not only in results, but it inquires into, and attempts to explain, the form of the process leading to these results. The problem of intellectual "progress" throughout the eighteenth century appears in this light. Perhaps no other century is so completely permeated by the idea of intellectual progress as that of the Enlightenment. But we mistake the essence of this conception, if we understand it merely in a quantitative sense as an extension of knowledge indefinitely. A qualitative determination always accompanies quantitative expansion; and an increasingly pronounced return to the characteristic center of knowledge corresponds to the extension of inquiry beyond the periphery of knowledge. One seeks multiplicity in order to be sure of unity; one accepts the breadth of knowledge in the sure anticipation that this breadth does not impede the intellect, but that, on the contrary, it leads the intellect back to, and concentrates it in, itself. For we see again and again that the divergence of the paths followed by the intellect in its attempt to encompass all of reality is merely apparent. If these paths viewed objectively seem to diverge, their divergence is, nevertheless, no mere dispersion. All the various energies of the mind are, rather, held together in a common center of force. Variety and diversity of shapes are simply the full unfolding of an essentially homogeneous formative power. When the eighteenth century wants to characterize this power in a single word, it calls it "reason." "Reason" becomes the unifying and central point of this century, expressing all that it longs and strives for, and all that it achieves. But the historian of the eighteenth century would be guilty of error and hasty judgment if he were satisfied with this characterization and thought it a safe point of departure. For where the century itself sees an end, the historian finds merely a starting-point for his investigation; where the century seems to find an answer, the historian sees his real problem. The eighteenth century is imbued with a belief in the unity and immutability of reason. Reason is the same for all thinking subjects, all nations, all epochs, and all cultures. From the changeability of religious creeds, of moral maxims and convictions, of theoretical opinions and judgments, a firm and lasting element can be extracted which is permanent in itself, and which in this identity and permanence expresses the real essence of reason. For us the word "reason" has long since lost its unequivocal simplicity even if we are in essential agreement with the basic aims of the philosophy of the Enlightenment. We can scarcely use this word any longer without being conscious of its history; and time and again we see how great a change of meaning the term has undergone. This circumstance constantly reminds us how little meaning the terms "reason" and "rationalism" still retain, even in the sense of purely historical characteristics. The general concept is vague, and it becomes clear and distinct only when the right "differentia specifica" is added. Where are we to look for this specific difference in the eighteenth century? If it liked to call itself a "century of reason," a "philosophic century," wherein lies the characteristic and distinguishing feature of this designation? In what sense is the word "philosophy" used here? What are its special tasks, and what means are at its disposal for accomplishing these tasks in order to place the doctrines of the world and of man on a firm foundation?

If we compare the answers of the eighteenth century to these questions with the answers prevailing at the time when that century began its intellectual labors, we arrive at a negative distinction. The seventeenth century had seen the real task of philosophy in the construction of the philosophical "system." Truly "philosophical" knowledge had seemed attainable only when thought, starting from a highest being and from a highest, intuitively grasped certainty, succeeded in spreading the light of this certainty over all derived being and all derived knowledge. This was done by the method of proof and rigorous inference, which added other propositions to the first original certainty and in this way pieced out and linked together the whole chain of possible knowledge. No link of this chain could be removed from the whole; none was explicable by itself. The only real explanation possible consisted in its "derivation," in the strict, systematic deduction by which any link might be traced back to the source of being and certainty, by which its distance from this source might be determined, and by which the number of intermediate links separating a given link from this source might be specified. The eighteenth century abandons this kind of deduction and proof. It no longer vies with Descartes and Malebranche, with Leibniz and Spinoza for the prize of systematic rigor and completeness. It seeks another concept of truth and philosophy whose function is to extend the boundaries of both and make them more elastic, concrete, and vital. The Enlightenment does not take the ideal of this mode of thinking from the philosophical doctrines of the past; on the contrary, it constructs its ideal according to the model and pattern of contemporary natural science.

The attempt to solve the central problem of philosophic method involves recourse to Newton's "Rules of Philosophizing" rather than to Descartes' *Discourse on Method*, with the result that philosophy presently takes an entirely new direction. For Newton's method is not that of pure deduction, but that of analysis. He does not begin by setting up certain principles, certain general concepts and axioms, in order, by virtue of abstract inferences, to pave the way to the knowledge of the particular, the "factual." Newton's approach moves in just the opposite direction. His phenomena are the data of experience; his principles are the goal of his investigation. If the latter are first according to nature ($\pi\rho\acute{o}\tau\epsilon\rho ov$ $\tau\hat{\eta}$ $\phi\acute{v}\sigma\epsilon\iota$), then the former must always be first to us ($\pi\rho\acute{o}\tau\epsilon\rho ov$ $\pi\rho\grave{o}s$ $\acute{\eta}\mu\hat{a}s$). Hence the true method of physics can never consist in proceeding from any arbitrary *a priori* starting-point, from a hypothesis, and in completely developing the logical conclusions implicit in it. For such hypotheses can be invented and modified as desired; logically, any one of them is as valid as any other. We can progress from this logical indifference to the truth and precision of physical science only by applying the measuring stick elsewhere.

The Mind of the Enlightenment

A scientific abstraction or "definition" cannot serve as a really unambiguous starting-point, for such a starting-point can only be obtained from experience and observation. This does not mean that Newton and his disciples and followers saw a cleavage between experience and thinking, that is, between the realm of bare fact and that of pure thought. No such conflicting modes of validity, no such dualism between "relations of ideas" and "matters of fact" as we find in Hume's *Enquiry concerning Human Understanding*, is to be found among the Newtonian thinkers. For the goal and basic presupposition of Newtonian research is universal order and law in the material world. Such regularity means that facts as such are not mere matter, they are not a jumble of discrete elements; on the contrary, facts exhibit an all-pervasive form. This form appears in mathematical determinations and in arrangements according to measure and number. But such arrangements cannot be foreseen in the mere concept; they must rather be shown to exist in the facts themselves. The procedure is thus not from concepts and axioms to phenomena, but vice versa. Observation produces the datum of science; the principle and law are the object of the investigation.

This new methodological order characterizes all eighteenth century thought. The value of system, the *"esprit systématique,"* is neither underestimated nor neglected; but it is sharply distinguished from the love of system for its own sake, the *"esprit de système."* The whole theory of knowledge of the eighteenth century strives to confirm this distinction. D'Alembert in his "Preliminary Discourse" to the French *Encyclopedia* makes this distinction the central point of his argument, and Condillac in his *Treatise on Systems* gives it explicit form and justification. Condillac tries to subject the great systems of the seventeenth century to the test of historical criticism. He tries to show that each of them failed because, instead of sticking to the facts and developing its concepts from them, it raised some individual concept to the status of a dogma. In opposition to the "spirit of systems" a new alliance is now called for between the "positive" and the "rational" spirit. The positive and the rational are never in conflict, but their true synthesis can only

8

be achieved by the right sort of mediation. One should not seek order, law, and "reason" as a rule that may be grasped and expressed prior to the phenomena, as their *a priori*; one should rather discover such regularity in the phenomena themselves, as the form of their immanent connection. Nor should one attempt to anticipate from the outset such "reason" in the form of a closed system; one should rather permit this reason to unfold gradually, with ever increasing clarity and perfection, as knowledge of the facts progresses. The new logic that is now sought in the conviction that it is everywhere present on the path of knowledge is neither the logic of the scholastic nor of the purely mathematical concept; it is rather the "logic of facts." The mind must abandon itself to the abundance of phenomena and gauge itself constantly by them. For it may be sure that it will not get lost, but that instead it will find here its own real truth and standard. Only in this way can the genuine correlation of subject and object, of truth and reality, be achieved; only so can the correspondence between these concepts, which is the condition of all scientific knowledge, be brought about.

From the actual course of scientific thinking since its revival in modern times the Enlightenment derives its concrete, self-evident proof that this synthesis of the "positive" and the "rational" is not a mere postulate, but that the goal set up is attainable and the ideal fully realizable. In the progress of natural science and the various phases it has gone through, the philosophy of the Enlightenment believes it can, as it were, tangibly grasp its ideal. For here it can follow step by step the triumphal march of the modern analytical spirit. It had been this spirit that in the course of barely a century and a half had conquered all reality, and that now seemed finally to have accomplished its great task of reducing the multiplicity of natural phenomena to a single universal rule. And this cosmological formula, as contained in Newton's general law of attraction, was not found by accident, nor as the result of sporadic experimentation; its discovery shows the rigorous application of scientific method. Newton finished what Kepler and Galileo had begun. All three names signify not only great scientific

personalities, but they have also become symbols and milestones of scientific knowledge and thought. Kepler pushes the
observation of celestial phenomena to a degree of precision
never achieved before his time. By indefatigable toil he arrived
at the laws which describe the form of the planetary orbits and
determine the relation between the revolution periods of the
individual planets and their respective distances from the sun.
But this factual insight is only a first step. Galileo envisages a
more general problem: his doctrine of motion marks an advance
to a broader and deeper stratum of the logic of scientific concepts. It is no longer a question of describing a field of natural
phenomena, however broad and important; a general foundation of dynamics, of the theory of nature as such, has now to be
evolved. And Galileo is aware that direct observation of nature
cannot accomplish this task, and that other cognitive means must
be invoked. The phenomena of nature present themselves to
perception as uniform events, as undivided wholes. Perception
grasps only the surface of these events, it can describe them in
broad outline and in the manner of their taking place; but this
form of description is not sufficient for a real explanation. For
the explanation of a natural event is not merely the realization
of its existence thus and so; such an explanation consists rather in
specifying the conditions of the event, and in recognizing exactly how it depends on these conditions. This demand can only
be satisfied by an analysis of the uniform presentation of the
event as given in perception and direct observation, and by its
resolution into its constitutive elements. This analytical process,
according to Galileo, is the presupposition of all exact knowledge of nature. The method of formulation of scientific concepts
is both analytical and synthetic. It is only by splitting an apparently simple event into its elements and by reconstructing it
from these that we can arrive at an understanding of it. Galileo
has given us a classical example of this process in his discovery
of the ballistic parabola. The path of a projectile could not be
described directly from observation; it could not simply be
abstracted from a great number of observations. Observation
gives us to be sure certain general characteristics; it shows us
that a phase of ascent is followed by a phase of descent, etc. But

observation fails to produce any precise determination of the path of a projectile. We arrive at a truly mathematical conception of an event by tracing the phenomenon itself back to its peculiar conditions, by isolating each set of conditions simultaneously affecting the event, and by investigating these sets of conditions with respect to their laws. The law of the parabolic path of the projectile may be found, and the increase and decrease of velocity may be exactly recorded once the phenomenon of projection has been shown to be a complex event, the determination of which depends on two different forces, that of the original impulse and that of gravity. In this simple example, as in a preliminary sketch, we have the whole future development of physics and its complete methodological structure. Newton's theory retains and substantiates all those features which are clearly recognizable here. For it is founded on the interdependence of the analytical and synthetic methods. Taking the three laws of Kepler as its point of departure, Newton's theory is not content merely to interpret them as expressing the factual results of observation. It seeks to derive these results from their presuppositions and to show that they are the necessary effect of the concurrence of various conditions. Each of these sets of conditions must be investigated by itself and its function known. Thus the phenomenon of planetary motion, which Kepler had regarded as a simple entity, is proved to be a complex structure. It is reduced to two fundamental forms of natural law: to the laws of freely falling bodies and to the laws of centrifugal force. Both forms of law had been investigated independently by Galileo and Huygens and precisely determined; now it was a question of reducing these discoveries to one comprehensive principle. Newton's great achievement lay in this reduction; it was not so much the discovery of hitherto unknown facts or the acquisition of new material but rather the intellectual transformation of empirical material which Newton achieved. The structure of the cosmos is no longer merely to be looked at, but to be penetrated. It yields to this approach only when mathematics is applied and it is subjected to the mathematical form of analysis. In as much as Newton's theory of fluxions and Leibniz's infinitesimal calculus provide a universal instrument for this procedure, the comprehensibility of nature seems for the first time to be strictly demonstrated. The path of natural science traverses indefinite distances; but its direction remains constant, for its point of departure and its goal are not exclusively determined by the nature of the objective world but by the nature and powers of reason as well.

The philosophy of the eighteenth century takes up this particular case, the methodological pattern of Newton's physics, though it immediately begins to generalize. It is not content to look upon analysis as the great intellectual tool of mathematico-physical knowledge; eighteenth century thought sees analysis rather as the necessary and indispensable instrument of all thinking in general. This view triumphs in the middle of the century. However much individual thinkers and schools differ in their results, they agree in this epistemological premise. Voltaire's *Treatise on Metaphysics*, d'Alembert's *Preliminary Discourse*, and Kant's *Inquiry concerning the Principles of Natural Theology and Morality* all concur on this point. All these works represent the true method of metaphysics as in fundamental agreement with the method which Newton, with such fruitful results, introduced into natural science. Voltaire says that man, if he presumes to see into the life of things and know them as they really are in themselves, immediately becomes aware of the limits of his faculties; he finds himself in the position of a blind man who must judge the nature of color. But analysis is the staff which a benevolent nature has placed in the blind man's hands. Equipped with this instrument he can feel his way forward among appearances, discovering their sequence and arrangement; and this is all he needs for his intellectual orientation to life and knowledge. "We must never make hypotheses; we must never say: Let us begin by inventing principles according to which we attempt to explain everything. We should say rather: Let us make an exact analysis of things. . . . When we cannot utilize the compass of mathematics or the torch of experience and physics, it is certain that we cannot take a single step forward."[2] But provided with such instruments as these, we can and should venture upon the high seas of knowl-

[2] Voltaire, *Traité de Métaphysique*, chs. III and V.

edge. We must, of course, abandon all hope of ever wresting from things their ultimate mystery, of ever penetrating to the absolute being of matter or of the human soul. If, however, we refer to empirical law and order, the "inner core of nature" proves by no means inaccessible. In this realm we can establish ourselves and proceed in every direction. The power of reason does not consist in enabling us to transcend the empirical world but rather in teaching us to feel at home in it. Here again is evident a characteristic change of meaning in the concept of reason as compared with seventeenth century usage. In the great metaphysical systems of that century—those of Descartes and Malebranche, of Spinoza and Leibniz—reason is the realm of the "eternal verities," of those truths held in common by the human and the divine mind. What we know through reason, we therefore behold "in God." Every act of reason means participation in the divine nature; it gives access to the intelligible world. The eighteenth century takes reason in a different and more modest sense. It is no longer the sum total of "innate ideas" given prior to all experience, which reveal the absolute essence of things. Reason is now looked upon rather as an acquisition than as a heritage. It is not the treasury of the mind in which the truth like a minted coin lies stored; it is rather the original intellectual force which guides the discovery and determination of truth. This determination is the seed and the indispensable presupposition of all real certainty. The whole eighteenth century understands reason in this sense; not as a sound body of knowledge, principles, and truths, but as a kind of energy, a force which is fully comprehensible only in its agency and effects. What reason is, and what it can do, can never be known by its results but only by its function. And its most important function consists in its power to bind and to dissolve. It dissolves everything merely factual, all simple data of experience, and everything believed on the evidence of revelation, tradition and authority; and it does not rest content until it has analyzed all these things into their simplest component parts and into their last elements of belief and opinion. Following this work of dissolution begins the work of construction. Reason cannot stop with the dispersed parts; it has to build from them a new structure, a true whole. But since reason creates this whole and fits the parts together according to its own rule, it gains complete knowledge of the structure of its product. Reason understands this structure because it can reproduce it in its totality and in the ordered sequence of its individual elements. Only in this twofold intellectual movement can the concept of reason be fully characterized, namely, as a concept of agency, not of being.

This conviction gains a foothold in the most varied fields of eighteenth century culture. Lessing's famous saying that the real power of reason is to be found not in the possession but in the acquisition of truth has its parallels everywhere in the intellectual history of the eighteenth century. Montesquieu attempts to give a theoretical justification for the presence in the human soul of an innate thirst for knowledge, an insatiable intellectual curiosity, which never allows us to be satisfied with any conception we have arrived at, but drives us on from idea to idea. "Our soul is made for thinking, that is, for perceiving," said Montesquieu; "but such a being must have curiosity, for just as all things form a chain in which every idea precedes one idea and follows another, so one cannot want to see the one without desiring to see the other." The lust for knowledge, the *libido sciendi*, which theological dogmatism had outlawed and branded as intellectual pride, is now called a necessary quality of the soul as such and restored to its original rights. The defense, reinforcement, and consolidation of this way of thinking is the cardinal aim of eighteenth century culture; and in this mode of thinking, not in the mere acquisition and extension of specific information, the century sees its major task. This fundamental tendency can also be traced unambiguously in the *Encyclopedia*, which became the arsenal of all such information. Diderot himself, originator of the *Encyclopedia*, states that its purpose is not only to supply a certain body of knowledge but also to bring about a change in the mode of thinking—*pour changer la façon commune de penser*.[2a] Consciousness of this task affects all the minds of the age and gives rise to a new sense of inner tension. Even the calmest and most discreet thinkers, the real "scientists," are swayed by this movement. They do not

[2a] Cf. Ducros, *Les Encyclopédistes*, Paris, 1900, p. 138.

dare as yet to specify its final aim; but they cannot escape its force, and they think they feel in this trend the rise of a new future for mankind. "I do not think that I have too good an idea of my century," writes Duclos in his *Thoughts on the Customs of this Century*, "but it seems to me there is a certain universal fermentation whose progress one could direct or hasten by the proper education." For one does not want simply to catch the contagion of the time and to be driven blindly on by whatever forces it may contain. One wants to understand these forces and control them in the light of such understanding. One does not care merely to dive into the eddies and whirlpools of the new thoughts; one prefers to seize the helm of the intellect and to guide its course toward definite goals.

The first step which the eighteenth century took in this direction was to seek a clear line of demarcation between the mathematical and the philosophical spirit. Here was a difficult and intrinsically dialectic task, for two different and apparently contradictory claims were to be equally satisfied. The bond between mathematics and philosophy could not be severed, or even loosened, for mathematics was the "pride of human reason," its touchstone and real guarantee. Yet it became increasingly clear that there was also a certain limitation inherent in this self-contained power of mathematics; that mathematics to be sure formed the prototype of reason, and yet it could not with respect to content completely survey and exhaust reason. A strange process of thinking now develops which seems to be motivated by diametrically opposed forces. Philosophical thinking tries at the same time to separate itself from, and to hold fast to, mathematics; it seeks to free itself from the authority of mathematics, and yet in so doing not to contest or violate this authority but rather to justify it from a new angle. In both its efforts it is successful; for pure analysis is recognized in its essential meaning as the basis for mathematical thinking in the modern era; and yet at the same time, precisely because of its universal function, such analysis is extended beyond the limits of the purely mathematical, beyond quantity and number. The beginnings of this trend are already discernible in the seventeenth century. Pascal's work *Of the Geometric Spirit* seriously attempts to draw a clear and distinct line between mathematical science and philosophy. He contrasts the "geometric spirit" with the "subtle spirit" (*esprit fin*) and tries to show how they differ both in structure and in function. But this sharp line of demarcation is soon obliterated. "The geometric spirit," says, for instance, Fontenelle in the preface to his work *On the Usefulness of Mathematics and Physics*,[3] "is not so exclusively bound to geometry that it could not be separated from it and applied to other fields. A work on ethics, politics, criticism, or even eloquence, other things being equal, is merely so much more beautiful and perfect if it is written in the geometric spirit." The eighteenth century grapples with this problem and decides that, as long as it is understood as the spirit of pure analysis, the "geometric spirit" is absolutely unlimited in its application and by no means bound to any particular field of knowledge.

Proof of this thesis is sought in two different directions. Analysis, whose force had hitherto been tried only in the realm of number and quantity, is now applied, on the one hand, to psychological and, on the other, to sociological problems. In both cases it is a matter of showing that here too new vistas open up, and that a new field of knowledge of the highest importance becomes accessible to reason as soon as reason learns to subject this field to its special method of analytic dissection and synthetic reconstruction. But psychological reality, concretely given and immediately experienced, seems to elude any such attempt. It appears to us in unlimited abundance and infinite variety; no element, no form, of psychological experience is like any other, and no content ever recurs in the same way. In the flux of psychological events no two waves exhibit the same form; each wave emerges, as it were, out of nothingness, and threatens to disappear into nothingness again. Yet, according to the prevailing view of psychology in the eighteenth century, this complete diversity, this heterogeneity and fluidity, of psychological content is illusory. Closer inspection reveals the solid ground and the permanent elements underlying the almost unlimited mutability of psychological phenomena. It is

[3] *Oeuvres*, Paris, 1818, vol. I, p. 34.

the task of science to discover those elements which escape immediate experience, and to present them clearly and individually. In psychological events there is no diversity and no heterogeneity which cannot be reduced to a sum of individual parts; there is no becoming which is not founded in constant being. If we trace psychological forms to their sources and origins, we always find such unity and relative simplicity. In this conviction eighteenth century psychology goes one step beyond its guide and master, Locke. Locke had been content to indicate two major sources of psychological phenomena; in addition to "sensation" Locke recognizes "reflection" as an independent and irreducible form of psychological experience. But his pupils and followers attempt in various ways to eliminate this dualism and to arrive at a strictly monistic foundation of psychology. Berkeley and Hume combine "sensation" and "reflection" in the expression "perception," and they try to show that this expression exhausts both our internal and external experience, the data of nature and those of our own mind. Condillac considers his real merit and his advance beyond Locke to be that, while retaining Locke's general method, he extended it into a new field of psychological facts. Locke's analytical art is effective in the dissection of ideas, but it goes no farther. It shows how every idea, be it ever so complex, is composed of the materials of sensation or reflection, and how these materials must be fitted together in order to produce the various forms of psychological phenomena. But, as Condillac points out, Locke stops with his analysis of psychological forms. He limits his investigation to these forms but does not extend it to the whole realm of psychological events and activity, or to their origin. Here then is a province for research hitherto scarcely touched and of untold riches. In Locke the different classes of psychological activity were left alone, as original and irreducible wholes like the simple data of sense, the data of sight, hearing, touch, motion, taste, and smell. Observing, comparing, distinguishing, combining, desiring, and willing are looked upon by Locke as individual independent acts existing only in immediate experience and not reducible to anything else. But this view robs the whole method of derivation of its real fruits. For psychological being remains an irreducible manifold which can be described in its particular forms but can no longer be explained and derived from simple original qualities. If such derivation is to be taken seriously, then the maxim which Locke applied to the realm of ideas must be applied to all operations of the mind. It must also be shown that the apparent immediacy of these ideas is an illusion which does not withstand scientific analysis. Individual acts of the mind, when analyzed, are in no sense original, but rather derivative and mediate. In order to understand their structure and true nature, one must examine their genesis; one must observe how, from the simple sense data which it receives, the mind gradually acquires the capacity to focus its attention on them, to compare and distinguish, to separate and combine them. Such is the task of Condillac's *Treatise on Sensation*. Here the analytical method seems to celebrate a new triumph in the scientific explanation of the corporeal world, a triumph not inferior to its performances in the realm of natural science. The material and mental spheres are now, as it were, reduced to a common denominator; they are composed of the same elements and are combined according to the same laws.[4]

But in addition to these two spheres of reality there is a third which, similarly, must not be accepted as consisting of simple sense data, but which must be traced to its origins. For we can only succeed in reducing this reality to the rule of law and reason by an inquiry into its sources. The third sphere of reality is that which we find in the structure of the state and of society. Man is born into this world; he neither creates nor shapes it, but finds it ready-made about him; and he is expected to adapt himself to the existing order. But here too passive acceptance and obedience have their limits. As soon as the power of thought awakens in man, it advances irresistibly against this form of reality, summoning it before the tribunal of thought and challenging its legal titles to truth and validity. And society must submit to being treated like physical reality under investigation. Analysis into component parts begins once

---

[4] Cf. Condillac, *Traité des sensations*, and also the "Extrait raisonné" which Condillac added to later editions of his treatise (ed. Georges Lyon, Paris, 1921, especially pp. 32 ff.).

more, and the general will of the state is treated as if it were composed of the wills of individuals and had come into being as a result of the union of these wills. Only by virtue of this basic supposition can we make a "body" of the state and subject it to that method which had proved its fruitfulness in the discovery of universal law in the physical world. Hobbes had already done this. The fundamental principle of his political theory, that the state is a "body," means just this: that the same process of thought which guides us to an exact insight into the nature of physical body is also applicable without reservation to the state. Hobbes's assertion that thinking in general is "calculation" and that all calculation is either addition or subtraction also holds for all political thinking. Such thinking too must sever the bond which unites the individual wills, in order to join them again by virtue of its own special method. Thus Hobbes resolves the "civic state" into the "natural state"; and in thought he dissolves all bonds of individual wills only to find their complete antagonism, the "war of all against all," remaining. But from this very negation is derived the positive content of the law of the land in its unconditional and unlimited validity. The emergence of the will of the state from the form of the covenant is set forth because this will can only be known by, and founded in, the covenant. Here is the bond which connects Hobbes's doctrine of nature with his doctrine of the state. These doctrines are different applications of Hobbes's logical basic assumption, according to which the human mind really only understands that which it can construct from the original elements. Every true formulation of a concept, every complete definition, must therefore start from this point; it can only be a "causal" definition. Philosophy as a whole is understood as the sum total of such causal definitions; it is simply the complete knowledge of effects from their causes, of derivative results from the totality of their antecedents and conditions.

The eighteenth century doctrine of the state and society only rarely accepted without reservations the content of Hobbes's teaching, but the form in which Hobbes embodied this content exerted a powerful and lasting influence. Eighteenth century political thought is based on that theory of the contract whose underlying assumptions are derived from ancient and medieval thought, but it develops and transforms these assumptions in a manner characteristic of the influence exerted by the modern scientific view of the world. In this field too the analytic and synthetic method is henceforth victorious. Sociology is modeled on physics and analytical psychology. Its method, states Condillac in his *Treatise on Systems*, consists in teaching us to recognize in society an "artificial body" composed of parts exerting a reciprocal influence on one another. This body as a whole must be so shaped that no individual class of citizens by their special prerogatives shall disturb the equilibrium and harmony of the whole, that on the contrary all special interests shall contribute and be subordinated to the welfare of the whole.[5] This formulation in a certain sense transforms the problem of sociology and politics into a problem in statics. Montesquieu's *Spirit of the Laws* looks upon this same transformation as its highest task. The aim of Montesquieu's work is not simply to describe the forms and types of state constitutions—despotism, constitutional monarchy, and the republican constitution—and to present them empirically, it is also to construct them from the forces of which they are composed. Knowledge of these forces is necessary if they are to be put to their proper use, if we are to show how they can be employed in the making of a state constitution which realizes the demand of the greatest possible freedom. Such freedom, as Montesquieu tries to show, is possible only when every individual force is limited and restrained by a counterforce. Montesquieu's famous doctrine of the "division of powers" is nothing but the consistent development and the concrete application of this basic principle. It seeks to transform that unstable equilibrium which exists in, and is characteristic of, imperfect forms of the state into a static equilibrium; it attempts further to show what ties must exist between individual forces in order that none shall gain the ascendancy over any other, but that all, by counterbalancing one another, shall permit the widest possible margin for freedom. The ideal which Montesquieu portrays in his theory of the state is thus the ideal of a "mixed government," in which, as a

[5] Condillac, *Traité des systèmes*, part II, ch. XV.

safeguard against a relapse into despotism, the form of the mixture is so wisely and cautiously selected that the exertion of a force in one direction immediately releases a counterforce, and hence automatically restores the desired equilibrium. By this approach Montesquieu believes he can fit the great variety and diversity of the existing forms of the state into one sound intellectual structure within which they can be controlled. Such a basic arrangement and foundation is Montesquieu's primary aim. "I have established principles," he points out in the preface to the *Spirit of the Laws*, "and I have observed how individual cases, as if by themselves, yielded to these principles, and I have seen that the histories of all nations are but sequences, and that each individual law is connected with another law or depends on a more general law."

The method of reason is thus exactly the same in this branch of knowledge as it is in natural science and psychology. It consists in starting with solid facts based on observation, but not in remaining within the bounds of bare facts. The mere togetherness of the facts must be transformed into a conjuncture; the initial mere co-existence of the data must upon closer inspection reveal an interdependence; and the form of an aggregate must become that of a system. To be sure, the facts cannot simply be coerced into a system; such form must arise from the facts themselves. The principles, which are to be sought everywhere, and without which no sound knowledge is possible in any field, are not arbitrarily chosen points of departure in thinking, applied by force to concrete experience which is so altered as to suit them; they are rather the general conditions to which a complete analysis of the given facts themselves must lead. The path of thought then, in physics as in psychology and politics, leads from the particular to the general; but not even this progression would be possible unless every particular as such were already subordinated to a universal rule, unless from the first the general were contained, so to speak embodied, in the particular. The concept of the "principle" in itself excludes that absolute character which it asserted in the great metaphysical systems of the seventeenth century. It resigns itself to a relative validity; it now pretends only to mark a provisional farthest point at which the progress of thought has arrived—with the reservation that thought can also abandon and supersede it. According to this relativity, the scientific principle is dependent on the status and form of knowledge, so that one and the same proposition can appear in one science as a principle and in another as a deduced corrollary. "Hence we conclude that the point at which the investigation of the principles of a science must stop is determined by the nature of the science itself, that is to say, by the point of view from which the particular science approaches its object. . . . I admit that in this case the principles from which we proceed are themselves perhaps scarcely more than very remote derivations from the true principles which are unknown to us, and that, accordingly, they would perhaps merit rather the name of conclusions than that of principles. But it is not necessary that these conclusions be principles in themselves; it suffices that they be such for us."[6] Such a relativity does not imply any skeptical perils in itself; it is, on the contrary, merely the expression of the fact that reason in its steady progress knows no hard and fast barriers, but that every apparent goal attained by reason is but a fresh starting-point.

Thus it is evident that, if we compare the thought of the eighteenth century with that of the seventeenth, there is no real chasm anywhere separating the two periods. The new ideal of knowledge develops steadily and consistently from the presuppositions which the logic and theory of knowledge of the seventeenth century—especially in the works of Descartes and Leibniz—had established. The difference in the mode of thinking does not mean a radical transformation; it amounts merely to a shifting of emphasis. This emphasis is constantly moving from the general to the particular, from principles to phenomena. But the basic assumption remains; that is the assumption that between the two realms of thought there is no opposition, but rather complete correlation—except for Hume's skepticism which offers an entirely different approach. The self-confidence of reason is nowhere shaken. The rationalistic postulate of unity dominates the minds of this age. The concept

---

[6] D'Alembert, "Éléments des Sciences," *Encyclopédie*, Paris, 1755, V, 493. Cf. *Éléments de Philosophie*, IV; *Mélanges de littérature, d'histoire et de philosophie*, IV, 35 f.

of unity and that of science are mutually dependent. "All sciences put together," says d'Alembert repeating the opening sentences of Descartes' *Rules for the Conduct of the Understanding*, "are nothing but human intelligence, which always remains one and the same, and is always identical with itself, however different the objects may be to which it is applied." The seventeenth century owed its inner solidarity, particularly as exemplified in French classical culture, to the consistency and rigor with which it clung to this postulate of unity and extended its application to all the spheres of knowledge and living. This postulate prevailed not only in science, but in religion, politics and literature as well. "One king, one law, one faith"— such was the motto of the epoch. With the advent of the eighteenth century the absolutism of the unity principle seems to lose its grip and to accept some limitations and concessions. But these modifications do not touch the core of the thought itself. For the function of unification continues to be recognized as the basic role of reason. Rational order and control of the data of experience are not possible without strict unification. To "know" a manifold of experience is to place its component parts in such a relationship to one another that, starting from a given point, we can run through them according to a constant and general rule. This form of discursive understanding had been established by Descartes as the fundamental norm of mathematical knowledge. Every mathematical operation, according to Descartes, aims in the last analysis to determine the proportion between an unknown quantity and other known quantities. And this proportion can only be strictly determined when the unknown and the known participate in a "common nature." Both elements, the unknown and the known, must be reducible to quantity and as such they must be derivable from the repetition of one and the same numerical unit. Thus the discursive form of knowledge always resembles a reduction; it proceeds from the complex to the simple, from apparent diversity to its basic identity. Eighteenth century thought holds firmly to this fundamental method, and attempts to apply it to broader and broader fields of knowledge. The very concept of "calculus" thus loses its exclusively mathematical meaning. It is not merely applicable to quantities and numbers; from the realm of quantities it invades the realm of pure qualities. For qualities too may be placed in such a relationship to one another that they are derivable from one another in a strict order. Whenever this is possible, the determination of the general laws of this order enables us to gain a clear view of the whole field of their validity. The concept of "calculus," therefore, is co-extensive with that of science itself; and it is applicable wherever the conditions of a manifold of experience can be reduced to certain fundamental relations and thus completely determined. Condillac, who first clearly formulated this general scientific concept in his essay *The Language of Calculus*, attempted in his psychology to give a characteristic sample and a fruitful application of the concept. For Condillac, who supports the Cartesian concept of the immateriality and spirituality of the soul, there can be no doubt that a direct mathematical treatment of psychological experience is impossible. For such a direct application of the concepts of quantity is valid only where the object itself consists of parts and can be constructed from these parts; and this can take place only in the realm of corporeal substance, which is defined as pure extension, but not in the realm of thinking "indivisible" substance. However, this fundamental and unalterable opposition between body and soul is no insurmountable barrier for the pure function of analytical knowledge. This function ignores material differences for, by virtue of the purity of its form and the formal nature of its operation, it is bound by no presuppositions regarding content. Even if psychological experience cannot like corporeal experience be divided into parts, yet in thought it can be analyzed into its constitutive elements. To this end it is only necessary that the apparent diversity of such experience be resolved by showing that it is a continuous development from a common source of all psychological phenomena. As proof, Condillac introduces the famous illustration which he places at the center of his psychology. Assuming a marble statue, he describes how it progressively comes to life and acquires an increasingly rich spiritual content because the individual senses engrave their special qualities on the marble. Condillac tries to show that the continuous series of "impressions" and the temporal order in which they are produced are sufficient to build up the totality of psychological experience and to produce it in all its wealth and subtle shadings. If we succeed in producing psychological experience in this manner, we have at the same time reduced it to the quantitative concept. Now everything that we call psychological reality and that we experience as such proves to be fundamentally a mere repetition and transformation of a certain basic quality which is contained in the simplest sense perception. Sense perception forms the borderline between the marble as dead matter and a living being endowed with a soul. But once this borderline has been passed, there is no need of any further assumptions or of any essentially new creations. What we commonly regard as the "higher" powers of the mind, contrasting these powers with sensation, is in reality only a transformation of the basic element of sense perception. All thinking and judging, all desiring and willing, all powers of the imagination and all artistic creation, qualitatively considered, add nothing new, nothing essentially different to this fundamental element. The mind neither creates nor invents; it repeats and constructs. But in this repetition it can exhibit almost inexhaustible powers. It extends the visible universe beyond all bounds; it traverses the infinity of space and time; and yet it is unceasingly engaged in the production of ever new shapes within itself. But throughout its activities the mind is concerned only with itself and its "simple ideas." These constitute the solid ground on which the entire edifice constructed by the mind, both in its "external" and in its "internal" aspects, rests—and from which the mind can never depart.

Condillac's attempt to show that all psychological reality is a transformation, a metamorphosis, of simple sense perception is continued by Helvetius in his book *On the Mind* (*De l'Esprit*). The influence which this weak and unoriginal work exerted on the philosophical literature of the eighteenth century is explicable in that the epoch found here a basic element of its thought expressed with pregnant clarity, and indeed with an exaggeration which parodies this thought. In Helvetius's exaggeration the methodological limitation and danger of this mode of thinking is clearly presented. The limitation consists in a leveling process which threatens to deny the living wealth of human consciousness and to look upon it merely as a disguise. Analytical thinking removes this disguise from psychological phenomena; it exposes them, and in so doing reveals their naked sameness rather than their apparent diversity and inner differentiation. Differences in form as well as in value vanish and prove to be delusions. As a result, there is no longer a "top" and "bottom" or a "higher" and a "lower" in the realm of psychological phenomena. Everything is on the same plane— equal in value and in validity. Helvetius develops this line of thought especially in the field of ethics. His main intention was to sweep away all those artificial differentiations which convention had erected and was trying hard to maintain. Wherever traditional ethics spoke of a special class of "moral" sensations, wherever it thought it found in man an original "feeling of sympathy" which rules over and restrains his sensual and egotistical appetites, Helvetius tries to show how poorly such a hypothesis corresponds to the simple reality of human feeling and action. Whoever approaches this reality without prejudice will find none of that apparent dualism. He will find everywhere and always the same absolutely uniform motivation. He will see that all those qualities which we refer to as unselfishness, magnanimity, and self-sacrifice are different only in name, not in reality, from the elementary impulses of human nature, from the "lower" appetites and passions. No moral greatness rises above this plane. For no matter how high the aims of the will may be, no matter what supernatural values and supersensible goals it may imagine, it remains nonetheless confined within the narrow circle of egotism, ambition, and vanity. Society does not achieve the suppression of these elemental impulses, but only their sublimation; and in so far as society understands its own function, this is all it can ever expect or ask of the individual. Consideration of the theoretical world should be guided by the same viewpoint. According to Helvetius there are neither fundamental gradations in the scale of ethical values nor radical gradations of theoretical form. On the contrary, all such distinctions boil down to the same undifferentiated mass of sensation. The so-called faculties of judgment and cognition, imagination and memory, and understanding and reason, are by no means specific original powers of the soul. Here again we have been subject to the same delusion. We think we have transcended the sphere of sense perception when we have only slightly modified its appearance. The criticism which explains away this modification also applies to theoretical distinctions. All operations of the mind can be reduced to judgment, and judgment consists only in grasping similarities and differences between individual ideas. But the recognition of similarity and difference presupposes an original act of awareness which is analogous to, or indeed identical with, the perception of a sense quality. "I judge or I perceive that of two objects the one I call 'fathom' makes a different impression on me from the one I call 'foot,' and that the color I call 'red' affects my eyes differently from the color I call 'yellow.' Hence I conclude that in such a case to judge is simply to perceive."[7] Here, as one sees, both the edifice of ethical values and the logically graded structure of knowledge are demolished. Both structures are, as it were, razed to the ground because it is thought that the only unshakable foundation of knowledge lies in sensation.

It would be erroneous to consider the fundamental viewpoint represented by Helvetius as typical of the content of the philosophy of the Enlightenment, as has often been done; and it is equally erroneous to regard it as typical of the thought of the French Encyclopaedists. For the sharpest criticism of Helvetius's work was exercised by precisely this school of thought; and this criticism originated among the best minds in French philosophical literature, as, for instance, Turgot and Diderot. But one thing is undeniable, namely, that in Helvetius as well as in Condillac a certain methodology appears, a methodology characteristic of and decisive for the entire eighteenth century. Here was a form of thinking whose positive achievement and immanent limitations, whose triumphs and defeats, were so to speak predetermined.

2

Thus far we have considered eighteenth century thought principally in its connection with the development of the ana-

[7] Helvetius, *De l'Esprit*, Paris, 1759, p. 8.

lytical spirit, especially as it evolved in France. France was the birthplace and the truly classical land of analysis, for Descartes had based his revolutionary transformation of philosophy on analysis. After the middle of the seventeenth century the Cartesian spirit permeates all fields of knowledge until it dominates not only philosophy, but also literature, morals, political science, and sociology, asserting itself even in the realm of theology to which it imparted a new form.[8] But neither in philosophy nor in general intellectual history does this influence remain unchallenged. With the philosophy of Leibniz a new intellectual power emerges. Leibniz not merely alters the content of the prevailing world picture, but he also endows thinking in general with a new form and a new basic direction. At first, to be sure, it seemed as if Leibniz were merely continuing the work of Descartes, as if his intention were simply to free the forces latent in that work in order to bring about their complete development. Just as Leibniz's mathematical achievement, his analysis of the infinite, stems directly from Descartes; just as this is merely a consistent continuation and a systematic completion of Descartes' analytical geometry, so the same appears to hold for Leibniz's logic. For this logic begins with the science of permutations and combinations, and it attempts to develop this to a general science of the forms of thought. And Leibniz is convinced that the progress of this theory of the forms of thought, the realization of the ideal of a *scientia generalis*, as he imagined it, can only be looked for as a result of the progress of analysis. From now on all of Leibniz's logical studies are concentrated on this one point. His goal is to arrive at an "alphabet of ideas," to resolve all complex forms of thought into their elements, into the last simple basic operations, just as in the theory of numbers every number can be understood and represented as a product of prime numbers. Thus here again unity, uniformity, simplicity, and logical equality seem to form the ultimate and highest goal of thought. All true statements, so far as they belong to the realm of strictly rational "eternal" truths,

[8] For more detailed information see Gustave Lanson's excellent account entitled "L'influence de la philosophie cartésienne sur la littérature française," in *Revue de métaphysique et de morale*, 1896; now also in *Études d'histoire littéraire*, Paris, 1929, pp. 58 ff.

are "virtually identical" and can be reduced to the principle of identity and contradiction. One can—as Louis Couturat did in his excellent presentation—try to see Leibniz's logic as a whole from this viewpoint; or one can go further and include his theory of knowledge, his philosophy of nature, and his metaphysics. In doing the latter one would seem merely to be pursuing Leibniz's own direction, for he always declared that there was no cleavage between his logic and mathematics and his metaphysics, that his entire philosophy was mathematical and had sprung from the innermost core of mathematics.

And yet, if one studies this general and indissoluble connection between the various parts of Leibniz's philosophy, one sees that the tendency hitherto considered basic, however essential it may be to the structure of Leibniz's system, does not exhaust this philosophy as a whole. For the deeper one penetrates into the originality and meaning of the Leibnizian concept of substance, the more distinctly one sees that this concept, both in content and form, represents a new trend of thought. A logic based exclusively on the principle of identity, and considering the whole significance of knowledge to consist in the reduction of diversity to unity, of change to stability, of difference to strict uniformity—such a logic would not do justice to the new concept of substance. Leibniz's metaphysics differs from that of Descartes and Spinoza in that it substitutes for Descartes' dualism and Spinoza's monism a "pluralistic universe." The Leibnizian "monad" is no arithmetical, no merely numerical, unit, but a dynamic one. The true correlate of this unit is not particularity but infinity. Every monad is a living center of energy, and it is the infinite abundance and diversity of monads which constitute the unity of the world. The monad "is" only in so far as it is active, and its activity consists in a continuous transition from one new state to another as it produces these states out of itself in unceasing succession. "The nature of the monad consists in being fruitful, and in giving birth to an ever new variety." Thus every simple element of the monad contains its own past and is pregnant with its future. Never is one of these elements just like another; never can it be resolved into the same sum of purely static qualities. Anything we may find in the monad is to be understood rather as in transition. Its recognizability, its rational determinability is not owing to the fact that we can grasp it by a single characteristic criterion, but that we can grasp the rule of this transition and understand the laws according to which it takes place. If we carry this thought through to its conclusion, we see that the fundamental motive pervading and dominating Leibniz's philosophy is only apparently the motive of identity. In place of the analytical identity of Descartes and Spinoza, we now have the principle of *continuity*. Leibniz's mathematics and his entire metaphysics are based on this principle. Continuity means unity in multiplicity, being in becoming, constancy in change. It signifies a connection which becomes manifest only in change and amid the unceasing mutation of qualities—a connection, therefore, which requires diversity just as fundamentally as unity. The relation between the general and the particular is now also seen in a new light. To be sure, Leibniz still seems unconditionally to uphold the logical primacy of the general. The ultimate aim of all knowledge lies in the "eternal truths" which express a general and necessary relation between ideas, between the subject and predicate of a judgment. The factual, merely contingent, truths do not have the same logical dignity as this logical model; they are more clearly and distinctly known the more we succeed in reducing them to rational factors, until we can finally resolve them entirely into such factors. But this goal is attainable only for a divine intellect, not for finite human knowledge. It constitutes, nevertheless, the norm and lodestar of human knowledge. And yet, according to the fundamental viewpoint which dominates Leibniz's logic and epistemology, the relation between the general and the particular is not one of subsumption. It is not only a case of subordinating the particular to the general, but also of knowing how the one is contained and grounded in the other. Side by side with the law of identity there therefore appears the equally valid and indispensable norm of truth, the "law of sufficient reason," which according to Leibniz is the presupposition of all factual truth. As mathematics is governed by the law of identity, so physics is governed by the law of sufficient reason. Physics is not exclusively concerned with purely conceptual relations; it does not stop when it has found agreement or disagreement of ideas. Physics must take as its starting point observation and sense experience; but it cannot be satisfied with the mere arrangement of these observations and the study of their accumulation. A system, not an aggregate, is the requirement of physics; and it can only realize this system when it succeeds in so relating its assemblage of facts that they appear as a complex of causes and effects. Only in this manner do spatial contiguity and temporal sequence represent a true connection in which every member determines and conditions every other according to definite rules, so that from any particular state of the universe, if completely known, the totality of the phenomena of the universe could be deduced.

We will not dwell on the special content of this fundamental conception; let it suffice to consider merely its categorical structure. It is at once clear that within this new general conception the concept of the *whole* has gained a different and deeper significance. For the universal whole which is to be grasped can no longer be reduced to a mere sum of its parts. The new whole is organic, not mechanical; its nature does not consist in the sum of its parts but is presupposed by its parts and constitutes the condition of the possibility of their nature and being. Herein lies the decisive distinction between the unity of the monad and that of the atom. The atom is a fundamental substance of things in the sense that it is what remains when matter is divided into its ultimate parts. It is a unit which, so to speak, resists multiplicity and retains its indivisibility despite every attempt to resolve it into subdivisions. The monad, on the other hand, knows no such opposition; for with the monad there is no alternative between unity and multiplicity, but only their inner reciprocity and necessary correlation. It is neither merely one nor merely many, but rather the "expression of multiplicity in unity" (*multorum in uno expressio*). It is a whole which is not the sum of its parts but which constantly unfolds into multiple aspects. The individuality of the monad manifests itself in these progressive acts of individuation—an individuation which is only possible and understandable under the presupposition that the monad as a whole is self-containing and self-sufficient. The nature and being of the form as a whole is not weakened or divided in the sequence of these distinctions but is contained undiminished in each of them. Leibniz sums up this fundamental conception, both conceptually and terminologically, in his concept of *force*. For, according to Leibniz, force is the present state of being in so far as this tends toward a future state or contains that state in itself (*status ipse praesens, dum tendit ad sequentem seu sequentem praeinvolvit*). The monad is not an aggregate but a dynamic whole which can only manifest itself in a profusion, in an infinity, of different effects. In this very infinity it preserves its identity as the same living center of force. This conception, which is no longer based on the concept of being but on that of action, lends an entirely new significance to the problem of the individual entity. Within the limits of analytical logic, of the logic of identity, this problem can only be mastered if the individual entity can be reduced to general concepts and shown to be a special case of these concepts. Such an entity is only "thinkable," can only be clearly and distinctly known, when it can be referred back to general concepts. Taken by itself every individual entity as presented in sense perception or direct intuition must remain an indistinct impression. To be sure, we can ascertain *that* such an impression exists, but we cannot with real precision and assurance say *what* it is. Knowledge of this "what" is reserved for the general concept; it can be gained only from an insight into the nature of the genus or from the definition which offers a general criterion. The individual entity, accordingly, can only be understood when it is included in, and subsumed under, the general concept. Leibniz's doctrine of the concept remains for the most part within this traditional framework yet it was his philosophy that criticized it decisively and implicitly transformed it. For in Leibniz's philosophy an inalienable prerogative is first gained for the individual entity. The individual no longer functions merely as a special case, as an example; it now expresses something essential in itself and valuable through itself. For in Leibniz's system every individual substance is not only a fragment of the universe, it is the universe itself seen from a particular viewpoint. And only the totality of these unique points of view gives us the truth of reality. This truth is not determined by the fact that the various monadological philosophies share certain portions of their content on which they agree, and these points of agreement form a common core of objectivity. Such truth can be grasped and explained only if every substance, remaining within itself and developing its conceptions according to a law peculiar to its own nature, through this characteristic creation stands in relation to the totality of all other substances and is as it were attuned to their pitch. The central thought of Leibniz's philosophy is therefore to be looked for neither in the concept of individuality nor in that of universality. These concepts are explicable only in mutual relationship; they reflect one another, and in this reflection they beget the fundamental concept of harmony which constitutes the beginning and end of the system. "In our own being," says Leibniz in his essay *Of the True Mystical Theology*, "is contained a germ, a footprint, a symbol of the divine nature and its true image." This means that only the highest development of all individual energies—not their leveling, equalization, and extinction—leads to the truth of being, to the highest harmony, and to the most intensive fullness of reality. This fundamental conception calls for a new intellectual orientation because not only has a transformation in individual results taken place, but the ideal center of gravity of all philosophy has shifted.

To be sure, this inner transformation seems at first to have no immediate, historically demonstrable significance for eighteenth century philosophy. For the whole body of Leibniz's thought does not act immediately as a living and pervading force. At first the eighteenth century knows the Leibnizian philosophy only in a very imperfect, in a purely "exoteric" form. It depends for its knowledge of Leibniz's teachings on a few writings which, like the *Monadology* and the *Theodicy*, owe their existence to external and accidental occasions and hence do not contain these teachings in a strictly conceptual treatment, but only in an abbreviated popular version. The chief work of Leibniz's theory of knowledge, *New Essays on the Human Understanding*, did not become known to the eighteenth century until the year 1765 when it was published by Raspe from the manuscript in Hanover at a time when the evolution and formulation of eighteenth century thought had for the most part already reached completion. The influence of Leibnizian ideas is therefore indirect, namely, by way of the transformation they underwent in the system of Wolff. Wolff's logic and methodology differ from those of Leibniz in that they attempt to reduce the variety of their deductions to as simple and uniform an arrangement as possible. The idea of harmony, the principle of continuity, and the law of sufficient reason have their specified place within Wolff's system, but Wolff tries to limit their original significance and independence and to show that they are inferences and deductions from the law of contradiction. Thus the concepts and basic tendencies of the Leibnizian system are transmitted to the eighteenth century with certain limitations, and they appear here, as it were, through a glass darkly. Gradually, however, a movement gets under way which endeavors to abolish this barrier to full comprehension. In Germany it is Wolff's most important pupil, Alexander Baumgarten, who shows his intellectual independence and originality in this matter also. In his metaphysics, and especially in the outline of his aesthetics, Baumgarten finds his way back to certain central conceptions of Leibniz which hitherto had lain fallow. The development of aesthetics and the philosophy of history in Germany now leads us back to the original and profound conception of the problem of individuality as first set forth in Leibniz's monadology and in his "system of pre-established harmony." But in eighteenth century French culture too, in which the Cartesian influence is still predominant, certain basic conceptions and problems of Leibniz appear with increasing frequency. The development does not proceed via aesthetics and the theory of art, which only with difficulty free themselves from the spell of seventeenth century classicism; but rather via the philosophy of nature and the descriptive sciences within which the rigid concept of form gradually breaks down. Leibniz's conception of evolution now receives more and more stress, and it gradually transforms from within the eighteenth century system of nature which had been dominated by the idea of fixed species. Steady progress can be traced from Maupertuis' revival of the basic idea of Leibniz's dynamics and from his defense and interpretation of the principle of continuity to Diderot's physics and metaphysics of the organic and to the beginnings of a comprehensive descriptive natural science in Buffon's *Natural History*. In *Candide* Voltaire parodies Leibniz's *Theodicy*, and in his essay on the elements of the Newtonian philosophy he charges that in natural science too Leibniz's concepts had been obstacles to progress. "His insufficient reason, his continuity, his plenum, his monads, etc.," writes Voltaire in 1741, "are the germs of confusion from which Mr. Wolff has methodically hatched fifteen quarto volumes which more than ever will put German heads to reading much and understanding little."[9] But Voltaire did not always judge in this manner. When, as in his *Age of Louis XIV*, he wanted to present the intellectual structure of the seventeenth century and to understand this structure in the light of its basic forces, he could not overlook Leibniz; and here in fact he acknowledges without reserve the universal significance of Leibniz's total achievement. This change of opinion becomes even more apparent in the generation after Voltaire, namely, among the French Encyclopaedists. While opposing the principles of Leibniz's metaphysics, d'Alembert shows the deepest admiration for Leibniz's philosophical and mathematical genius. And Diderot's article on Leibniz in the *Encyclopaedia* bestows enthusiastic praise on the philosopher. Diderot agrees with Fontenelle that Germany has gained as much honor through this one mind as Greece did through Plato, Aristotle, and Archimedes together. From such personal expressions of praise to a deeper understanding of the principles of the Leibnizian philosophy is still, to be sure, a long way. Yet if one wishes to grasp the entire intellectual structure of the eighteenth century and see it in its genesis, one must clearly separate the two streams of thought which converge at this point. The classical Cartesian form of analysis and that new form of philosophical synthesis which originates in Leibniz are now integrated. From the logic of "clear and distinct ideas" the way leads to the logic of "origin"

[9] Cf. Voltaire's correspondence, especially his letters to Mairan (May 5, 1741) and to Maupertuis (August 10, 1741).

and to the logic of individuality; it leads from mere geometry to a dynamic philosophy of nature, from mechanism to organism, from the principle of identity to that of infinity, from continuity to harmony. In this fundamental opposition lay the great intellectual tasks which eighteenth century thought had to accomplish, and which the century approaches from different angles in its theory of knowledge and in its philosophy of nature, in its psychology and in its theory of the state and society, in its philosophy of religion and in its aesthetics.

CHAPTER II

Nature and Natural Science

IN ESTIMATING the importance of natural science in the genesis and formation of the modern picture of the universe, we must not confine ourselves to a consideration of individual features which science has added to, and by virtue of which it has decisively transformed, the world around us. The extent of these influences seems almost immeasurable and yet it does not fully indicate the formative force which originated in natural science. The real achievement of science lies elsewhere; it is not so much in the new objective content which science has made accessible to the human mind as in the new *function* which it attributes to the mind of man. The knowledge of nature does not simply lead us out into the world of objects; it serves rather as a medium in which the mind develops its own self-knowledge. A process is thus initiated which is more significant than all increase and extension of the mere material with which newly awakened natural science has enriched human knowledge. As early as the sixteenth and seventeenth centuries the accumulation of the materials of knowledge seemed to be approaching the illimitable. The clear-cut form of the classical and medieval conception of the world crumbles, and the world ceases to be a "cosmos" in the sense of an immediately accessible order of things. Space and time are extended indefinitely; they can no longer be comprehended within that clearly defined scheme which classical cosmology possessed in Plato's doctrine of the five regular heavenly bodies or in Aristotle's hierarchical cosmos, nor can they be represented by finite measures and numbers. One world and one Being are replaced by an infinity of worlds constantly springing from the womb of becoming, each one of which embodies but a single transitory phase of the inexhaustible vital process of the universe. But the important aspect of the transformation does not lie in this boundless expansion, but in the fact that the mind now becomes aware of a new force within itself. All extensive growth would remain fruitless and could only lead the mind to a vacuum if it did not acquire a new intensity and concentration within itself. And it is this intensity which informs the mind of its real nature. The highest energy and deepest truth of the mind do not consist in going out into the infinite, but in the mind's maintaining itself against the infinite and proving in its pure unity equal to the infinity of being. Giordano Bruno, in whom this new climate of opinion first appears, defines the relation between the ego and the world, between subject and object in this sense. For him the infinite process of becoming, the great spectacle of the world forever unrolling before our eyes, is the guaranty of that deepest meaning which the ego can find only in itself. The power of reason is our only access to the infinite; it assures us of the presence of the infinite and teaches us to place it within measure and bound, not in order to limit its realm but in order to know it in its all-comprehensive and all-pervasive law. Universal law, which is discovered and formulated in thought, forms the necessary correlate of the intuitively experienced boundlessness of the universe. Thus the new conception of nature, seen in the perspective of the history of thought, owes its origin to a double motive and is shaped and determined by apparently opposing forces. It contains both the impulse toward the particular, the concrete, and the factual, and the impulse toward the absolutely universal; thus it harbors the elemental impulse to hold fast to the things of this world as well as the impulse to rise above them in order to see them in their proper perspective. The desire and joy of the senses unite here with the power of the intellect to break away from all the objects of concrete experience and to risk flight into the land of possibilities. The modern concept of nature, as its shape becomes increasingly articulate from the Renaissance on and as it seeks philosophical foundation and justification in the great systems of the seventeenth century—in Descartes, Spinoza, and Leibniz—is characterized above all by the new relationship which develops between sensibility and intellect, between experience and thought, between the sensible world and the intelligible world.

This change in the method of natural science involves also a decisive transformation in pure ontology; it substitutes new measuring sticks for the ones hitherto applied to the order of being. The task of medieval thought had consisted largely in tracing the architectonics of being and in delineating its main design. In the religious system of the Middle Ages as it is crystallized in scholasticism every phase of reality is assigned its unique place; and with its place goes a complete determination of its value, which is based on the greater or lesser distance which separates it from the First Cause. There is no room here for doubt, and in all thinking there is the consciousness of being sheltered by this inviolable order which it is not the business of thought to create but only to accept. God, the soul, and the world are the three great points on which all being hinges, and the system of knowledge is oriented to them. Knowledge of nature is by no means excluded from this system; but from the first it remains confined within a definite circle of existence, from which it cannot depart without getting lost—without darkening the light which illuminates it within its prescribed sphere. Knowledge of "nature" is synonymous with knowledge of creation. It is knowledge so far as it is accessible to a finite, created, dependent being, and it includes no other content than the finite objects of sense. Thus such knowledge is limited both subjectively and objectively. Especially in medieval thought the limits of natural knowledge do not, of course, coincide with those of physical and corporeal, of material existence. Not only is there natural knowledge of the corporeal world and its forces but there is also natural knowledge of law, of the state, and even of religion and its fundamental truths. For the extent of natural knowledge is not determined by the object but by its origin. All knowledge, no matter what its content, is "natural" so long as it springs from human reason alone and does not rely on other foundations of certainty. "Nature" therefore does not so much signify a given group of objects as a certain "horizon" of knowledge, of the comprehension of reality. To nature belongs everything in the sphere of "natural light" (*lumen naturale*), everything whose understanding and confirmation require no other aid than the natural forces of knowledge. The "realm of nature" is thus opposed to the "realm of grace." The one is communicated to us through sense perception and its supplementary processes of logical judgment and inference, of the discursive use of the understanding; the other is accessible only through the power of revelation. There need be no opposition between belief and knowledge, between revelation and reason. The great systems of scholasticism look upon it as their chief task to reconcile the two and to harmonize them according to their content. The realm of grace does not negate the realm of nature. Though the former, so to speak, overshadows the latter, it does not impinge on the existence of the latter as such: "Grace does not abolish nature, but completes it" (*gratia naturam non tollit, sed perficit*). But the fact remains that the real perfection of nature is not to be found in nature itself but must be sought beyond the natural sphere. Neither science nor morality, neither law nor state, can be erected on its own foundations. Supernatural assistance is always needed to bring them to true perfection. For "natural light" no longer harbors any real truth; it has been darkened and cannot be restored by any efforts of its own. In medieval thought there remains, in theory as well as in practice, side by side with divine law a relatively independent sphere of natural law accessible to and dominated by human reason. But "natural law" (*lex naturalis*) can never be more than the point of departure for "divine law" (*lex divina*), which alone is capable of restoring the original knowledge lost through the fall of man. Reason is and remains the servant of revelation (*tanquam famula et ministra*); within the sphere of natural intellectual and psychological forces, reason leads toward, and prepares the ground for, revelation.

The nature philosophy of the Renaissance attacks from two angles this viewpoint which long survived the age of scholasticism, and which still went unchallenged[1] at the foundation of Protestant theology in the sixteenth and seventeenth centuries. This philosophy takes the lead in destroying the old conception of nature. Its basic tendency and principle can be expressed in the formula that the true essence of nature is not to be sought in the realm of the created (*natura naturata*), but in that of the creative process (*natura naturans*). Nature is more than mere creation; it participates in original divine essence be-

[1] See especially Ernst Troeltsch, *Vernunft und Offenbarung bei Johann Gerhard und Melanchthon*, Göttingen, 1891.

cause the divine power pervades nature itself. The dualism between creator and creation is thus abolished. Nature as that which is moved is no longer set over against the divine mover; it is now an original formative principle which moves from within. Through its capacity to unfold and take on form from within itself, nature bears the stamp of the divine. For God is not to be conceived as a force intervening from without and exerting its influence as a moving cause on matter foreign to itself; God Himself enters directly into the processes of nature. Such a "presence" is appropriate to the divine and is alone worthy of its dignity. "God is not an external intelligence rolling around and leading around; it is more worthy for him to be the internal principle of motion, which is his own nature, his own appearance, his own soul than that as many entities as live in His bosom should have motion."[2] A radical transformation of the concept of nature appears in these words of Giordano Bruno. Nature is elevated to the sphere of the divine and seems to be resolved into the infinity of the divine nature, but on the other hand it implies the individuality, the independence and particularity of objects. And from this characteristic force, which radiates from every object as a special center of activity, is derived also the inalienable worth which belongs to it in the totality of being. All this is now summed up in the word "nature," which signifies the integration of all parts into one all-inclusive whole of activity and life which, nevertheless, no longer means mere subordination. For the part not only exists within the whole but asserts itself against it, constituting a specific element of individuality and necessity. The law which governs individual entities is not prescribed by a foreign lawgiver, nor thrust upon them by force; it is founded in, and completely knowable through, their own nature. This conclusion marks the second important step; in it the transition from the dynamic philosophy of nature of the Renaissance to the mathematical science of nature is implicitly accomplished. For the latter too is based entirely on the fundamental conception

[2] "Non est Deus vel intelligentia exterior circumrotans et circumducens; dignius enim illi debet esse internum principium motus, quod est natura propria, species propria, anima propria quam habeant tot quot in illius gremio vivunt."

of law whose meaning is now indeed more strictly determined. The requirement is now, not merely to sense dimly the law of activity in nature, but to know this law precisely and to express it in clear concepts. Neither feeling nor sense perception nor imagination can satisfy this requirement; it can be fulfilled only if the connection between the individual and the whole, between "appearance" and "idea," is looked for in a hitherto untried manner. Sense observation must be combined with exact measurement, and the new theory of nature must grow out of these two factors. This theory too, as established in the works of Kepler and Galileo, is still imbued with a strong religious impulse which acts as a driving force. Its constant aim is to find signs of the divinity of nature in natural law. But precisely because of its underlying religious tendency this theory of nature inevitably comes into conflict with traditional forms of belief. Looked at from this viewpoint, the fight which the Church carried on against the advance of the modern spirit of mathematical science now becomes quite understandable. The Church was not assailing individual accomplishments of scientific investigation. Reconciliation would have been possible between these and church doctrine. Galileo himself for a long time believed in such a reconciliation and honestly strove for it. But the tragic misunderstanding which was his eventual downfall was the fact that he looked in the wrong place for the opposition he was endeavoring to reconcile, and that he himself underestimated the radical innovation in methodological attitude which had taken place within him. Hence he did not approach the conflict at its real foundation but merely tried to adjust and balance results derived from his basic standpoint. In reality it was not the new cosmology which church authorities so vehemently opposed; for as a mere mathematical "hypothesis" they could just as well accept the Copernican as the Ptolemaic system. But what was not to be tolerated, what threatened the very foundations of the Church, was the new concept of truth proclaimed by Galileo.[3] Alongside of the truth of revelation comes now an independent and original truth of nature.

[3] For a fuller presentation of this subject see the author's book *Das Erkenntnis-problem*, third edition, vol. I, pp. 276 ff.

This truth is revealed not in God's word but in his work; it is not based on the testimony of Scripture or tradition but is visible to us at all times. But it is understandable only to those who know nature's handwriting and can decipher her text. The truth of nature cannot be expressed in mere words; the only suitable expression lies in mathematical constructions, figures and numbers. And in these symbols nature presents itself in perfect form and clarity. Revelation by means of the sacred word can never achieve such brightness and transparency, such precision, for words as such are always varicolored and ambiguous admitting a variety of interpretations. Their meaning must always be given them by man and must therefore be fragmentary. In nature, on the other hand, the whole plan of the universe lies before us in its undivided and inviolable unity, evidently waiting for the human mind to recognize and express it.

And according to the judgment of the eighteenth century such a mind had meantime appeared. What Galileo had called for became reality in Newton; the problem posed by the Renaissance seemed to have been solved in a surprisingly short time. Galileo and Kepler had grasped the idea of natural law in all its breadth and depth, and in its fundamental methodological meaning; but they had only been able to illustrate the application of this law in individual cases, in the phenomena of freely falling bodies and of planetary motion. Room for doubt remained; for proof was still lacking that the strict law, which had been shown to govern the parts, was also valid for the whole, and that the universe as such could be approached and adequately understood by way of the exact concepts of mathematical knowledge. Newton's work offered such proof. Here it was no longer a matter of a particular natural phenomenon, it was not merely the reduction of a limited field of phenomena to rule and order; on the contrary, in Newton it was a question of establishing and clearly expressing a—rather *the*—cosmic law. This law seemed assured in Newton's theory of gravitation. Thus was the victory of human knowledge decided and an elemental power of knowledge had been discovered which seemed equal to the elemental power of nature. In this sense the whole eighteenth century understood and esteemed Newton's achievement. In Newton it honored the great empirical scientist; it does not, however, stop here, but more and more emphatically points out that Newton not only gave hard and fast rules to nature but to philosophy as well. Not less important than the results of Newton's investigations are his so-called rules of philosophy (*regulae philosophandi*) which he found valid in natural science and established forever in this field of knowledge. The unreserved admiration and veneration of the eighteenth century for Newton is derived from this conception of his achievement. By virtue of its results and its aim alone this achievement appears great and incomparable but, in the light of the method by which its aim had been accomplished, it seems even greater. Newton first showed science the way leading from arbitrary and phantastic assumptions to the clarity of the concept, from darkness to light:

"Nature and Nature's laws lay hid in night,
    God said: 'Let Newton be,' and all was light."

These verses from Pope express most effectively the kind of veneration which Newton enjoys in the thinking of the Enlightenment. Thanks to Newton, it believed it stood finally on firm ground which could never again be shaken by any future revolution of natural science. The correlation between nature and human knowledge has now been established once and for all and the bond between them is henceforth inseverable. Both members of the correlation are quite independent but by virtue of their independence they are, nevertheless, in complete harmony. Nature in man, as it were, meets nature in the cosmos half way and finds its own essence there. Whoever finds the one is sure to find the other. The philosophy of nature of the Renaissance understood by "nature" the law which springs from the essence of things and with which they are originally endowed, not the law they receive from without. "Nature is nothing but a force implanted in things and the law by which all entities proceed along their proper paths."[4] To find this law

---

[4] Natura estque nihil, nisi virtus insita rebus
    Et lex qua peragunt proprium cuncta entia cursum.
Giordano Bruno, *De Immenso*, liber VIII, cap. 9, *Opera latina*, Naples, 1879-1891, vol. I, part II, p. 310.

we must not project our own ideas and subjective imaginings into nature; we must rather follow nature's own course and determine it by observation and experiment, by measurement and calculation. But our basic standards for measurement are not to be derived from sense data alone. They originate in those universal functions of comparing and counting, of combining and differentiating, which constitute the nature of the intellect. Thus the autonomy of the intellect corresponds to the pure autonomy of nature. In one and the same intellectual process of emancipation the philosophy of the Enlightenment attempts to show the self-sufficiency of both nature and intellect. Both are now to be recognized as elemental and to be firmly connected with one another. Thus any mediation between the two which is based on a transcendent power or a transcendent being becomes superfluous. Such mediation cannot further strengthen the bond between nature and mind. On the contrary, the intervention of a transcendent being, by the mere approach to the problem which it involves and by the questioning to which it subjects nature and mind, loosens this bond and must in the long run sever it completely. And indeed the metaphysics of "occasionalism" in modern times had taken just this step; it had sacrificed the autonomous action of nature and the autonomous form of the mind to the omnipotence of the divine First Cause. Against this relapse into transcendence the philosophy of the Enlightenment proclaims the pure principle of immanence both for nature and for knowledge. Both must be understood in terms of their own essence, and this is no dark, mysterious "something," impenetrable to intellect; this essence consists rather in principles which are perfectly accessible to the mind since the mind is able to educe them from itself and to enunciate them systematically.

By this basic conception is to be explained the almost unlimited power which scientific knowledge gains over all the thought of the Enlightenment. D'Alembert called the eighteenth century the philosophical century but with equal justification and pride this era often labeled itself the century of natural science. The organization of natural science had already made great progress in the seventeenth century, and even then it had reached a certain inner completion. In England, the founding of the Royal Society in 1660 created a fixed center for all scientific pursuits. It had functioned even earlier as a free organization of individual scientists; and so, even before the royal decree of foundation gave it official sanction and an official constitution, it had been active as an "invisible college." And even then it represented a certain methodological viewpoint; it emphasized time and again that no concept in physics was admissible which had not first passed the empirical test and proved itself by experiment. The movement which starts here soon reaches France, where it finds its first support in the Académie des Sciences founded by Colbert in 1666. But not until the eighteenth century does the movement achieve its full breadth and effectiveness in all fields of intellectual life. It now goes beyond the sphere of the academies and learned societies. From a mere matter of scholarly interest it now becomes the concern of all civilization. It is no longer merely the empirical scientists, the mathematicians and physicists, who participate in this movement but also those thinkers who are seeking a new orientation of all the intellectual sciences. A renewal of these sciences, deeper insight into the spirit of laws, of society, of politics, and even of poetry, seems impossible unless it is pursued in the light of the great model of the natural sciences. Again it is d'Alembert who not only personally brought about this alliance between the natural and the intellectual sciences but who also in his *Elements of Philosophy* expressed with the greatest clarity the principle on which the alliance rests: "Natural science from day to day accumulates new riches. Geometry, by extending its limits, has borne its torch into the regions of physical science which lay nearest at hand. The true system of the world has been recognized. . . . In short, from the earth to Saturn, from the history of the heavens to that of insects, natural philosophy has been revolutionized; and nearly all other fields of knowledge have assumed new forms . . . the discovery and application of a new method of philosophizing, the kind of enthusiasm which accompanies discoveries, a certain exaltation of ideas which the spectacle of the universe produces in us; all these causes have brought about a lively fermentation of minds.

Nature and Natural Science

Spreading throughout nature in all directions, this fermentation has swept with a sort of violence everything before it which stood in its way, like a river which has burst its dams. . . . Thus, from the principles of the secular sciences to the foundations of religious revelation, from metaphysics to matters of taste, from music to morals, from the scholastic disputes of theologians to matters of commerce, from natural law to the arbitrary laws of nations . . . everything has been discussed, analyzed, or at least mentioned. The fruit or sequel of this general effervescence of minds has been to cast new light on some matters and new shadows on others, just as the effect of the ebb and flow of the tides leaves some things on the shore and washes others away."[5] No reputable thinker of the eighteenth century entirely escaped the influence of this basic tendency. Voltaire marks a new epoch in France, not through his creative writings or his first philosophical essays, but through his defense of Newton in his *Elements of the Philosophy of Newton*. Similarly, among Diderot's writings there is a work on the elements of physiology and among Rousseau's a treatise on the fundamental laws of chemistry. Montesquieu's first writings deal with physical and physiological problems, and he was apparently kept from a continuation of such studies only by the external circumstance of an eye ailment which developed at this time and made scientific observation difficult. In the style typical of his youthful writings Montesquieu says: "One would say that Nature acted like those virgins who long preserved their most precious possession, and then allowed themselves to be ravished in a moment of that they had preserved with such care, and defended with such constancy."[6] The whole eighteenth century is permeated by this conviction, namely, that in the history of humanity the time had now arrived to deprive nature of its carefully guarded secret, to leave it no longer in the dark to be marveled at as an incomprehensible mystery but to bring it under the bright light of reason and analyze it with all its fundamental forces.

[5] D'Alembert, *Éléments de Philosophie*; see above p. 4.

[6] Sainte-Beuve, "Montesquieu," *Causeries du Lundi*; cited from Sainte-Beuve, *Portraits of the Eighteenth Century*, tr. Katharine P. Wormeley, G. P. Putnam's Sons, New York and London, 1905, p. 115.

To do this, however, it was above all necessary to sever the bond between theology and physics once and for all. Much as this bond had been loosened in the eighteenth century, it had by no means been entirely broken. The authority of Scripture was still eagerly defended even in matters of pure natural science. The ridicule to which again and again Voltaire subjected "Biblical physics" seems to us today obsolete and shallow; but the impartial historical judge must not forget that in the eighteenth century this ridicule was directed at a dangerous antagonist. Orthodoxy had by no means given up the principle of verbal inspiration, and in this principle the inference was implied that a genuine science of nature was contained in the Mosaic story of the creation whose basic features are not to be tampered with. Not only theologians, but physicists and biologists, endeavor to support and explain this science. In 1726 appears in French translation a book by the Englishman Derham entitled *Physical Theology*, and this is followed later by Derham's *Astronomical Theology*, by Fabricius's *The Theology of Water* and Lesser's *Insect Theology*.[7] Voltaire not only combats the ostensible results of theological physics but he tries especially to show the falsity of the method applied to nature by theologians and to discredit their physics as a monstrous offspring of the theological spirit, a bastard of faith and science. "One writer wants to persuade me by means of physics to believe in the Trinity; he tells me the three persons of the deity are like the three dimensions of space. Another claims he will give me palpable proof of transubstantiation and shows me through the laws of motion how an accidental property can exist without its subject." Clear methodological differentiation between theology and science makes its way slowly. Geology takes the lead in this matter by breaking down the temporal framework of the Biblical story of the creation. Even in the seventeenth century attacks had centered on this framework. Fontenelle compares the belief of the ancients in the immutability of the celestial bodies with the belief of a rose protesting that, as long as roses can remember, no gardener ever died.

[7] Regarding the extent and content of the literature of "theological physics" see D. Mornet, *Les sciences de la nature en France au XVIIIe siècle*, Paris, 1911, pp. 31 ff.

Nature and Natural Science

Criticism becomes more serious after definite empirical results, especially paleontological discoveries, are there to support it. In his works *The Sacred Theory of the Earth* (*Telluris sacra theoria*) in 1680 and *Philosophical Archaeology* (*Archaeologia philosophica*) in 1692 Thomas Burnet is still striving to confirm the objective truth of the Biblical account of creation. But to this end he has to abandon the principle of verbal inspiration and take refuge in an allegorical interpretation which permits him to disregard all measurements of time in the Bible. In place of the individual days of the Biblical creation Burnet assumes whole epochs or periods to which any length of time required by the empirical findings can be attributed. In Buffon's great work *The Epochs of Nature* this approach is later raised to the dignity of an ultimate principle of scientific research. Buffon was not looking for trouble with theology, and when the first attacks on his work came out he submitted to the decision of the Sorbonne. But his silence regarding the creation story was more eloquent than an open declaration of war could have been. For now for the first time a physical account of the world had been outlined which avoided religious dogmatism and claimed as its sole basis the observable facts and general principles of natural science. The stronghold of the traditional system had finally been breached, and Voltaire's busy mind did not rest until it had taken down the whole structure stone by stone in a work extending over more than half a century. Such demolition was the indispensable precondition of the new edifice of physics. For not until now had science with full consciousness of the implications taken up again the case against Galileo. It had summoned him before its own court and decided his case according to its own basic principles. And this decision has never since been seriously contested; even its opponents finally accepted it in silence. This was the first important victory of the philosophy of the Enlightenment. It finished in this respect what the Renaissance had begun; it marked off a definite field for rational knowledge within which there was to be no more restraint and authoritative coercion but free movement in all directions. By virtue of this freedom philosophy could attain to full self-knowledge and to knowledge of its inherent forces.

Nature and Natural Science

2

In his *Conversations on the Plurality of Worlds* Fontenelle tries to explain Cartesian cosmology by comparing the events of nature with those of a large stage. The spectator in the orchestra sees a series of events which come and go in varied sequence. He is absorbed in the contemplation of these events and delighted with the profusion of pictures which pass before him, without wondering how they are produced. But if perchance there is a mechanic among the audience, he will not be satisfied with merely beholding these pictures. He will not rest until he has discovered the causes of these phenomena, until he has penetrated the mechanism behind all these changing scenes. The behavior of the philosopher is like that of the mechanic. But here the difficulty is increased by the circumstance that nature, in the spectacle it constantly presents, has so carefully hidden its mechanism that it has taken us centuries to come upon its mysterious springs of action. Not until modern times was man permitted to look behind the scenes; science sees not only phenomena themselves, but also the clockworks which bring them about. Far from diminishing the charm of the drama, such insight materially enhances its value. Many people erroneously hold the opinion that knowledge of the mechanics according to which the universe behaves detracts from its dignity because such knowledge reduces the universe to a clockwork. "I esteem the universe all the more," writes Fontenelle, "since I have known that it is like a watch. It is surprising that nature, admirable as it is, is based on such simple things."[8]

The comparison which Fontenelle draws here is no mere play of wit; it involves an idea of decisive importance for the entire structure of natural science in the seventeenth century. Descartes' philosophy of nature had given this idea its form and universal application. Nature cannot be understood if it is taken merely as a sum total of phenomena, if one considers only the extension of its events in space or their temporal sequence. One must trace the phenomena back to their principles, and

---

[8] Fontenelle, *Entretiens sur la pluralité des mondes*, premier soir, *Oeuvres de Fontenelle*, Paris, 1818, vol. II, pp. 10 f.

the principles are nowhere else to be found than in the laws of motion. Once these laws have been discovered and reduced to exact mathematical expression, the path of all future knowledge is marked out. We only have to develop completely what is implicitly contained in these laws in order to have a synopsis of all nature and to understand the universe in its innermost structure. Descartes' treatise on the system of the world was intended as the execution of this basic theoretical plan. Its motto was: "Give me matter and I will build you a world." Thought no longer wants to accept the world simply as empirically given; it sets itself the task of analyzing the structure of the universe, in fact, of producing this structure with its own resources. Beginning with its own clear and distinct ideas, it finds in them the model for all reality. Mathematical principles and axioms of thought lead it safely through the entire realm of nature. For there is a definite path, a single uninterrupted chain of deduction, which stretches from the highest and most general causes of natural events down to the special laws of nature and even to every individual effect, no matter how complex. There is no barrier between the realm of clear and distinct concepts and the realm of facts, between geometry and physics. Since the substance of physical body consists in pure extension, knowledge of this extension, that is, geometry, is master of physics. Geometry expresses the nature of the corporeal world and its general fundamental properties in exact definitions and proceeds from these by an uninterrupted chain of thought to the determination of the particular and the factual.

But this ambitious project of Cartesian physics had not passed the empirical test. The further Descartes proceeded along this path and the more closely he approached the special phenomena of nature, the greater were the difficulties which he encountered. He met these difficulties only because he constantly resorted to new and more complicated mechanisms and entangled himself in a network of hypotheses. This finely spun texture is torn to pieces by Newton. He too seeks universal mathematical principles in nature but he no longer believes it possible to reduce physics to geometry. He advocates rather the independent function and the unique character of physical investigation, and this character is founded in the method of experimentation and the method of inductive reasoning. The path of physical investigation does not lead from top to bottom, from axioms and principles to facts, but rather from the latter to the former. We cannot begin with general assumptions about the nature of things and then derive from them a knowledge of particular events; we must rather begin with this knowledge, as given us in direct observation, and in a gradual ascent try to get back to the first causes and to the simple elements of natural processes. The ideal of deduction is now confronted with the ideal of analysis. And analysis is by nature unending; it cannot be limited to a definite, verifiable chain of thought which could be anticipated *a priori*. It must rather be taken up anew at every stage of empirical science. Analysis knows no absolute end but only relative and provisional stopping points. Newton also looked upon his fundamental doctrine, the general theory of gravitation, only as such a provisional point of rest. For he is satisfied to show that gravity is a universal phenomenon of nature without inquiring after its ultimate causes. Newton expressly rejects a mechanical theory of gravitation because experience does not offer sufficient evidence for such a theory. Nor does he claim any metaphysical foundation for gravity, for this too for the physicist would mean an unjustifiable transgression of boundaries. He is concerned solely with the phenomena of gravity; and he tries to express these phenomena not in a mere concept, in an abstract definition, but in a comprehensive mathematical formula which implicitly contains them as concrete individual cases and completely describes them. Physical theory neither pretends to, nor should, venture beyond pure description of natural phenomena.[9] Seen from this standpoint gravity is of course a general property of matter but it does not have to be regarded as one of its essential properties. Natural philosophy that undertakes to construct the world in pure thought, out of mere concepts, is according to Newton always exposed to a double temptation and danger. Wherever

[9] For a fuller account of the opposition between the "explanation of nature" and the "description of nature," between definition and description, in Newton and his school, see the author's *Erkenntnisproblem*, vol. II, p. 401.

it finds any general, universally recurring quality of things, it must either hypostatize this quality, that is, make it an absolutely real, original quality of being; or it must resolve and reduce it to a derivative of general antecedent causes. But to genuine empiricism the one procedure is as foreign as the other. Empiricism is satisfied with establishing the phenomena; but it knows, on the other hand, that no phenomenon is absolutely final and incapable of further analysis. This analysis must not, however, take place prematurely in thought; it must rather be awaited in the course of experimental progress. In this sense Newton insists that gravity is for the time being a "last" element of nature, a provisionally irreducible quality which cannot be sufficiently explained on the basis of any known mechanism; but this does not exclude the possibility that on the basis of future observations this quality too may become reducible to simpler natural phenomena. The assumption of some kind of occult qualities, to which scholastic physics appealed, is of course arbitrary and meaningless. On the other hand, it would mark an important advance for scientific insight if we were to succeed in reducing the wealth of natural phenomena to a few fundamental properties of matter and to definite principles of motion, even if the causes of these properties and principles should meantime remain unknown.

In these classical dicta, as they appear, for instance, at the end of his *Optics*,[10] Newton clearly outlined the program for all natural science in the eighteenth century. The crucial point in the natural science of this time is that at which it consciously and energetically advances from Descartes to Newton. The ideal of a purely mechanical philosophy of nature, such as Fontenelle in the statements quoted above had proclaimed, was gradually superseded until it was finally abandoned entirely by the epistemologists of modern physics. Condillac in his *Treatise on Systems* which appeared in 1759 vigorously urges that the "spirit of systems" which had produced the great metaphysical edifices of the seventeenth century be banished from physics. Instead of any general, but arbitrary, explanation based on the apparent "nature of things," there must appear simple observa-

---

[10] *Optice*, ed. Samuel Clarke, 1740, liber III, quaestio 31.

tion of phenomena and clear designation of their empirical connection. The physicist must finally give up trying to explain the mechanism of the universe; he has done enough if he succeeds in establishing definite general relations in nature. The ideal of natural science, accordingly, is no longer shaped after the pattern of geometry, but rather after that of arithmetic; for the doctrine of numbers, according to Condillac, represents the clearest and simplest example for the theory of relations as well as for the general logic of relations.[11] This ideal of knowledge achieves its widest dissemination and its greatest effectiveness, however, because Voltaire makes it the battle cry of his war on Cartesian physics. With his characteristic ability to simplify and to universalize, Voltaire at once makes this a general question. Newton's method is by no means confined to physics; it holds as well for all knowledge in general, and from the first limits such knowledge within certain boundaries and to certain conditions. For if we do not use the compass of mathematics and if the light of experience does not guide us, we cannot take a single step forward. It is vain to imagine that we shall ever see into the essence of things. We cannot know from general concepts how it is possible for one material object to affect another, any more than we can gain a clear insight into the genesis of our ideas. In the one case as in the other we must be satisfied if we can verify the "what" without any knowledge of the "how." To ask *how* we think and feel or how our limbs obey the command of our will, is to inquire into the mystery of creation. Here all knowledge fails us, for there is no knowledge of first principles. We can never know completely anything really elementary or absolutely primary, said Voltaire.[12] On the question of the certainty or uncertainty of knowledge the roles have been switched about strangely as a result of this transition from the constructive to the analytical ideal of natural science. For Descartes the certainty and stability of all knowledge was founded in its first principles, while everything factual as such remained uncertain and problematical. We cannot trust the appearances of things

[11] Condillac, *Traité des systèmes; Logique*, part II, ch. vii and *passim*.
[12] Voltaire, *Le philosophe ignorant* (1766), x. Cf. *Traité de métaphysique* (1734), especially ch. III ff.

to the senses, for sense perception always involves the possibility of sense deception. We can escape such deception only by penetrating beyond mere appearance, by relating the empirically given to concepts and expressing it in concepts which carry their proof within themselves. There is then an immediate and intuitive certainty regarding principles; regarding facts knowledge is mediate and derivative. The certainty of the facts is subordinated to that of the principles and dependent on the latter. The new physical theory of knowledge, which owes its existence to Newton and Locke, reverses, however, this relationship. The principle is derivative; the fact as such is original. No principle is certain in itself; every principle owes its truth and inner reliability solely to the use to which we can put it, and this use consists only in the aid we receive from the principle in comprehending the manifold of given phenomena and arranging them according to certain points of view. If we overlook the function of arrangement, then every principle is useless. For a principle cannot be based on itself; its truth and certainty must be found in the body of knowledge which the principle validates. Just as this body of knowledge must belong to the sphere of the observable and factual, so no principle, however general, can absolutely abandon this sphere or transcend it. By the middle of the century this view gained general recognition through Newton's pupils and followers in France—through Voltaire, Maupertuis, and d'Alembert. It is customary to consider the turn toward mechanism and materialism as characteristic of the philosophy of nature of the eighteenth century, and in so doing it is often believed that the basic trend of the French spirit has been exhaustively characterized. Yet in truth this materialism, as it appears in Holbach's *System of Nature* and Lamettrie's *Man a Machine* (*L'homme machine*), is an isolated phenomenon of no characteristic significance. Both works represent special cases and exemplify a retrogression into that dogmatic mode of thinking which the leading scientific minds of the eighteenth century oppose and endeavor to eliminate. The scientific sentiments of the Encyclopaedists are not represented by Holbach and Lamettrie, but by d'Alembert. And in the latter we find the vehement renunciation of mechanism and materialism as the ultimate principle for the explanation of things, as the ostensible solution of the riddles of the universe. D'Alembert never deviates from the Newtonian method. He too rejects all questions regarding the absolute nature of things and their metaphysical origin. "What difference does it make to us fundamentally whether or not we penetrate to the essence of bodies provided that, matter being supposed such as we conceive it, we can deduce from properties which we regard as primitive, other secondary properties which we perceive in matter; and that the general system of phenomena, always uniform and continuous, nowhere shows us a contradiction? Let us stop here then, and let us not seek to minimize by subtle sophisms the extent of our clear and certain knowledge, which is already too scanty." Concerning the questions of the unity of soul and body and their reciprocal relations, concerning the questions of our simple ideas and of the ultimate grounds of motion, he said: "the supreme Intelligence has drawn a veil before our feeble vision which we try in vain to remove. It is a sad lot for our curiosity and our pride, but it is the lot of humanity. We should conclude therefrom at any rate that the systems, or rather, the dreams of the philosophers on most metaphysical questions deserve no place in a work exclusively intended to contain the real knowledge acquired by the human mind."[13]

With this critical self-denial in respect to certain spheres of knowledge we are already at the threshold of a more difficult and profound problem. D'Alembert's philosophy gives up all claim to establish a metaphysical formula which could reveal to us the nature of things in themselves; its aim is to remain within the realm of phenomena and simply to reveal the system, the constant and general order, of these phenomena. But how can we rely on the truth of this system, or on the existence of such an order at all? Where is the guarantee, the decisive proof, that at least this general system of phenomena is completely self-contained, homogeneous and uniform? D'Alembert postulates such uniformity, but nowhere does he justify it more explicitly. But is not this postulate simply faith in disguise?

[13] D'Alembert, *Éléments de Philosophie*, VI; *Mélanges de Philosophie*, vol. IV, pp. 59, 63 f.

Does it not contain an unproven and undemonstrable metaphysical presupposition? Classical rationalism in Descartes, Spinoza, and Leibniz had already faced this fundamental question. This school of thought believed it could answer the question by carrying the problem of the unity of nature back to the problem of the unity of the divine First Cause. Just as surely as nature is a work of God, so too it radiates the image of the divine spirit; it mirrors God's immutability and eternity. Hence it is in its origin that nature finds assurance of its real and profound truth. The uniformity of nature springs from the essential form of God; from the very concept of God it is clear that He can be thought of only as One, as in harmony with himself, as unchangeable in all his thoughts and acts of will. To suppose a change of existence as possible in God, would be tantamount to a negation of his essence. Spinoza's equation of God and nature, his formula: "God or nature" (*deus sive natura*) rests entirely on this fundamental conception. To assume, even in thought, that another order of nature were possible, would be equivalent to the assumption that God could be or become other than He is: "If, therefore, things could have been of another nature, or could have been determined in another manner to action, so that the order of nature would have been different, the nature of God might then be different to that which it now is. . . ."[14] Hence we are only using different expressions for the same thing when we speak of the laws of nature and the laws of God. For "the general laws of nature which govern and determine all phenomena are nothing but the eternal decrees of God which always entail eternal truth and necessity."[15]

For Leibniz too there is no other definite proof of the stability of nature, of the harmony between the ideal and the real, of the agreement between facts and the eternal verities, than recourse to the unity of the highest principle from which the sensible world as well as the conceptual world is derived. In order to prove that the fundamental principles of infinitesimal

[14] Spinoza, *Ethic*, Book I, Prop. XXXIII, Demonstration, translated by W. Hale White, revised by Amelia Hutchison Stirling, Humphrey Milford, Oxford University Press, London, 1930, p. 33.
[15] Spinoza, *Tractatus Theologico-Politicus*, cap. III, sect. 7.

calculus are applicable without restriction to nature, and that the principle of continuity has not merely an abstract mathematical but also a concrete physical significance, Leibniz assumes that the laws of reality cannot deviate from the purely ideal laws of mathematics and logic: "This is because all things are governed by reason and because otherwise there would be no knowledge, which would be contrary to the nature of the sovereign principle."[16] But does not this reasoning contain an obvious vicious circle? Are we justified in inferring the absolute unity and immutability of God from the empirical homogeneity which nature seems to exhibit? And may we in turn use the unity and immutability of God as an argument for perfect homogeneity in the order of nature? Do we not offend against the most elementary laws of logic by converting the very thing which is to be proved into our weightiest argument, and by supporting all certainty of our judgments and conclusions on a metaphysical assumption which is more problematical than empirical certainty itself? Our thinking is here confronted with a decision involving a more difficult task and a greater responsibility than all mere questions of content in the philosophy of nature. For it is now a question not of the content of nature, but of its concept; not of the results of experience, but of its form. The task of freeing natural science from the domination of theology appeared as a relatively simple matter to Enlightenment thought. To accomplish this task it was merely necessary to utilize the heritage of preceding centuries; the separation which had already taken place in fact, had now to be realized conceptually. Thus everything that is achieved in this direction is rather a conclusion than a really new intellectual beginning; it is merely the clarification of a methodological development which could be looked upon as established by the progress of science in the seventeenth and eighteenth centuries. When, however, this same science is asked to justify itself, a new and more radical problem arises. What is the use of freeing natural science from all theologico-metaphysical content and of limiting it to purely empirical statements, if we do not, on the other

[16] Leibniz's letter to Varignon, Feb. 2, 1702, *Mathematische Schriften*, ed. Gerhardt, IV, 94.

hand, succeed in eliminating metaphysical elements from its structure? And does not every statement which goes beyond the simple affirmation of an immediate object of sense perception contain just such an element? Is the systematic structure of nature, the absolute homogeneity of experience, itself a result of experience? Is it deducible from, and demonstrable by, experience? Or does it not rather constitute a premise of experience? And is not this premise, this logical *a priori*, just as questionable as any metaphysical or theological *a priori* could be? One should not only eliminate all individual concepts and judgments from the realm of empirical science; one should finally have the courage to pursue this tendency to its logical conclusion: one should even withdraw from the concept of nature the support of the concept of God. What will then become of the apparent necessity of nature, of its general, eternal, and inviolable laws? Is this necessity based upon an intuitive certainty, or upon any other rigorous deductive proof? Or must we forego all such proofs and make up our minds to take the last step, namely, to acknowledge that the world of facts can only support itself and that we seek in vain for any other firmer foundation, for a rational ground, for this world?

In all these questions we have anticipated the development from the phenomenalism of mathematical natural science to the skepticism of Hume. This is not merely a question of an intellectual construction, but of a concrete historical process which can be traced step by step in eighteenth century thought and elucidated in all its relations and ramifications. Hitherto historians of thought have failed on this point, and hence have missed the real source of Hume's skepticism. Hume's point of departure does not appear if, as has consistently been the case, we are satisfied with placing his teachings in the light of English empiricism and developing and deriving them historically from the presuppositions of empiricism. Hume's doctrine is not to be understood as an end but as a new beginning; it is more than a mere link in that chain of thought which leads from Bacon to Hobbes, from Hobbes to Locke, and from Locke to Berkeley. From all these thinkers Hume has, to be sure, adopted certain tools of thought, namely, the conceptual and systematic apparatus of empiricism and sensationalism. But his characteristic and specific question derives from another source, namely, from the continuity and linear progression of scientific thought in the seventeenth and eighteenth centuries. An important link in this chain is the contribution of the Newtonian school, especially the systematic treatment which Newton's fundamental conceptions received at the hands of Dutch philosophers and scientists.[17] These conceptions were developed with remarkable consistency and constancy; the Dutch scholars attempted to base on them a logic of the experimental sciences. In seventeenth century Holland the trend toward exact observation of facts and the development of a strictly experimental method were combined in exemplary fashion with a critical mode of thinking whose objective was a clear determination of the meaning and value of scientific hypotheses. The great Dutch scientist, Christian Huygens, is the classic example of such a combination. In his *Treatise on Light* (*Traité de la lumière*, 1690) Huygens formulates principles of the relation of experience and thought, of theory and observation, which far surpass Descartes in their clarity and precision. He emphasizes that one cannot attain the same clarity in physics as is possible in mathematical demonstrations and inferences, and that there can be no intuitive certainty of the fundamental truths of physics. Physics requires simply a "moral certainty," which, however, can be raised to such a high degree of probability that for all practical purposes it is as good as a rigorous proof. For if the conclusions reached under the assumption of a certain hypothesis are completely verified by experience, and especially if on the basis of these conclusions one can predict new observations which are verifiable by experiment, then that kind of truth has been attained to which alone physics may lay claim.[18] The Dutch physicists of the eighteenth century build on these foundations in the belief that in the Newtonian theory they have the highest and final confirmation of their viewpoint. For no other hypothetical elements are sup-

[17] For the significance of these Dutch scientists in the development of French thought, and for the influence they exerted especially on Voltaire, see Pierre Brunet, *Les physiciens hollandais et la méthode expérimentale en France au XVIIIe siècle*, Paris, 1926.

[18] Huygens, *Traité de la lumière*, German tr. by Lommel, Leipzig, 1890, pp. 3 f.

posed to have been introduced in this theory than those which can be put to the test of immediate experience. S'Gravesande, when in the year 1717 he is called to a professorship of mathematics and astronomy at the University of Leyden, attempts in his inaugural address to develop and elucidate in detail the Newtonian theory. But in so doing he encountered a strange and difficult problem. When as a result of certain observations we anticipate other cases which we have not directly observed, our prediction is based on the axiom of the uniformity of nature. Without this axiom, without this assumption that the laws which pertain in nature today will continue to be valid, there would obviously be no foundation for conclusions about the future which are based on past experience. But how can this axiom itself be proved? S'Gravesande replies: This is not a strictly logical, but a pragmatic, axiom; its validity does not lie in the necessity of thought, but in that of action. For all action, all practical relationships with things, would be impossible, if we could not assume that the lessons of former experience will be valid in the future. Scientific prediction does not then involve the syllogistically necessary conclusions of formal logic; it is, nevertheless, a valid and indispensable conclusion by analogy. But we must and can be content with such a conclusion, for that must indeed be true whose denial would imply the negation of all man's empirical existence and of all his social life.[19]

Thus quite suddenly things have taken a strange turn; the certainty of physics is no longer based on purely logical presuppositions but on a biological and sociological presupposition. S'Gravesande himself tries to belittle the novelty and radicalism of this idea by taking refuge once more in a metaphysical interpretation and explanation. "The author of nature," he declares, "has made it necessary for us to reason by analogy, which consequently can be a legitimate basis for our reasoning."[20] In this conclusion s'Gravesande's transition to another kind of reasoning becomes distinctly noticeable. For

---

[19] Cf. s'Gravesande's inaugural address *De Matheseos in omnibus scientiis praecipue in physicis usu*, 1717; and his work *Physices Elementa . . . sive Introductio ad philosophiam Newtoniam*, Leyden, 1720 f.

[20] S'Gravesande, *Physices Elementa*, French tr. by Joncourt; cf. Brunet, *op.cit.*, pp. 56 f.

does the psychological and biological necessity of an inference by analogy predicate anything with respect to the logical necessity or the objective truth of the inference? Mathematical empiricism here stands on the threshold of skeptical empiricism, and the step from Newton to Hume is henceforth inevitable. The two viewpoints are now separated only by a wall so thin a mere breath could blow it down. In order to lay the keystone of his doctrine of the certainty of knowledge, Descartes had to appeal to the "truthfulness of God." To deny the absolute validity of the concepts and principles of pure mathematics which we grasp with the greatest clarity would be tantamount to doubting this truthfulness. Now, however, in order to make sure of the truth of the highest physical principles—in other words, of the truth of experience—we must indeed have recourse to God, but to his goodness rather than his truthfulness. For it follows from God's goodness that a conviction which is vital and necessary to man must have some objective foundation in the nature of things. If we consider the goodness of the creator, we can rely on conclusions by analogy, says s'Gravesande: "For the certainty of analogy is based on the invariability of those laws which could not be subject to change without the human race feeling it and perishing in a short time."[21] But the fundamental problem of physical method now becomes a problem of theodicy. If one eliminates the question of theodicy or answers it in the negative, then the question of the certainty of physical induction appears in an entirely new light. And it is just this transformation that takes place in Hume. Mathematical empiricism had reached the point where the uniformity of nature rested only on a sort of belief. Hume accepts this conclusion, but he robs the belief of its metaphysical disguise and removes all its transcendent elements. It is no longer based on religious, but on purely psychological grounds; it springs from a purely immanent necessity of human nature. In this sense Hume's doctrine of belief is a continuation and an ironic resolution of lines of thought which had attempted to give a

---

[21] S'Gravesande, "Speech on Evidence"; cf. Joncourt's introduction to the French tr. of *Physices Elementa*.

62

religious foundation to the science of experience. This resolution consists in an exchange of roles in the relation between science and religion. Now it is not religion which, thanks to its higher, "absolute" truth, can provide a solid foundation for science; it is rather the relativity of scientific knowledge which draws religion also into its magic circle. Religion, like science, is incapable of a rational, strictly objective justification; we must be satisfied with deriving them both from their subjective sources, and if not with justifying them, at least with understanding them, as manifestations of certain fundamental and original instincts of human nature.

And the same conclusion, toward which we are driven on the one hand by the problem of causality, is urged upon us on the other hand by the problem of substance. Here, too, mathematical empiricism had anticipated a decisive development. It had disputed the idea that among the various fundamental qualities of matter which we encounter in experience there exists no definite relationship of sequence and consubstantiality, and that any one quality could be deduced from any other according to the rules of formal logic. Such a deduction was the ideal which Descartes had set up for physics. Beginning with the purely geometrical qualities, Descartes tries to show how these contain all other properties which we ordinarily attribute to the corporeal world. All qualities of matter, including its impenetrability and weight, can be reduced to mere extension. Extension is thus the truth, the essence, the substance of the corporeal world, while all other qualities are reduced to the status of mere accidents, that is, of contingent qualities. But Newton and his school oppose to Descartes' deductive ideal a purely inductive ideal. They insist that, as long as we follow experience closely, we never arrive at anything but the regular co-existence of properties, and we do not succeed in deriving one property from the other. For the development of this problem, too, it is especially instructive to observe the teachings of the Dutch physicists. Both s'Gravesande and his pupil and successor, Musschenbroek, repeatedly stress the fact that it is meaningless to distinguish between essential and non-essential properties of matter. For we can never know whether or not some natural law which is universally confirmed by experience and hence acknowledged as a general law of nature—for instance, the law of inertia—will reveal to us some essential and necessary property of physical bodies. "We simply do not know whether these laws are derived from the nature of matter; whether they are to be derived merely from certain fundamental properties with which God has endowed physical bodies, but which are in no sense essential and necessary; or, finally, whether the effects we see are produced by external causes." We can regard extension and shape, motion and rest, weight and inertia with empirical certainty as fundamental properties of matter; but there is nothing to prevent the existence, along with these qualities which are known to us, of other qualities which we shall perhaps discover in the future, and which we shall have equal or greater reason to look upon as elementary and original.[22] Thus, with respect also to any ultimate distinctions among the properties of physical bodies, we must realize once and for all that there can be no final decision. Instead of distinguishing between essence and appearance and of deriving the latter from the former, we must operate entirely within the phenomenal world; instead of trying to explain one property in terms of another, we must rest content with the empirical co-existence of the various characteristics exhibited by experience. In terms of actual knowledge we shall lose nothing by rejecting all transcendent qualities of physical bodies; we shall only rid ourselves of an ideal which again and again has been an obstacle to the progress of empirical science. Obviously, then, it is only a step from this view to the complete abandonment of the concept of substance, to the assumption that the idea of a thing is simply the idea of a mere sum or aggregate of qualities. The transition takes place gradually and unnoticed. The attempt to eliminate all metaphysical elements from empirical philosophy finally gains so much ground that it casts doubt upon the logical foundations of this philosophy as well.

[22] Cf. s'Gravesande, *Physices Elementa Mathematica*, Praefatio, and Musschenbroek's inaugural address as rector, *De methodo instituendi experimenta physica*, 1730.

Nature and Natural Science

While mathematical physics remains within the limits of strict phenomenalism, or even advances to skeptical conclusions, the popular philosophy of natural science proceeds in exactly the opposite direction. Untouched by any critical doubts or scruples, this philosophy shows no inclination toward any epistemological renunciation. It feels the urge to know what holds the world together at its innermost core, and it thinks the solution of the riddle of the world is within its grasp. To this end no more positive exertions are required; all we have to do is put aside the hindrances which heretofore have delayed the progress of natural science and prevented it from resolutely pursuing its path to the end. What always prevented the human mind from achieving a real conquest of nature and from feeling quite at home there was the unfortunate tendency to ask for a realm beyond. If we set aside this question of transcendence, nature ceases at once to be a mystery. Nature is not mysterious and unknowable, but the human mind has enveloped it in artificial darkness. If we remove the mask of words, of arbitrary concepts, of phantastic prejudices from the face of nature, it will reveal itself as it really is, as an organic whole, self-supporting and self-explanatory. No explanation from without, which seeks the principle of nature in a realm beyond, can ever achieve its aim. For man is the work of nature, and he has no existence except in nature. He strives in vain to free himself from nature's law, for even in thought he can only apparently transcend that law. Much as his mind may strive to go beyond the world of sense, it must always return to this world since its only power consists in the joining of sense data. In this process lies all the knowledge we can gain from nature, but in it too an order appears which is so clear and complete that nothing dark and dubious remains. The riddle of nature vanishes for the mind which dares to stand its ground and cope with it. For such a mind finds no contradictions and partitions but only one being and one form of law. All the processes of nature, including those commonly called "intellectual," the whole physical and moral order of things, are reducible to matter and motion and are completely explicable in terms of these two concepts. "To exist is to experience the movements proper for a finite species. To preserve oneself is to give and receive the movements from which the maintenance of existence results; it is to attract matter suitable for strengthening one's being and to repel matter which could weaken or damage it." What we are and what we shall be, our ideas, volitions, and actions are nothing but the necessary effects of the being and fundamental properties with which nature has endowed us and of the circumstances by virtue of which these properties develop and change.[23]

Therefore, the conclusion which alone can assure us of the truth of nature is not deductive, logical, or mathematical; it is an inference from the part to the whole. The essence of nature as a whole can be deciphered and determined only if we take the nature of man as our starting point. Accordingly, the physiology of man becomes the point of departure and the key for the study of nature. Mathematics and mathematical physics are banished from their central position and superseded, in the works of the founders of materialistic doctrine, by biology and general physiology. Lamettrie begins with medical observations; Holbach appeals especially to chemistry and the sciences of organic life. Diderot raises the objection to the philosophy of Condillac that it is not enough to take mere sensation as the fundamental element of all reality. Science must go beyond this limitation and show the cause of our sensations, which can nowhere be found but in our physical organization. Thus the basis of philosophy does not lie in the analysis of sensations but in natural history, in physiology, and in medicine. Lamettrie's first book is entitled *The Natural History of the Soul*. He points out that such a history can only be written by following strictly the physical processes and taking no step not demanded and justified by exact observations. It was such observations made during an attack of fever—when he became most emphatically aware that his whole emotional and intellectual life was undergoing a complete revolution—which, as he says himself, determined the nature of his studies and the tendency of his whole philosophy.[24]

[23] Holbach, *Système de la nature*. See especially pp. 1 ff., 53 ff.
[24] Cf. Lamettrie, *Histoire naturelle de l'âme*, 1745; the book later appeared under the title, *Traité de l'âme*.

Sensory, corporeal experience was to be his only guide from now on; he used to say of the senses: "Here are my philosophers" (*Voilà mes philosophes*).[25] According to Diderot, anyone who in this world is not satisfied with the visible and seeks the invisible causes of visible effects, is no wiser than a peasant who attributes the motion of a clock whose mechanism he does not understand to a spiritual being concealed in it.

Dogmatic materialism now joins the course of phenomenalism and makes use of the weapons of the latter without accepting its conclusions. For materialism, too, assures us it has no intention of determining the absolute nature of matter, and that this question is of no decisive importance for its conclusions. "I am just as resigned," writes Lamettrie, "to being ignorant of how inert and simple matter becomes active and composed of organisms as I am to not being able to look at the sun without a red glass; and I feel the same way about the other incomprehensible wonders of nature, about the emergence of feeling and thought in a being which appeared otherwise to our weak eyes as a mere bit of dust. One must grant me only that organized matter is endowed with a principle of motion which alone differentiates it from matter which is not organized, and that all animal life depends on the diversity of this organization. . . ." With respect to apes and the other highest types of animals the behavior of man stands in the same relationship as the planetary clock constructed by Huyghens does to a primitive timepiece. "If more instruments, more cogwheels, and more springs are required to register the movements of the planets than to denote the hours; if Vaucanson had to employ more art to produce his flutist than his duck, if he had employed still more energy he might have produced a being with the power of speech. . . . The human body is a clock, but an immense one and constructed with so much artifice and skill that if the wheel which turns the second hand should stop, then the minute hand would still turn and continue on its way. . . ."[26] It is characteristic of the method of materialism in the eighteenth century that it no longer considers the relation between body and soul from the viewpoint of

[25] *Traité de l'âme*, ch. I.
[26] Lamettrie, *L'homme machine*, ed. Maurice Solovine, Paris, 1921, pp. 129 f.

substance, as was the case in the great seventeenth century systems, but almost exclusively from the viewpoint of causality. The question of the relation of the "essences" of body and soul need not disturb us; it is sufficient that we are sure of the indissoluble connection of their effects. Here no line of demarcation can be drawn between them, for the separation of corporeal and psychological phenomena is a mere abstraction without proof or support in experience. No matter how much we refine our observations or how far we may go in our experimental analysis, we shall never reach the point where we can separate the psychological from the corporeal. Both are so completely of one cast that the elimination of the one is never possible without the destruction of the other. Since we cannot grasp and judge the nature of things except by its effects, we have no choice but to infer the identity of their nature from the necessary and inseparable connection of their effects. The apparent chasm between dead matter and vital phenomena, between motion and sensation, is insignificant. To be sure, we are ignorant of the manner in which sensation arises from motion, but does not the same ignorance prevail where we are concerned with matter itself and its basic phenomena? Nor can we understand conceptually the process of a mechanical impulse or the transmission of a certain momentum from one mass to another; we must be content to observe them in experience. Similarly, empirical observation is possible in the case of the so-called psycho-physical problem. In the first case as in the second the problem is on the one hand enigmatic, but on the other, plain. If we are satisfied with what we learn from experience and do not look beyond this realm, then experience shows us the same constant connection between corporeal and psychological being and processes as between different material properties. If we do not find it strange to attribute to matter, besides its fundamental quality of extension, other properties as well, then why should we hesitate to attribute to it the capacity for sensation, memory, and thought? Thought as such is as incompatible with organized matter as is, for instance, impenetrability, electricity, magnetism, or weight, which, similarly, cannot be reduced to mere extension but represent something new to, and different from, extension.[27] And what holds for sensations and ideas, is also true of our appetites and desires, and of our decisions and moral acts. Nor do we need any transcendent and immaterial principle, or a simple substance, which is only an empty word, to understand these phenomena. "If we assume the least principle of motion, then animated bodies will have all they require in order to move, to feel, to think, to repent, and in short to conduct themselves physically and, which is dependent on this, morally."[28]

But with these well known conclusions of the materialistic system, we only have so far its outside, not its real conceptual core. For, paradoxical as it may appear at first glance, this core is not to be found in natural philosophy, but in ethics. Materialism as it appears in the eighteenth century, as it is justified and defended, is no mere scientific or metaphysical dogma; it is rather an imperative. It not only aims to establish a thesis concerning the nature of things but also to command and to forbid. This feature is especially evident in Holbach's *System of Nature*. Viewed superficially Holbach's doctrine looks like a system of the strictest and most consistent determinism. No aspect of nature is to be introduced into the philosophy of nature which is explicable only in terms of man and his appetites and desires. In nature nothing is just or unjust, good or bad; here all beings and all happenings are equal in value and in validity. All phenomena are necessary; and in view of its given qualities and of the specific circumstances of its existence, no being can act otherwise than it actually does. Hence there is no evil, no guilt, no disorder in nature: "All is in order in a nature, no part of which can ever deviate from the certain and necessary rules which issue from the essence it has received."[29] If man believes himself free, he is merely exhibiting a dangerous delusion and an intellectual weakness. It is the structure of the atoms that forms him, and their motion that propels him forward; conditions not dependent on him determine his nature and direct his fate.[30]

[27] Lamettrie, *L'homme machine*, p. 134.
[28] *Ibid.*, p. 113.
[29] Holbach, *Système de la nature*, Pt. I, ch. IV and V, pp. 50 f., 58 ff.
[30] *Ibid.*, p. 274. Cf. Lamettrie, "Discours sur le bonheur," *Oeuvres philosophiques*, p. 211: "I am, and I am proud of it, a zealous citizen; but it is not in

But with this content of the materialistic thesis, its presentation becomes involved in a curious antagonism. For it by no means follows Spinoza's motto: "not to laugh at, not to lament, nor to detest, but to understand." Superficially considered Holbach's philosophy of nature is only intended as an introduction to a more comprehensive whole. His *System of Nature* merely forms the basis for his *Social System* and for his *Universal Morality*, and the real tendency which dominates his thought clearly appears only in these last two books. Man must free himself from all idols, from all illusions concerning the original cause of things, for only by so doing can he succeed in ordering and establishing the world according to his own ideas. Hitherto theological spiritualism has prevented any truly autonomous regulation of the politico-social system. It is the dragon of the sciences, obstructing their development at every stage. "As the born enemy of experience, theology, the science of the supernatural, has been an insuperable obstacle to the progress of the natural sciences. Physics, natural history, and anatomy were not allowed to see anything except through the malevolent eyes of superstition."[31] But this rule of superstition becomes even more dangerous if it is permitted to shape the moral order. For here it not only annuls human knowledge but robs human happiness of its real foundation. It frightens man with a thousand phantoms and deprives him of every uninhibited joy of existence. Only a resolute and radical break with all spiritualism can cure this situation. The notions of God, freedom and immortality are to be uprooted once and for all, so that the rational order of nature shall not be threatened and overthrown by constant intervention from the supernatural world which these notions seem to construct. The same line of reasoning is to be found in Lamettrie's *Man a Machine*. The world will never be happy so long as it does not decide to become atheistic. When the belief in God vanishes, all theological disputes and religious wars will cease too: "nature, hitherto infected with a sacred

---

this quality that I write, it is as a philosopher; as such, I see that Cartouche was Cartouche and Pyrrhus, Pyrrhus: counsels are useless to one born with a thirst for carnage and blood."

[31] *Système de la nature*, p. 311.

poison, would resume its rights and purity."[32] The *System of Nature* itself encounters a difficult dilemma when it appears thus as challenger and accuser, and when it is not content with theoretical conclusions but rather sets up a norm for human thought and faith. The doctrine of the absolute necessity of the events of nature gets caught in the net of its own reasoning. For on the basis of this doctrine what right have we to speak of norms at all, what right to demand and evaluate? Does not this doctrine see in every "ought" a mere delusion which it transforms into a "must"? And is there any alternative but to yield to this "must"? Can we guide it and prescribe its course? Even eighteenth century criticism of the *System of Nature* bared this fundamental weakness of its argument. Frederick the Great's reply to the book calls attention emphatically to this point. "After the author has exhausted all evidence," this reply objects, "to show that men are guided by a fatalistic necessity in all their actions, he had to draw the conclusion that we are only a sort of machine, only marionettes moved by the hand of a blind power. And yet he flies into a passion against priests, governments, and against our whole educational system; he believes indeed that the men who exercise these functions are free, even while he proves to them that they are slaves. What foolishness and what nonsense! If everything is moved by necessary causes, then all counsel, all instruction, all rewards and punishments are as superfluous as inexplicable; for one might just as well preach to an oak and try to persuade it to turn into an orange tree." A more subtle and elastic dialectic than Holbach's could of course endeavor to overcome this objection and weave it skillfully into its own argument. Diderot saw and expressed clearly all the antinomies into which the system of fatalism finally leads; but he utilizes these antinomies as the motivating force, as the vehicle, for his own thoroughly dialectic thought. He admits a vicious circle but he transforms this situation into a grand jest. A most ingenious and original book took this impulse as its inspiration. The novel *Jack the Fatalist* endeavors to show that the concept of fate is the alpha and omega of all human thinking; but it also shows how thought time

[32] *L'homme machine*, p. 111.

and again comes into conflict with this concept, how it is forced implicitly to deny and revoke the concept even while affirming it. There is no alternative but to recognize this situation as inevitable, and to extend our very idea of necessity so as to include that inconsistency with respect to this idea of which we are guilty in all our thoughts and judgments, in all our affirmations and negations. According to Diderot it is this oscillation between the two poles of freedom and necessity which brings the circle of our thought and existence to completion. By such oscillation, not by a simple assertion or denial, we can discover the all-inclusive concept of nature, that concept which in the last analysis is just as much beyond agreement and contradiction and beyond truth and falsehood as it is beyond good and evil because it includes both extremes without differentiation.

The eighteenth century as a whole remained aloof from this whirlpool of Diderot's dialectic which carries him along from atheism to pantheism, from materialism to dynamic panpsychism, and back again by turns. The *System of Nature* played a relatively unimportant part in the general development of Diderot's thought. Even the thinkers closest to Holbach's circle not only rejected the radical conclusions of his work but denied his very premises. Voltaire's sure judgment appeared when he at once attacked Holbach's book at its weakest point. With ruthless clarity he pointed to the contradiction in the fact that Holbach, who dedicated his banner to the fight against dogmatism and intolerance, in turn set up his own thesis as dogma and defended it with fanatical zeal. Voltaire refused to permit his viewpoint as a free thinker to be based on such arguments, and he was unwilling to receive from the hands of Holbach and his followers the "patent of an atheist" (*le brevet d'athée*). And Voltaire was even more critical of Holbach's presentation of his views and of the literary value of the book. He classified the work as belonging to the only literary genre he could not tolerate, namely, the "boring genre" (*genre ennuyeux*).[33] In fact Holbach's style, apart from its prolixity and digressiveness, is peculiarly harsh and dry. Its objective is to

[33] Cf. Voltaire's poem "Les Cabales" (1772), *Oeuvres*, Paris, ed. Lequien, 1825, vol. XIV, pp. 236 ff.

eliminate from the philosophy of nature not only all religious, but all aesthetic elements as well, and to neutralize all the forces of feeling and phantasy. It is silly to adore and worship a nature which operates absolutely blindly and mechanically. "Let us consider that we are the sensitive parts of a whole which is entirely devoid of feeling, of a whole all of whose forms and combinations will perish after they have arisen and endured for a longer or shorter period. Let us regard nature as a huge work-shop which contains everything required to produce all those formations we see before us, and let us not attribute nature's works to an imaginary cause which exists only in our own brain."[34] Words like these were no doubt in Goethe's mind when he says that he and his youthful friends in Strasbourg, when they heard of the Encyclopaedists, felt as if they were walking among countless moving spools and looms in a great factory where the bewilderment produced by the machinery, the incomprehensibility of the complicated interlocking process, and the consideration of all that goes into the production of a piece of cloth, caused them to grow disgusted with the very coats they had on. Of the *System of Nature* Goethe relates that he and his friends could not understand how such a book could be dangerous: "It seemed to us so grey, so Cimmerian, so deathlike that we could hardly stand its presence, and we shuddered at it as if it were a ghost." The reaction against Holbach's work, which began soon after its appearance, is owing to the fact that it drew the fire not only of all the religious but of all the most vital artistic forces of the epoch. These were the forces which were not only urging a reformation of systematic aesthetics but which were also active in the formation of the philosophy of nature of the eighteenth century. From them arose a movement destined to exercise an epoch-making influence on the growth of modern science.

4

In his essay *On the Interpretation of Nature* (1754) Diderot, who among the thinkers of the eighteenth century probably

[34] *Système de la Nature*, p. 205.

possessed the keenest sense for all intellectual movements and transitions of that epoch, remarks that the century seems to have reached a decisive turning-point. A great revolution in the field of science is now in the offing. "I dare almost assert that in less than a century we shall not have three great geometers left in Europe. This science will very soon come to a standstill where Bernoullis, Eulers, Maupertuis, Clairants, Fontaines, d'Alemberts, and La Granges will have left it. They will have erected the columns of Hercules. We shall not go beyond that point." We know how far this prophecy came from fulfillment so far as the history of pure mathematics is concerned. Diderot's hundred years had not yet elapsed before the death of Gauss—who had revolutionized mathematics and extended its frontiers both in content and method in a manner the eighteenth century could not foresee. Yet there was, nonetheless, a genuine sentiment behind Diderot's prediction. For the point he wishes to emphasize is that among the various natural sciences mathematics will not be able to maintain its sole mastery much longer. A rival is appearing on the horizon which mathematics will not be able to suppress entirely. However perfect mathematics may be within its own province and to whatever precision it may evolve its concepts, yet this perfection will necessarily remain its immanent limitation. For it cannot reach out beyond its own self-made concepts; it has no immediate access to empirical concrete reality. This reality becomes accessible to us only through experiment, through faithful exact observations. But if the experimental method is to be completely effective, we must grant it full autonomy and free it from all tutelage. It is therefore necessary in the field of natural science to combat the systematizing spirit in mathematics as well as in metaphysics. As soon as the mathematician develops not merely his own conceptual world, but is convinced that he can catch reality in the meshes of his concepts, he has himself become a metaphysician. "When geometers have decried metaphysicians, they were far from thinking that all their science was simply metaphysics." With this observation the ideal of mathematical natural science, which dominated all eighteenth century physics, begins to fade; and in its place a new ideal arises, the demand for a purely descriptive science of nature. Diderot had grasped and described this ideal in its general outlines long before it was realized in detail. Why, he asks, do we possess so little really reliable knowledge of nature despite all the striking progress of mathematical science? Have geniuses been lacking, or has there been a dearth of thought and study? By no means. The reason lies rather in a systematic neglect of the relation between conceptual and factual knowledge. "The abstract sciences have occupied the best minds for too long. Words have been multiplied endlessly, but factual knowledge has lagged behind.... Yet the true wealth of philosophy consists in facts, of whatever kind they may be. But it is a prejudice of rational philosophy that he who cannot count his crowns is scarcely richer than somebody who only possesses one crown. Unfortunately, rational philosophy is much more concerned with comparing and combining facts already known than with collecting new ones."[35] In these words Diderot formulates a new slogan which announces a new mode of thinking. The counting, systematizing, and calculating spirit of the seventeenth century is now challenged by a new tendency, a tendency to subdue the sheer profusion of reality by attacking it without reservations as to whether it can be described in clear and distinct concepts or reduced to measurement and number. Even though such systems may still be constructed, the delusion of their relation to reality vanishes. "Fortunate the systematic philosopher whom, like Epicurus and Lucretius or like Aristotle and Plato of old, nature has endowed with a lively imagination, great eloquence, and the art of expressing his ideas in striking and sublime pictures. The building he has erected may some day tumble down, but his statue will remain upright even beneath the ruins." The system thus possesses more individual than universal, more aesthetic than objectively logical meaning. As a tool of knowledge it is indispensable, but one must beware of becoming the slave of a mere tool. One should possess a system without being possessed by it: "May you have Lais, provided Lais does not

---

[35] Diderot, *De l'Interprétation de la Nature*, sections IV, XVII, XX, XXI; *Oeuvres*, ed. Assézat, vol. II.

have you."[36] A new scientific trend, a new temper in research, now emerges which demands recognition and justification for itself as such and for its method.

This justification can begin with a consideration which had already been employed in mathematical physics. The followers and pupils of Newton in their controversy with Descartes' "rational" physics had emphasized again and again that the demand for an explanation of nature was to be superseded by the demand for a full description of nature's processes.[37] Instead of definition, as known in pure mathematics, there will have to be description. For the physicist, of course, exact description of an event is the same thing as its measurement; only that which can be determined in purely numerical values and expressed in terms of such values can be described with real precision. As we go from physics to biology the postulate of pure description takes on a different meaning. It is no longer a question of transforming directly observed reality into an aggregate of quantities, into a network of numbers and measures; it is now rather a matter of retaining the specific form of empirical reality. It is this specific form which is supposed to lie before us in all the wealth and variety of its being as well as in the profusion of becoming. The logical structure of those concepts of classes and species, by virtue of which we usually seek insight into nature, are directly opposed to the actual profusion of nature. These concepts must necessarily limit direct observation; instead of leading to complete understanding of its content, they lead to impoverishment. This impoverishment is to be counteracted by seeking a method of forming concepts which permits us to come into direct contact with the specific welter of phenomena and individual instances of the forms of nature, and to focus our attention here while our concepts remain as flexible as the phenomena themselves. Diderot offered a model for such a formation of concepts in his formulation of botanical science. "If I dared," he writes here, "I should like to make the paradoxical statement that under certain circumstances there is nothing more laborious and wasteful than method. Method is a guide to truth

---

[36] *Ibid.*, sections XXI, XXVII: "Laidem habeto, dummodo te Lais non habeat."
[37] See above pp. 51 ff.

which one cannot afford to dispense with, for as soon as one loses sight of it one must necessarily go astray. If one were to undertake to teach a child to speak by starting with the words that begin with A, then by proceeding to those that begin with B, etc., half a lifetime could go by before the child would finish the alphabet. Method is excellent in the realm of reasoning, but in my estimation it is detrimental in the case of natural history in general and in botany in particular."[38] This does not mean that these sciences can dispense with system and method; it means rather that their form of system must not be borrowed from that of the rational disciplines, but that it must be derived from, and adapted to, the specific subject matter of these sciences.

Diderot could hardly have expressed this postulate with such clarity and decisiveness if it had not been in some measure fulfilled at the time he set down his thoughts on the interpretation of nature. For just at this time the first three volumes of Buffon's *Natural History* had appeared. Buffon's work established a new type of natural science and presented, as it were, a companion-piece to Newton's *Mathematical Principles of Natural Philosophy (Philosophiae naturalis principia mathematica)*. To be sure, in substance, originality, and creative force Buffon's contribution is not to be compared with Newton's; but from the point of view of method it is scarcely inferior in so far as it expresses with perfect clarity a definite basic tendency in the formation of the concepts of natural science, presenting this tendency with the magnificent breadth of a universal plan. Buffon declares in his introduction that it is futile and wrong to establish a strictly monistic ideal of natural science and to subordinate all other branches of scientific research to this ideal. Any such methodological monism fails because of the opposition between mathematics and physics. For the truth of mathematics consists merely in a system of purely analytical propositions connected by the bond of strict necessity, which in the last analysis express one and the same content of knowledge in diverse forms. But this concept of truth loses its meaning and

<hr>

[38] "La Botanique mise à la portée de tout le monde," *Oeuvres*, ed. Assézat, vol. VI, p. 375.

force as soon as we approach the sphere of the real and try to acclimate ourselves to this sphere. Here, where we are no longer dealing with concepts of our own making whose form and structure we can prescribe and which we can derive from one another by deduction, the clarity which is present while comparing mere ideas abandons us; here we can never go beyond the realm of the probable. We must commit ourselves to the exclusive guidance of experience, for only experience can yield that kind of certainty of which the truth of physical objects is capable. We must increase and sharpen our observations; we must generalize from facts and combine them in conclusions by analogy until we finally reach a stage of knowledge whence we can see how particulars are connected with the whole, and how special effects are dependent on general ones. Now we are no longer comparing nature with our concepts but, as it were, with itself; we see how each of nature's operations dovetails with other operations and how, finally, they are joined in the totality of one activity.[39] We do not understand this unity if we attempt to divide it into classes and species. For such classifications result in a system of nomenclature, not in a system of nature. They may be useful, indeed indispensable, for surveying the facts; but nothing is more dangerous than to confuse these mere signs with that which they signify, than to make real definitions of merely nominal ones, and then to expect from them some kind of explanation of the nature of things. On this rock, according to Buffon, even Linnaeus's *Philosophy of Botany* was shipwrecked. Linnaeus selects arbitrarily certain qualities and features according to which he tries to group the plant world, and he thinks he can give us a picture of the sequence, organization, and structure of this world on the basis of this procedure of mere arrangement, of analytical classification. Such a picture is only possible by a reversal of his procedure. We must apply the principle of connection rather than that of analytical differentiation; instead of assigning living creatures to sharply distinguished species, we must study them in relation to their kinship, their transition from one type to another, their evolution and transformations. For these are the things which constitute life as we find it in

---

[39] Buffon, *Histoire naturelle*, 1749, premier discours.

nature. Since nature proceeds from one species, and often from one genus, to another by imperceptible steps so that there are many intermediate stages which seem to belong partly to this, and partly to that, genus, no other alternative remains than to trace all these subtle transitions, than to make our concepts elastic in order to represent the flexibility of natural forms. Henceforth Buffon tends toward outright nominalism; he states that in nature there are only individuals, there are no species and genera. And he is convinced that this view is universally confirmed by observation. Animals of one continent are not to be found on another continent, and if we think we find the same classes they are so changed that we scarcely recognize them. Do we need further evidence to be convinced that biological types are not unalterable, that animal traits can change completely in the course of time, and that the less perfect species, those least fit for survival, have already become extinct or will vanish in time?[40]

The importance of Buffon's views as an introduction to a general theory of evolution need not be discussed here. In relation to our problem they are less important for their content than for their form and advocacy of a certain ideal of knowledge which is more and more concretely realized as Buffon's work as a whole progresses. The independent structure of biological knowledge begins here for the first time to appear in clear outline and to assert itself against the form of theoretical physics. Scientific method is no longer exclusively dominated by mathematics; it is now, so to speak, provided with a second focal point in the fundamental form of historical knowledge. The well known passage in Kant's *Critique of Judgment*, in which the idea of an archeology of nature is for the first time clearly developed, seems to have been written with direct reference to Buffon's work. "Just as in human history one consults documents, examines coins and medals, and deciphers ancient inscriptions in order to determine the revolutions and epochs in the intellectual life of man, so in natural history one must search the archives of the world, unearth the oldest relics, col-

[40] For Buffon's position in the history of the theory of evolution, see Perrier, *Philosophie zoologique avant Darwin*.

lect remnants, and unite all signs of physical changes which are traceable to the various ages of nature into one corpus of evidence. This is the only way to determine any fixed points in the infinity of space and to leave behind a few milestones on the unending pathway of time."[41] In this procedure lies the strength of a purely descriptive natural science, which in biology is gradually to supersede the former method of scholastic logic, of definition according to *genus proximum* and *differentia specifica*. In the true sense of the word only what has been *defined*, that is, clearly known and sharply delineated, has been exactly described: "il n'y a de bien défini que ce qui est exactement décrit." With this changed conception of the nature and aim of the formation of scientific concepts, the attitude toward the essential content of natural processes also undergoes a transformation. Even in Descartes the logico-mathematical doctrine of definition demanded as its counterpart and corollary a strictly mechanical explanation of nature. But as the center of gravity of thought shifts from definition to description, from the species to the individual, mechanism can no longer be considered as the sole and sufficient basis of explanation; there is in the making a transition to a conception of nature which no longer seeks to derive and explain becoming from being, but being from becoming.

5

The Cartesian system of physics in France quickly overcame the opposition of church doctrine and of the scholastic followers of the physics of substantial forms. From the middle of the seventeenth century on, its advance is rapid; it gains acceptance not merely in learned circles but, as a result of Fontenelle's *Conversations on the Plurality of Worlds*, it also becomes a part of the general culture of society. The influence of Cartesianism is so strong and so persistent that even those thinkers who are essentially opposed to its aims cannot escape it. In the seventeenth century the doctrine of Descartes imprints upon the French mind its characteristic form, and this form proves so hardy that it can even conquer and absorb quite heterogeneous

[41] Buffon, *Histoire naturelle*, cited from Joseph Fabre, *Les Pères de la Révolution*, Paris, 1910, pp. 167 f.

content.[42] Cartesianism never gained such almost unlimited sway either in England or in Germany. The growth of German thought is guided by the influence of Leibniz. The main trend of Leibniz's thought gains recognition very slowly, fighting for every inch of ground; but its penetration is, nevertheless, deep and effective. In England not only the systems of empiricism become increasingly critical of the Cartesian system, especially of its doctrine of innate ideas and of the form of Descartes' concept of substance; but here too a form of natural philosophy is kept alive which is directly related to the dynamism of the Renaissance, and which seeks to go back beyond that to its ancient sources, especially the Neo-Platonic teachings. These tendencies receive their first summary expression and systematic presentation in the writings of the Cambridge School. One of the leading thinkers of this school, Henry More, greeted the Cartesian philosophy enthusiastically on its first appearance because he saw in it the decisive triumph of spiritualism, the radical separation of matter and mind, of extended and thinking substance. But in the later development of his doctrine of nature More opposes Descartes on this very point. For, as More objects, Descartes had not only distinguished between the two substances, but he had separated them from one another; and he had gone so far with his logical distinction that he had rendered any real connection between them impossible. And yet the unity and life of nature are based on the connection between mind and matter, on the unity of their interaction. But this unity and life are destroyed if one permits the sphere of the mind to begin only with human self-consciousness, if one limits it to the region of "clear and distinct" ideas. Insight into the continuity of the forms of nature refutes this limitation and makes it fundamentally impossible. Between the various forms of life, as we meet them everywhere in organic nature, and the form of self-consciousness, there is no gap. One uninterrupted series of stages leads from the most elementary processes of life to the highest processes of thought, from dark and blurry sensa-

[42] For a fuller account see G. Lanson, "L'influence de la Philosophie Cartésienne sur la littérature française," *Revue de Métaphysique*, 1896 (*Études d'histoire littéraire*, Paris, 1929, pp. 58 ff.).

tions to the highest form of reflective knowledge. Where experience discloses such a connection, we must heed its evidence; where the phenomena form an unbroken sequence, the principles must not stand in glaring opposition, as they do in Descartes' thought. Descartes simply rules out the life of plants and animals; he declares that animals are machines, thus sacrificing them to mechanism. Opposed to this viewpoint is the doctrine of "plastic natures" entertained by More and Cudworth. Life is not limited to thinking and self-consciousness; it manifests itself more fundamentally and universally as a forming power. We must attribute life to all those creatures which in the manner of their existence, in their external shapes as they appear to our senses give evidence of forming forces working within them of which they are the embodiment. This hierarchy of "plastic natures" extends from the simplest to the most complex processes of nature, from the elements to the highest organisms; and the order and connection of the universe can only be grounded in these plastic natures, not in mere mass and motion.[43]

Leibniz attacked the philosophy of Descartes from another angle, expressly rejecting the doctrine of plastic natures.[44] For, although as a biologist and metaphysician he centers his attention on the phenomenon of organic life, he is very much concerned not to interfere with the great principle of mathematical physics which Descartes had established. If therefore the thinkers of the Cambridge School speak of the "mathematical sickness" (*morbus mathematicus*) of Descartes, and if they look upon this sickness as a fundamental flaw in his doctrine of nature, Leibniz, on the other hand, stresses the point that the doctrine of life must be so formulated that it does not stand in contradiction to the basic principles of mathematical physics. The harmony between the two ways of thinking, according to Leibniz, can only be assured if one realizes that all the phenomena of nature, without exception, are capable of a strictly

[43] For an account of the philosophy of nature of the Cambridge School see the author's book *Die platonische Renaissance in England und die Schule von Cambridge*, Studien der Bibliothek Warburg, Leipzig, 1932, ch. v.

[44] See Leibniz's essay "Considérations sur les Principes de Vie et sur les Natures Plastiques," *Philos. Schriften*, ed. Gerhardt, vol. VI, pp. 539 ff.

mathematical and mechanical explanation. However, the principles of mechanism themselves are not to be looked for in mere extension, shape, and motion, but as issuing from another source. Mechanism is the intellectual compass which guides us along the only sure path through the realm of phenomena, which subjects all phenomena to the "principle of sufficient reason" and so makes them rationally comprehensible and completely explicable. But comprehension of the world does not achieve its goal by virtue of this sort of explanation. Such comprehension cannot be content with a hasty survey of the phenomena and with a knowledge of their temporal and spatial order. Instead of proceeding from one element of the process to another which is adjacent in space and time, instead of tracing step by step the various stages through which an organic body passes during its development, connecting the stages according to the law of cause and effect, this comprehension must raise the question of the common ground of the entire series. This ground itself does not however belong to the series as one of its elements, but lies beyond it. In order to understand this ground we must leave the mathematico-physical order of phenomena and proceed to the metaphysical order of substances; we must find the basis for derivative forces in original forces. This is what Leibniz attempts to accomplish in his system of monadology. The monads are the subjects from which all events originate, and the principle of their activity, of their progressive development, is not the mechanical connection of causes and effects, but a teleological relationship. Every monad is a true entelechy; each strives to develop and improve its being, to rise from one stage of its development to another which is more complete. What we call mechanical processes are thus merely the outside, the presentation to sense, of those dynamic processes that go on within the substantial entities, within the internal teleological forces. Thus extension, in which Descartes thought he saw the substance of matter, is derived from the non-extended; the extensive is derived from the intensive, and the mechanical from the vital. "That which is exhibited mechanically or extensively in matter is concentrated dynamically and monadically in the entelechy itself, in which it is the source of mechanism and the representation of mechanical things; for phenomena result from the monads."[45]

Thus, with all due recognition of the merits of a mathematical explanation of nature, the foundation for a new philosophy of the organic was laid—at least a new problem was faced whose effects are recognizable throughout the development of the philosophy of nature in the eighteenth century. It is not merely theoretical considerations and abstract speculations which keep this problem alive. Of no less importance is the new aesthetic philosophy represented by artistically inclined minds. The blending of the two elements is already observable in the fundamental position which Leibniz assigns to his concept of harmony. And the importance of this aesthetic trend in the structure of a new conception of nature appears even more clearly in Shaftesbury. Shaftesbury bases his philosophy of nature on the doctrine of "plastic natures" as propounded by the Cambridge School. But he rejects all those mystical conclusions which Henry More, especially, had drawn from this doctrine. For Shaftesbury's purpose is so to state his concept of form that its intellectual, supersensible origin will be recognizable, retaining, however, the purely intuitive aspect of this concept. Shaftesbury looks upon the world as a work of art, and he wants to go back from the work of art to the artist who formed it and who is immediately present in all its manifestations of form. This artist does not work from an external model which he would simply have to copy, nor does he follow a prescribed plan in his creations. His activity is determined entirely from within; accordingly, it cannot be described by analogy with external processes, or by the action which one body exerts on another. The concept of purpose, which permeates and dominates Shaftesbury's whole philosophy, now assumes a new position and a different meaning. Just as artistic creation and aesthetic appreciation are not governed by ulterior purposes, as the purpose of such activity is found in the activity itself—in creation and contemplation—the same is true for the "genius" of nature.

[45] Leibniz's letter to Christian Wolff, *Briefwechsel zwischen Leibniz und Wolff*, ed. Gerhardt, Halle, 1860, p. 139. For fuller treatment see the author's book *Leibniz' System*, Marburg, 1902, especially pp. 283 ff. and 384 ff.

It *is* only in so far as it is active. But its essence is not exhausted in any particular work, nor in the infinite profusion of its works; it manifests itself solely in the creating and forming process. And this act is also the source of all beauty: "The beautifying, not the beautified, is the really beautiful." This immanent purpose, which is derived from his aesthetics, appears also in Shaftesbury's philosophy of nature and forms there a new fundamental tendency. Here too Shaftesbury goes beyond the model of the thinkers of the Cambridge School. For the Cambridge men conceive the "plastic natures," which they look upon as indispensable to all organic processes, principally as subordinate forces which they place under the guidance and rule of the divine will. God stands over the world as its "telos" and transcendent principle while the plastic natures act within the world, being, as it were, entrusted by the First Cause, which is merely concerned with general aims, with the task of executing the details of creation. In Shaftesbury this distinction between the lower and the higher, between the highest divine power and the "daemonic" forces of nature, disappears. He sees one in all and all in one. In support of this standpoint of aesthetic immanence we find no "above" or "below" in nature and no outside or inside, for the absolute contrast between the "here" and the "there," between this world and the world beyond, does not exist in the phenomenal world. The concept of "inward form" overcomes all oppositions of this sort. In Goethe's words: "For such is the content of nature that what was valid outside is also valid inside."[46] A powerful current of new feeling for nature flows from this source into the intellectual history of the eighteenth century. In the development of German thought Shaftesbury's apostrophes to nature exert a decisive influence; they give expression to those fundamental forces which shaped the philosophy of nature of Herder and the young Goethe.[47]

[46] "Denn das ist der Naturgehalt,
   Dass drinnen gilt was draussen galt."

[47] For fuller treatment see Dilthey's essay "Aus der Zeit der Spinoza-Studien Goethes," *Archiv fuer die Geschichte der Philosophie*, 1894: *Gesammelte Schriften*, vol. II, pp. 391 ff. Regarding Shaftesbury's view of nature and its relation to the thought of the Cambridge School, see the author's book, *Die platonische Renaissance in England und die Schule von Cambridge*, chap. VI.

Nature and Natural Science

Speaking of Herder's and Goethe's views of nature, we are of course beyond the limits of the epoch of the Enlightenment, but here again there is nowhere a gap in the continuity of eighteenth century thought. The epoch reaches its limits in a perfectly regular development. The unity and continuity of this development are assured from the first by Leibniz's system and the universality of his thought. In France, too, from the middle of the century on the influence of Leibniz's concept of the monad steadily gains strength. It was especially Maupertuis who brought Leibniz to France. His personal relation to Leibniz is not indeed free from contradictions, but the objective kinship of his metaphysics, his philosophy of nature, and his theory of knowledge with Leibniz's basic ideas is undeniable. His principle of the least action, his formulation and justification of the principle of continuity, as also his doctrine of the phenomenality of space and time, are traceable to Leibniz. Maupertuis attempted indeed to avoid a direct indebtedness to Leibniz on these points; despite his tacit adoption of Leibniz's fundamental doctrines he continues to criticize and to attack the Leibnizian system as such, especially in the form which it had received at the hands of Wolff and his pupils. This ambiguous position served him badly in his controversy with König.[48] But even more clearly than in Maupertuis' statement of the principle of least action (*"principe de la moindre action"*) is his indebtedness to Leibniz for his biological theories, as König pointed out. These theories are contained in a Latin treatise entitled *Dissertatio inauguralis metaphysica de universali Naturae systemate* (Inaugural Metaphysical Dissertation on the Universal System of Nature) which was published at Erlangen in 1751 as the work of a Dr. Baumann. The special significance of this work in the history of ideas lies in the circumstance that here for the first time the attempt is made to reconcile the two great opponents in the philosophy of nature of the seventeenth century. Maupertuis is the first great proponent of Newton's ideas in France; he even anticipates Voltaire in this matter, paving the

---

[48] For a fuller account of this controversy see Harnack, *Geschichte der Akademie der Wissenschaften zu Berlin*, Berlin, 1901, pp. 252 ff.

way for the latter.[49] But he soon realizes that Newton's principle of attraction cannot serve as a sufficient foundation for descriptive natural science, for the understanding and interpretation of organic life. Excellent as Newton's theory proved in astronomy and physics, as soon as one enters the field of chemistry he faces entirely new problems which can no longer be solved in terms of Newtonian thought. If we wish to retain the general principle of mass attraction also in chemistry as our ultimate basis of explanation, we must at least give a different and broader meaning to the concept of attraction than it has in physics. And we encounter a further change of meaning if we turn from chemistry to biology and try to explain the formation of a plant or of an animal. The problem of propagation of the species and all the complicated problems of heredity cannot be solved by the method of physics; these problems cannot even be formulated from this standpoint. We are here obliged to seek another fundamental concept of matter than that which the physicist assumes. Neither Cartesian extension nor Newtonian gravity is of any assistance in understanding the phenomena of life, to say nothing of the difficulties of deriving these phenomena from extension and gravity. There is nothing left to do but to add to the purely physical predicates of impenetrability, mobility, inertia and weight, others which stand in direct relation to the fact of life. And at this point Maupertuis turns to Leibniz, who had explained that the true and ultimate grounds of explanation of the processes of nature are not to be found simply in the concept of mass, but in the simple substances whose nature can only be described in terms of consciousness, that is, through the predicates of ideation and appetency. Maupertuis insists, moreover, that no explanation of nature can be complete unless one decides to include these predicates among the fundamental elements of being, rather than regard them as derivative qualities. On the other hand, Maupertuis does not wish to subscribe to that radicalism advocated by Leibniz which had divided the world into substances and phenomena,

---

[49] Concerning Maupertuis' defense of Newton and his first works in mathematical physics, see Brunet, *Maupertuis*, two volumes, Paris, 1929, vol. I, pp. 13 ff.

into simple and composite elements. In his approach to the concept of the monad Maupertuis does not attempt to conceive the fundamental units of which all natural processes consist as metaphysical points—as Leibniz had done—but as physical points. In order to arrive at these units we need not depart from the corporeal world as such, but we must enlarge the concept of matter in such a way that it does not exclude the basic facts of consciousness. In other words, we must admit into the definition of matter not only the qualities of extension, impenetrability, gravity, etc., but also those of desire, aversion, and memory. The objection that such a combination involves a contradiction, that such completely heterogeneous, indeed such opposite predicates cannot be joined in the same subject, need not disturb us. For this objection is valid only on the assumption that the explanations employed by the scientist are definitions of realities which exhaustively characterize the essence of things. If with Descartes and his followers we regard consciousness and thinking as essential properties of the soul, and extension as the essential property of body; then it is of course consistent to set up an absolute barrier between soul and body, since these two types of properties have nothing in common, and to ascribe to the one type only such properties as are denied to the other. But this mutual exclusion ceases to be valid the moment we are aware that all thinking is limited to the recognition of empirical properties. How these properties are inwardly connected, and whether they are essentially compatible or incompatible, we cannot and do not wish to ask; it is sufficient if experience always reveals them together, if we can observe their regular coexistence. Since thought and extension "are only properties, they can both belong to one subject whose real nature is unknown to us; all the reasoning of those philosophers is fruitless, it no more proves the impossibility of the coexistence of thought and extension than it might prove that it would be impossible that extension should be found together with mobility. For if it is true that we feel less repugnance to conceive thought and extension in one and the same subject than to conceive extension and mobility, that is because experience constantly places the one combination before our eyes, and only permits us to know the other by inference and induction."[50]

If the logical and metaphysical objections which can be raised against the coexistence and direct co-ordination of psychological and physical properties in the concept of matter can thus be eliminated, the construction of a philosophy of nature can proceed without hesitation. We can never imagine deriving the conscious from the unconscious, for in so doing we should have asserted a real creation out of nothing. It is quite absurd to think that the origin of the soul can be explained in terms of a combination of atoms, none of which possesses either sensation or intelligence, or any other psychological quality.[51] Hence there is no alternative but to assume consciousness as an original phenomenon, in the atoms themselves; we cannot assume that consciousness emerges from atoms as a creation, but that it develops within the atoms and rises to higher and higher degrees of clarity. As Maupertuis works out his thought, nothing remains of the fundamental principle of Leibniz's philosophy of nature. The spiritualism of Leibniz now degenerates into a vague sort of hylozoism. Matter as such is animate; it is endowed with sensation and desire, with certain sympathies and antipathies. Corresponding to each particle of matter is an "instinct" which causes it to seek that which is suitable and to flee the opposite; but each particle is also possessed of a certain self-awareness. When one particle is combined with others to make up larger masses, it does not thereby relinquish its self-awareness; from this accumulation of animated molecules a new general consciousness arises in which the elements forming the whole participate and are fused. "Perception being an essential property of the elements, it evidently cannot perish, diminish, or increase. It can indeed undergo different modifications as a result of various combinations of elements; but in the universe as a whole perception must always amount to the same sum total, even though we cannot isolate and verify this sum. . . . Every element through its union with other elements having

---

[50] Maupertuis, *Système de la Nature*, sect. III, IV, XIV, XXII, *Oeuvres*, Lyons, 1756, tome II, pp. 139 ff.
[51] *Ibid.*, sect. LXIII and LXIV; pp. 166 f.

mingled its consciousness (perception) with theirs and lost its specific self-awareness, we lack all recollection of the primitive state of the elements, and our origin must remain entirely lost to us."[52]

Maupertuis' doctrine is pursued further by Diderot in his *Thoughts on the Interpretation of Nature*, but Diderot was too incisive a critic not to see its weaknesses. He quite correctly sees in this attempt to transcend materialism but another variety of the same thing. And against this sublimated form of materialism Diderot advocates a different, a purely dynamic philosophy. It is of course dangerous when speaking of Diderot to try to characterize his philosophy as a whole at any given time by a certain term and, so to speak, to nail it down in this way. For Diderot's thought can only be grasped on the wing, that is, in the stages of its unceasing transitions. These transitions never end when any particular goal has been achieved, and at no point of their course can one designate their nature or their purpose. In the course of his life Diderot changed his viewpoint countless times, but the change in itself is neither accidental nor arbitrary. It is an indication of Diderot's belief that no particular viewpoint from which we contemplate the universe can do justice to its profusion, its inner variety, its constant mutations. Thus Diderot's thinking does not strive for crystallization, for expression in definitive formulas. It is and remains a fluid and fleeting element; but it is precisely in this elasticity that Diderot believes he can come nearer to reality, which itself knows no rest but is forever in flux. This infinitely changeable universe can only be understood by a flexible manner of thinking, by a kind of thinking which permits itself to be borne and driven from one flight to the next, which does not rest content with what is present and given, but which rather luxuriates in the abundance of possibilities and wants to explore and test them.[53] By virtue of this fundamental characteristic Diderot becomes one of the first to divorce himself from the static philosophy of the eighteenth century and to change this philosophy into a truly

[52] *Ibid.*, sect. LIII, LIV; pp. 155 f.

[53] See Bernhardt Groethuysen's excellent characterization of Diderot in his article, "La Pensée de Diderot," *La Grande Revue*, vol. 82 (1913), pp. 322 ff.

dynamic view of the world. All conceptual schemes, all attempts at mere classification, appear to Diderot as narrow-minded and inadequate; they seem to him useful only to describe the state of knowledge at a particular moment. No limits are to be imposed upon knowledge by such procedures, and no predictions regarding the future of knowledge are to be deduced from them. Our minds must remain open to all new possibilities; we must not allow the horizon of experience to be narrowed by any systems or rules. These considerations lead Diderot to a new conception of the philosophy of nature. It is vain to confine nature within limits, vain to seek to subject it to our human classifications. Nature knows only diversity and absolute heterogeneity. None of its forms retains its identity; each form represents merely a transitory state of equilibrium of its shaping forces which can and will cease to be. "Just as in the animal and vegetable kingdoms, an individual so to speak begins, develops, endures, perishes and vanishes. Might it not be the same with whole species? . . . Could not the philosopher . . . suspect that from all eternity the animal kingdom has had its peculiar elements, sporadic and buried in the mass of matter; that these elements have chanced to unite because it was possible for them to do so; that the embryo formed from these elements has passed through an infinite number of structures and stages; that it has possessed successively movement, sensation, ideas, thought, reflection; . . . that millions of years have elapsed between each of these developments; and that the embryo perhaps still has more transitions to undergo."[54] "Who knows all the animal species which have gone before us? Who knows the species which will follow ours? Everything changes, everything passes away; only the whole is permanent. The world is constantly waxing and waning; it begins and ends at every instant. . . . In the immeasurable ocean of matter there is no molecule which resembles any other molecule—nay, not even itself—for a single moment. 'A new order of things is born': such is the eternal motto of the universe." For the philosopher no delusion is more dangerous than the "sophism of the ephem-

[54] Diderot, "De l'Interprétation de la Nature," sect. LVIII, *Oeuvres*, ed. Assézat, vol. II, pp. 57 f.

eral" (*le sophisme de l'éphémère*), than the belief that the world must necessarily be that which it now is. The world's being is but a fleeting moment in the infinity of its becoming, and no thought can measure *a priori* the wealth which this becoming may sometimes produce.[55] "A new order of things is born" (*rerum novus nascitur ordo*), the motto by which Diderot characterizes nature, also applies to Diderot's own position in the history of eighteenth century thought. He introduces a new order of ideas; he not only goes beyond previous achievements, but he changes the very forms of thought which had made these achievements possible and given them permanence.

[55] Diderot, "Rêve d'Alembert," *Oeuvres*, vol. II, pp. 132, 154, and *passim*.

CHAPTER III

Psychology and Epistemology

I T IS characteristic of eighteenth century thought that the problem of nature and the problem of knowledge are very closely connected with, indeed inseparably linked to, one another. Thought cannot turn toward the world of external objects without at the same time reverting to itself; in the same act it attempts to ascertain the truth of nature and its own truth. Knowledge is not merely applied as an instrument and employed unreservedly as such, but time and again with growing insistence the question of the justification of this use of knowledge and of the quality of the instrument arises. Kant was by no means the first to raise this question; he merely gave it a new formulation, a deeper meaning, and a radically new solution. The general task of defining the limits of the mind (*ingenii limites definire*) had already been clearly grasped by Descartes. Locke places the same question at the foundation of his whole empirical philosophy. Even Locke's empiricism reveals a deliberately "critical" tendency. According to Locke an investigation of the function of experience should precede any determination of its object. We must not grasp at any objects whatever and seek to investigate their nature on the basis of our knowledge; our first question must be what kind of objects is commensurate with, and determinable by, our knowledge. But the solution of this question, that is to say, exact insight into the specific character of the human understanding, cannot otherwise be attained than by examining the whole extent of its realm and by tracing the whole course of its development from its first elements to its highest forms. Thus the critical problem has its roots in a genetic problem. A really adequate explanation of the human mind is only to be found in its evolution. Hence psychology is designated as the foundation of epistemology, and up to Kant's *Critique of Pure Reason* psychology held this position almost unchallenged. The reaction against this viewpoint, which originates with Leibniz's *New Essays on the Human Understanding*, sets in several decades too late because this work was not published until 1765, when it was edited from the manuscripts in the Hannover Library; and even then this reaction is confined for some time to the sphere of German intellectual history. The sharp distinction between the transcendental and psychological methods, between the question of the beginning of experience and its origin, as Kant systematically develops it, cannot be retained in a historical presentation of the fundamental problems of eighteenth century thought. For there is constant overlapping of the two methods, and transcendental deduction is never separated from psychological deduction. The objective validity of the fundamental concepts of knowledge is to be determined and judged by their origin. Psychological origin thus becomes a logical criterion; but there are, on the other hand, certain logical norms which permeate, and give direction to, the problems of psychology. Psychology thus receives a predominantly reflexive character; it is not content with a mere understanding of forms and processes of the operations of the mind, but it seeks to go back to their ultimate ground, to their very elements, in order to analyze them into their constituent parts. In view of this method psychology feels that it belongs to the natural sciences. Its highest ideal is to become the "analyst of the soul" just as chemistry is the analyst of the inorganic world, and anatomy of the organic world. Voltaire writes of Locke: "So many philosophers having written the romance of the soul, a sage has arrived who has modestly written its history. Locke has set forth human reason just as an excellent anatomist explains the parts of the human body."[1]

The fundamental question of the truth of knowledge, of the agreement between concepts and objects, had been solved by the great rationalistic systems of the seventeenth century by reducing both the realm of concepts and that of objects to the same original stratum of being. In this stratum concepts and objects meet and from this original mingling is derived all their later correspondence. The nature of human knowledge can only be explained in terms of the ideas which the mind finds within itself. These innate ideas are the seal that is from

---

[1] Voltaire, *Lettres sur les Anglais*, Lettre XIII, *Oeuvres*, Paris, Lequien, 1821, vol. XXVI, p. 65.

Psychology and Epistemology

the first stamped upon the mind, assuring it once and for all of its origin and destiny. According to Descartes all philosophy begins with a consideration of those "primitive notions" in our minds which are the models for all other knowledge. Among these notions are the concepts of being, number, and duration, which are valid for any thought content; while in the corporeal world there are the additional concepts of extension, form, and motion, and in the realm of the mind there is the concept of thought.[2] In these simple models and prototypes are included all empirical reality, all the variety of physical bodies, and all the diversity of psychological processes. These models and prototypes point forward to empirical reality, but they can do so only because at the same time they point backward to its origin. Innate ideas are the trademark which the divine workman has imprinted on his product: "les marques de l'ouvrier empreintes sur son ouvrage." There is now no need to ask further concerning their connection with reality or concerning the possibility of their application to it. They are applicable to reality because they spring from the same source and because, accordingly, there is nowhere any opposition between their own structure and the structure of things. Reason, as the system of clear and distinct ideas, and the world, as the totality of created being, can nowhere fail to harmonize; for they merely represent different versions or different expressions of the same essence. The "archetypal intellect" of God thus becomes the bond between thinking and being, between truth and reality in the philosophy of Descartes. This basic aspect of Descartes' thought is even more apparent in his immediate pupils and successors. In the development beyond Descartes all immediate connection between reality and the human mind, between thinking substance and extended substance is denied and completely broken off. There is no union between soul and body, between our ideas and reality, except that which is given or produced by the being of God. The way never leads from the one pole of being to the other, but always through the center of divine being and activity. It is only through this medium that we recognize and

[2] Cf. especially Descartes' letter of May 21, 1643, to Countess Elizabeth of Palatine, *Oeuvres*, ed. Adam-Tannery, vol. III, p. 665.

act upon external objects. Thus Descartes' doctrine of innate ideas is intensified in Malebranche to the assertion that we see all things in God. There is no true knowledge of things except in so far as we relate our sense perceptions to ideas of pure reason. It is only through this relation that our ideas gain objective meaning, only thus that they cease to be mere modifications of the ego and come to represent objective reality and order. Sense qualities, sensations of color and tone, of smell and taste, contain no trace whatever of any knowledge of being or of the world, for through the immediacy with which we experience them they represent merely states of mind which change from moment to moment. Scientific method alone can perceive in these states of mind the objectively subsisting and objectively valid order of nature. But such perception is possible only by the procedure of relating the accidental to the necessary, the merely factual to something rational, the temporal to the eternal. We attain to knowledge of the physical world by reducing matter to extension rather than by attributing to it any quality perceptible to sense. But this reduction must then be followed by a further reduction which penetrates more deeply. For it is not sufficient to understand extension in the sense in which it is given in concrete perception, in the imagination. In order to grasp the exact meaning of extension, we must free it from all pictorial content, we must proceed from a merely imaginative to an intelligible extension.[3] The human mind can only know nature and physical reality through the concept of intelligible extension, but the mind can only grasp this concept by relating it to God as the "place of ideas." In this sense every genuine act of cognition, every act of reason, brings about an immediate union between God and the human soul. The validity, the value, and the certainty of the fundamental concepts of our knowledge are placed beyond doubt by virtue of the fact that in and through them we participate in divine being. All logical truth and certainty are based ultimately on such metaphysical participation, which indeed they require for their complete proof. The light that illumines the path of knowledge shines

[3] For a fuller treatment of Malebranche's concept of "intelligible extension" see the author's book *Das Erkenntnisproblem*, vol. I, pp. 573 ff.

from within, not from without; it radiates from the realm of ideas and eternal truths, not from that of things of sense. Yet this inner light is not wholly ours, but points back to another and higher source of light: "It is a refulgence of the luminous substance of our common master."[4]

As we consider this development of Cartesian rationalism, we can see most distinctly the point at which opposition to the philosophy of the Enlightenment was sure to arise. In the problem of knowledge this philosophy found the same task it had encountered and, as it believed, successfully solved in the problem of nature. Nature and knowledge are to be placed on their own foundations and explained in terms of their own conditions. In both cases flights into transcendent worlds must be avoided. No foreign element may be permitted to come between knowledge and reality, between subject and object. The problem must be placed on the ground of experience and solved there, for any step beyond experience would signify a mock solution, an explanation of the unknown in terms of that which is still less known. That mediation which apriorism and rationalism had looked upon as forming the basis of the highest certainty of knowledge is thus decisively rejected. The great process of secularization of thought, in which the philosophy of the Enlightenment sees its main task, is felt at this point with particular intensity. The logical and epistemological problem of the relation of knowledge to its object cannot be solved by the introduction of metaphysical considerations; these can only confuse the issue. In his famous letter to Markus Herz, which contains the first precise formulation of his critical problem, Kant emphatically spurned any attempt at such a solution. "Plato took an older conception of the divine being as the source of principles and pure concepts of the understanding, while Malebranche took a conception of God which still prevails.... But a *deus ex machina* in the determination of the origin and validity of our knowledge is the most preposterous device that one can choose; and, besides the vicious circle in the sequence of inferences from it, it has the further disadvantage that it fosters

---

[4] Malebranche, *Entretiens sur la Métaphysique*, ch. v, sect. 12.

every pious or brooding whim."[5] In this negative part of his thesis Kant is still defending the general conviction of the Enlightenment. This age had again and again opposed the attempt to solve the problem of knowledge by means of a transcendent world. Voltaire, too, in his constant struggle against such tendencies appeals frequently to the system of Malebranche. In Malebranche he sees one of the most profound metaphysicians of all times;[6] and for this very reason Voltaire repeatedly refers to Malebranche in order to prove the impotence of the metaphysical system-building spirit.[7] In Voltaire and in the whole French Encyclopaedist movement this negative approach implies, to be sure, a definite position, henceforth looked upon as unassailable. For what relation remains between the ego and the external world, between subject and object, if we eliminate transcendence as our bridge? What conceivable connection is there between subject and object other than that of a direct influence of the one upon the other? If the ego and the physical world belong to different strata of reality, and if despite this fact they are to come into contact and establish a connection, then such a connection would seem possible only if external reality were to partake of consciousness. The only known empirical form of such a participation is, however, that of a direct influence. This alone can bridge the gap between idea and object. The assertion that every idea that we find in our minds is based on a previous impression and can only be explained on this basis, is now exalted to the rank of an indubitable principle. Even Hume's skepticism, however much it assails the universal validity of the causal relation in general, does not reject this special form of causality. Even though the original of a given idea cannot always be produced, though it be ever so hidden, yet there can be no doubt that it exists and that we are to seek it. Any such doubt would signify merely superficiality and lack of consistent thinking.[8]

[5] Kant's letter to Markus Herz, Feb. 21, 1772, *Werke*, ed. Cassirer, vol. IX, pp. 104 f.

[6] See Voltaire's *Siècle de Louis XIV*, *Oeuvres*, ed. Lequien, vol. XIX, p. 140.

[7] See Voltaire's satirical poem "Les Systèmes," *Oeuvres*, vol. XIV, pp. 231 ff., and also his treatise "Tout en Dieu, Commentaire sur Malebranche" (1769), *Oeuvres*, vol. XXXI, pp. 201 ff.

[8] Hume, *Treatise of Human Nature*, part III, sect. 2.

Psychology and Epistemology

Here we have then the astonishing and systematically paradoxical result that psychological empiricism itself, in order to be able to develop its thesis, finds itself forced to base its doctrine on a psychological axiom. The maxim "Nothing is in the intellect which was not first in sense" (*nihil est in intellectu quod non antea fuerit in sensu*) can by no means lay claim to factual truth as tested by a thorough-going induction. Yet not only empirical probability, but complete and indubitable certainty—indeed, a sort of necessity—are attributed to this maxim. Diderot expressly states: "Nothing is proved in metaphysics, and we know nothing either concerning our intellectual faculties or concerning the origin and progress of our knowledge, if the old principle: *nihil est in intellectu,* etc., is not evidence of a first axiom."[9] This statement is typical, for it shows that not even empiricism has entirely foregone the appeal to general principles and their *a priori* evidence. But this evidence has now changed its position; it no longer asserts a connection between pure concepts but rather insight into a factual context. The metaphysics of the soul is to be replaced by a history of the soul, by that "historical, plain method" which Locke had maintained against Descartes.[10] On all questions of psychology and the theory of knowledge Locke's authority remained practically unchallenged throughout the first half of the eighteenth century. Voltaire places Locke above Plato, and d'Alembert in his introduction to the French Encyclopaedia says that Locke is the creator of scientific philosophy just as Newton is the originator of scientific physics. Condillac in a brief survey of the history of psychology proceeds immediately from Aristotle to Locke declaring that, from the viewpoint of real contributions to the solution of psychological problems, all that lay between these two thinkers is insignificant.[11] Only in one respect does English as well as French psychology attempt to go beyond Locke. Both these psychologies want to get rid of the last remnants of dualism which had remained in Locke's psychological prin-

[9] Diderot, *Apologie de l'Abbé de Prades,* sect. XII.

[10] Locke, *Essay concerning Human Understanding,* Book I, ch. I, sect. 2.

[11] "Immediately after Aristotle comes Locke; for it is not necessary to count the other philosophers who have written on the same subject." Condillac, *Extrait raisonné du Traité des Sensations,* ed. Georges Lyon, Paris, 1921, p. 32.

ciples; they want to do away with the distinction between internal and external experience and reduce all human knowledge to a single source. The difference between sensation and reflection is only apparent and it vanishes upon further analysis. The development of empirical philosophy from Locke to Berkeley and from Berkeley to Hume represents a series of attempts to minimize the difference between sensation and reflection, and finally to wipe it out altogether. French philosophical criticism of the eighteenth century hammered at this same point also in an attempt to eliminate the last vestige of independence which Locke had attributed to reflection. Reflection is supposed to be the mind's knowledge of its own states, of its own nature; but is there in truth any real empirical datum to support such knowledge? Do we ever experience ourselves without finding in this experience some sensation which is related to something physical, to some quality or condition of our body? Can a pure sensation of self, an abstract self-consciousness, ever be found in experience? Maupertuis, who raises this question, does not wish to answer it dogmatically but he tends toward a negative reply. The more deeply one considers the idea of pure existence and the more closely one analyzes it, the more impossible it appears to separate it from all sense data. One sees that the sense of touch especially plays a decisive role in the development of this idea.[12] The same conclusion is expressed by Condillac in a much more radical form, and it leads him to a sharp criticism of the foundations of Lockean psychology and theory of knowledge. Without doubt Locke took an important step forward and first blazed the trail for empirical investigation. But he stopped half way and recoiled before the most difficult problem. For where the higher functions of the mind—those of comparing, distinguishing, judging, and willing—are concerned, Locke suddenly proves unfaithful to his genetic method. He is content merely to enumerate these faculties and to leave them as fundamental powers of the mind without tracing them to their source. Hence the thread of the investigation breaks just at the most

[12] Cf. Maupertuis, *Examen philosophique de la preuve de l'existence de Dieu employée dans l'Essai de Cosmologie*, Mémoires de l'Académie de Berlin, 1756, § xix f.

critical point. Locke successfully attacked innate ideas but he permitted the prejudice regarding innate operations of the mind to survive. He did not see that, like seeing and hearing, observing, understanding, etc., are not ultimate indivisible qualities, but late developments which we acquire through experience and learning.[13] The investigation must therefore be pursued further. No upper limits must be set for the process of constant growth of the mind. This process must not stop short of the so-called "higher" intellectual energies; on the contrary, it exerts all its forces only when it reaches these energies. Here too there is nothing which is not completely contained in the original sense elements. Mental operations represent nothing really new and therefore mysterious; they are indeed merely transformed sensations. If we trace step by step the genesis of the operations of the mind and the process of transformation of sense elements which these operations involve, then we see that there is never any clear line of demarcation between individual phases of mental activity, but that these phases imperceptibly melt into one another. If we consider these mental metamorphoses as a whole, we find in one and the same series acts of thinking and willing as well as acts of feeling and perceiving. Condillac is not a sensationalist in the sense that like Hume he wants to reduce the ego to a mere "bundle or collection of different perceptions." He maintains the simple structure of the soul, emphasizing that the real subject of consciousness can be looked for only in such a structure. Unity of person necessarily presupposes the unity of a sentient being; it presupposes the soul as a simple substance which is variously modified according to the different impressions received by the body.[14] Thus, strictly speaking, the senses are not the cause but the occasion of all our knowledge. For it is not the senses which perceive; it is rather the mind which perceives when modifications of bodily organs take place. We must carefully observe the first sensations of which we become aware; we must discover the foundation of

[13] "Locke did not know how much we need to learn by touching, seeing, hearing, etc. All the faculties of the soul appeared to him to be innate qualities, and he did not suspect that they could have their origin in sensation itself." Condillac, *Extrait raisonné*, p. 33.

[14] Condillac, *Traité des animaux* (1755), ch. II.

the first operations of the mind, watch them in their development, and pursue them to their extreme limits. In short, as
Bacon said, we must, as it were, create the whole human mind
anew in order really to understand its structure.[15]

In his attempt to create the mind anew Condillac does not, of
course, confine himself to mere empirical observation. The
Treatise on Sensations does not merely attempt to set forth a
list of observations; it follows rather a strict systematic plan
and proceeds from a systematic assumption to which it tries to
adhere and which it tries to prove step by step. The illustration
of the statue which is awakened to life by means of the impressions impinging upon it, and which in this way advances to increasingly rich and differentiated forms of life, shows clearly
that the "natural history of the soul" which Condillac endeavors
to give is not free from speculative and constructive considerations. Nor is Condillac content merely to present the growth of
the mind and the progressive variety of its forms; he wants
rather to elucidate the tendency of this growth and to penetrate
into its real moving forces. We find in Condillac a new and
fruitful approach. He realizes that so long as we remain in the
realm of mere concepts and ideas, that is, in the realm of theoretical knowledge, the ultimate forces in the growth of the
mind cannot be made manifest. Recourse to another dimension
of the mental world now becomes necessary. The activity of
the mind and the vital source of all its manifold energies do
not lie in speculation or in mere contemplation. For motion cannot be explained in terms of rest; nor can the dynamics of the
mind be based on its statics. In order to understand the latent
energy behind all the metamorphoses of the mind, which does
not permit it to retain any form but drives it on to ever new
shapes and operations, one must assume in the mind an original
moving principle. This principle is not to be found in mere ideation and thought but only in desiring and striving. Thus the
impulse precedes knowledge and forms its indispensable presupposition. Locke, in his analysis of the phenomena of the will,
had stressed that that which incites man to a certain act of willing, and which in every individual case is the concrete cause of

[15] *Extrait raisonné*, p. 31.

his decision, is not at all the mere idea of a future good toward which the act is supposed to serve as a means. There is no moving power whatever in this idea and in the purely theoretical consideration of the various possible goals of the will from the standpoint of the better or the worse choice. This power does not work by anticipation of a future good; it originates rather in the remembrance of displeasure and uneasiness which the mind feels under certain conditions, and which irresistibly incite it to shun these conditions. Locke considers this uneasiness, therefore, as the real motivating force, as the decisive impulse, in all our acts of the will.[16] Condillac starts with these arguments, but he seeks to pursue them far beyond the sphere of the phenomena of the will and to extend them over the whole field of the operations of the mind. Uneasiness (*inquiétude*) is for him not merely the starting-point of our desires and wishes, of our willing and acting, but also of all our feeling and perceiving and of our thinking and judging, indeed of the highest acts of reflection to which the mind can rise.[17] The usual order of ideas, which had been reaffirmed and sanctioned by Cartesian psychology, is thus reversed. The will is not founded on the idea, but the idea on the will. Here we meet for the first time that voluntaristic tendency whose development can be traced through Schopenhauer in the field of metaphysics and the theories of modern pragmatism in the field of epistemology. In the purely theoretical order of phenomena we have, according to Condillac, the first activity of the mind; this is the simple act of grasping what the senses present, that is, the act of perception. The act of perception is immediately followed by the act of attention which requires dwelling on certain perceptions and singling out individual sense experiences from the totality of the psychological process. But this very selection of, and emphasis on, certain perceptions would not be possible if there were no ground of preference for one perception rather than another,

[16] Locke, *Essay*, Book II, ch. XXI, sect. 30 ff.

[17] "It remained to be shown that this uneasiness is the first principle which gives us the habits of touching, seeing, hearing, feeling, tasting, comparing, judging, reflecting, desiring, loving, fearing, hoping, wishing; and that, in a word, it is through uneasiness that all the habits of the mind and body are born." *Extrait Raisonné*, p. 34.

and this ground of preference as such no longer belongs to the sphere of the purely theoretical, but to that of the practical. Attention focuses on that which in some sense immediately concerns the individual, that is, which answers his needs and inclinations. Similarly, our needs and inclinations determine the direction of our memory. This faculty cannot be explained on the basis of the mere mechanical association of ideas; it is determined and directed rather by our appetites and desires. It is our need which recalls some forgotten idea from its darkness and causes it to live again: "Ideas are reborn by the action of the needs which produced them." Ideas form, so to speak, vortices in the mind, and these vortices multiply as our emotional drives grow and are differentiated. Each vortex can be considered as the center of a certain motion which is continuous from the center to the periphery of the sphere of mental activity, that is, to the clear and conscious ideas. "These vortices gain ascendancy by turns over one another according as their needs become more urgent. They accomplish their revolutions with amazing variations. They crowd one another, destroy one another, or come into being again according as the feelings to which they owe their power weaken, are eclipsed, or appear in a form hitherto unknown. From one instant to the next the vortex, which but now drew others into its orbit, can itself be consumed; and as soon as the need vanishes, all vortices are fused into one. Chaos alone remains. Ideas come and go without order, forming only moving tableaux which offer bizarre and imperfect images. It is our needs which must lend them definite character again and place them in their true light."[18] The logical order of our ideas, according to Condillac, is not a primary, but a derived fact; it is only a sort of reflection of the biological order. What on a given occasion seems to be essential, depends not so much on the nature of things as on the direction of our interest; and our interest is determined by that which is advantageous for us and necessary for our self-preservation.

We have now arrived at a problem of importance to a general characterization of the philosophy of the Enlightenment. It is customary, under the influence of a too narrow conception of

[18] Condillac, *Traité des animaux*, Part II, ch. II, pp. 398 f.

the idea of "enlightenment," to accuse the psychology of the eighteenth century of being wholly intellectualistic, and of limiting its analyses principally to the realm of ideas and theoretical knowledge, while neglecting the force and specific quality of the emotional life. But this conception will not bear unbiased historical scrutiny. Nearly all the psychological systems of the eighteenth century at least clearly recognized and sketched the problem raised here. Even in the seventeenth century the analysis of the affects and passions had again become the focus of interest both of psychology and of philosophy in general. Descartes' essay on the passions of the soul and Spinoza's presentation of his doctrine of the affects in the third book of his *Ethics* are not simply occasional writings; they form integral parts of their systems. On the whole, however, the idea prevails in these systems that the pure essence of the soul cannot be grasped and determined from this angle. For this essence consists in thought, and only as such does it manifest itself in its purity. The clear and distinct idea, not the inarticulate affect, is characteristic of the real nature of the soul. Desires and appetites, the passions of sense, belong only indirectly to the soul; they are not its original properties and tendencies, but rather disturbances which the soul suffers as a result of its union with the body. The psychology and ethics of the seventeenth century are in the main based on this conception of the affects as "perturbations of the mind" (*perturbationes animi*). Only that action has ethical value which overcomes these disturbances, which illustrates the triumph of the active over the passive part of the soul, of reason over the passions. This Stoic view not merely dominates the philosophy of the seventeenth century, but it permeates the intellectual life of the age in general. On this point Descartes' teaching agrees with that of Corneille.[19] The rule of the rational will over all desires of sense, over appetites and passions, proclaims and expresses the freedom of man. The eighteenth century advances beyond this negative characterization and evaluation of the affects. It looks upon the affects not as a mere obstacle, but seeks to show that they are the origi-

[19] Cf. G. Lanson, *L'Influence de la Philosophie Cartésienne sur la littérature française* (see above p. 27).

nal and indispensable impulse of all the operations of the mind. In Germany the views of Leibniz were already exerting an influence in this direction. For Leibniz in his definition of the monad by no means tried to reduce its nature to the mere idea, to theoretical knowledge. The monad is not limited to ideation, but combines ideation with striving. Together with the concept of the idea appears the equally valid concept of the tendency, and with perception (*perceptio*) is "that which one is eager to perceive" (*percepturitio*).[20] German psychology in general upholds this basic presupposition, and it is thus enabled to gain for the phenomena of the will and of pure feeling an independent place in the system of psychology. But the same development, seen from another angle, takes place in France and England. Hume's epistemological skepticism, even in the realm of psychology, leads to the overthrow of all previously valid standards. It turns all scales of value upside down; for it shows that reason, in which one usually venerates the highest faculty of man, plays a quite subordinate role in our mental processes as a whole. Far from ruling the "lower" faculties of the mind, reason is constantly dependent on their aid; without the cooperation of sensibility and the imagination reason cannot take a single step forward. All rational knowledge is reducible to the one inference from effect to cause; but precisely this influence is indefensible on purely logical grounds. The only possible explanation for it is an indirect one, which consists in revealing its psychological origin, in tracing to its source our faith in the validity of the causal principle. Then we find that this faith is not based on certain universally valid and necessary principles of reason but that it is derived from a mere instinct of human nature. This instinct as such is blind, but in this blindness lies its real power, the power with which it dominates all our thinking. Utilizing this theoretical result of his investigation, Hume continues from this point his process of leveling the faculties of the mind until he has broadened it to include all phases of intellectual activity. The upper strata of the mind are removed by Hume according to a consistent plan. In his *Natural History of*

---

[20] For the distinction between *perceptio* and *percepturitio* in Leibniz, see especially the correspondence with Christian Wolff, ed. Gerhardt, Halle, 1860, p. 56.

Religion Hume tries to show how every claim of religion to convey and make accessible to man a "higher world" is illusory and untenable. The real sphere of religion, of the idea and veneration of God, lies elsewhere. We are not to seek this sphere in an innate idea, nor in an original intuitive certainty; nor can we arrive at it through thought and inference, through theoretical proofs and their corollaries. Here too there is no other way than to seek the deepest roots of religion among human instincts. The affect of fear is the beginning of all religion, and all the various shapes and forms of religion are derived from, and are explicable in terms of, this emotion. We have here a new trend of thought, one which also gains irresistible momentum in eighteenth century France. It sounds like a violent revolution when Vauvenargues, in his *Introduction to the Knowledge of the Human Mind* (1746), says that the true nature of man does not lie in reason, but in the passions. The Stoic demand for control of the passions by reason is and always will be a mere dream. Reason is not the dominating force in man; reason is comparable only to the hand that tells the time on the face of a clock. The mechanism that moves this hand lies within; the motivating force and ultimate cause of knowledge lie in those primary and original impulses which we continually receive from another, a completely irrational realm. Even the most dispassionate thinkers of the French Enlightenment, the champions and spokesmen of a purely rational culture, support this thesis. Voltaire says in his *Treatise on Metaphysics* that without the passions, without the desire for fame, without ambition and vanity, no progress of humanity, no refinement of taste and no improvement of the arts and sciences is thinkable: "It is with this motivating force that God, whom Plato called the eternal geometer, and whom I call the eternal machinist, has animated and embellished nature: the passions are the wheels which make all these machines go."[21] Helvetius in his essay *On the Mind* adopts the same attitude. And Diderot's first independent enterprise as a thinker, his *Philosophical Thoughts*, begins similarly with this idea. It is of no avail to

[21] Voltaire, *Traité de Métaphysique* (1734), ch. VIII, *Oeuvres*, ed. Lequien, vol. XXXI, p. 61.

oppose the passions, and it would be the height of the ridiculous to try to destroy them since in so doing we should undermine the proud foundations of reason. Everything excellent in poetry, painting, and music, everything sublime in art and morals, is derived from this source. Hence the affects must not be weakened but strengthened; for the true power of the soul springs from the harmonious balance of the passions, not from their destruction.[22] Thus a gradual change in psychological orientation and evaluation becomes apparent, a transformation which appears before the chief works of Rousseau were published, and which develops independently of them. We shall see that this transformation is not only important for the system of theoretical knowledge but that its effects are felt in all directions and that it exerts its influence on the ethics, the philosophy of religion, and the aesthetics of the age of the Enlightenment, giving new significance to the major problems of these fields of knowledge.

2

A survey of the special problems of eighteenth century epistemology and psychology shows that in all their variety and inner diversity they are grouped around a common center. The investigation of individual problems in all their abundance and apparent dispersion comes back again and again to a general theoretical problem in which all the threads of the study unite.[23] This is the problem which Molyneux first formulated in his *Optics*, and which soon awakened the greatest philosophical interest. Is the experience derived from one field of sense perception a sufficient basis on which to construct another field of perception that is of qualitatively different content and of specifically different structure? Is there an inner connection which permits us to make a direct transition from one such field to another, from the world of touch, for instance, to that of vision? Will a person born blind—who has acquired an exact knowledge of certain corporeal forms by means of experience and so can

---

[22] Diderot, *Pensées philosophiques* (1746), sect. 1 ff.

[23] There is no place here for discussion of these problems. For a fuller treatment, see the author's *Erkenntnisproblem*, vol. II.

distinguish accurately among them—have the same power to distinguish objects if, as a result of a successful operation, he gains possession of his visual faculty, and is required to judge concerning these forms on the basis of purely optical data without the aid of his sense of touch? Will he be able immediately to distinguish a cube from a sphere by sight, or will a long and difficult period of adjustment be necessary before he succeeds in establishing a connection between the tactile impression and the visual form of these two objects? No uniform solution of all these problems was found at once, but now that the problems had been formulated, their influence reached far beyond the sphere of the special sciences. Berkeley's philosophical diary shows how much these problems occupied his mind, and how they form, as it were, germinating cells from which his whole theory of perception developed. The *Essay towards a New Theory of Vision*, which forms the prelude to Berkeley's philosophy and contains all of his ideas implicitly, is nothing but an attempt at a complete systematic development and elucidation of Molyneux's problem. For decades thereafter the strength and fruitfulness of this problem are still evident in French philosophy. Voltaire, in his *Elements of the Philosophy of Newton*, gives an extensive exposition of the problem;[24] Diderot makes it the central point of his first psychological and epistemological essay, *Letter on the Blind* (1749). As for Condillac, he is so much under the spell of this question that he even declares that it contains the source and key to all modern psychology; for it was this question which drew attention to the decisive role of the faculty of judgment in the simplest act of perception as well as in the developing structure of the perceptual world.[25] The decisive systematic significance of Molyneux's problem is thus clearly indicated; the individual example which this problem presents called attention to the general question as to whether sense as such can produce the physical world which we find in consciousness, or whether to this end it requires the cooperation of other powers of the mind, and as to how these powers are to be determined.

[24] *Éléments de la Philosophie de Newton*, ch. VII, *Oeuvres*, vol. XXX, pp. 138 ff.
[25] Condillac, *Traité des sensations*, ed. Lyon, p. 33.

Psychology and Epistemology

Berkeley in his *New Theory of Vision* and his *Principles of Human Knowledge* had proceeded from the paradox that the only material available for the erection of the structure of our perceptual world consists in simple sense perceptions, but that, on the other hand, these perceptions do not contain the slightest indication of those "forms" in which perceptual reality is given. We believe that we see this reality before us as a solid structure in which every individual element has its assigned place, and in which its relation to all other parts is exactly determined. The fundamental character of all reality lies in this definite relationship. Without the presence of order in the co-existence and sequence of our individual perceptions, without a definite spatial and temporal relationship among the various perceptions, there can be no objective world, no "nature of things." And not even the most determined idealist can deny this nature of things; for he too must postulate an inviolable order among phenomena, or else his phenomenal world will dissolve into mere illusion.[26] Thus the cardinal question of all theory of knowledge is that of the meaning of this order, while the cardinal question of all genetic psychology is that of its derivation. But here experience, from which alone we can expect reliable guidance, seems to leave us in the lurch. For it always shows us the world of products, not the world of process; it confronts us with objects bearing definite shapes, especially in respect to a certain spatial arrangement, without telling us how they acquired these shapes. The first glance we cast on things enables us to discover not only certain sense qualities, but certain spatial relations as well; we ascribe to every individual object a certain magnitude, a certain position, and a certain distance from other objects. But if we try to establish the foundation of all these assertions, we find that it is not to be discovered among the data given us by the visual sense. For these data are merely differentiated according to quality and intensity and contain nothing that would lead us to the concept of magnitude or of pure quantity. The ray of light which passes from the object to my eye can tell me nothing directly about the object's

[26] Cf. Berkeley, *A Treatise concerning the Principles of Human Knowledge*, sect. 34; *Three Dialogues between Hylas and Philonous*, Third Dialogue.

shape or its distance from me. For all the eye knows is the impression on the retina. But from the quality of this impression no knowledge can be had of the cause which produced it, nor of the distance of the object from the eye. The conclusion to be drawn from all this is that what we call distance, position, and magnitude of objects is itself something invisible. Berkeley's fundamental thesis now seems to be reduced to an absurdity; the equation of being (*esse*) and being perceived (*percipi*) seems to have vanished. In the midst of phenomena which are immediately perceived by our senses, and which we cannot avoid, something has been discovered which lies beyond all the limits of perception. The distance between objects appears by its very nature to be imperceptible, and yet it is an element which is absolutely essential to the structure of our conception of the world. The spatial form of perceptions is fused with its sense material; and yet it is not given in the material alone, nor can it be analytically reduced to this material. Thus the form of perceptions constitutes a foreign body in the only accessible world of immediate sense data which cannot be eliminated without causing this world to collapse. In the assertion: ". . . distance is in its own nature imperceptible and yet it is perceived by sight,"[27] Berkeley in his *New Theory of Vision* gives the most poignant expression of the dilemma with which sensationalist psychology and epistemology are confronted at the very start.

Berkeley overcomes this dilemma by giving a broader meaning to his basic concept of perception, by including in its definition not only simple sensation but also the activity of representation. Every sense impression possesses such a power of representation, of indirect reference. It not only presents itself with its specific content to consciousness but it causes all other content with which it is joined by a strong empirical bond to be visible and present in consciousness. And this reciprocal play of sense impressions, this regularity, with which they recall each other and represent each other in consciousness, is also the ultimate basis of the idea of space. This idea is not given as such in a particular perception; it belongs neither to the sense of vision nor to that of touch alone. Space is no specific qualitative ele-

[27] Berkeley, *New Theory of Vision*, sect. 11.

ment as originally given as color or tone; it is that which results from the relationship among various sense data. Since in
the course of experience visual and tactile impressions are firmly
joined, consciousness acquires the ability to pass from one type
of sensation to another according to certain rules. It is in this
transition that we must look for the origin of the idea of space.
The transition itself must of course be understood as a purely
empirical, not as a rational, transition. It is not a bond of a
logical and mathematical kind; it is not reasoning which leads
us from certain perceptions of visual sensation to those of touch,
or from the latter to the former. Habit and practice alone weave
this bond, and they make it progressively firmer. The idea of
space is not, therefore, strictly speaking an element of sense
consciousness but an expression of a process which goes on in
consciousness. Only the speed and regularity of this process
cause us to overlook the intermediate stages in ordinary introspection and to anticipate the end of the process at the very
start. But closer psychological and epistemological analysis reveals these intermediary steps and teaches us how indispensable
they are. It shows us that the same connection exists between
different fields of sensory experience as between the symbols
of our language and their meaning. Just as the speech symbol
is in no sense similar to the content to which it refers nor is connected with it by any objective necessity, yet fulfills its function
nevertheless, so the same relation holds for the connection
among generically different and qualitatively disparate impressions. It is only the universality and regularity of their arrangement which distinguish the symbols of sense impressions from
those of speech. Elucidating Berkeley's idea Voltaire writes:
"We learn to see just as we learn to speak and read. . . . The
quick and almost uniform judgments which all our minds form
at a certain age with regard to distances, magnitudes, and positions make us think that we need only open our eyes in order to
see things as we actually do perceive them. This is an illusion.
. . . If all men spoke the same language, we should always be
inclined to believe that there is a necessary connection between
words and ideas. But all men speak the same language with respect to the imagination. Nature says to all: When you have

seen colors for a certain length of time, your imagination will represent to you in the same manner the bodies to which these colors seem to belong. The prompt and involuntary judgment which you will form, will be useful to you in the course of your life."[28]

Berkeley's theory of vision was recognized and adopted in its main aspects by almost all leading psychologists of the eighteenth century. Condillac and Diderot[29] modify it in certain details; both point out, for instance, that visual impressions in themselves include a certain "spatiality." To the sense of touch they attribute merely the function of clarification and fixation of our visual experience; they consider tactile sensations as indispensable not for the origin, but for the growth of our conception of space. But this modification does not affect Berkeley's strictly empirical thesis as such. All apriority of space is vigorously rejected; hence the question of its generality and necessity appears in a new light. If we owe our insight into the structural relations of space merely to experience, it is not inconceivable that a change of experience, as for instance in the event of an alteration of our psychophysical organization, would affect the whole nature of space. Henceforth the concept of space is indefatigably pursued through all its ramifications. What is the significance of that constancy and objectivity which we are accustomed to attribute to the forms of perception and of the understanding? Does this constancy predicate anything concerning the nature of things, or is not all that we understand by this term related and limited to our own nature? Are the judgments which we base on this conception valid, as Bacon would say, by analogy with the universe (*ex analogia universi*) or rather exclusively by analogy with man (*ex analogia hominis*)? With this question the problem of the origin of the idea of space develops far beyond its initial limits. We see now the circumstance which caused psychological and epistemological thought in the eighteenth century to recur again and again to this problem. For on it the fate of the concept of truth in gen-

[28] Voltaire, *Éléments de la Philosophie de Newton*, part II, ch. VII; *Oeuvres*, vol. XXX, p. 147.

[29] See Diderot, *Lettre sur les Aveugles*, and Condillac, *Traité des Sensations*, part I, chaps. VII, XI ff.

eral seemed to depend. If space, which is a fundamental element of all human perception, consists merely of the fusion and correlation of various sensory impressions, then it cannot lay claim to any other necessity and any higher logical dignity than the original elements of which it is composed. The subjectivity of sensory qualities, which is known to and generally acknowledged by modern science, accordingly draws space too into its sphere. But the development cannot stop here, for what is true of space is true in the same sense and with the same justification of all the other factors on which the "form" of knowledge is based. Even the psychology of antiquity distinguished sharply among the various classes of sensory content, between colors and sounds, tastes and smells, on the one hand, and between the pure "form concepts" on the other. The latter—among which were included, besides space, especially duration, number, motion, and rest—were given a special place in that they were not attributed to a particular sense but to a "common sense," αἰσθη-τήριον κοινόν. The rationalistic theory of knowledge in modern times went back to this psychological distinction among the sources of sense impressions in order to establish a specific difference in validity between the ideas derived from the two classes of sensory content. Leibniz points out that the ideas which one usually attributes to "common sense" (*sensus communis*), really belong to and are derived from the mind: ". . . they are ideas of pure reason, but such as have an external reference and are perceivable by the senses; hence they are capable of definitions and proofs."[30] This view appeared to have been conclusively overthrown by the exact analysis of Molyneux's problem. In the year 1728, when Cheselden successfully operated on a fourteen year old boy who had been blind from birth, Molyneux's theoretical problem seemed to have found an empirical solution. Observations on this boy who had suddenly acquired visual organs seemed to confirm the empirical argument on all points. Berkeley's theoretical predictions were completely verified. It was found that the patient by no means obtained full visual power as soon as his eyesight began to function, and that he had to learn gradually and laboriously to distinguish between the

---

[30] Leibniz, *Nouveaux Essais sur l'entendement humain*, Book II, ch. v.

corporeal forms which were presented to his vision. The theory that there is no inner affinity between the data of touch and those of vision but that the relation between them is merely the result of their habitual connection is thus verified by experience. But if this conclusion is valid, then we can no longer speak of a uniform space underlying all the senses and serving, as it were, as a homogeneous substratum. This homogeneous space, which Leibniz had looked upon as a creation of the mind, now proves to be a mere abstraction. We do not find any such unity and uniformity of space in experience but rather just as many qualitatively different kinds of space as we have different fields of sensory experience. Optical space, tactile space, kinesthetic space, all have their own unique structure; they are not connected or related by virtue of a common essence or an abstract form but merely by the regular empirical connection existing between them, by means of which they can reciprocally represent one another. A further conclusion now seems inescapable. The question as to which of all these sensory spaces is to be considered the "true" space, now loses all meaning. They all possess equal validity; none can claim a higher degree of certainty, objectivity, and generality than any other. Accordingly, what we call objectivity or truth or necessity, has no absolute, but merely a relative meaning. Each sense has its own world, and there is no other alternative than to understand and analyze all these worlds in a purely empirical manner without attempting to reduce them to a common denominator. The philosophy of the Enlightenment never tires of inculcating this relativity. This is a theme which not only permeates scientific thought but which is also popularized in general literature. Swift treated the subject with great satirical power and intellectual acumen in his *Gulliver's Travels*, and from here its influence spread to French literature where it is especially felt in Voltaire's *Micromégas*. Diderot, too, in his letters on the blind and on the deaf and dumb gives us elaborate variants of this thought. The basic tendency of the first of these essays is to show by the example of Saunderson, the famous blind geometer, how every deviation in the organic disposition of man must necessarily result in a complete change in his spiritual life. Not merely the sense world, the pattern of perceptual reality, is affected by such a deviation; if we look more deeply into the matter, we shall find the same alteration taking place in all phases of personality, in the intellectual as in the moral, and in the aesthetic as in the religious phases. Relativity extends into the sphere of the highest, the so-called purely intellectual ideas. The concept and word "God" cannot mean the same thing for the blind as for those who can see. Is there then a logic, a metaphysics, or an ethics which can emancipate itself from the bondage of our sense organs? Or are not all our statements about the physical world as well as the intellectual merely about ourselves and the peculiarity of our organization? Would not our being have to undergo a fundamental change if we were endowed with a new sense, or deprived of one of the senses we already have? The philosophers of the eighteenth century love to enlarge upon and explain such psychological speculations in terms of cosmological speculations. A uniform tendency can be traced from Fontenelle's *Conversations on the Plurality of Worlds* to Kant's *General Natural History and Theory of the Heavens*. Perhaps the wealth of possibilities which we can imagine and construct in the abstract is realized in the universe in such a way that to every celestial body there corresponds a specific psycho-physiological quality in the inhabitants. "They say we lack a sixth sense which would explain to us many things of which at present we know nothing. This sixth sense is apparently in some other world in which one of our five senses is lacking. . . . Our knowledge has certain limits beyond which the human mind was never able to go . . . the rest is for other worlds where things we know are unknown."[31] This idea recurs innumerable times in the psychological and epistemological literature of the Enlightenment.[32] And logic, ethics, and theology seem to fade more and more into mere anthropology. In his essay *The Physical Causes of Truth*, Johann Christian Lossius takes the last step in this direction. Lossius maintains

[31] Fontenelle, *Entretiens sur la pluralité des mondes*, Third Evening, *Oeuvres*, Paris, 1818, vol. II, p. 44.
[32] Among writers of the German Enlightenment, Sulzer can be mentioned in this connection. Cf. Sulzer, "Zergliederung des Begriffs der Vernunft" (1758), *Vermischte philosophische Schriften*, vol. I, p. 249.

that we should substitute the useful doctrine of the growth of our ideas for the useless doctrine of logical propositions and conclusions, and that in so doing we should classify our concepts not according to their content or the objects they embrace but according to the organs which appear to be made for this or that concept. In this way we should understand the nature of human ideas, to be sure, not perfectly, yet ever so much more clearly than by means of all the explanations from Aristotle to Leibniz. We shall of course have to renounce all claims to general validity and objectivity; but it will do as little harm to truth as to beauty if we recognize and admit that both are "of a more subjective than objective nature," and that they are not a property of the things but merely a relation of the things to us who think them.[33]

From this fundamental viewpoint it was only one more step to the full recognition of "subjective idealism," but this last step was only rarely taken and the inescapable conclusion only reluctantly drawn. Berkeley had no immediate successor, and those who pursued his psychological method tried to avoid its metaphysical consequences. This becomes especially apparent in Condillac's essay on the origin of human knowledge and in his *Treatise on the Sensations*. Condillac at first believes he can find proof for the reality of the external world simply in the experiences of the sense of touch. The evidence of the other senses, of smell and taste, of sight and hearing, are in his opinion insufficient proof. For in experiences of these senses all we ever grasp is modifications of our own ego without any conclusive indication of an external cause from which these modifications are derived. In seeing, smelling, tasting, hearing, the mind perceives without being aware that there are physical organs for all these activities. It is absorbed in the pure act of perception and knows nothing of any physical substratum of its activity. The situation changes only when we come to the sense of touch, for every tactile sensation exhibits necessarily a double relation. It reminds us in every single phenomenon also of a particular part of the body; thus it represents, so to speak, the

---

[33] Lossius, *Physische Ursachen des Wahren*, Gotha, 1775, pp. 8 ff., 56. Cf. the author's account in *Das Erkenntnisproblem*, vol. II, pp. 575 f.

first penetration into the world of objective reality. But Condillac did not stand by his first solution of the problem; in the later edition of his *Treatise on the Sensations* he deliberately attempted to supplement and improve it. There is now a more radical turn in Condillac's thinking. We must admit on the one hand that all knowledge comes from the senses; on the other hand it is clear that all our sensations are merely expressions of our own modes of being (*manières d'être*). How then can we ever perceive objects outside ourselves? We may ascend to the highest heavens or descend to the deepest abyss, yet we shall never transcend the bounds of our ego, since we shall always encounter merely ourselves and our own thoughts. Condillac thus faces the problem squarely, but the means for its consistent solution are not available to his sensationalistic method.[34] Diderot clearly recognized this weakness; he says that Condillac adopted Berkeley's principles, but tried to avoid his consequences. But psychological idealism cannot really be overcome in this manner. Diderot sees in this idealism, as Kant does later, a "scandal of human reason": "a system which, to the shame of the human mind, is the most difficult to combat, though the most absurd of all."[35]

In Maupertuis' philosophical letters and in his thoughts on the origin of language we find the same inner lack of assurance. Here again the problem is clearly and boldly stated. Maupertuis not only declares that extension, so far as its objective reality is concerned, is exactly like all other sensory qualities, he not only maintains that there is basically no difference between pure space and the phenomena of color and tone so far as their content and psychological development are concerned, but he proceeds to an examination of the general meaning of the predication of reality, to the meaning of the judgment: "There is." What sense does this judgment convey; what are its real content and basis? What do we mean when we say not merely that we see or touch a tree but when we make the further assertion that a tree "exists"? What does this attribution of

---

[34] For a more detailed account of Condillac's vacillating attitude toward the problem of the reality of the external world, see George Lyon's introduction to his edition of the *Traité des sensations*, pp. 14 ff.

[35] Diderot, *Lettre sur les Aveugles, Oeuvres*, ed. Naigeon, vol. II, p. 218.

existence add to the simple sense data? Can it be shown that there is a perception of existence which is just as simple and original as the perception of color or tone? Since this is obviously not so, what other meaning is contained in this predication of existence? If one reflects on these questions, he is led to the conclusion that what we mean by "existence" is not so much a new reality as a new symbol. This symbol permits us to apply a single term to a complicated series of sense impressions and so to crystallize the series for consciousness. A complex of immediate impressions, of recollections and expectations, is expressed by the symbol. The experience to which it refers is composed of a repetition of several similar experiences and of certain accompanying circumstances which bind them firmly together and so seem to give them greater reality. The perception "I have seen a tree" is connected with the other perception that I was at a certain place; I returned to this place and found the tree again, etc. A new awareness thus arises: "I shall always see a tree, if I return to this place," which means: "There is a tree." This reasoning seems to confute any narrowly sensationalistic explanation of the problem of being, for the concept of being cannot be reduced to a simple sensation. Yet very little ground has been gained, for we have now simply exchanged a sensationalistic for a purely nominalistic interpretation of experience. Maupertuis is clearly aware that this is not a solution, but merely a transference of the problem. Hence his analysis too ends in skepticism. The perception "There is a tree," declares Maupertuis, "conveys, so to speak, reality to its object and constitutes a proposition regarding the existence of the tree as independent of me. Yet it would perhaps be very difficult to find in this proposition anything more than was contained in the preceding propositions, which were merely the symbols for my perceptions. If I had never had but once each perception: 'I see a tree,' 'I see a horse,' then, however vivid these perceptions might have been, I am not sure that I could ever have inferred the proposition: 'There is.' If my memory had been sufficiently comprehensive as not to fear multiplying the symbols of my perceptions and such that I could have employed only simple expressions for each perception, such as

A, B, C, D, etc., then perhaps I should never have arrived at the proposition: 'There is,' even though I should have had all the same perceptions as made me formulate it. Would not this proposition be merely an abbreviation of all the perceptions: 'I see,' 'I have seen,' 'I shall see,' etc."[36] The progress here attained lies in the transference of the focal point of the problem of reality from mere sensation to judgment. But judgment is not understood in its characteristic logical significance; Maupertuis tries to transform judgment into a mere accretion, a coexistence and sequence of perceptions. A fundamental transformation and a critical solution of the question here raised could only be achieved after this obstacle had been removed, that is, after Kant had analyzed judgment into the "unity of action" and recognized it by virtue of its inherent spontaneity as the expression of the "objective unity of self-conciousness." The "problem of the relation of an idea to its object" was thus established on a new foundation; it was raised above the importance of a merely psychological question and made the focal point of a "transcendental logic."

3

But, revolutionary as it appears, this last development in philosophical method does not take place without historical preparations. For the doctrines of Locke and Berkeley, of Hume and Condillac, never gained unchallenged recognition in Germany. Much as Locke's influence seems to dominate here for a time, it was from the first confined within certain limits as a result of the systematic development of psychology by Christian Wolff. Wolff's rational and empirical psychology goes its own way, and it remains faithful to the fundamental principles of Leibniz. It bases the doctrine of the soul on the doctrine of the spontaneity, self-sufficiency, and independence of the monad which receives nothing from without but which produces all its content according to a law peculiar to itself. This kind of spontaneity is irreconcilable with the idea of a "physical influx" (*influxus physicus*), with the concept of "impression" as this is

---

[36] Maupertuis, *Réflexions Philosophiques sur l'Origine des Langues et la Signification des Mots*, sect. XXIV, XXV; *Oeuvres*, vol. I, pp. 178 ff.

Psychology and Epistemology

maintained by English and French psychology. According to Leibniz and Wolff, a psychology which attempts to find the basis of the mind in the impression has simply misunderstood the whole problem. It misses the fundamental phenomenon of the mind, whose nature consists in activity not in mere passivity. A functional psychology is now opposed to the psychology of sensation. One does not do justice to functional psychology if, according to a wide-spread view, one treats it simply as a "faculty psychology." For in Leibniz there is no such thing as a "faculty" in the sense of a mere possibility, of an empty potentiality; nor is there a rigid separation of individual capacities of the mind from one another and a hypostasis of these capacities to independent forces. Wolff also consistently upheld the postulate of the unity of the soul, although his tendency to distinguish sharply between concepts sometimes seems to favor an isolating approach. The division of the mind into various faculties, and their definition and nomenclature, are for Wolff chiefly a matter of presentation; actually, however, as he repeatedly emphasizes, all these faculties are not independent forces, but only the various tendencies and expressions of a single basic force, that of representation.[37]

This representation is not to be understood as a mere reflection of an externally existing reality but as a purely active energy. The nature of substance, says Leibniz, lies in its fertility, that is, in its capacity to produce an unending series of ideas. The ego, then, is not merely the scene of ideas but rather their source and origin: "the fountain and source of ideas by a prescribed law of things about to be created."[38] And herein lies the real perfection of the ego; it is more perfect the more freely this production takes place. In his treatise *On Wisdom* Leibniz writes: "All intensification of being I call perfection, for just as sickness is a diminution of health, so is perfection something which rises above health. . . . Now just as sickness comes from injured action, as medical men well know, so perfection appears in the power to act. Indeed all being consists in

[37] Cf., for instance, Wolff's *Psychologia rationalis*, § 184 ff. and his *Psychologia empirica*, § 11 ff. and *passim*.

[38] Leibniz's letter to de Volder, March 24, 1699, *Philosophische Schriften*, ed. Gerhardt, vol. II, p. 172.

a certain force, and the greater this force, the higher and freer the being. Furthermore, the greater the force, the more we see *multiplicity from unity and in unity* since the one governs the many outside itself and pre-forms the many inside itself. Now unity in multiplicity is nothing but harmony, and because one thing agrees more nearly with this than with that, order arises, and from order beauty, and beauty awakens love. Thus it appears that happiness, joy, love, perfection, being, force, freedom, harmony, order, and beauty are all linked together, a fact which few people rightly understand. Now when the soul feels within itself a great harmony, order, freedom, force, or perfection, and is accordingly delighted, this causes joy. . . . Such joy is constant and cannot deceive or cause future sorrow if it is the result of knowledge and accompanied by light; from this joy there arises in the will an inclination toward the good, that is, virtue. . . . Thence follows that nothing serves happiness more than the light of reason and the exercise of the will to act at all times according to reason, and that such light is especially to be sought in the knowledge of these things which can bring our minds more and more toward a higher light because from this light springs an ever-enduring progress in wisdom and virtue, and also, as a consequence, in perfection and joy whose efficacy will remain with the soul even after this life."[39]

In these brief characteristic sentences Leibniz outlined the whole development of German philosophy during the era of the Enlightenment; he defined the central concept of the Enlightenment and sketched its theoretical program. These sentences themselves represent a real "unity in multiplicity," for they epitomize all that the German Enlightenment contributes in the fields of psychology, epistemology, ethics, aesthetics, and the philosophy of religion, and all that it was to bring to completion later. It was this beginning which rescued German philosophy in the eighteenth century from the perils of mere eclecticism. Much as popular philosophy was exposed to these perils and often as it succumbed to them, science and systematic philosophy

[39] Leibniz, "Von der Weisheit," *Deutsche Schriften*, ed. Guhrauer, vol. I, pp. 422 f.

always found their way back to those fundamental questions first raised by Leibniz. Wolff was and remained the "preceptor of Germany," and Kant's statement that he had been the real originator of the spirit of thoroughness in Germany is perfectly true. That Kant could not only start from the thinking of the German Enlightenment, but that his formulation of problems and systematic method were a direct outgrowth of this thinking, are owing to the fact that the philosophy of this era had clearly seen and recorded one of the great possibilities of the development of a uniform theoretical system of thought. To reveal this basic tendency we can start with the opposition which we have already remarked. French and English philosophy of the eighteenth century had been imbued with and guided by the tendency to develop all philosophical knowledge so that, in characteristic words of Locke, it would no longer have to stand on borrowed ground.[40] The whole structure of knowledge was to bear itself and to stand on its own foundation. Because of this postulate of autonomy, the system of innate ideas was rejected, for the appeal to the innate seemed equivalent to an appeal to a foreign arbiter—equivalent indeed to founding knowledge on the being and nature of God. This appeal had become manifest in Descartes when he had traced the meaning of the innate back to God's creative force, and when he had found ideas and eternal truths to be the effects of this force.[41] With Malebranche a really substantial union had replaced this causality; he had maintained that the contemplation of ideas and eternal truths is proof of direct participation of the human mind in God's nature. In rejecting this form of transcendence, empirical philosophy had no other foundation for knowledge than experience, than the "nature of things."[42] But even this nature of things

---

[40] Cf. Locke, *Essay*, Book I, ch. IV, § 24 f.

[41] Cf. Descartes' letter to Mersenne, May 1630; *Oeuvres*, ed. Adam-Tannery, vol. I, p. 151: "You ask me in which kind of cause God has placed the eternal verities. I answer you that it is in the same kind of cause as all things He has created, that is to say, efficient and total cause. For it is certain that He is also the Author of the essence as well as the existence of creatures; but this essence is nothing else than those eternal verities which I do not imagine as emanating from God like the rays of the sun. But I know that God is the Author of all things, and that these verities are something, consequently that God is their author."

[42] Cf. above pp. 55 ff.

now threatens the independence of the mind from another angle. Henceforth the mind must find its real task in holding a mirror up to nature—a mirror which can only reflect images, but cannot create or form them independently. "In this part the understanding is merely passive; and whether or no it will have these beginnings and as it were materials of knowledge, is not in its own power. . . . These simple ideas, when offered to the mind, the understanding can no more refuse to have, nor alter when they are imprinted, nor blot them out and make new ones itself, than a mirror can refuse, alter or obliterate the images or ideas, which the objects set before it do therein produce."[43]

To both doctrines, that of metaphysical "transcendence" as well as the empirical form of "immanence," Leibniz opposes his own viewpoint. He upholds the postulate of immanence, for everything in the monad is to be derived from within itself. But in that he intensifies this principle, he not only finds it impossible to return to God, but equally difficult to return to nature in the usual sense of the word. A difference between the nature of the mind and the nature of things and a one-sided dependence of the former on the latter can no longer be maintained. "What we call the contemplation of the nature of things is very often nothing but the knowledge of the nature of our own mind and of those innate ideas which one does not need to seek outside."[44] When the mind becomes a mirror of reality, it is and remains a living mirror of the universe, and it is not simply a sum total of mere images but a whole composed of formative forces. The basic task of psychology and epistemology will henceforth be to elucidate these forces in their specific structure and to understand their reciprocal relations. And this is the task which the thinkers of the German Enlightenment now undertake and which they endeavor to accomplish by patient toil. If this toil tends to be diffuse, and if second-rate minds often enough lose sight of the goal entirely, it never lacks its peculiar depth; for throughout their diversity of problems these philosophers always aim to validate a certain principle and to elucidate and

[43] Locke, *Essay*, Book II, ch. I, sect. 25.
[44] Leibniz, *Nouveaux Essais*, Book I, ch. I, sect. 21.

prove it from various angles. The psychological formulation and defense of the spontaneity of the ego now prepare the ground for a new conception of knowledge and of art; new pathways and new goals are revealed for the advancement of both epistemology and aesthetics.

The division of the mind into its individual "faculties" contributes not merely toward an empirical analysis of phenomena, but forms the beginning and outline of a future universal system, a real "phenomenology of the spirit." The most original and ingenious psychological analyst of this circle saw and maintained this possibility: Tetens' work entitled *Philosophical Essays on Human Nature* is different in its method from Berkeley's and Hume's works bearing similar names in that Tetens endeavors to classify and describe not only the phenomena of the individual mind but in that he treats such a description as the prelude to a general theory of the "objective spirit." We ought not merely to observe the faculty of understanding as it gathers experiences and produces its first sense ideas from perceptions, but also as it soars to greater heights, as it formulates theories and combines truths into sciences. In such activity the power of the mind reveals its highest energy; and now the question of the fundamental rules must be raised according to which the mind erects such immense structures as geometry, optics, and astronomy. Tetens is dissatisfied with the contributions of Bacon, Locke, Condillac, Bonnet, and Hume to a solution of this problem; he maintains that these thinkers had not even understood the problem of rational knowledge in its specific meaning and that, because of their preoccupation with the problem of sense knowledge, this problem had been almost entirely neglected.[45] Similarly, Tetens' most original contribution to the doctrine of the "faculties of the soul," the basic concept with which he enriched this doctrine, points in the same direction. When he demands precise characterization of feeling, distinguishing it sharply from sense perception, he does not take this distinction simply from introspection; on the contrary, he is

[45] Tetens, *Philosophische Versuche über die menschliche Natur und ihre Entwicklung*, Riga, 1777, vol. I, pp. 427 ff. (Neudruck der Kantgesellschaft, Berlin, 1913, pp. 416 f.)

led to it by the consideration that two entirely different modes
of object relations are involved in feeling and sense perception.
Perceptions, to be sure, are ours; yet their essential definition
does not lie in the fact that they express a state of our own being
but that they express a quality of the object. Feeling, on the
other hand, represents a different, a much more radical and
purely subjective relation; we know only that it represents a
mutation within ourselves, and we accept it as immediately given
without relating it to external objects. But that this relation is by
no means subjective in the sense that it is purely arbitrary, that
rather it contains its own rule and law within itself, and that feeling constitutes a genuine microcosm, a world by itself—German
philosophy of the Enlightenment accepts these propositions as
proved by the phenomenon of art in which the representation
and development of this microcosm is accomplished. At this
point Mendelssohn's doctrine of the mental faculties comes in.
This doctrine proceeds by a method of reconstruction and
draws conclusions from the images in the mind and their specifically differentiated shapes regarding the forces underlying
such mental activity. In order clearly and surely to distinguish
between the object of art and that of theoretical knowledge, in
order to discriminate between the beautiful and the true, Mendelssohn finds it necessary to recognize a special class of psychological phenomena. The beautiful object is neither one of mere
knowledge nor one of mere desire. It slips through our fingers
if we try to treat it as an object of knowledge and to approach
it by means of scientific method, by the process of analysis and
definition. But the nature of the beautiful object also escapes
us if we approach it from the "practical" viewpoint, making it
the object of wishing or acting, because as soon as an object is
desired or striven for, it ceases to be a beautiful object, an object
of artistic contemplation and enjoyment. On the basis of these
considerations Mendelssohn postulates an independent faculty
of the mind to which he gives the name "faculty of approval"
(*Billigungsvermögen*). No element of desire enters into the
approval of the beautiful: "It seems to be a special sign of
beauty that it is contemplated with calm pleasure, that it pleases
even if we do not possess it, and if we are ever so far removed

from the desire to possess it. Only when we consider the beautiful in relation to ourselves and regard its possession as advantageous, does the desire for possession awake in us; and this desire is very different from the enjoyment of beauty."[46] Thus the doctrine of the faculties—and herein lies its systematic value—always endeavors to treat psychology not only as a doctrine of the elements of consciousness, that is, as a doctrine of sensations and impressions, but rather as a comprehensive theory of attitudes and behavior. Not the content, but the energies of the mind should be studied and accurately described. We can understand from this viewpoint the close alliance which now develops between psychology and aesthetics. Since Dubos' *Critical Reflections on Poetry, Painting, and Music* (1719), the same theory of mental energies had prevailed in aesthetics. Dubos' thoughts and observations could be cited in confirmation of Leibniz's ideas, for Leibniz looked upon all aesthetic pleasure as an "exaltation of being," as an animation and intensification of the powers of the mind. The pleasure of the sheer sense of being alive can infinitely outweigh the displeasure which might arise from the contemplation of the object as a mere object. "I need not tell you," Lessing writes to Mendelssohn, "that the pleasure which accompanies a livelier exercise of our energies can be so infinitely outweighed by the displeasure arising from the objects toward which our energies are directed that we are no longer aware of that pleasure."[47] Sulzer, too, in his treatise *On Energy in Works of Fine Art*[48] presents the same basic conception, and under its presupposition he attempts to discriminate among the energies of theoretical thinking, aesthetic contemplation, and the activity of the will.

From yet another angle, aesthetic theory now enters the realm of pure epistemology. In conquering a place for the

---

[46] Mendelssohn, *Morgenstunden*, Abschnitt VII.

[47] Letter to Mendelssohn, Feb. 2, 1757, *Werke*, ed. Lachmann-Muncker, vol. XVII, p. 90. (In his introductory sentence the author seems to contradict the quoted passage. That he does not in fact do so is evident from a consideration of Lessing's statements before and after the words cited. Lessing wrote: "All passions, even the most disagreeable ones, are pleasing as passions. . . . When we suddenly see a painted snake, it pleases us all the better, the more violently we are frightened by it."—Tr.)

[48] *Von der Kraft in den Werken der schönen Künste.*

pure "imagination," and in endeavoring to show that the "poetic faculty" is not a combining, but an original creative faculty, aesthetics also brings about a change in logic, in the conception of the meaning and origin of concepts. Berkeley, Hume, and Condillac consider a concept merely as a shower of impressions, that is, as a simple summation or the symbol we use for such a summation. No independent significance can be attributed to this symbol; it only represents indirectly for the memory that which was concretely given in perception. Yet even if we consider concepts of relation rather than concepts of things, this situation remains unaltered. For the mind cannot establish any sort of connection without first having experienced its reality; it cannot truly conceive any unity or difference without first having tested it in the realm of fact. But functional psychology criticizes this view. Again it is Tetens who emphatically disputes this doctrine of thought as a mere "transposition of phantasms." No matter how much thinking may be stimulated by the sense impression, by the empirical datum, it is never content to stop here. For thinking not only forms concepts as mere aggregates but it rises to ideals. And these ideals are not comprehensible without the aid of the "plastic power of the imagination." "Psychologists usually explain poetic creation as a mere analysis and synthesis of ideas which are recalled in memory after having been acquired through sense perception. . . . If such is the case, then poetry too is nothing but a transposition of phantasms and can give rise to no new simple ideas in our consciousness." However, this explanation is completely inadequate for any real work of art. One cannot do justice to a Klopstock or Milton, "if one considers the images breathed forth by these poets in their animated poetic language as nothing but an accumulated mass of perceptual ideas, whether contiguous to one another or following each other in rapid succession." And the same is true of scientific ideals as we encounter them, for instance, in all exact mathematical knowledge. They likewise can never be explained by mere addition and subtraction of individual perceptions, by combination or abstraction; on the contrary, they are "true products of the poetic imagination." "It is known that this is so in the case of general geometrical concepts. But the same thing is in fact true of all other concepts." The mere process of empirical generalization is then not yet sufficient to raise what just now was simply a sense image to the level of a pure concept. For general sense representations are not yet general ideas, nor are they concepts of the poetic imagination or of the understanding. They are merely raw material for such concepts; their form, however, cannot be understood or derived from them alone. Yet it is the form on which the real exactness of the concept depends. "There is, for example, the idea of a curved line bending back on itself, which is taken from perceptions of the visual sense, and the idea has received its own form from the various perceptions which by their combination produced this form. But now something more happens. The conception of extension is in our power; we can modify ideal extension as we wish. The imagination, therefore, so arranges the image of the circle that every point is equally distant from the center, and no point is the least bit nearer or farther away. The last addition to the sense image is contributed by the creative imagination, as is the case with all our ideals."[49]

This transcendence beyond that which is immediately given in the sense impression, this power of the theoretical imagination, is by no means restricted to pure mathematics. It appears equally clearly in the formation of our concepts of experience, for the concepts on which theoretical physics is based cannot be explained in terms of a combination of perceptual ideas. To be sure, they begin with such ideas, but they do not end there; they use these ideas of sense as a starting point but they transform them by means of the inner autonomous activity of the understanding. This autonomous activity, not the mere habit that comes from the regularity of the perceptions, is what constitutes the real core and substance of the first laws of motion. The general principles of natural science can never be derived *a priori* from mere concepts. But it is wrong to think one can infer from this fact that they must have originated in a mere

---

[49] Cf. Tetens, *Philosophische Versuche über die menschliche Natur*, erster Versuch: "Ueber die Natur der Vorstellungen," No. xv. Neudruck der Kant-Gesellschaft, pp. 112 ff.; see author's *Erkenntnisproblem*, vol. II, pp. 567 ff.

induction in the sense of a simple aggregation of individual observations. Even a law like that of inertia cannot be completely derived or explained in this manner. "The idea of a body set in motion, which neither acts upon any other body nor is acted upon, leads the mind to the idea that the motion of the body will continue unchanged; and even though the latter idea be derived from perceptions, yet its connection with the former idea is an effect of the power of thought, which according to its nature brings about in us this relation between the two ideas; and the connection between predicate and subject, which is made by this operation of the mind, is far more reason for the conviction that our judgment is true than the association of ideas based on perceptions."[50] In general it can be said that, wherever a certain relation between ideas is conceived, recourse to mere sensation, to passive impressions, is insufficient to explain the idea of the relation in its specific nature. That such a specific nature exists is undeniable, for by no means all relations and connections between phases of consciousness can be reduced to identity and diversity, to agreement and contradiction. The succession of things, their contiguity, the particular nature of their co-existence, and the dependence of one thing on another; all these relations obviously embrace more than mere uniformity and diversity. Thus in all thinking, specific, sharply distinguished forms of relations appear and in each of them a certain direction is observable; this direction is like a path which thought follows spontaneously without being driven into it by the mechanical force of impressions and habit. What we call judging and combining, or inferring and concluding, is accordingly different from arranging ideas in sequence and connection; it is more than simply observing similarity and agreement among them. "For even if a rational conclusion is explained by the derivation of the similarity and difference of two ideas from their similarities and differences with respect to a third idea, yet this derivation of similarity and difference from other relations of the same kind is an activity peculiar to the understanding; it amounts to the active production of one idea of relation

<hr>

[50] Tetens, *op.cit.*, vierter Versuch: "Über die Denkkraft und das Denken," IV, Neudruck der Kant-Gesellschaft, pp. 310 ff.

from another, which . . . is more than the perception of two relations in succession."[51]

Here we have reached a point where the inner unity and systematic completeness which characterize the thought of the German Enlightenment despite all the apparent dispersal of individual problems become clearly manifest. For from two different sides, from psychology as well as logic, we now approach the same central problem. The convergence comes when the question of the nature and origin of the pure idea of relation arises. Just as Tetens approaches this problem as a psychological analyst, Lambert makes it a focal point of his logic and general doctrine of method. He too goes back to Leibniz, and his rediscovery of certain Leibnizian principles in their true originality and depth is a real historical service. He is not satisfied with the Leibnizian heritage in philosophy as it had been formulated by Wolff and his school; he goes in quest of the sources from which Leibniz had developed his system. It is Leibniz's plan for a universal logic which permanently fascinates Lambert and on which he bases the outline of his semeiology. He seeks a system of the forms of thought, and he undertakes to treat these in such a way that each will have a special symbolic language comparable to the algorisms of infinitesimal calculus. Exact thinking will not be possible until this has been accomplished, until a definite symbolic operation corresponds to every definite conceptual relation and, finally, until we possess general rules for these operations. Lambert wants to extend the prevalence of this kind of thinking far beyond the sphere of pure geometry. For according to him it shows prejudice to believe that only the ideas of extension and magnitude can be clearly explained and deductively developed. The certainty and conclusiveness of this development are not exclusively found in the realm of quantity; they are also attainable where purely qualitative relations are concerned. From this position Lambert also believes he can clearly sketch the limitations of the Lockean philosophy and its analysis of the basic concepts of knowledge. He does not care to dispute Locke's

[51] *Ibid.*, fünfter Versuch: "Von der Verschiedenheit der Verhältnisse und der allgemeinen Verhältnisbegriffe," in *op.cit.*, pp. 319 ff.

"anatomy of concepts"; he acknowledges that those concepts in which we wish to express the elements of reality cannot be simply invented, but must be found in experience. Genuine knowledge of reality can never be founded on a merely formal, a purely conceptual proposition, such, for instance, as the law of sufficient reason; for such complete agreement of all the parts in one logical whole also belongs to the merely possible. But the knowledge of reality has to do with material properties, with "solids and forces"; and the nature and quality of a real basic force can never be construed in terms of concepts but only in terms of experience. For the sake of experience we must give up any standard definition and rest content with description; in "good anatomical fashion" we must go back by means of an analysis of the given to its ultimate constituents, but without raising any claim that we can make these constituents more comprehensible as a result of such an explanation of concepts. If any further clarification is possible here, it can only be accomplished along Lockean lines, that is, not by means of further logical elaboration but by means of a genetic analysis of simple ideas. It is, however, another matter once we have ascertained the basic concepts in this way and arrived at some idea of their number and order. Then we find that a wealth of further distinctions is contained in the simple and specific nature of each of these concepts—distinctions which are inherent in this nature and follow from it directly. In order to develop these distinctions completely we do not need to refer back to experience. We see that the various fundamental concepts stand in certain relationships of agreement or contradiction, of dependence, etc., which can be determined by a consideration of their nature. The knowledge of these relations as such is not, therefore, empirically inductive but *a priori* knowledge. According to Lambert, such apriority is not to be restricted to pure geometry. What never occurred to Locke was to try to accomplish for the other simple ideas what geometers had done for space, namely, to show its systematic structural qualities in a deductive way.[52] At

[52] See Lambert, *Anlage zur Architektonik oder Theorie des Einfachen und Ersten in der philosophischen und mathematischen Erkenntnis*, Riga, 1771, § 10. For a fuller account of Lambert's method, see the author's *Erkenntnisproblem*, vol. II, pp. 534 ff.

this point Lambert brings his "alethiology" to bear on the problem. This is a general doctrine of the truth, that is, of the relations and connections existing among simple ideas, which Lambert formulated on the model of Leibniz's "universal logic" (*mathesis universalis*). He refers not only to geometry but especially to arithmetic and to pure chronometry and pure phoronomy for evidence and examples of a certain type of science which, although it owes its material to experience, nevertheless shows in this very material not merely accidental but necessary properties. Thus Lambert's doctrine of truth forms, as it were, the logical correlate of Tetens' findings concerning the nature of the pure idea of relation. When these two separate streams of thought of the German Enlightenment joined in Kant, their relative goal was achieved; and with achievement the goal vanished to be supplanted by a new principle and new problems.

CHAPTER IV

Religion

IF WE were to look for a general characterization of the age of the Enlightenment, the traditional answer would be that its fundamental feature is obviously a critical and skeptical attitude toward religion. If we attempt to test this traditional view by concrete historical facts, we soon come to entertain the gravest doubts and reservations so far as German and English thought of the Enlightenment is concerned. Yet French philosophy of the eighteenth century seems to confirm the traditional view all the more stubbornly. In this judgment opponents and enemies, admirers and devoted followers have all agreed. Voltaire in his writings and letters never tires of repeating his old battle cry: *Écrasez l'infâme.* And if he cautiously adds that his struggle is not with faith but with superstition, not with religion but with the Church, yet the next generation, which saw in Voltaire its spiritual leader, did not uphold this distinction. French Encyclopaedism declares war openly on religion, on its claims to validity and truth. It accuses religion, of having been an eternal hindrance to intellectual progress and of having been incapable of founding a genuine morality and a just social and political order. Holbach in his *Natural Politics* recurs untiringly to this point. His indictment of religion is climaxed in the charge that while religion educated men to fear invisible tyrants, it also made men slavish and cowardly toward earthly despots, stifling all initiative to the independent guidance of their own destiny.[1] Deism too is now denounced as an amorphous hybrid and a weak compromise. Diderot states that deism had cut off a dozen heads from the Hydra of religion, but that from the one head it had spared, all the others would grow again.[2] This complete rejection of religious faith in general, in whatever historical form it may appear and no matter what

---

[1] Cf. Holbach, *Politique Naturelle*, Discourse III, especially sects. XII ff.; cited from Hubert, *D'Holbach et ses Amis*, Paris, no date, pp. 163 ff.

[2] Diderot, *Traité de la Tolérance*, ed. D. Tourneux and Cathérine II, pp. 292 f.

arguments may support it, seems henceforth to be the only means to free man from slavery and prejudice and to open up the way to his real happiness. Diderot has Nature say to man: "In vain, O slave of superstition, do you seek your happiness beyond the limits of the world in which I have placed you. Have the courage to free yourself from the yoke of religion, my haughty rival, which does not recognize my prerogatives. Cast out the Gods who have usurped my power, and return to my laws. Return to nature from which you have fled; she will console you and dispel all those fears which now oppress you. Submit to nature, to humanity, and to yourself again; and you will find flowers strewn all along the pathway of your life." "Examine the history of all nations and all centuries and you will always find men subject to three codes: the code of nature, the code of society, and the code of religion; and constrained to infringe upon all three codes in succession, for these codes never were in harmony. The result of this has been that there never was in any country . . . a real man, a real citizen, or a real believer."[3] Whoever has understood this fact, can never return to the previous state of things. There can be no compromise and no reconciliation; one must choose between freedom and slavery, between clear consciousness and vague emotion, between knowledge and belief. And for modern man, for the man of the Enlightenment, there can be no hesitation about this choice. He must and should renounce all help from above; he must blaze his own way to a truth which he will possess only in so far as he can win and establish it by his own efforts.

Yet it is doubtful if on the basis of such declarations by its champions and spokesmen we can consider the Enlightenment as an age basically irreligious and inimical to religion. For such a view runs the risk of overlooking precisely the highest positive achievements of the period. Skepticism as such is incapable of such achievements. The strongest intellectual forces of the Enlightenment do not lie in its rejection of belief but rather in the new form of faith which it proclaims, and in the new form of

---

[3] Diderot, *Supplément au Voyage de Bougainville* (1771), *Oeuvres*, ed. Assézat, vol. II, pp. 199 ff. and especially pp. 240 f.

religion which it embodies. Goethe's saying about belief and disbelief also applies in all its depth and truth to the Enlightenment. If Goethe calls the conflict between belief and disbelief the deepest, indeed the only, theme of the history of the world and humanity, and if he adds that all epochs in which belief dominates are brilliant, uplifting, and fruitful both for the contemporary world and for posterity, while those in which disbelief holds its wretched sway vanish in the years to come because nobody cares to devote himself to the knowledge of the unfruitful, then we cannot for a moment hesitate as to which side of this conflict the Enlightenment represents. This era is permeated by genuine creative feeling and an unquestionable faith in the reformation of the world. And just such a reformation is now expected of religion. All apparent opposition to religion which we meet in this age should not blind us to the fact that all intellectual problems are fused with religious problems, and that the former find their constant and deepest inspiration in the latter. The more insufficient one finds previous religious answers to basic questions of knowledge and morality, the more intensive and passionate become these questions themselves. The controversy from now on is no longer concerned with particular religious dogmas and their interpretation, but with the nature of religious certainty; it no longer deals with what is merely believed but with the nature, tendency, and function of belief as such. Thus, especially among the thinkers of the German Enlightenment, the fundamental objective is not the dissolution of religion but its "transcendental" justification and foundation. In the light of this objective the specific nature of the religiosity of the epoch of the Enlightenment appears, both in its negative and its positive tendency, in its disbelief and in its belief. It is only when one takes both tendencies together and recognizes their mutual dependence that one can understand the historical development of the philosophy of religion of the eighteenth century as a real unity, as a movement whose point of departure lies in a fixed intellectual center and which strives toward a definite ideal goal.

Religion

I. THE DOGMA OF ORIGINAL SIN AND THE PROBLEM OF THEODICY

Amid all the wealth and confusing diversity of the literature of religion and theology in the eighteenth century—even on the one question of deism the number of polemic writings produced on both sides presents an insurmountable difficulty to their complete examination—a certain central point can be found to which the discussion always returns. The philosophy of the Enlightenment did not have to raise this point itself; it inherited it from previous centuries and merely had to approach it with new intellectual weapons. Not even the Renaissance claimed to be simply a rebirth of antiquity and of the scientific spirit; its aim was rather the transformation or renovation of religion. The Renaissance strove for a religion of affirmation of the world and of the intellect, a religion which conceded to both their specific value, and which found the real proof and seal of divinity not in the degradation and destruction of the world and the human intellect but in their exaltation. In this manner universal theism was founded as it appears in humanistic theology of the sixteenth and seventeenth centuries. This theology is founded on the conception that divinity can be grasped only in the totality of its manifestations, and that each of these manifestations has, therefore, an inalienable and independent value. No form or name can express the absolute being of God, for form and name are modes of limitation and hence are incommensurable with the nature of the infinite. But the reverse of this is also implied. Since all particular forms are equally remote from the nature of the Absolute, they are also near it. Every expression of the divine, in so far as it is in itself genuine and true, may be compared with every other; they are equivalent so long as they do not pretend to express that being itself but merely to indicate it in a parable or a symbol. The growth and constant intensification of this humanistic religious spirit can be traced from Nicholas of Cusa to Marsilio Ficino, and from Ficino to Erasmus and Thomas More. In the first decades of the sixteenth century this development seemed to have reached its goal, and a "religion within the bounds of humanity" seemed to have been founded. It does not approach Christian dogma in an inimical or skeptical manner; it attempts rather to understand and to interpret the dogma itself in such a way that it becomes the expression of a new religious attitude. Nicholas of Cusa finds his fundamental conception of humanity (*humanitas*) embodied in the idea of Christ. The humanity of Christ becomes the bond of the world and the highest proof of its inner unity; for it is Christ's humanity which bridges the chasm between the infinite and the finite, between the creative first principle and created being. The religious universalism which is now established can comprehend also the universe of new intellectual forms which spring up in the Renaissance and re-interpret them from one philosophical viewpoint. This universalism is likewise accessible to mathematics, to the new natural science, and to cosmology, and it lays the foundation for a fresh conception of the meaning of history in opposition to that of Augustine and the Middle Ages. All this seemed possible within the sphere of religion and seemed to have been achieved not in opposition to, but by virtue of, it. In the breadth which religion now gained, its real and ultimate depth seemed for the first time to become truly manifest. The problem of the reconciliation of man and God, with whose solution the great scholastic systems and all medieval mysticism had wrestled, appeared now in a new light. This reconciliation was no longer looked for exclusively in an act of divine grace; it was supposed to take place amid the activity of the human spirit and its process of self-development.[4]

But the Reformation proved to be an irreconcilable opponent of this humanistic religion. The Reformation seems to agree with the Renaissance in giving new value and new sanction to life on earth. It too calls for a spiritualization of the content of faith; and this spiritualization is not confined to the ego, the religious subject, but encompasses also the being of the world, placing it in a new relation to the basis of religious certainty. The world is now to be justified on grounds of the certainty of faith. Thus again the ascetic demand for negation of this world

[4] For a fuller account see the author's book *Individuum und Cosmos in der Philosophie der Renaissance*, Studien der Warburger Bibliothek X, Leipzig, 1927.

is met by a demand for world affirmation. This affirmation is to be realized in one's daily occupation, that is, in activity within the secular social order. But if humanism and the Reformation in this wise meet on the same plane, they are nonetheless miles apart. Faith as understood by the Reformation remains alien to the religious ideals of humanism both in its origin and its aim. The core of this opposition lies in the radically different attitude of humanism and the Reformation toward the problem of original sin. Humanism never dared openly assail the dogma of the fall of man but its basic intellectual tendency was toward undermining the force of this dogma. The influence of Pelagianism in the religious position of humanism becomes increasingly evident; efforts to throw off the hard yoke of Augustinian tradition become more and more deliberate. The return to antiquity was not the least factor in this struggle; Plato's doctrine of Eros and the Stoic doctrine of the self-determination of the will are matched against the Augustinian view of the radical corruption of human nature and its inability to attain divinity by its own efforts. Religious universalism, toward which Humanism strives, could only be maintained along these lines; only in this way could a type of revelation be justified which did not appear in a temporally and geographically limited proclamation of the divine.[5] But the sharpest objections of Reformation thought are directed against this broadening of doctrine. For all schools of Reformation thought stand or fall with their belief in the absolute and unique truth of the Biblical word. All their inclinations toward life in this world can and must not shake this belief; both this world and the world beyond are postulated and established by belief in the Bible. The Bible in its transcendence, in its supernatural origin, and in its absolute authority is the only basis for certainty of salvation. Thus the religious individualism of the Reformation remains throughout oriented and confined to purely objective, supernaturally binding realities.[6] And the more it tries to strengthen this bond, the more it finds itself thrust back upon the Augus-

[5] For details see the author's book *Die platonische Renaissance in England und die Schule von Cambridge*, chs. II and IV.

[6] See Troeltsch, *Renaissance und Reformation, Gesammelte Werke*, vol. IV, pp. 275 f.

tinian conception of dogma. For Luther, as also for Calvin, dogma becomes the real support and core of theology. The break with humanism had thus become inevitable. It is consummated in Luther's work *On the Enslaved Will*[7] with unstinting clarity. The cautious defense of human freedom by Erasmus, his support of the autonomy of the will, which was not completely forfeited by the fall, seem to Luther to be nothing less than an unmasked expression of religious skepticism. There is no more dangerous error than belief in any such independence of man as could be looked upon as a special power in addition to divine grace, as a power which can effect the least thing either against or in cooperation with divine grace. We must absolutely distinguish between God's power and ours, between His work and ours; for on this distinction depends self-knowledge and the knowledge and glory of God. "For so long as a man is convinced that he can do something for his own salvation, he retains his self-confidence and does not completely despair; for this reason he does not humble himself before God, but asserts himself, or at least hopes and wishes for opportunity, time, and work in order finally to attain his salvation. But he who never doubts that all depends on the will of God, despairs completely of helping himself, does not choose us, but awaits an act of God; he is nearest to Grace and salvation."

In these words we have the verdict of the faith of the Reformation on humanism, and the seventeenth century tried in vain to contest this sentence. To be sure, the ideals of the Renaissance were kept alive in this century and they found new defenders especially among philosophers. But the great religious movements passed these tendencies by unheeded. The hope of a universal religion, as it had been entertained by Cusa and expressed in his work *On the Peace of Faith*,[8] had perished; peace of faith had been supplanted by the most implacable spirit of religious controversy. And in this controversy victory seemed everywhere to go to the most rigid dogmatism. If Hugo Grotius in the Netherlands and the Cambridge School in England try once more to revive the spirit of the Renaissance, their immediate influence remains confined to a relatively narrow sphere.

---

[7] *De servo arbitrio.*   [8] *De Pace fidei.*

Religion

Grotius succumbs to the attack of Gomarism which gained final victory over Dutch Arminianism, just as Cudworth and More are unable to check the advance of Puritanism and of orthodox Calvinism. Yet the work of these men was not without its fruits both in religion and in general intellectual history, for it paved the way for the "Enlightenment" in the eighteenth century. The theology of the era of the Enlightenment was distinctly aware of this general context. The charge that is usually brought against this era, that it felt as if it were the first period in world history, and that it underestimated the achievements of the past, does not hold here at all. Semler, one of the leaders of German theology of the Enlightenment, exhibits the spirit of historical criticism, for which he prepares the ground through his Biblical criticism, when he recognizes and expresses the historical connections among Biblical events. In his controversy with orthodoxy he goes back directly to Erasmus, whom he calls the father of protestant theology. The old questions regarding the self-determination of reason and the autonomy of the moral will arise again with full force, but now they are to be answered independently of all authority, irrespective of the Bible and the Church. And with this approach the power of medieval dogma is broken for the first time; for Augustinianism is now attacked not in its consequences and direct influences but at its very heart. The concept of original sin is the common opponent against which all the different trends of the philosophy of the Enlightenment join forces. In this struggle Hume is on the side of English deism, and Rousseau of Voltaire; the unity of the goal seems for a time to outweigh all differences as to the means of attaining it.

First let us trace the problem as it appears in the intellectual history of France where it achieves its most fruitful formulation. With a perfection possible only to the French analytical mind, all the various aspects of the problem are elucidated and their logical consequences developed. The diverse possible approaches are set over against each other in a clear-cut antithesis, and the dialectical solution seems to spring spontaneously from this antithesis. The problem of original sin is again raised in French philosophy of the seventeenth century by one of its most profound thinkers. With almost unrivaled vigor and with the greatest clarity of presentation the problem appears in Pascal's *Thoughts* (*Pensées*). Its content seemed scarcely to have changed since Augustine, for through the mediation of Jansen's great work on Augustine the formulation of the idea of original sin invariably recurs to this source. But the form and method of Pascal's reasoning distinguish him from Augustine and mark him as a thinker of modern times. Method in the age of Pascal is dominated by Descartes' logical ideal of the clear and distinct idea, and the Cartesian doctrine is applied even to the mysteries of faith. The result of this combination of Augustinian content with Cartesian method is a paradoxical mixture of ideas because the doctrine Pascal seeks to establish stands in sharp contrast to the procedure by which he reaches his conclusions. The thesis he defends is the absolute powerlessness of reason which is incapable of any kind of certainty by its own efforts, and which can arrive at the truth only by means of an unconditional surrender to faith. But the very necessity of this surrender is not demanded and preached; he sets out to prove it. He does not address the believers but the unbelievers, and he meets the latter on their own ground. He speaks their own language and offers to fight them with their own weapons. Pascal is an unrivaled master of the instrument of modern analytical logic which he had brought to a high degree of perfection in his mathematical works; he now wields this instrument in the service of a fundamental religious question. He approaches his problem, then, with the same methodological means which he had employed in his work on conic sections in the field of geometry, and which he had applied to a problem of physics in his essay on empty space. Here too the important thing is exact observation of phenomena and the power of hypothetical thinking. We possess no other means, and need no other means, to bring about a decision. Just as the physicist, in answering the question of the character of a certain natural force, has no other resource than to survey the phenomena involved and to consult them in systematic array, so too the fundamental mystery of human nature must be solved. Here, similarly, we must require of every hypothesis that it do justice to the phenomena, and that it describe them completely. The postulate of the "rescue of the phenomena" (σώζειν τὰ φαινόμενα) is no less valid for theology than for astronomy. And it is on this point that Pascal challenges his opponents—the doubters and the unbelievers. If they reject the religious solution of the problem and refuse to accept the doctrine of the fall of man and of man's dual nature, then it is their responsibility to give another more probable explanation. It becomes their task to introduce simplicity in place of duality and harmony in place of discord. But this alleged unity and harmony will immediately clash with all the facts of human experience. For wherever we encounter man, we find him not as a complete and harmonious being but as a being divided against himself and burdened with the most profound contradictions. These contradictions are the stigma of human nature. As soon as he attempts to understand his position in the cosmos, man finds himself caught between the infinite and nothingness; in the presence of both, he is incapable of belonging to either one of them alone. Elevated above all other beings, he is also degraded below all; man is sublime and abject, great and wretched, strong and powerless, all in one. His consciousness always places before him a goal he can never reach, and his existence is torn between his incessant striving beyond himself and his constant relapses beneath himself. We cannot escape this conflict which we find in every single phenomenon of human nature, and there is no other way to explain it than to transfer it from the phenomena to their intelligible origin, from the facts to their principle. The irreducible dualism of human nature is resolved only in the mystery of the fall. Through this mystery that which had been cloaked in impenetrable darkness becomes at once manifest. Though this hypothesis is in itself an absolute mystery, it is, on the other hand, the only key to our deepest being. Human nature becomes comprehensible only by virtue of the incomprehensible mystery which underlies it. Thus all the standards of logical and rational knowledge are reversed. In this knowledge the unknown is explained by reducing it to a known quantity, but Pascal bases immediately given and existing phenomena on the absolutely unknown. This overthrow of all rational means and measures teaches us that we are dealing not with an accidental but with a necessary, not with a subjective but with an objective, limit of knowledge. It is not merely the weakness of our insight that prevents us from arriving at an adequate knowledge of the object, it is the object itself which defies rationality and is absolutely contradictory. Every rational measure as such is an immanent measure, for the form of rational knowledge consists in drawing conclusions from the real nature of a thing regarding properties which necessarily belong to it. But here we are dealing with a nature which contradicts itself; here it is immanence which turns into transcendence and negates itself as soon as we attempt to understand it completely. "Who will disentangle this turmoil? Nature confounds Pyrrhonists and reason confounds dogmatists. What will become of you then, O man, who try by your natural reason to discover what is your true condition? . . . Know then, proud creature, what a paradox you are to yourself. Be humble, impotent reason; be quiet, imbecile nature: *know that man surpasses man infinitely* and learn from your Master of our true condition, of which you are ignorant. Hearken unto God!"[9]

The most difficult and profound problem of eighteenth century philosophy is posed in these words of Pascal. In him this philosophy found an opponent of equal strength, who had to be reckoned with if it were to take a single step forward. If the spell of transcendence could not be broken at this point, and if man was and remained "self-transcendent," then any natural explanation of the world and of existence was checked at the start. It is, therefore, understandable that French philosophy of the Enlightenment recurs to Pascal's *Thoughts* again and again as if it were impelled from within, and that it repeatedly tests its critical strength on this work. Criticism of Pascal continues through all periods of Voltaire's career as a writer. This criticism begins in his first philosophical work, *Letters on the English*, and half a century later he comes back to this product of his youth in order to supplement it and support it with new

[9] Pascal, *Pensées*, art. VIII (ed. Ernest Havet, fifth edition, Paris, 1897, vol. I, p. 114).

arguments.[10] He accepted Pascal's challenge; he said he wanted to defend humanity against this "sublime misanthrope." But if one inspects his various arguments, it would seem as if he were trying to avoid an open fight. For Voltaire carefully avoids pursuing Pascal to the real core of his religious thinking and to the ultimate depths of his problem. He tries to keep Pascal on the surface of human existence; he wants to show that this surface is self-sufficient and self-explanatory. Voltaire treats Pascal's deep seriousness in his typical urbane manner; he answers the terse precision of Pascal's reasoning with intellectual agility, and the mystical depth of his feeling with the superficiality of the worldling. Common sense is invoked against the subtleties of metaphysics and made judge of these subtleties. What Pascal had called the contradictions of human nature become for Voltaire merely a proof of its wealth and abundance, of its variety and versatility. Human nature, to be sure, is not simple in the sense that it has a definite being and must follow a prescribed course; for it is forever venturing upon new possibilities. But according to Voltaire not the weakness but the strength of human nature lies in this almost unlimited versatility. However diverse the activity of man may appear, however difficult it may be to hold fast to any one accomplishment and not be driven on from one goal to another and from one task to another, the true intensity and highest power of which human nature is capable is demonstrated by this very manysidedness. In the display and unhampered development of all the various forces at work within him, man is what he can and should be: "Those apparent contrarieties, which you call *contradictions*, are the necessary ingredients which enter into the composite of man, who is, like the rest of nature, what he ought to be."

But Voltaire's philosophy of "common sense" is not his last word on this question. Little as he concedes to Pascal's arguments, one feels nevertheless that he is constantly disturbed by them. In fact we have now reached a point at which mere negation did not suffice, at which a clear positive decision was ex-

[10] Cf. Voltaire, *Remarques sur les Pensées de M. Pascal, Oeuvres*, ed. Lequien, Paris, 1921, vol. XXXI, pp. 281 ff.

pected of the philosophy of the Enlightenment. If it rejected the mystery of original sin, it had to shift the cause and origin of evil to another quarter; it had to recognize and prove the necessity of the source of evil in the eyes of reason. There seemed, therefore, no escape at this point from metaphysics as such; for doubts regarding dogma compel us all the more inexorably toward the riddle of theodicy. This riddle exists too for Voltaire since he looks upon the existence of God as a strictly demonstrable truth. The proposition: "I exist; therefore a necessary and eternal being exists," has lost none of its force for Voltaire.[11] But if the Gordian knot of the problem of theodicy remains uncut as ever, how can we escape Pascal's conclusion that the coils of this knot lead us back to the "abyss" of faith?[12] Optimism, the philosophical solution of Leibniz and Shaftesbury, was consistently rejected by Voltaire; he looked upon optimism not as a philosophical doctrine but as something on a par with mythical phantasies and romances.[13] Those who maintain that all is well with the world are mere charlatans; we must admit that evil exists and not add to the horrors of life the absurd bigotry of denying them.[14] But if Voltaire here takes his stand against theology and metaphysics in favor of a theoretical skepticism, he is yielding indirectly to the reasoning of Pascal whom he intended to refute. For at least with respect to his achievement he now stands at exactly the same point where Pascal had stood. Pascal had come to the conclusion, which he never tired of stressing, that philosophy as such, that reason left to its own resources and deprived of the support of revelation, must necessarily end in skepticism: "Pyrrhonism is the truth."[15] Since on the problem of the origin of evil Voltaire had deprived himself of all the weapons against skepticism, he finds

[11] Cf. *Additions aux remarques sur les Pensées de Pascal* (1743) in *op.cit.*, vol. XXXI, p. 334: "*I exist, therefore something exists throughout eternity*, is an evident proposition."

[12] *Pensées*, art. VIII, *op.cit.*, p. 115: "The node of our condition has its folds and coils in that abyss, in such a way that man is more inconceivable without this mystery than this mystery is inconceivable to man."

[13] Cf. especially, *Il faut prendre un parti ou le principe d'action* (1772), sect. XVII: "Des romans inventés pour deviner l'origine du mal," *Oeuvres*, vol. XXXI, p. 177.

[14] *Ibid.*, sect. XVI, *Oeuvres*, XXXI, 174 ff.

[15] Cf. *Pensées*, ed. Havet, XXIV, 1; XXV, 34; vol. II, pp. 87, 156.

himself henceforth driven hither and yon in the skeptical whirlpool. He embraces all solutions and he rejects them all.
Schopenhauer often referred to Voltaire's *Candide* and he tried
to use it as his most powerful weapon against optimism. But in
a systematic sense Voltaire was no more a pessimist than an
optimist. His position on the problem of evil is never the upshot of a sound doctrine; it is, and this is all it pretends to be,
merely the expression of the transient mood in which he contemplates the world and man. This mood is capable of all
nuances, and Voltaire likes to indulge in the play of nuances.
In his youth Voltaire knows no pessimistic moments. He advocates a purely hedonistic philosophy whose justification consists in the maximum enjoyment of all the pleasures of life. To
pursue any other wisdom seems to him as difficult as it is useless: "True wisdom lies in knowing how to flee sadness in the
arms of pleasure."[16] Voltaire means only to be the apologist of
his time in these words, the apologist of luxury, of taste, and of
sensuous enjoyment undeterred by any prejudice.[17] Later on,
however, as a result of the earthquake of Lisbon, Voltaire expressly retracts his glorification of pleasure. The axiom: "All is
well," is now absolutely rejected as a doctrine.[18] It is foolish
self-deception to close our eyes to the evils which everywhere
confront us; all we can do is turn our eyes to the future hoping
it will bring the solution of the riddle which is now insoluble:
"*Some day all will be well*, is our hope; *all is well today*, is
illusion." Again Voltaire accepts a compromise both in the
theoretical and in the ethical respect. Moral evil too is undeniable but its justification consists in the fact that it is inevitable
to human nature as it is. For were it not for our weaknesses,
life would be condemned to stagnation, since the strongest

[16] "La véritable sagesse
   Est de savoir fuir la tristesse,
   Dans les bras de la volupté."
[17] Cf. the poem "Le Mondain" (1736) and "Défense du Mondain ou l'Apologie du Luxe," *Oeuvres*, vol. XIV, pp. 112 ff., 122 ff.—The following treatment
of Voltaire and Rousseau has already been published in part in a somewhat different form. Cf. the author's essay: "Das Problem Jean-Jacques Rousseau," *Archiv
fuer Geschichte der Philosophie*, ed. Arthur Stein, vol. XLI (1932), pp. 210 ff.
[18] "Poême sur le désastre de Lisbonne ou examen de cet axiome: Tout est bien"
(1756), *Oeuvres*, vol. XII, pp. 179 ff.

impulses of life arise from our appetites and passions, that is, ethically considered, from our shortcomings. Voltaire gave his most pregnant expression of this outlook on the world and life in his philosophical tale *The World as It Is, Vision of Babouc* (*Le Monde comme il va, Vision de Babouc*, 1746). Babouc receives an order from the angel Ithuriel to go to the capital of his country and observe the manners and customs there, and his judgment is to decide whether the city will be destroyed or spared. He acquaints himself with all the weaknesses and faults of the city and with its grave moral shortcomings, but also with the full splendor of its culture and refined society. And on this basis he passes judgment. He has a small statue made by the best goldsmith in the city; it is composed of all metals, the most precious and the most inferior. He brings this to Ithuriel and asks him: "Would you destroy this pretty statue because it is not composed entirely of gold or diamonds?" Ithuriel understands: "He resolves not to think of correcting Persepolis and to *permit it to go on as it is*; for, says he, if all is not well, all is tolerable." In *Candide* too, in which Voltaire pours out all his scorn for optimism, he does not deviate from this basic attitude. We cannot avoid evil and we cannot eradicate it. We should let the physical and moral world take their course and so adjust ourselves that we can keep up a constant struggle against the world; for from this struggle arises that happiness of which man alone is capable.

Elsewhere in eighteenth century thought we find the same uncertainty which Voltaire's position on the problem of theodicy reveals. The literature of this problem is immense, for philosophers still feel that the fate of metaphysics and religion must hinge on this fundamental problem. Hence they recur untiringly to this question, without, however, contributing any essential enrichment of the matter. Leibniz's arguments are repeated innumerable times and elucidated from all angles, but they are scarcely better understood in their vital connection with the basic concepts and presuppositions of his philosophy. Systematic consideration is gradually superseded by eclectic treatment.[19] A new trend appears when empirical psychology attacks the problem with its special instruments. A new way seemed to open up for overcoming former vagueness on the question of the primacy of pleasure or pain in human existence and for placing this question on a sound scientific basis. If this question was to be solved, one could not be satisfied with a vague supposition; one would have to discover a definite scale to which the individual values of pleasure and pain could be related. Here the problem arose of reconciling diametrical opposites by a new methodological procedure. The vague flux of the pleasure-pain sensation was to be brought to clarity and reduced to exact expression. Only a combination of psychology and mathematics, of empirical observation and purely conceptual analysis seemed capable of solving this problem. Maupertuis, in his *Essay on Moral Philosophy*, attempted such a synthesis. He starts off with a certain definition of pleasure and pain which he tries to formulate in such a way that it is possible to give these emotions a fixed quantitative value on the basis of which they can be numerically compared with one another. Our knowledge of the physical world depends on our success in reducing its phenomena—whose qualitative differences only are given in perception—to purely quantitative differences. The same is true of our knowledge of psychological phenomena. Here, too, the heterogeneity which we observe in immediate experience must not prevent us from considering the content of experience as conceptually homogeneous. However diverse the modes of pleasure and pain may be, they have this much in common, that each of them possesses a certain intensity and duration. If we can succeed in reducing these two factors to measurement and in establishing a relation according to which the quantitative value of the whole proves to be dependent on these individual factors, then the way to a solution has been found. A calculus of sensation and feeling could then be formulated which would be no less precise than that of arithmetic, geometry, and physics.

[19] Details of the eclectic treatment of the theodicy problem will not be discussed here. The reader is referred to J. Kremer, *Das Problem der Theodizee in der Philosophie und Literatur des 18. Jahrhunderts*, Berlin, 1909, and K. Wolff, *Schillers Theodizee*, which has an introduction on the theodicy problem in the philosophy and literature of the eighteenth century, Leipzig, 1909.

Thus the problem of a "mathematics of intensive quantities" (*mathesis intensorum*), as Leibniz had conceived it in connection with the fundamental questions of his new analysis of the infinite, is now extended to include the field of psychology. Maupertuis now tries to formulate a law exactly analogous to the fundamental rules of statics and dynamics. In order to perform a calculation with pleasure and pain, we must first consider that the quantity of these emotions is dependent on the one hand on their intensity and, on the other, on the time during which they are present and active in the mind. A double intensity during one unit of time can, therefore, have the same result as a single unit of intensity during two units of time. In general, the quantitative value of the pleasurable and painful conditions of life can be defined as the product of the intensity of pleasure and pain and their duration. On the basis of this formula Maupertuis now undertakes to evaluate the various ethical systems with respect to their truth content. All such systems on closer analysis are distinguishable from one another only in terms of their different calculuses of happiness. They all attempt to tell us how to attain the highest good, that is, the greatest possible amount of pleasure out of life. Some seek to attain this end by multiplying the good things of life, while others seek it by avoiding life's evils. The Epicurean strives for an increase of the sum of his pleasures, the Stoic for a reduction of pains; the former teaches that the goal of life lies in attaining happiness, the latter that it lies in avoiding unhappiness.[20] The whole upshot of this calculation leads Maupertuis to pessimism, for it proves that in the course of an ordinary life the sum of the evils always is greater than the sum of the goods.[21] Kant in his pre-critical *Attempt to Introduce the Concept of Negative Quantities into Philosophy* refers to Maupertuis' calculation, disputing both the results and the method. Kant asserts that this task cannot be solved by man because only homogeneous sensations can be added together, while feeling appears very differently according to the variety of emotions aroused by the ex-

[20] Maupertuis, *Essai de Philosophie morale*, chs. I, IV, V, *Oeuvres*, vol. I, pp. 193 ff.
[21] *Ibid.*, ch. II, pp. 201 ff.

ceedingly complex conditions of life.[22] But Kant's really decisive objection came only when he developed his own ethical theory. This theory was destined to undermine once and for all that treatment of the theodicy problem which still completely dominated the popular philosophy of the eighteenth century. By rejecting eudaemonism as the basis of ethics, it deprived the calculus of pleasure and pain of all moral or religious significance. The question of the value of life was seen henceforth in an entirely new perspective. "It is easy to decide what value life would have for us if its value were estimated in terms of what we enjoy, that is, according to the natural end of the sum of all inclinations or of happiness. This value would sink below zero; for who would start life anew under the same conditions, or even according to a plan of his own (though according to the natural course of things), if life's purpose were merely pleasure? . . . Hence there is evidently nothing left but the value which we ourselves place upon our lives, not only through what we ourselves do, but through what we perform independently of nature in a purposive manner, if the existence of nature is to be meaningful only under this condition."[23]

The popular philosophy of the Enlightenment was not ripe for the idea of a purpose which reaches beyond the dimension of pleasure and pain. Only two thinkers of the eighteenth century, approaching the matter from quite different angles, grasped this idea and in a certain sense anticipated Kant by their formulations of the problem. Through them the theodicy problem was subjected to a new treatment and gained essentially new meaning. In the abundance of its fruitless ventures metaphysics had exhausted its possibilities; it had reached a point at which it could neither advance nor retreat. Unless, then, the question was simply to be relegated completely to the sphere of faith, to that "abyss" of the irrational of which Pascal had spoken, there was no alternative but to call upon other intellectual forces for a solution and to entrust the matter to them. Enlightenment thought is thus forced to approach the basic question of theodicy by an apparent detour. It no longer starts

[22] Kant, *Werke*, ed. Cassirer, vol. II, pp. 219 f.
[23] *Ibid.*, vol. V, p. 514n. (*Critique of Judgment*, sect. 83).

with a metaphysical and theological exposition; nor does it take its point of departure in a definition of the concept of the divine being, deducing the various divine attributes from the definition. Concentration on the nature of the Absolute is now replaced by a complete analysis of the formative forces within the ego. An immanent solution of the problem can only be expected from these forces, that is, a solution which does not compel the intellect to transcend its limits. And here again those two fundamental motives are discernible which in the course of the intellectual history of the eighteenth century become increasingly important as they take on a recognizable shape of their own. On the one hand it is the aesthetic problem, on the other the problem of law and the state which now comes to the fore. Neither of these problems seems to stand in any direct relationship to the theodicy problem, and yet it can be shown that a characteristic transformation and deepening of this problem takes root in them. The initiator of this development is Shaftesbury. He founds a philosophy in which aesthetics not only represents a systematic province but occupies the central position of the whole intellectual structure. According to Shaftesbury, the question of the nature of truth is inseparable from that of the nature of beauty, for the two questions agree both in their grounds and in their ultimate principle. All beauty is truth, just as all truth can be understood basically only through the meaning of form, that is, the meaning of beauty. That everything real partakes of form, that it is no chaotic amorphous mass, but possesses rather an inner proportion and evidences in its nature a certain structure, and in its development and motion a rhythmic order and rule: this is the fundamental phenomenon in which the purely intellectual, the supersensible origin of the real manifests itself. Sense as such is not capable of perceiving this phenomenon, let alone understanding it in its ultimate origin. Where sense only is involved, where the relation we establish between ourselves and the world depends merely on our instincts and appetites, there is as yet no access to the realm of form. The animal that is affected by the objects of its environment merely as stimuli which awaken its instincts and occasion certain reactions, is ignorant of all knowledge of the form of things. This knowledge does not spring from the force of desire as a direct sense reaction but from the force of pure contemplation, which is free of all desire for possession and of any act of direct seizure of the object. In this faculty of pure contemplation and of a pleasure which is not motivated by any "interest," Shaftesbury finds the fundamental force behind all artistic enjoyment and all artistic creation. By virtue of this force man realizes his true self and partakes of the highest, indeed the only happiness of which he is capable. The standards applicable to the question of theodicy have now undergone a complete transformation. For now it becomes obvious that any calculus of the goods and evils of the world must necessarily fail to account for the deeper meaning of this question. The content of life must not be defined in terms of its matter, but only of its form. It does not depend on the degree of pleasure life grants us but on the pure energy of the formative forces from which it derives its form. Shaftesbury seeks the true theodicy, the ultimate justification of existence, not in the sphere of joy and sorrow but in that of the free inner activity of forming according to a purely intellectual prototype and archetype. This Promethean activity, which leaves all mere enjoyment behind, which is indeed incommensurable with all pleasure, reveals to us the true divinity of man, and thereby the divinity of the universe.[24]

Again we find a different perspective and a thoroughly original trend of thought when we consider Rousseau's attitude toward the theodicy problem.[25] No less a man than Kant expressly credited Rousseau with having taken the last step in this field. "Newton was the first to see order and regularity combined with great simplicity, where hitherto disorder and multiplicity had reigned, and since then comets move in geometric paths. Rousseau first discovered beneath the diversity of human shapes the deeply hidden nature of man and the latent law according to which Providence is justified by Rousseau's

[24] For a fuller account of the form and basis of Shaftesbury's theodicy, see the author's work *Die platonische Renaissance in England*, ch. VI, pp. 110 ff.

[25] The following passage is based in part on the author's essay "Das Problem Jean-Jacques Rousseau," to which the reader is referred. See above p. 147, note 17.

observations. Previously the objections of Alphonsus and Manes were believed to be valid. Since Newton and Rousseau, God has been justified and Pope's thesis has come true."[26] These sentences are at first sight hard to understand and to interpret because the writings of Rousseau contain no such explicit treatment, no such purely analytical exposition of the problem of theodicy, as we find in Leibniz, Shaftesbury, or Pope. Rousseau's real originality and significance lie in an entirely different sphere; it is not the problem of God but the problem of law and society which occupies all his thinking. But in this respect he establishes a new relation and welds a new connecting-link. Rousseau is the first to carry this problem beyond the sphere of individual human existence and to turn it expressly toward the problem of society. In society Rousseau believed he had found the decisive feature of the meaning of human existence, of human happiness or misery. Such was the conclusion he derived from his study and criticism of political and social institutions. In the *Confessions* he says of himself: "I saw that everything depended basically on political science, and that, no matter how one views the problem, every people is just what its government makes it. The great question of the best possible form of government seemed to lead me back to the other question: 'What form of government is most suited to produce a nation which is virtuous, enlightened, wise—in short, in the highest sense of the word, as perfect as possible?' " A new norm for human existence appears here; instead of the mere desire for happiness, the idea of law and social justice is made the standard by which human existence is to be measured and tested. At first the application of this standard leads Rousseau to a completely negative decision. All the assets which mankind believes it has acquired in the course of its development—all the treasures of knowledge, of art, of increased refinement and enjoyment of life—vanish before Rousseau's inexorable criticism. Far from having given life new value and substance, these supposed benefits have drawn it farther and farther away from its source until they have finally robbed it of its real meaning. In his presentation of the traditional and conventional forms of life and of human existence in

[26] Kant, *Werke*, ed. Hartenstein, vol. VIII, p. 630.

society Rousseau to a surprising degree finds himself in agreement with Pascal. He is the first thinker in the eighteenth century to take Pascal's accusation against man seriously and to feel its full force. Instead of softening it, instead of attributing it to the self-torturing mood of a brooding misanthropist, as Voltaire had done, Rousseau grasps its cardinal point. The description of the greatness and misery of man which occurs in Pascal's *Thoughts* is revived in Rousseau's early writings, in his prize essay on the arts and sciences, and in his *Discourse on Inequality*. Amid the dazzling luster with which civilization has adorned the life of man Rousseau, like Pascal, sees only illusion and tinsel. Rousseau, too, insists that all this wealth is calculated only to blind man to his own inner poverty. Man takes refuge in society, in a variety of activities and diversions only because he cannot bear his own thoughts and the sight of himself. All this restless and aimless activity arises from his fear of quiet; for if he were to stop for only a single moment to reflect upon his own condition, he would fall prey to the deepest and most hopeless despair. Regarding the forces which, in the present state of society, tend to bring individuals together, Rousseau entertains the same opinion as Pascal. He stresses repeatedly that there is no original moral impulse, no desire for community in its true sense in the present state of society, nor any natural sympathy uniting one man to another. All social ties are based on mere illusion. Egotism and vanity, the impulse to dominate and to impress others; such are the real bonds that hold society together.[27] "Just a lacquer of words everywhere, just a mad scramble for a happiness which exists only in appearance. Nobody is concerned with reality any more; all suppose it to lie in illusion. They drift along through life as slaves of self-love; not in order to live, but in order to make others believe they have lived."[28]

Rousseau thus admits all the premises on which Pascal had based his reasoning. He undertakes no embellishment or attenu-

[27] Compare Rousseau's development of the problem in his two prize essays for the Academy of Dijon with Pascal's *Pensées*, especially articles II, IV; ed. Havet, vol. I, pp. 26 ff., 48 ff.

[28] Cf. Rousseau's autobiographical sketch: *Rousseau juge de Jean-Jacques*, third Dialogue.

ation; like Pascal he depicts the present state of mankind as one of extreme decadence. But although Rousseau recognizes the phenomenon on which Pascal bases his argument, he stoutly rejects the interpretation which Pascal's mysticism and religious metaphysics had offered for it. Rousseau's feeling and thinking both rebel against Pascal's hypothesis of an original perversion of the human will. The idea of the fall of man has lost all its force and validity for Rousseau. On this point he opposed orthodoxy no less severely and radically than did Voltaire and the French Encyclopaedists. It was indeed this dogma which brought about his irreconcilable conflict and final break with the teachings of the Church. In its judgment concerning Rousseau's writings the Church itself stresses this central point at once clearly and confidently as the really decisive problem. The mandate in which Christophe de Beaumont, archbishop of Paris, condemns *Émile* points out that Rousseau's thesis that the first impulses of human nature are always innocent and good stands in sharpest conflict with all the doctrines of the Bible and the Church concerning the nature of man. But Rousseau himself now faces a dilemma from which there seems to be no escape. If he admits the fact of human degeneration, if he indeed repeatedly insists on this fact and paints it out in the darkest colors, how can he escape the cause of degeneration, how evade the conclusion of radical evil? Rousseau extricates himself from this dilemma by introducing at this point his doctrine of nature and the "state of nature." Every time we pronounce judgment on man, we must distinguish most carefully as to whether our statement applies to "natural man" (*l'homme naturel*) or to "civilized man" (*l'homme artificiel*). Whereas Pascal had explained the insoluble contradictions of human nature by asserting that, metaphysically considered, man has a twofold nature, Rousseau on the other hand finds this conflict in human nature in the midst of empirical existence and development. This development had indeed compelled man to adopt a compulsory form of society, thus exposing him to all moral evils; it had fostered in him all the vices of vanity, arrogance, and boundless greed for power. Rousseau's *Émile* begins with the words: "All is well when it leaves the hands of the Creator of things; all degenerates in the hands of man." Thus God is condoned and guilt for all evil is attributed to man. But since guilt belongs to this world, not to the world beyond; since it does not exist before the empirical, historical existence of mankind, but arises out of this existence, we must therefore seek redemption solely in this world. No help from above can bring us deliverance. We must bring it about ourselves and be answerable for it. With this conclusion Rousseau finds the new approach to the problem of evil which he follows in his political writings undeviatingly to its logical consequences. Rousseau's ethical and political theory places responsibility where it had never been looked for prior to his time. Its historical significance and systematic value lie in the fact that it creates a new subject of "imputability." This subject is not individual man but society. The individual as such, as he comes from nature's workshop, is still without the pale of good and evil. He follows his natural instinct of self-preservation, and he is governed by his "self-love" (*amour de soi*); but this self-love has not yet degenerated into "selfish love" (*amour propre*) whose only satisfaction lies in the subjection of others to its will. Society alone is responsible for this kind of selfish love. It is such egotism which causes man to turn tyrant against nature and even against himself. It awakens in him wants and passions which natural man knew nothing of, and it also provides him with the new means with which he can gratify these desires and passions without restraint. Eagerness to be talked of and the passion to distinguish ourselves before others, prevent us from knowing ourselves and lure us, so to speak, out of ourselves.[29] But is this self-estrangement grounded in the nature of every society? Is not a truly human community conceivable which no longer depends on these motives of power, greed, and vanity, but which is entirely based on a law recognized as inwardly binding and necessary? Such is the question which Rousseau now raises and which he attempts to answer in his *Social Contract*. When the compulsory form of society, which has hitherto prevailed, falls and is replaced by a new form of political and ethical community—a community in which

---

[29] Cf. "Discours sur l'origine de l'inégalité parmi les hommes," *Oeuvres*, Zweibruecken, 1782, pp. 75 ff., 90 ff., 138 ff.

every member, instead of being subjected to the arbitrary will of others, obeys only the general will which he recognizes and acknowledges as his own—then the hour of deliverance has arrived. But it is futile to expect this deliverance from without. No God can bring it about for us; man must rather become his own deliverer and in the ethical sense his own creator. Society heretofore has inflicted the deepest wounds on mankind; yet it is society too which through a transformation and reformation can and should heal these wounds. Such is Rousseau's solution of the problem of theodicy in his philosophy of law.[30] And he has in fact placed this problem on an entirely new footing, removing it from the sphere of metaphysics and making it the focal point of ethics and politics.

If at this stage we survey once more the whole development of the theodicy problem in the eighteenth century, one general fundamental characteristic feature stands out. The eighteenth century did not formulate the problem of theodicy alone; it received it rather in the form in which it had been handed down by the great philosophical systems of the seventeenth century. Leibniz especially seemed to have exhausted all its possibilities, and the philosophy of the Enlightenment added nothing essential to his theoretical concepts and viewpoints. This philosophy speaks throughout the language of metaphysics and utilizes the intellectual apparatus of this province of thought. But the metaphysical form now gradually receives new content. The problem moves from the realm of theology and theological metaphysics and assumes a new orientation. An inner transformation takes place as the concrete content of the thought of the age enters into the problem and gradually reshapes it. The same process of secularization that we observed above in the field of natural science now takes place in the realm of philosophy. The systematic concepts developed by seventeenth century metaphysics are still firmly anchored in theological thinking with all their originality and independence. For Descartes and Malebranche and for Spinoza and Leibniz there is no solution of the problem of truth independently of the problem of

[30] Concerning the content and basic principle of Rousseau's philosophy of law, see below ch. VI.

God because knowledge of the divine being forms the highest principle of knowledge from which all other certainties are deduced. But in eighteenth century thought the intellectual center of gravity changes its position. The various fields of knowledge—natural science, history, law, politics, art—gradually withdraw from the domination and tutelage of traditional metaphysics and theology. They no longer look to the concept of God for their justification and legitimation; the various sciences themselves now determine that concept on the basis of their specific form. The relations between the concept of God and the concepts of truth, morality, law are by no means abandoned, but their direction changes. An exchange of index symbols takes place, as it were. That which formerly had established other concepts, now moves into the position of that which is to be established, and that which hitherto had justified other concepts, now finds itself in the position of a concept which requires justification. Finally even the theology of the eighteenth century is affected by this trend. It gives up the absolute primacy it had previously enjoyed; it no longer sets the standard but submits to certain basic norms derived from another source which are furnished it by reason as the epitome of independent intellectual forces. In this change of position theology also rejects the dogma of original sin. The rejection of this dogma is the typical indication of the basic direction of the theology of the Enlightenment, especially as it develops in Germany where it has its most important representatives. These advocates of the new theology all consider the idea of an original sin which is visited upon succeeding generations as absolutely absurd, as an insult to the first laws of logic and ethics. This is all the more significant since these men in general by no means abandon dogmatics. Even where the attempt is made to retain the fundamental ingredients of dogmatics with a few modifications and reinterpretations, the opinion that man through the fall has lost all his ability to attain the good and the true without divine grace is most emphatically rejected. Increasingly sharp polemics against Augustine are found throughout this whole "neological" literature.[31] Even Reimarus in his *Apology* stresses the point

[31] Examples of these polemics are to be found in Jerusalem's sermons as also in

that sin is an act of thoughts, desires, or works, that it is therefore closely bound to the consciousness of the subject of the action and cannot be inherited in a purely physical way, nor can it be transmitted from one subject to another. And the same thing holds for redemption and justification; for just as no one else can incur moral guilt for me, neither can he acquire moral merit for me. With this reasoning an important change takes place in the inner development of Protestantism. For now the controversy between Luther and Erasmus arises again, but this time it is decided in favor of the latter. The deep gulf between the Renaissance and the Reformation, between the humanistic ideal of human freedom and dignity and the doctrine of the bondage and depravity of the human will has now been bridged. The epoch of the Enlightenment ventures to go back to those basic postulates from which the Renaissance struggle against the fetters of the medieval system had arisen. That conception of Protestantism has now been reached whose true nature and substance Hegel expresses in his philosophy of history. In its reconciliation with humanism, Protestantism became the religion of freedom. While the controversy over the dogma of original sin in France led to the sharpest separation between religion and philosophy, the idea of Protestantism in Germany proved capable of such a transformation that it was able to absorb the fresh trends of thought and the attitude from which they had sprung, and to abandon the previous historical form of Protestantism in order the more effectively to validate its ideal significance.[32]

II. TOLERANCE AND THE FOUNDATION
OF NATURAL RELIGION

A general axiom which frequently recurs in varying guises in the philosophy of the Enlightenment asserts that the gravest

---

his posthumous writings, and also in Semler's *Autobiographie*. A fuller account of this development is contained in Aner, *Theologie der Lessing-Zeit*, pp. 50 ff., 158 ff., 223, and *passim*.

[32] Cf. especially Troeltsch, *Die Bedeutung des Protestantismus fuer die moderne Welt*, third edition, Munich and Berlin, 1927, and also "Renaissance und Reformation," *Gesammelte Werke*, vol. IV, pp. 261 ff.

obstacle to the investigation of truth is not to be looked for in the mere lack of knowledge. Without doubt all our knowledge suffers from such shortcomings, and at every step we become painfully aware of its uncertainty and its loopholes. But this barrier represents no real danger as soon as we have noticed it. The mistakes of science are corrected by science itself in the course of its immanent progress; the errors in which it entangles us eliminate themselves in so far as we permit it to proceed freely on its course. Of much deeper effect are those divergences from truth which do not arise from a mere insufficiency of knowledge but from a perverted direction of knowledge. It is not mere negation so much as this perversion which is most to be feared. And the falsification of the true standards of knowledge appears as soon as we attempt to anticipate the goal which knowledge must attain and to establish this goal prior to investigation. Not doubt, but dogma, is the most dreaded foe of knowledge; not ignorance as such, but ignorance which pretends to be truth and wants to pass for truth, is the force which inflicts the mortal wound on knowledge. For here it is not a matter of error but of deception; not a matter of an illusion arising inadvertently but of a delusion of the intellect into which it falls by its own fault and in which it becomes more and more completely enmeshed. And this axiom holds not only for knowledge but also for faith. The real radical opposite of belief is not disbelief, but superstition; for superstition gnaws at the very roots of faith and dries up the source from which religion springs. In superstition, therefore, knowledge and faith encounter a common enemy and the fight against him is their first and most urgent task. They can and should unite to perform this task and on the basis of this union a treaty between knowledge and faith and a determination of their mutual boundaries can be accomplished.

Bayle is the first thinker to become an out-and-out advocate of this truth. In his *Historical and Critical Dictionary* he laid the foundation on which all later attempts at its justification and realization have been based. Bayle's skepticism is rooted in this insight, and here it proves its fruitfulness, its eminently positive significance. "I do not know whether one could not say that the obstacles to a good examination do not come so much from the fact that the mind is void of knowledge as that it is full of prejudice." This statement, which is in the article on Pellison in the *Dictionary*, could be made the motto of Bayle's complete works. He does not wish to disturb the content of faith, and he refrains from any explicit criticism of this content. But he violently assails that attitude which considers every means fair in the defense of faith, which mixes up truth and fancy, insight and prejudice, reason and passion, in so far as they can be useful in any sense in the achievement of the main goal of apologetics. In this way the content of faith is not saved but destroyed; for it can only survive in its purity. Not atheism, but superstition, is the major evil to be attacked. In this maxim Bayle anticipated the main thesis of the religious criticism of French Encyclopaedism. Diderot constantly refers to Bayle. In his article on Pyrrhonism in the *Encyclopaedia* Diderot says that in the art of reasoning Bayle has few peers, and perhaps no superior. Although he piles doubt on doubt, he always proceeds in methodical order; one article of his dictionary is like a living polyp that splits itself into a number of other polyps which are all alive and produced by one another. Similarly, Diderot constantly repeats the assertion that superstition is a graver misunderstanding of and a worse insult to God than atheism, that ignorance is not so far from the truth as prejudice.[33] One grasps the sense and substance of this declaration only if he calls to mind the methodological and epistemological presuppositions on which it rests. These presuppositions can be distinctly seen in Descartes' original foundation of rationalism. Descartes assumes that human knowledge is subject to manifold delusions, but that knowledge itself is at fault if it permits itself to be led from the path of truth by these delusions. For deception has its origin in the senses or in the imagination; error, however, signifies a lapse of judgment; and judgment is a free act of the intellect which the latter must answer for independently. The in-

---

[33] Cf. Diderot's *Lettre sur les sourds et muets*, also his *Pensées philosophiques*, sect. XII: "Superstition is more harmful than atheism."

tellect can decide for itself whether it wishes to follow an impulse of the senses or surrender to the imagination, or refuse to do either. It can and should reserve its decision if available data are insufficient for a genuine formation of judgment and for the attainment of complete certainty. It is only when the intellect decides prematurely, when it permits itself to be forced to make an assertion without having in hand the necessary premises, that it falls prey to error and uncertainty; no mere shortcomings of the mind are now involved but rather guilt of the will. It is the task of the will to guide the path of knowledge; and this faculty possesses the power to protect knowledge from all aberration in that it confronts knowledge with the general and inviolable demand never to pronounce judgment except on the basis of clear and distinct ideas. This Cartesian principle is adopted by the philosophy of the Enlightenment, and by this principle the Enlightenment is led to the rule in which Kant sees the true nature of the age. "Enlightenment is man's exodus from his self-incurred tutelage. Tutelage is the inability to use one's understanding without the guidance of another person. This tutelage is self-incurred if its cause lies not in any weakness of the understanding, but in indecision and lack of courage to use the mind without the guidance of another. 'Dare to know' (*sapere aude*)! Have the courage to use your own understanding; this is the motto of the Enlightenment."[34] The different attitude of and evaluation by Enlightenment philosophers of the individual conditions from which error can arise, are explicable on the basis of this motto. Not every mistake of knowledge denotes failure, for those mistakes which merely express the limits of our being are necessary and unavoidable. How could God hold a being to which He has given certain absolute limits responsible for remaining within its prescribed limits and not striving for omniscience? We are not responsible for such limitations of knowledge; on the contrary, it is madness to transcend our limits and to venture with dogmatic assurance to pronounce judgment on the universe and its origin. Real unbelief is not therefore evidenced by doubt; it expresses rather

[34] "Beantwortung der Frage: Was ist Aufklärung?" *Werke*, ed. Cassirer, vol. IV, p. 169.

reserve, the simple and honest humility of knowledge. Unbelief appears rather in the apparent certainty which tolerates only its own opinion disallowing all others. The loopholes in our knowledge and the shortcomings of thought itself with respect to the highest Being do not count in an ethical and religious sense: "The Author of nature," says Diderot, "who will not reward me for having been a man of wit, will not damn me for having been a sot."[35] But what counts and is subject to ethical standards, is that blind belief which deliberately closes its mind to all investigation and opposes all examination; for such belief not only limits the content of knowledge, but negates its being, its form, and its principle.

It is clear then that the demand for tolerance, as made by the philosophy of the Enlightenment, is completely misunderstood if it is given a purely negative interpretation. Tolerance means anything but a recommendation of laxity and indifference to fundamental questions of religion. Only among individual unimportant thinkers do we find a form of defense of tolerance which tends to indifference. On the whole, however, the opposite tendency prevails; the principle of the freedom of faith and conscience is the expression of a new and positive religious force which uniquely characterizes the century of the Enlightenment. In this principle was embodied a new form of religious awareness which asserts itself thereafter clearly and confidently. The new form was indeed attainable only as a result of a complete change of religious aims and sentiment. The decisive transformation took place when a genuine religious ethos superseded the religious pathos which had motivated the preceding centuries of religious controversy. Henceforth religion is not to be a matter of mere receptivity; it is to originate from, and to be chiefly characterized by, activity. Man is not merely seized and overwhelmed by this activity as by a strange power, but he in turn influences and shapes the activity from within. It is not supernatural power nor divine grace which produces religious conviction in man; he himself must rise to it and maintain it. From this theoretical principle all the conclusions which the

[35] *Additions aux Pensées philosophiques*, sect. XI.

epoch of the Enlightenment drew, and all the concrete and practical demands which the epoch raised, follow of themselves and by an inner necessity. A consequence now appears which must seem strange at first glance to those accustomed to the traditional conception of the Enlightenment. If there is any one formula by which the period of the Enlightenment can be characterized and which can be attributed to the period with absolute certainty, it would seem to be that it is an era of pure intellectualism, that it unconditionally upholds the primacy of thought and pure theory. In the formation and development of its religious ideals, however, this view is by no means confirmed. The opposite tendency clearly prevails here; for however much the Enlightenment strives to found a "religion within the bounds of mere reason," it attempts on the other hand to emancipate religion from the domination of the understanding. This is precisely the charge which the Enlightenment constantly brings against the dogmatic system of theology which it opposes, namely, that it has missed the important point of religious certainty in that it considered belief as a mere acceptance of certain theoretical propositions and wanted to confine belief to these propositions by force. Such a limitation is neither possible nor desirable because it would change religion into mere opinion, and thus deprive it of its real moral and practical force. Where this force is active and pure, we transcend all differences of religious ideas and concepts. These ideas and concepts must never be taken for anything other than the outside wrapping of religious certainty. They are infinitely varied, but we need not therefore despair of the unity of religion. For diversity concerns only the sense symbols, not the supersensible content which seeks representation, though necessarily inadequate, in these symbols. The Enlightenment thus revives that principle which Nicholas of Cusa had formulated three centuries earlier; it emphatically proclaims the identity of religion amid all its different rites and despite all controversies regarding ideas and opinions. But the horizon of the Enlightenment is broader than that of the Renaissance, and the variety of religious phenomena which the Enlightenment tries to comprehend under this principle is even greater than at the time of the Renaissance. Yet even in Cusa's work *On the Peace of Faith* the controversy about the true religion is fought out not merely among Christians, Jews, and Mohammedans; the pagan world, the Tartar and the Scythian, also claim their shares of true knowledge of God. In the eighteenth century, however, the peoples of the Orient especially attract attention and demand equal recognition for their religious convictions.[36] Leibniz had already called attention to Chinese civilization; and Wolff in a speech on Chinese wisdom had praised Confucius as a prophet of pure morality and ranked him next to Christ. Voltaire takes up this strain and uses it as his main proof that the core of religion and morality depends very little on particular points of faith. In Montesquieu's *Persian Letters* the comparison between Orient and Occident by no means favors the latter; the unbiased observation and criticism of the Persian reveals everywhere the arbitrary, conventional, and accidental elements in all those things which in the opinion of the Occident are supposed to be most certain and sacred. In this work Montesquieu created a literary model which thereafter served criticism and polemics on many occasions. But this controversial literature does not have as its purpose destruction; it seeks rather to make positive use of destructive criticism. In contrast to the narrow-mindedness of dogma, the critical literature of the eighteenth century strives for the freedom of an all-comprehensive, a truly universal awareness of God. Diderot, in his *Philosophical Thoughts*, gave the most incisive expression to this fundamental attitude of the epoch: "Men have banished divinity from their midst; they have relegated it to a sanctuary; the walls of a temple are the limits of its view; beyond these walls it does not exist. Madmen that you are, destroy these enclosures which obstruct your horizon; liberate God; see Him everywhere where He actually is, or else say that He does not exist at all."[37]

The struggle for the expansion of the concept of God which

[36] Concerning the importance of the Orient for French civilization of the eighteenth century, see Martino, *L'Orient dans la littérature française au XVIIe et XVIIIe siècle*, Paris, 1906.

[37] Diderot, *Pensées philosophiques*, sect. XXVI, *Oeuvres*, ed. Assézat, vol. I, p. 138.

is fought by the century of the Enlightenment with the exertion of all its intellectual and moral energies, cannot be taken up in detail here. A sketch of its main trend and its general aspects will have to suffice. The arms for this struggle had already been forged in the seventeenth century; and here again it was Bayle's *Dictionary* which constituted the real arsenal of all Enlightenment philosophy. In his writings against Louis XIV on the occasion of the revocation of the Edict of Nantes, Bayle commences with a special demand, namely, for the recognition of freedom of faith and conscience for Protestants. But the presentation and justification of this demand far outgrow his immediate task; they become so acrimonious that they even offend Bayle's allies and make of Jurieu, a leading Protestant theologian, an implacable opponent. For Bayle expressly states that his defense of the freedom of religion is not intended to serve any particular faith, but that it establishes a universal, purely philosophical goal and represents a principle which is equally valid and binding for every form of belief. In a purely ethical sense on the basis of the criteria of moral reason, according to Bayle, coercion is absurd and reprehensible; hence it appears impossible ever to justify the use of force for the sake of religion. For there can and must be no radical difference between morality and religion. If a conflict arises between them, if the testimony of the Bible contradicts the testimony of the moral conscience, this dispute should be settled in a way that respects the absolute primacy of the moral consciousness. For if we relinquish this primacy, we forego any criterion of religious truth; then we no longer have any standard by which to measure the claims to certainty of an alleged revelation or distinguish, within religion itself, between reality and deception. Every literal interpretation of the Bible must therefore be rejected which commands us to act contrary to the first principles of morality. In these principles, not in a mere communication of the literal sense, we have the real inviolable maxims of interpretation, which should not be set aside for the sake of any literalism, however well documented: "It is better to reject the testimony of criticism and grammar than that of reason." The underlying principle of all exegesis of the Bible must therefore

be that any interpretation is wrong which violates the highest
and most certain moral principles and recommends or justifies
a crime: "Any literal sense which contains an obligation to commit crimes is false."[38] Here was a regulative maxim to whose
content the philosophy of the Enlightenment had to add nothing, but which it needed only to develop to its logical conclusion,
in order to achieve its essential goal. But to this achievement one
more thing was of course necessary, and this was contributed by
Voltaire. He dug up the treasure which lay buried beneath an
unwieldy mass of historical and theological learning in Bayle's
Dictionary. The principle of ethical criticism of the Bible, which
was vehemently disputed in the seventeenth century and denounced by both Protestants and Catholics, is brought by Voltaire to the common storehouse for the learning of the age.
When in the year 1763 in his *Treatise on Tolerance* Voltaire
looks back on this struggle, it is with the assurance of final
victory. We are living in an era in which reason from day to day
is becoming a more frequent guest both in the palaces of the
great and in the shops of citizens and merchants, Voltaire states.
This progress is irresistible; the fruits of reason will and must
reach full maturity. Reverence for the past must not prevent us
from reaping these fruits. For it is a fundamental law of the
intellectual world that it only exists and persists if we daily
create it anew. "Past times are as if they had never been. It is
always necessary to start at the point at which one already stands,
and at which nations have arrived." This saying belongs to those
thoughts which only Voltaire could express with such brevity
and clarity; it focuses in one point all the intellectual convictions and tendencies of the Enlightenment. Another outstanding feature of Voltaire's *Treatise on Tolerance* is the serious and
sober detachment with which he approaches his fundamental
problem—an attitude rarely found in Voltaire's religious writings. Here, where he is motivated by a perfectly concrete
purpose, namely, the reopening of the case against Jean Calas,
his style is characterized by unusual austerity and force. He
restrains his playful humor completely, and more than usually, he

---

[38] Bayle, *Commentaire philosophique sur les paroles de l'Évangile: contrains
les d'entrer, Oeuvres diverses*, The Hague, 1727, vol. II, pp. 367, 374.

dispenses with polemics. The personal ethos which always motivates Voltaire's invective was seldom expressed as effectively as in this work of his advanced years. Tolerance, which religious fanatics dare to call a dangerous error and a monstrous demand, is termed the "appanage of reason" (*l'appanage de la raison*) by Voltaire. Tolerance is not a particular postulate of philosophy, but rather an expression of its principle; tolerance is of the very essence of philosophy. It expresses the affinity of philosophy and religion. It is the greatest triumph of philosophy if today the period of religious wars is over—if Jew, Catholic, Lutheran, Greek, Calvinist, Anabaptist, and Socinian now live together as brothers and serve the welfare of society in the same way. "Philosophy, philosophy alone, that sister of religion, has disarmed the hands of superstition which have so long been reddened with gore; the human spirit awakened from its intoxication is astonished at the excesses it committed under the influence of fanaticism."[39] There are still of course zealots and fanatics enough, but if we let reason do its work, it will slowly, but unfailingly cure this evil. "It is mild, it is humane; it teaches us forbearance and dispels discord; it fosters virtue and makes obedience to the laws agreeable rather than compulsory."

Here again it appears that purely intellectual standards are felt more and more to be insufficient. The truth of religion cannot be determined according to purely theoretical criteria; its validity cannot be decided abstractly without regard to its moral effect. Lessing's fable of the rings (*Nathan the wise*) is foreshadowed in the idea that the ultimate truth of religion cannot be shown by external demonstration but only by internal conviction. All demonstration is inadequate, whether it is based on historical facts or on logical and metaphysical premises; for religion in the last analysis is only what it does, and its essential nature can be realized in no other way than through feeling and action. Here we have the touchstone of all true religion. Diderot goes back to this basic argument to prove the advantages of natural over revealed religion. He argues that a direct decision in the dispute over the individual historical religions cannot be

[39] Voltaire, *Traité sur la tolérance à l'occasion de la mort de Jean Calas*, chs. I, IV, *Oeuvres*, vol. XXIX, pp. 63, 74 f.

reached because each religion claims absolute superiority over all others and therefore dogmatically repudiates all other beliefs. But this purely negative attitude, nevertheless, has its limits. Despite its policy of exclusion toward all other religions, no religion can and wants completely to deny its relation to natural religion. For this is the native soil to which every religion feels itself attached, and from which it can never entirely break away. If then one asks the various creeds to which religion they would concede second place without yielding their own supremacy, their reply would be unanimous. They would all at least grant second place to natural religion, but never to any other; the dispute is thus decided so far as persons of unbiased and purely philosophical judgment are concerned. For such persons it is now clear where they must seek true generality and true eternity: "Everything that has a beginning will sometime have an end, and, vice versa, that which has never had a beginning can never perish. Now the Jewish and Christian religions have had beginnings, and there is no religion on earth the date of whose origin is not known with the exception of natural religion. This religion alone then will never end, while all the others will perish." Jews and Christians, Mohammedans and heathen, are all heretics and schismatics of natural religion, which alone can really be shown to be authentic. For the truth of natural religion is to that of the revealed religions as testimony which I give myself is to that which I receive from others, as that which I feel immediately within myself is to that which I have been taught. "The former testimony I find within myself inscribed by the hand of God; the latter has been written on parchment and marble by superstitious people. The former I bear within myself, and I find it always the same; the latter lies outside myself and differs with every country and clime. The former brings together and unites civilized man and barbarian, Christian and heathen, philosopher and people, scholar and uneducated, old man and child; the latter estranges father and son, arms man against man, and exposes the wise to the hatred and persecution of the ignorant and fanatic." Nor does the objection that natural religion as the oldest is the most imperfect withstand examination; for is it not likely that what is oldest is also truest, that it is the *a priori* of all religion? And even if one accepts the idea of development and perfection, the question is not decided in favor of any particular revealed religion or its articles of faith. For how do we know that we are already at the end of this development? If natural law could be superseded by Mosaic law, and this in turn by Christian law; why should not Christian law be succeeded by some other which God has not yet revealed to man?[40] In these sentences from Diderot's essay *On the Sufficiency of Natural Religion* we can already hear overtones of Lessing's ideas. We are also reminded of Lessing by the sharp distinction which Diderot draws between rational and historical proofs, and by the trenchancy with which he emphasizes that factual testimony, however sound it may appear, can never reach the degree of certainty necessary for it to serve as a basis for proof of general and necessary truths.[41] By such arguments, the proofs of the existence of God, on which theology and metaphysics of the seventeenth century had founded their systems, are robbed of their force; the center of religious certainty is transferred to another point where it is neither accessible to, nor dependent on, such proofs.

English deism, despite all the variety and deviations within individual presentations, shows essentially the same basic tendency. Deism begins as a strictly intellectualist system; its aim is to banish mysteries, miracles, and secrets from religion and to expose religion to the light of knowledge. Toland's book *Christianity Not Mysterious* (1696) describes in its title the theme which hereafter appears over and over again in the writings of the deistic movement. The philosophic meaning of deism consists primarily in that it maintains a new principle in the formulation of its problem. For deism assumes that the question of the content of faith cannot be isolated from that of the form of faith, that both questions are soluble only in common. It is then not only the truth content of individual dogmas, it is rather the religious type of certainty as such toward which the question is now directed. On this matter Toland believes he can refer to

[40] Diderot, *De la suffisance de la religion naturelle*, sects. IV, XVIII, XXV ff.
[41] Cf. for instance Diderot's "Introduction aux grands principes" and his answer to objections to this essay, *Oeuvres*, ed. Naigeon, 1798, vol. I, p. 350.

Locke and introduce the basic concepts and principles of Locke's theory of knowledge into the problems of religion. For what is true of religious knowledge in general, must also hold for religious knowledge in particular. Locke had defined the act of knowing in general as an awareness of agreement or disagreement between ideas. Hence it follows that knowledge by nature involves a relation; above all, the terms of the relation must be given in, and clearly understood by, our consciousness. For without such understanding of the basic elements of the relation it loses all meaning. According to Toland this methodological consideration represents an essential principle and a necessary limit for the objects of religious faith. Absolute transcendence of these objects is forestalled; for how could our consciousness, as a knowing, believing and judging subject, concentrate on an object if this object were not somehow present in some phenomenon of consciousness? But the absolutely irrational which transcends all human understanding cannot present itself in consciousness; of the irrational, then, we can no more say *that* it is than we can determine *what* it is. The objection that one can be very sure of the existence of a thing without knowing any of its predicates is unsound. For even if such a form of knowledge were possible, what religious significance could we attribute to it? If belief is not to become completely vain and meaningless, its object must somehow be meaningful—it must include certain elements which can be clearly understood. That which is in every respect mysterious and by definition beyond all understanding, must therefore remain as alien to faith as to knowledge. "Could that Person justly value himself upon being wiser than his Neighbors, who having infallible Assurance that something call'd *Blictri* had a Being in Nature, in the mean time knew not what this *Blictri* was?"[42] Toland concludes that there can be mysteries only in a relative, not in an absolute, sense. He refers to content which is beyond the reach of a certain mode of comprehension, not to content which is beyond all possibility of understanding. So far as the word "mystery" is concerned, Toland declares that it had originally meant a doctrine which

[42] Toland, *Christianity Not Mysterious*, London, 1696, p. 133.

was not contrary to reason but which involved a known truth that for some reason was to be kept secret from a part of mankind. The concept "revelation," accordingly, cannot be opposed to that of natural religion in the sense that the two terms are different in their specific content. It is not the content of that which is manifested which distinguishes these concepts but the nature and manner of the manifestation. Revelation is not a unique ground of certainty; it is only a particular form of communication of a truth whose ultimate proof and verification must be sought in reason itself.

Tindal, too, in his book *Christianity as Old as the Creation* (1730), starts from this principle. He points out that natural and revealed religion do not differ in substance but in the manner of their becoming known; the former is the inner, the latter the outer manifestation of the will of an infinitely wise and good being. In order to conceive such a being, it is necessary to free it from all merely anthropomorphic limitations. It would indicate an incomprehensible narrow-mindedness in this being to withhold part of its nature and activity, or to employ them to the advantage of a particular time and of a particular people above all other peoples. Just as God is always the same and human nature is one and unalterable in itself, revelation too must dispense its light equally in all directions. God would not be God if, as for example the dogma of election by grace has it, He could, as it were, conceal his nature within Himself—if He could enlighten one part of mankind and leave the other in darkness. The most important criterion of the genuineness of all revelation can therefore consist only in its universality, in its transcendence of all local and temporal limitations. Christianity is, therefore, true to the extent that it satisfies this fundamental condition. It exists in so far as it is bound to no particular place or time, in so far as it is as old as the world. Between natural law and Christian law, so far as content is concerned, there is no difference; the latter claims to be nothing more than the reassertion of that which is set down in the first. Such a "republication of the Law of Nature" is given to man especially in his knowledge of morality. Here then lies the truly infallible revelation which exceeds all others in value and certainty. Tindal thus arrives at a definition of religion which Kant later could adopt unchanged in his work on *Religion within the Bounds of Mere Reason*. For Tindal religion is the recognition of our duties as divine commands; it consists in starting with generally valid and generally accessible norms and then in relating these to a divine Author and looking upon them as expressions of His will. The center of gravity has now shifted, even in the development of English deism, from the sphere of the purely intellectual to that of "practical reason"; and "moral" deism has now replaced "constructive" deism.[43]

The extraordinary effect which English deism had on the whole intellectual life of the eighteenth century depends essentially on this transition. In the light of its purely theoretical content the intensity of this effect is scarcely credible. For among the leaders of this movement there is no thinker of real depth and of truly original stamp, and the purely theoretical deductions on which deism bases the defense of its viewpoint are often questionable and involved in half-truths. The attitude of deism, the honest desire for truth and the moral seriousness with which it undertook its criticism of dogma, were more effective than all these deductions. Such are the real inner motivating forces. Bayle, who lived at the beginning of the deistic movement, recognized this clearly and prophesied victory for the ethos of deism. In his attack on the revocation of the Edict of Nantes Bayle says: "Our age . . . is full of freethinkers and deists. People wonder at this. But for my part I am surprised that there are not more of such persons in view of the ravages which religion is producing in the world and the extinction of our virtue which it is bringing about as an almost inevitable consequence by authorizing for its temporal prosperity all the crimes imaginable: homicide, robbery, banishment, abduction, etc., which in turn produce an infinite number of other abominations, hypoc-

---

[43] Concerning the details of this development see especially Leslie Stephen, *History of English Thought in the Eighteenth Century*, two volumes, second edition, London, 1881; see also Troeltsch, "Deismus," *Gesammelte Schriften*, vol. IV, pp. 429 ff. and Hermann Schwarz, "Deismus," *Paedagogisches Lexikon*, ed. Velhagen and Klasing.

risy, the sacrilegious profanation of the sacraments, etc."[44] Deism springs from the inner repudiation of the spirit in which the religious quarrels of the preceding centuries had been conducted; it gives expression to a deep longing for that "peace of faith" which had been hoped for and promised by the Renaissance but never attained. Not in religious war, but only in religious peace can and will the truth and the nature of God be revealed to us; such is the general conviction of the deistic movement. For God, as Bayle had already argued, is too benevolent a being to be the author of anything so pernicious as the revealed religions which carry in themselves the inexterminable seeds of war, slaughter, and injustice. In Germany too it is primarily this motive to which deism owes its uninterrupted progress. In German intellectual history in the eighteenth century the growth of the deistic movement can be traced from decade to decade. Bibliographies and reviews of the literature of the English freethinkers become a regular section of the periodicals.[45] To be sure, the controversy over natural religion and the relation between reason and revelation never became as acrimonious in Germany as it did in France. For here it faces a different opponent. It no longer opposes an orthodoxy and ecclesiastical hierarchy which attempts with its authority and claim to absolute power to suppress freedom of thought; on the contrary, the task of German deism lay in perfecting a religious system which bore the most diverse seeds of new thought. Leibnizian philosophy in Germany acts as the intellectual medium within which religious thought develops, and this medium can comprehend and reconcile the most antagonistic principles. The fundamental tendency of Leibniz's thought, the tendency toward harmony, also remained alive in German deism. In the system of Christian Wolff there is no sharp differentiation between the content of faith and that of knowledge, between revelation and reason. The claims of both are to be carefully balanced and exactly determined. As in Locke and Leibniz, the

---

[44] Bayle, *Commentaire Philosophique, Oeuvres Diverses*, The Hague, 1737, vol. II, p. 366.
[45] For the spread of deism in Germany see, for instance, Hettner, *Literaturgeschichte des achtzehnten Jahrhunderts*, third edition, vol. III, pp. 264 ff.

irrationality of the content of faith is disputed, but no one asserts that this content can be derived from reason alone or that there are no supra-rational elements in faith. Reason and revelation remain the original sources of knowledge; they should not oppose, they should supplement, one another; and they can be sure that as a result of this collaboration a uniform meaning of religious truth will ensue. These two forces are not to be aroused against each other but so combined that their harmony appears. Within the school of Wolff there remained room for an orthodoxy which did not permit any alterations of the basic content of revealed faith even if the form in which this faith was presented gradually changed, and the claim to, and the method of, demonstration by degrees assumed greater importance.[46] The tendency of the real theological innovators in Germany—so-called "neology," as it is represented by such men as Semler, Sack, Spalding, Jerusalem, etc.—soon goes beyond this stage. It not merely employs reason as a support and as formal proof of a matter of faith upheld by other sources, but by means of reason it seeks to define such points of faith. This school of thought removes from dogma all ingredients which cannot be derived from its definitions, and tries to show by means of investigations of the history of dogma that these ingredients are later and heterogeneous additions to the originally pure faith. The content of revelation is thus substantially reduced, while the concept of revelation remains for the time being still unchanged. But this concept is now used only to support and sanction those truths which are comprehensible to, and quite in keeping with, reason. Demonstration in the strict sense, real syllogistic proof, is now more and more supplanted by empirical proof, which does not, however, look for its basis in particular historical facts but in inner certainties. "My experience is my proof," writes Jerusalem; and the essential experience, on which all proof of religion must be based, is peace of mind, which makes us happier than reason as a theoretical faculty can

---

[46] For a fuller account see, for instance, Troeltsch, "Aufklaerung," *Gesammelte Schriften*, vol. IV, pp. 370 ff. Regarding the trend of earlier Wolffian thought cf. the works of Canz, *Usus Philosophiae Leibnitianae et Wolffianae in Theologia* (1733) and *Philosophiae Wolffianae consensus cum Theologia* (1735).

ever do.[47] With this appeal to subjectivity as the true principle of all religious certainty the authority of any apparently objective source is repudiated, and only one step remains to be taken in order to renounce this authority explicitly as well. Later theological rationalism took this step; it called the whole body of faith before the forum of reason and declared revelation as an independent source of knowledge to be dispensable. And thus the basic demand of deism had found its way into theology and triumphed over all resistance. Sack had once declared that revelation was the "telescope of reason" without which reason could not see at all, or only very dimly, the most important religious truths. Reimarus could reply that this analogy too has its limits. For as in the field of sensory awareness the organs of perception can be sharpened while they cannot be dispensed with, and as a telescope or a microscope is useless without the aid of natural vision, so it is also in the field of intellectual endeavor, where knowledge must always be referred ultimately to and measured by the natural powers of the mind.[48]

Deism thus finally overcame all obstacles placed in its path. Despite the exertion of all energies and despite the flood of polemical literature which grew from year to year, the final victory of deism seemed inevitable. But now fresh and unexpected aid came to the rescue of the threatened system of orthodoxy. One of the bitterest opponents of this system became an ally on this point. It was not theological dogmatics but radical philosophical skepticism which repelled the attacks of deism and stalled its advance. In England Samuel Clarke with all his logical acumen had once more undertaken to establish the truth of the whole body of Christianity by deducing it from uni-

[47] Regarding the development of "neology" in Germany, see especially the wealth of material in Aner, *Theologie der Lessingzeit*, Halle, 1929. From a historical viewpoint the close relation between the German "neologists" of the eighteenth century and the English theologians of the seventeenth century is particularly interesting. The concept of "religious experience," as it is found in Jerusalem, for instance, was anticipated in detail by the thinkers of the Cambridge School. Cf. the author's book *Die platonische Renaissance in England*, especially pp. 19 ff.

[48] Cf. Reimarus's preface to his *Abhandlung von den vornehmsten Wahrheiten der natuerlichen Religion*.

versally valid premises.[49] Even Voltaire was compelled to admire Clarke's ability; in his *Letters on the English* he describes Clarke as a "real thinking machine" (*une vraie machine à raisonnements*) capable of the most difficult tasks.[50] Nor did Voltaire retract this judgment later on; in his *Treatise on Metaphysics* he ranks Clarke along with Locke as one of the first "artists of reason."[51] But all this labor with strictly logical demonstrations seemed to make no impression on deism; it seemed rather to make the weakness of orthodox doctrine stand out more conspicuously than before. In his defense of freethinking Anthony Collins remarks ironically that until Clarke undertook to demonstrate the existence of God nobody had ever entertained any doubts on this point.[52] Yet what the logician and metaphysician could not do, the radical opponent of all logical and metaphysical dogmatism succeeded in doing. It was Hume who confronted deism with a new problem, and in doing so he broke its hold on contemporary thought. In founding its concept of natural religion, deism proceeds from the presupposition that there is a human nature which is everywhere the same, and which is endowed with certain fundamental knowledge of a theoretical as well as of a practical sort on which it can absolutely rely. But where do we find such a human nature? Is it an empirically given fact, or is it not rather simply a hypothesis? And does not the main weakness of deism lie in the fact that it trusts implicitly in this hypothesis, and that it raises a hypothesis to the status of a dogma? Hume assails this dogma. His opposition to deism is concerned neither with its doctrine of reason nor of revelation; he aims merely to evaluate it from the viewpoint of the standards of experience, of pure factual knowledge. His evaluation proves that the whole proud structure of deism stands on feet of clay. For that apparent "human nature" on which deism proposed to base natural religion is itself no reality, but a mere fiction. Experience reveals human nature to us in an

[49] Cf. Clarke, *A Demonstration of the Being and Attributes of God*, London, 1705/06.

[50] See *Lettres sur les Anglais*, Letter VII, *Oeuvres*, vol. XXVI, pp. 33 ff.

[51] *Traité de Métaphysique*, ch. II, *Oeuvres*, vol. XXXI, pp. 20 ff.

[52] Collins, *A Discourse of Freethinking Occasioned by the Rise and Growth of a Sect Called Freethinkers*, London, 1713. See Leslie Stephen, *op.cit.*, vol. I, p. 80.

entirely different light from all the constructive attempts of the
deists. Here we find human nature not as a storehouse of fundamental truths, of *a priori* verities, but as a dull confusion of instincts; not as a cosmos, but as a chaos. The more penetrating
our knowledge of the nature of man and the more accurate our
description of this nature, the more it loses the appearance of
rationality and order. Hume had reached this conclusion even
in the realm of theoretical ideas. We usually consider the law
of sufficient reason as the principle of all theoretical knowledge
and we think this principle gives unity and inner stability to all
our knowledge in general. But sharper analysis of concepts
dispels this illusion. For the very concept of cause, which was
supposed to stabilize our knowledge, is itself without foundation. It is supported by no immediate evidence, and by no *a
priori* significance and necessity; it is itself merely a product of
the play of ideas which are connected by no objective, rational
principles, but in their combination simply follow the workings
of the imagination and obey its mechanical laws. And the same
is true to an even greater degree of our religious ideas. Their
apparently objective content and sublime sense resolve into
mere appearance as soon as we trace them back to their origin
and examine their growth and development. We then find
neither an originally speculative nor an originally ethical content. It was not brooding over the first principles of being and
the foundations of the world order, nor devotion to a being of
infinite wisdom and goodness, which brought forth the first
conceptions of God, and which still supports and maintains
them. Such purely philosophical considerations have no power
over the multitude. Man did not begin as a philosopher and it
is a delusive and vain hope that he will ever end as a philosopher. He is not subject to the domination of an abstract reason,
but to the power of appetites and passions. And appetites and
passions are not only the source of the first religious ideas and
dogmas; they are still the root of all religion. Religious conceptions are not shaped and fostered by thinking and by the moral
will. It is the emotions of hope and fear which have led men to
adopt beliefs and which support their continuance in faith.
Here we have the real foundation of religion. Religion is

rooted neither in logical nor in ethical grounds; it merely has an anthropological cause. It arises from the fear of supernatural powers and from man's desire to propitiate these powers and subject them to his will. Here too it is the play of passion and of the imagination which controls and guides the currents of our religious life. Superstition and the fear of demons are the real roots of our conception of God. We should not think that we can escape this conclusion by referring to the higher, purely "spiritual" religions which have risen far above these beginnings with their "primitive" conception of God. For this argument too collapses if, instead of observing religion in its rational transformation and in its idealistic disguise, we consider it rather in its sober empirical reality. Here religion always remains the same from beginning to end and from the lowest to the highest points. The same fundamental psychological forces which prevailed at the origin of religion also determine its further progress and continue to influence its development. Superstition takes on diverse and increasingly subtle forms but its innermost being remains forever the same. If we venture to remove the veil of words, of abstract concepts and moral ideas, in which the "higher" religions are enshrouded, then we find that the pattern of religion is everywhere the same. The motto: "I believe because it is absurd" (*credo quia absurdum*) exhibits its old force here and everywhere. Can there be a greater logical absurdity than the dogma of transubstantiation? Is there anything ethically more pernicious, or more injurious to human society, than the articles of faith of the revealed religions? The distinction between the "higher" and the "lower" religions consists only in the fact that a third motive is added to those of hope and fear; this motive arises from intellectual refinement, but in the purely ethical sense it amounts rather to retrogression than to progress. This is the motive of flattery which causes man to elevate his gods beyond all measure of earthly perfection and to attribute to them more and more sublime properties. But if one looks more closely and examines human behavior rather than human ideas, then one finds that, despite all this intellectual and moral improvement, everything has remained just as it was before. The all-good, all-wise, and all-just God of

Christianity, as Calvinism has conceived Him, becomes just as much of a cruel, malicious, and arbitrary tyrant as any whom worshipers of a primitive religion ever feared and adored. The fear of demons is thus also at the bottom of all higher religious conceptions, and this fear has not diminished owing to the fact that it no longer comes out in the open, that it sees to it that all the weaknesses which primitive religions naively display are hypocritically concealed both from itself and from others.[53]

Such is the "natural history of religion," as Hume portrays it; he believes he has overthrown natural religion once and for all and shown that it is nothing but a philosophical dream. It was thus philosophy itself which rescued the system of revealed religion from its most dangerous opponent. But the incision made by the sharp instrument of Hume's analysis inflicted a mortal wound on the orthodox system as well. Skepticism has the last word against revealed as well as against natural religion. "What a noble privilege is it of human reason to attain the knowledge of the Supreme Being; and, from the visible works of nature, be enabled to infer so sublime a principle as its Supreme Creator! But turn the reverse of the medal. Survey most nations and most ages. Examine the religious principles which have, in fact, prevailed in the world. You will scarcely be persuaded that they are anything but sick men's dreams. . . . No theological absurdities so glaring that they have not sometimes been embraced by men of the greatest and most cultivated understanding. No religious precepts so vigorous that they have not been adopted by the most voluptuous and most abandoned of men. . . . The whole is a riddle, an enigma, an inexplicable mystery. Doubt, uncertainty, suspense of judgment, appear the only result of our most accurate scrutiny concerning this subject. But such is the frailty of human reason, and such the irresistible contagion of opinion, that even this deliberate doubt could scarcely be upheld, did we not enlarge our view, and opposing one species of superstition to another, set them a quarrelling; while we ourselves, during their fury and contention, happily make our escape in the calm, though obscure, regions of philosophy."[54]

[53] Hume, *The Natural History of Religion*, sect. I ff., XIII-XV.
[54] Hume, *op.cit.*, sect. XV.

Religion

The line of thought which Hume follows through to its logical consequences was not typical of the eighteenth century. This century placed too much faith in the power of reason to renounce it at this vital point. It did not want to surrender to doubt, but insisted on a clear and sure decision. Hume's *Natural History of Religion* remained an isolated phenomenon in the intellectual history of the Enlightenment. For one other possible way remained which did not lead to that abrupt separation of reason and experience as it exists in Hume's doctrine but which seemed rather to combine and reconcile the claims of both. The abstract concept of natural religion had to be related to a definite content in order to stand up against the skeptical attacks that had been directed against it. It could no longer remain a mere postulate; it had to be shown that what this concept seeks and asserts has its place in the real religious life. This concept of natural religion had to seek its foundation not in reason alone, but also in history. By virtue of this task, to which it is led as by an inner necessity, eighteenth century thought finds itself confronted with a general problem which it attacks with its methodological instruments. The relation between religion and history must be understood; it is necessary to know how these two concepts mutually condition one another, and how within this relation the concrete reality of religion originates.

III. RELIGION AND HISTORY

The still prevailing and apparently ineradicable view that the eighteenth century had no conception of the historical world, that its mode of thinking was simply unhistorical, is directly and convincingly contradicted by a glance at the development of religious thought. For the inner transformation of religion is conditioned by the fact that it frees itself from the domination of metaphysical and theological thinking and secures for itself a new standard, a new norm of judgment. This is not a simple norm, but one based on two different elements which religion tries to harmonize. The result is a synthesis of the rational and historical spirit. Reason is referred to history and history to reason, and from this correlation religion obtains a new general outlook and a new ideal of knowledge. Reason and history are clearly distinguished and kept in a state of constant tension on which the whole inner movement of religious thought in the eighteenth century depends. Far from attempting a simple leveling process by sacrificing history to reason, the polarity between these two concepts is recognized and precisely defined. But this polar relation does not, according to the fundamental conviction of the philosophy of the Enlightenment, exclude an ideal equilibrium between the two opposing forces; for one reality and one truth are after all revealed to us in reason as well as in history—in different forms, to be sure, but agreeing in essence. We must, therefore, hold up the mirror of reason to history and view its image of history in this reflection; but all rationality must also be seen in historical perspective. The two conceptions of reality and truth which result are in essential agreement both in tendency and objective. Consideration of the eternal and immutable norms of reason must go hand in hand with consideration of the manner in which they unfold historically, in which they have been realized in the course of empirical historical development. Real "enlightenment" of the mind can only emerge from the reconciliation and opposition of these two modes of contemplation. Sound understanding of the "being" of the intellect presupposes an understanding of its "becoming" as an integral element, but on the other hand the real meaning of this becoming cannot of course be grasped unless it is related to and measured by unchangeable being.

This conception of knowledge met its severest test when it was confronted with the very foundation of religious certainty, namely, with the problem of defining clearly and unmistakably the truth content of the Bible. The very raising of this question and the claim which it included meant a revolution of religious thought. For both the question and its claim involved a deliberate break with the principle of verbal inspiration which had never been rejected by the Reformation, which had in fact stressed this principle more than ever. The main endeavor of the Reformation went to prove that the truth of Scripture is in itself uniform and unique, unexceptionable and unlimited; and this truth could not otherwise be maintained than on the assumption that the Bible contains no inconsistency or discrepancy. Every word, indeed every letter, was supposed to be on a par with the whole in value and sanctity, and so could claim the same validity as revelation. Not even in the seventeenth century could this claim be upheld without difficulty in the light of the progress of philosophical thought. For the Cartesian method of doubt cannot stop at this point. To be sure, Descartes himself never tires of assuring us that his innovation is concerned solely with knowledge and not with belief; in every matter of theological dogma he expressly declares his submission to the authority of Scripture and the Church. But his immediate pupils and followers cast off this cautious restraint. Even those thinkers who are inspired by the purest personal zeal, and who wish to employ the principles of Cartesianism especially for the awakening and deepening of the religious spirit, cannot escape the effects of this movement. The first work which in its very title calls for a critical history of the books of the Bible originates in the circle of the Oratorians; its author, Richard Simon, was inspired by Malebranche, his personal friend. Simon examines the authenticity of the books of the Bible, and regarding their development he sets up hypotheses which shake the foundations of orthodoxy. This first historical analysis of the Bible remains within Church circles; indeed its indirect purpose had been to serve the ends of the Catholic Church. For Simon's purpose is to show that protestant reliance on the exclusive truth of the Bible, and its consequent rejection of all other religious authority, are indefensible positions. The Bible alone is no absolute protection against doubt; it must have the support of the concurring testimony of Christian tradition.[55] A freer historical conception and evaluation of Scripture is therefore not yet achieved, and the judgment of history is called upon only when it suits the ends of orthodoxy. Spinoza first dares to raise the really incisive question. His *Theologico-Political Treatise* is the first attempt at a philosophical justification and foundation of Biblical criticism. It would seem paradoxical at first glance

[55] Cf. Richard Simon, *Histoire critique du vieux Testament*, Paris, 1678.

that Spinoza should be the one to perform this task. For if one considers the whole body of his metaphysics and its logical foundation, they do not encourage any hopes of historical insight. For Spinoza the ultimate source of all certainty lies not in becoming, but in pure being; not in empirical change, but in the immutable grounds of being and in the self-contained unity of the nature of things. These concepts alone are susceptible of adequate determination, while all finite, derived, and particular existence can be understood only through the medium of the "imagination." All knowledge of time and of temporal relations belongs to this medium; it does not rise to the sphere of philosophical knowledge, that is, knowledge "under the aspect of eternity"; on the contrary, philosophical knowledge, in order to reach its own perfection, must eliminate all temporal elements. Spinoza's viewpoint seems to preclude recognition of "historical" truth in its narrower sense and, if strictly interpreted, to convert it necessarily to a "contradiction between noun and adjective" (*contradictio in adjecto*). And yet Spinoza was the originator of the idea of the historicity of the Bible, and the first to develop it with sober precision and clarity. If we pursue this idea to its place in Spinoza's system as a whole, we find that it arose from no immediate historical tendency, from no interest in historical method as such, but that it represents an indirect conclusion from the logical premises of the system. Spinoza's monism is offended by the special position of the Bible, indeed by the special place of thought in general. Extension and thought, nature and mind, the order of things and the order of ideas, are not two fundamentally different spheres; they are identical orders of being depending on the same basic law. Hence contemplation of historical being is not to be separated from contemplation of natural being; both orders of being are to be treated from the same standpoint. "I may sum up the matter by saying that the method of interpreting Scripture does not widely differ from the method of interpreting nature—in fact, it is almost the same. For as the interpretation of nature consists in the examination of the history of nature, and therefrom deducing definitions of natural phenomena on certain fixed axioms, so Scriptural interpretation proceeds by the examination of Scripture, and inferring the intention of its authors as a legitimate conclusion from its fundamental principles. By working in this manner everyone will always advance without danger of error—that is, if they admit no principles for interpreting Scripture, and discussing its contents save such as they find in Scripture itself—and will be able with equal security to discuss what surpasses our understanding, and what is known by the natural light of reason."[56] Such is the principle which Spinoza represents, so simple in its nature yet so decisive and far-reaching in its consequences; being, or the nature of things, is not to be understood through the Bible, but the Bible itself is to be understood as a portion of this being, and therefore as subject to its general laws. The Bible is not the key to nature but a part of it; it must therefore be considered according to the same rules as hold for any kind of empirical knowledge. How can absolute truths and metaphysical insight concerning the fundamental principle of things (*natura naturans*) be expected from the Bible since Scripture itself is something entirely conditional and derived, and therefore belongs altogether to the realm of derived being (*natura naturata*)? The way to interpret and understand Scripture, and to discover its relative truth, can be no other than analysis and treatment by means of the tools of empirical investigation. The difficulties it contains will be resolved, the undeniable contradictions will be eliminated, if one places every passage in its proper context; that is, if one does not consider it as timeless truth but rather to be explained in terms of the particular circumstances accompanying its development and of the individuality of its author. The *Theologico-Political Treatise* attempts to apply this method of explanation, and in the light of later scientific Biblical criticism its results often appear strange and arbitrary. But the method as such is not affected by these obvious shortcomings and, despite the hostile reception of Spinoza's treatise, it was generally adopted.

[56] Spinoza, *A Theologico-Political Treatise*, ch. VII, *Chief Works of Spinoza*, tr. R. H. M. Elwes, Bohn's Philosophical Library, London, 1900, vol. I, pp. 99-100.

Religion

Spinoza seems hardly to have had any direct influence on eighteenth century thought. His name is carefully avoided, and knowledge of his teachings flows only from diluted and often turbid springs. Bayle's account and his criticism did their part to turn discussion of Spinozism into false paths and to place it in a one-sided and wrong perspective. But historical criticism of the Bible develops undisturbed in spite of all this. Its advance depends less on general considerations of method or system than on the great model of humanism and its characteristic ideal of knowledge. Erasmus, not Spinoza, is the real leader of this movement. In his critical edition of the New Testament the religious attitude and ethos of humanism found their first classic expression. Erasmus is convinced that the restoration of the pure text of the Bible would also mean the restitution of pure Christian doctrine. If we succeed in purifying this text of all later additions and arbitrary falsifications, then the image of pure Christianity in its sublime simplicity and in its original moral meaning will shine forth. The same sentiment inspires the work of his greatest pupil, Hugo Grotius. The complete plan of scientific criticism of the Bible first arises in the comprehensive mind of Grotius which is nourished by all the sources of humanistic and theological scholarship, and his *Annotations* on the Old and New Testaments marked out the path, even in detail, of eighteenth century research. Ernesti speaks with the highest admiration of this work which he expressly calls his model. In Semler's *Treatise on the Free Investigation of the Canon* (1771) this development has already reached the end of its first phase. Philosophical criticism thereafter has little to add to this work; generally, it merely points to Semler's work and draws systematic conclusions from his results. In Diderot's article on the Bible in the French *Encyclopaedia* we have an almost complete sketch of the main tendencies and tasks of Biblical criticism. He describes the various criteria by which the authenticity of the individual books of the Bible must be determined; he calls for a careful analysis of the content of these books, an investigation of the circumstances under which they were written, and an exact determination of the time when they were composed. The principle of verbal inspiration has thus lost all its force, and the historical conception of Scripture has reached the heart of the theological system.

But, in spite of all assurances to the contrary, had not the real spirit of this system vanished? Had not theology received a dangerous poison along with this newly awakened historical sense? If we turn back to Spinoza, there can be no doubt that for him the idea of the historicity of the Bible involved a chiefly negative tendency. He looked upon all knowledge that is concerned with, and confined to, merely temporal relations as once and for all relegated to the "imagination." Such knowledge can never convey clear ideas or strictly objective insight. For it is limited to the realm of the merely subjective, of absolute anthropomorphism. To recognize and treat the Bible as something temporally conditioned is, to Spinoza's way of thinking, tantamount to considering it as an epitome of anthropomorphic thought. The Bible is thus finally expelled from the region of philosophic truth, for such truth is not grasped by the "imagination" but by reason and intuition. What religious thought and sentiment look upon as the highest guarantee of all inspiration, Spinoza considers as rather its ineradicable shortcoming. The violence with which inspiration seizes the individual and subjects him to its power and the manner in which it makes him an unconscious tool in the hands of an apparently higher power, destroy the possibility of its possessing any real truth. For all truth depends on the condition of inner freedom and rational insight. It can only be attained if the power of the emotions and of the imagination is limited and subjected to the strict law of reason. The intensity of emotion, the strength of the imagination as it appears in the religious seer or prophet, is therefore the surest proof that his visions have nothing to do either with the discovery of objective truth or with the announcement of a generally valid and obligatory command, but that all such announcements are subjective; and that the prophet, when he declares that he speaks of God, is in reality talking only of himself and revealing his own inner states. In the introductory chapters of Spinoza's *Theologico-Political Treatise*, which deal with prophecy, this thesis is strictly applied. We see how the image of God changes with every individual prophet, how it assumes the form of his imagination and the color of his sentiment. The messages of the prophets vary according to their temperaments, their imaginations, and their previous experiences. "As a man is, so is his God." To the mild man He is mild; to the angry, angry; to the melancholy and mournful, gloomy and severe; to the cheerful, kindly and forgiving.[57] If one wished to express the basic thought of Spinoza's Biblical criticism in the language of his system, which of course the treatise cannot do, then one might say that no prophetic vision can represent the "substance," the nature and being of God, but that it can only express a certain "mode." And here more than anywhere else the proposition holds that "all determination is negation." The core and meaning of the divine cannot be brought to light by any such form of utterance; they are rather destroyed by it. The character of the divine lies in its universality, which excludes all limitation by, and confinement to, the individual. The miracles of the Bible and its prophetic visions offend against this fundamental philosophical certainty. They seek God in the particular and the accidental instead of in the universal and necessary. The miracle, as an interference with the order of nature and its universal laws, is positively anti-theistic; for the truth and being of God manifest themselves in these very laws. "As everything is true with necessity only according to divine decision, it follows perfectly clearly that the general laws of nature are merely God's decisions, which follow from the necessity and perfection of the divine nature. If therefore something should happen in nature that is in contradiction to its general laws, it would also be in contradiction to the decision, reason, and nature of God, or if someone wished to maintain that God acted against the laws of nature, he would also have to maintain that He acted against His own nature, which is perfectly absurd."[58] Literal belief in miracles is thus to Spinoza's way of thinking a perversion of religion; to proclaim a miracle is to deny God. And the same thing is true of all those

---

[57] Cf. especially *Tractatus theologico-politicus*, ch. II.
[58] *Tractatus theologico-politicus*, ch. VI.

subjective religious prophecies and revelations issuing from individuals and expressing only their own peculiar nature. All particularity is a negation of generality; all historicity narrows, blurs, and wipes away rationality. Spinoza's introduction of historical treatment into religion cannot and is not meant to serve as its philosophical justification; on the contrary, it can only aid insight into the necessary limitations of religious certainty.

A remarkable turn of events in the intellectual history of the eighteenth century now takes place in that the only great thinker who really understood Spinoza's religious thought, and who found his whole philosophy congenial, advances beyond him precisely on this point of religious certainty. Lessing is the first to free Spinoza's character from all those distortions which had been occasioned by his theological and philosophical opponents. He is the first to see Spinoza's doctrine in its true shape, and he devotes himself to this doctrine without reservation and prejudice; toward the end of Lessing's life it would seem, indeed, as if he no longer had any essential objection to the logical necessity and systematic unity of this doctrine. At first sight the conversation with Jacobi presents Lessing as a convinced Spinozist. "The orthodox concepts of deity are no longer for me; I cannot enjoy them. 'One and all' (Ἓν καὶ Πᾶν): I know nothing else." But the real greatness of Lessing's thought, his magnificent impartiality and receptivity, as well as his originality and depth, are shown by the fact that in the very moment of his acknowledgment of his indebtedness he takes a first step toward an immanent, methodological advance beyond Spinoza's teachings. The fundamental productive feature of Lessing's criticism appears here no less clearly than in the realm of his aesthetic and literary criticism. Lessing seems to adopt the essential points of Spinoza's philosophy, but his adoption is permeated with his own nature and thoughts which radically transform the ideas of Spinoza. Lessing like Spinoza rejects the demonstrative power of miracles. He too sees authentic miracles henceforth in the universal, not in the particular, and in the necessary, not in the accidental. The "miracles of reason," as Leibniz had termed them, constitute the real evidence of the divine. With Spinoza,

Religion

Lessing maintains the unity and universality of the concept of nature and at the same time he defends the postulate of pure immanence. For Lessing, too, God is no extramundane but an intramundane power; God is not a force which intervenes in our world of experience but one which permeates and shapes this world from within. However, Lessing's concept of the nature of this forming process is entirely different from Spinoza's. He proclaims as a new and essential truth what Spinoza could not imagine as anything but delusion. The relation between the whole and the part, between the general and the particular, between the universal and the individual, is a different matter for Lessing than for Spinoza. The particular and individual in experience have for Lessing a decidedly positive significance rather than a merely negative one. In this respect Lessing was an unswerving follower of Leibniz. A typical saying of Leibniz which Lessing could have taken as his motto asserts: "Mind is not a part, but an image of divinity, a representation of the universe" (*mens non pars est, sed simulacrum divinitatis, repraesentativum universi*). To such a way of thinking individuality is not simply a quantitative limitation but a unique quality; it is not a mere fragment of reality but its perfect replica. Looked at from this point of view all temporal existence takes on an entirely different appearance from that of Spinoza's system. Just as Leibniz had defined the monad as the "expression of multiplicity in unity," so Lessing could have defined it as the expression of the temporal in the immutable. For the monad *is* only in so far as it is constantly evolving, and no phase of this evolution is absolutely dispensable for the whole. The form of temporality as such is not incompatible with being; for only in such form can being appear and reveal itself in its purest essence. In applying this fundamental concept to religion Lessing encounters a new problem. For the historicity of the sources of religion is no longer utilized merely for the purpose of criticizing, or of refuting, religious doctrine; it now becomes a fundamental element of the deepest sense of religious teachings. If Spinoza seeks to dispute the absolute truth of religious revelation by an investigation of its history, Lessing attempts by the same procedure to accomplish the opposite end, namely, the restitution of religion. The authentic, the only absolute religion is simply the religion which comprehends within itself the totality of the historical manifestations of the religious spirit. Within this religion no detail is completely lost; there is no opinion, however eccentric, and no error which does not indirectly serve and belong to the truth. Lessing's *Education of Humanity* (*Erziehung des Menschengeschlechts*), which applies the Leibnizian theodicy concept to a new field of knowledge, was inspired by this basic conception; for Lessing's view of religion as a divine plan for the education of humanity is nothing but a theodicy of history, a justification of religion not through a being which has existed from the beginning of time but through religious growth and the goal of this growth.

The difficulty with which this idea gains acceptance appears with especial clarity if we compare Lessing with Mendelssohn on this point. Similar as are the religious ideas of these two thinkers from the viewpoint of content, nevertheless a sharp cleavage develops as to method. In their systematic presuppositions Lessing and Mendelssohn are closely akin, for Leibnizian concepts are the starting-point for them both. At first the difference between them lies merely in that Mendelssohn is in general content to retain the traditional form of these concepts as transmitted in the system of Christian Wolff, while Lessing's historical and philosophical interest and his critical flair lead him further and do not permit him to rest until in this field too he has reached the sources. The general mode of thought, however, remains the same in both for it is given in Leibniz's distinction among the fundamental forms of truth.[59] Leibniz's theory of knowledge too draws a sharp line of demarcation between the eternal truths and the temporal ones, between the necessary truths and the contingent ones. The former express relations prevailing among pure ideas whether the object of these ideas is found in the empirically real world or not. The propositions of

[59] Compare the following pages with the author's fuller account in his essay, "Die Idee der Religion bei Lessing und Mendelssohn," *Festgabe zum zehnjährigen Bestehen der Akademie für die Wissenschaft des Judentums*, Berlin, 1929, pp. 22 ff. Parts of this essay appear in the above.

pure geometry or arithmetic remain equally true, eternal, and necessary, even though in the reality of space and time, in the world of physical bodies, there is not a single form which corresponds exactly to the strict concepts which mathematics formulates of number and of the various geometric figures. And what is true of mathematical truths, holds also, according to Leibniz, for the truths of logic, ethics, and metaphysics. These truths too are valid not only for the real world which is given here and now, but for every possible world; they are not concerned with unique existence in space or with a single event in time, but with the absolutely general form of reason itself. This reason is always and everywhere the same, and it knows no possibility of change or transformation because any transformation would signify a loss of its own super-temporal and everlasting nature. If one proceeds from this Leibnizian definition of truth and from the specific distinctions it draws, then the question arises as to how these distinctions are applicable to the problem of religious certainty, and as to what results they would have on this problem. To what kind of certainty does religious belief belong? Is it to be classified with the necessary or with the accidental truths; is it based on a timeless and rational or on a temporal and historical foundation? Lessing wrestled tirelessly with this problem, and at times he seems to despair of its solution. He can neither renounce the "rationality" of religion, nor can he entertain any doubt of the particularity and uniqueness of the forms of religion, or of their dependence on the places and times in which they have existed. The core of all belief does not consist in the acceptance of a conceptual system, in itself valid and timeless; religious belief is always related to unique elements of experience, to a particular historical process. No reconciliation seems possible between these two approaches to religion which are by nature differentiated: "Contingent historical truths can never serve as proof for necessary truths of reason." "If I have no grounds historically on which I can object to the statement that Christ resurrected a dead man, must I therefore consider it true that God has a son in His own image? . . . If I have no grounds historically on which I can deny that Christ rose from the dead, must I therefore consider it true that this resurrected Christ was the son of God? . . . To jump from that historical truth to an entirely different class of truths, and to ask me to alter all my metaphysical and moral concepts accordingly . . . if that is not a 'transformation to another kind' (μετάβασις εἰς ἄλλο γένος), then I do not know what else Aristotle meant by this term. . . . This is the ugly, wide ditch over which I cannot leap, however often and earnestly I try. If anyone can help me over, I pray, I conjure him to do so. God will recompense him."[60]

But neither the theology nor the systematic metaphysics of the eighteenth century contained a principle by virtue of which Lessing's question could really be answered and his demand truly satisfied. He had to pave his own way and attempt himself to fill in that "ugly, wide ditch" which stood in his path. Lessing's last work on the philosophy of religion accomplished this task. In his *Education of Humanity* Lessing created a new synthesis of the historical and the rational. The historical is no longer opposed to the rational; it is rather the way to the realization of the rational and the real, indeed the only possible place of its fulfillment. The elements, which Leibniz's analytical mind had separated with such incomparable precision and clarity, now tend toward reconciliation. For religion, according to Lessing, belongs neither to the sphere of the necessary and eternal nor to that of the merely accidental and temporal. It is both in one; it is the manifestation of the infinite in the finite, of the eternal and rational in the temporal process of becoming. With this thought and with its development in the *Education of Humanity*, Lessing has reached the turning-point of the real philosophy of the Enlightenment. Neither theological "neologism" nor academic rationalism could follow him along this path. For both these movements conceive "reason" as "analytical identity";[61] both see the unity and truth of reason in its uniformity, without which such unity would be impossible. Especially characteristic and illuminating for an understanding

---

[60] Lessing, "Über den Beweis des Geistes und der Kraft," *Schriften*, ed. Lachmann-Muncker, vol. XIII, pp. 5 ff.

[61] Cf. above ch. I, pp. 15 ff.

of this intellectual conflict is Mendelssohn's position with respect to Lessing's fundamental idea. Mendelssohn writes in his *Jerusalem*: "I for my part have no idea of the education of humanity with which I know not what historian fired the imagination of my late friend Lessing. Progress is for the individual whom Providence has destined to pass a portion of his eternity here on earth. . . . But that all mankind should always progress with the passage of time and perfect itself, this does not seem to me to have been the purpose of Providence; it is not at any rate so necessary for preserving the idea of God's Providence as one usually thinks." For Mendelssohn and typical Enlightenment philosophy as he embodies it, it remained to the last inconceivable that the attainment of the highest human goal could be entrusted to so unreliable a guide as history with all its irrationalities, its constant vacillations and errors. This philosophy shuns the arbitrary vicissitudes of history, taking refuge in the inviolable, eternal laws of reason. But Lessing in truth no longer recognizes any such reason. He always had been the great rationalist, and he remained so to the last; but he replaces analytical reason with synthetic reason, and static reason with dynamic reason. Reason does not exclude motion; it seeks rather to understand the immanent law of motion. It is reason itself that now plunges into the stream of becoming, not in order to be seized and carried along by its swirls but in order to find here its own security and to assert its stability and constancy. In this idea of reason we have the dawn of a new conception of the nature and truth of history which could not achieve maturity, perfection, and confirmation in the realm of theology and metaphysics. It is Herder who takes the last and decisive step in this development when he directs his question at historical reality as a whole and tries to answer it on the basis of the concrete evidence of its phenomena. But Herder's contribution is only in appearance an isolated achievement. It does not represent a break with the thought of the Enlightenment but evolves slowly and steadily from this thought and matures on its soil. The problem of history for the philosophy of the Enlightenment arises in the field of religious phenomena, and it is here that this problem first became urgent. Enlightenment thought could not, however, stop with this beginning; it was forced to draw new conclusions and to make new demands, which in turn opened up the whole horizon of the historical world.

CHAPTER V

The Conquest of the Historical World

THE common opinion that the eighteenth century was an "unhistorical" century, is not and cannot be historically justified. This opinion is rather a battle cry coined by the Romantic Movement when it entered the field against the philosophy of the Enlightenment. But if we examine this campaign more closely, it soon appears that the Enlightenment had forged the weapons for it. The concept of historical cultures, which Romanticism summons up against the Enlightenment and under whose banner it disputes the intellectual presuppositions of the preceding century, was discovered only as a result of the effectiveness of those presuppositions, that is to say, as a result of the ideas and ideals of the Enlightenment. Without the aid of the philosophy of the Enlightenment and without its intellectual heritage, Romanticism could not have achieved and maintained its own position. However remote from the Enlightenment the Romantic view of the content of history—its material "philosophy of history"—may be, in method it remains dependent on, and most deeply indebted to, the Enlightenment. For it was the eighteenth century which raised the central philosophical problem in this field of knowledge. It inquires concerning the "conditions of the possibility" of history, just as it inquires concerning the conditions of the possibility of natural science. To be sure, the eighteenth century seeks only to establish these conditions in preliminary outline. It tries to grasp the meaning of history by endeavoring to gain a clear and distinct concept of it, to ascertain the relation between the general and the particular, between idea and reality, and between laws and facts, and to draw the exact boundaries between these terms. If Romanticism largely failed to recognize this decisive pioneer work, and if it frequently brushed it aside scornfully, its judgment need no longer influence and dim ours. There is a strange irony in the fact that Romanticism, in the charge it brings against the Enlightenment in the name of history, makes the same mistake of which it accuses its opponent. Parts suddenly seem to be exchanged, and a complete dialectical reversal appears to take place. For Romanticism, which is incomparably superior to the eighteenth century in the breadth of its historical horizon and in its gift of the historical sense, loses its advantage in the very moment when it seeks to place this century in proper historical perspective. This movement, which devotes itself so whole-heartedly to the past in order to grasp its pristine reality, fails to live up to its ideal when it encounters that past with which it is still in direct contact. The principle which it establishes for the historically remote proves unmanageable when applied to the immediate past. Romanticism was historically blind to the generation of its own fathers. It never attempted to judge the Enlightenment by its own standards, and it was unable to view without polemical bias the conception of the historical world which the eighteenth century had formulated. And this polemical bias not infrequently approaches caricature. It was not until the period following Romanticism that this distortion was corrected. This period had had enough of the Romantic spirit, yet it firmly upheld the postulate of historicity which that spirit had established. It had also gained proper perspective in regard to the eighteenth century and so could now, as it were, extend the benefits of the historical approach to that age as well. Dilthey in his essay, "The Eighteenth Century and the Historical World,"[1] was one of the first to bestow this benefit in full measure on the epoch of the Enlightenment. Though this essay succeeded in dispelling the popular error concerning the unhistorical and anti-historical spirit of the eighteenth century, the concrete problem which arises at this point is still far from solved. For it is not sufficient simply to add the historical sense as a necessary and indispensable feature of the total picture of the Enlightenment; the specific tendency of the new force which now appears must be determined and its precise effect traced. The eighteenth century conception of history is less a finished form with clear outlines than a force exerting its in-

[1] "Das achtzehnte Jahrhundert und die geschichtliche Welt," first published in the *Deutsche Rundschau*, August and September 1901; now available in *Gesammelte Schriften*, vol. III (1927), pp. 209 ff.

fluence in all directions. The manner in which this force starts at a certain point in the sphere of theology and spreads from there until it pervades progressively all the fields of knowledge, is the subject of this chapter.

1

The philosophy of the eighteenth century from the outset treats the problems of nature and history as an indivisible unity. It tries to attack both types of problem with the same intellectual tools; it endeavors to ask the same questions and to apply the same universal method of "reason" to nature and to history. Above all, scientific and historical knowledge in their new form now encounter a common opponent. In both cases a purely immanent intellectual foundation is required; natural scientists and historians attempt to leave nature and history in their own spheres and to establish them on their own soil. Science as such refuses to recognize an absolutely supernatural or an absolutely super-historical sphere. We have already seen how a new form of the concept of God and of theology, and a new form of religiosity, spring from this refusal. The view of the theological innovators, the "neologists," of the eighteenth century is always based on the concept of and the demand for historical criticism of religious sources. In Germany, Mosheim and Michaelis, Ernesti and Semler became the real teachers of the generation of "neologists." History bears the torch for the Enlightenment; it frees the "neologists" from the bonds of Scripture dogmatically interpreted and of the orthodoxy of the preceding centuries.[2] But the relation to history was of course not so simple and unambiguous as in the field of natural science. For eighteenth century philosophy looked upon this field as an old and recognized possession. Here the decisive step had been taken at the time of the Renaissance; Galileo's "new science" had asserted and demonstrated the value and independence of scientific thought. Like Kant every philosopher of the Enlightenment could treat mathematical physics as a "fact" whose

[2] Cf. above pp. 176 ff. For a more detailed treatment see Aner, *op.cit.*, pp. 204 ff., 233, 309, and *passim*.

possibility could, to be sure, become an epistemological problem but whose reality remained unchallenged and unshakable. In the case of history, however, the task was different and more difficult. For here it was not possible to start with a scientific fact which in the nature of its certainty and the firmness of its foundation could be compared with theoretical physics. The world of historical phenomena had to be conquered and conceptually established in one and the same process of thought. It is clear that such a task could not be solved at once, but required long and laborious preparations. These preparations summoned up all the intellectual powers of the Enlightenment and proved the efficacy of these powers in a new field. The philosophy of the Enlightenment had to become creative and to produce; it could not be content with epitomizing and systematizing scientific results furnished by the various special disciplines; it had to accomplish something itself and to do the work of a basic science in a broad field. In natural science Voltaire is only the literary disciple of Newton and the popularizer of his ideas and principles; but in the field of history he ventures to formulate an original and independent conception, a new methodological plan, for which he paves the way in his *Essay on Manners*. All great historical works of the eighteenth century were henceforth written under the influence of this philosophical achievement. As in France Turgot and Condorcet are influenced by Voltaire, similarly in England Hume, Gibbon, and Robertson take Voltaire as their model. And Hume is a concrete illustration of the close personal union between history and philosophy. The epoch of "philosophical historiography" which begins in the eighteenth century endeavors to balance these two elements. It by no means subjects the writing of history one-sidedly to the constructive force of philosophy; it seeks rather to derive new philosophical problems immediately from history, from the vital wealth of historical detail. The exchange of ideas which is initiated in this way now steadily grows in intensity and in scope, and it proves fruitful for both philosophy and history. Just as mathematics becomes the prototype of exact knowledge, so history now becomes the methodological model from which the eighteenth century acquires new understanding for the general task and the specific structure of the abstract sciences. Here again the first step consisted in emancipating these sciences from the tutelage of theology. In permitting the use of historical method to an increasing degree and in treating the history of dogmatics and of the church as its own field, theology had recognized an ally which was to prove stronger than itself, and which in the end was to challenge it on its own grounds. Friendly competition turns into a controversy, and from this controversy the new form of history and of the abstract sciences develops.

The beginnings of this movement can, philosophically, be traced back as far as the seventeenth century. Cartesianism indeed, with its exclusively rational tendency, remained aloof from the sphere of history. According to this philosophy, nothing merely factual can claim any real certainty, and no kind of factual knowledge can be compared in value to the clear and distinct knowledge of logic, to pure mathematics, and to the exact natural sciences. Malebranche's thought also clings strictly to this rule; he too declares that only that belongs to philosophical knowledge which "could have been known by Adam." In Bayle, however, general methodology undergoes a change. In his first philosophical writings Bayle is a confirmed Cartesian, and he never ceased to admire Cartesian physics. But his method of doubt follows a new direction and sets up a new goal. Descartes' doubt is dominated by the principle that we cannot trust any source of certainty which has deceived us even once, or which involves the possibility of such deception. Measured by this standard, not only the testimony of sense perception, but all knowledge not strictly demonstrable, not reducible to self-evident axioms and logical proof, is to be rejected. The entire dimension of the historical is thus eliminated from the field of the Cartesian ideal of knowledge. No factual knowledge can lead to this ideal, to genuine wisdom (*sapientia universalis*). With respect to history Cartesian doubt retains a purely negative character; it rejects and ejects. Bayle, however, does not deny the factual as such; on the contrary, he makes it the real model of his doctrine of science. The accumulation of well established facts is for Bayle the Archimedean point on which he seeks to base all knowledge. He thus becomes the first confirmed and consistent "positivist" in the midst of a strictly rational and rationalistic century. D'Alembert's comment that metaphysics must either be a science of facts or it must become a science of illusions could also have been spoken by Bayle. He rejects all knowledge of the first absolute "grounds" of being; he merely wants to survey the phenomena as such and within this sphere to distinguish clearly and sharply between the certain and the uncertain, between the probable and the erroneous. He does not, therefore, direct his doubt against the historical; he uses it rather as an instrument for discovering the truth of history and for reaching that form of certainty of which history is capable. In this process of testing historical truth Bayle is indefatigable and insatiable. He is motivated by a desire to survey the factual and given world of history and to orient himself here. Within this world nothing is indifferent or unimportant; there are scarcely any gradations of value and significance. It is no accident that he chose for his critical work the form of a *Historical and Critical Dictionary*. For the dictionary allows the spirit of mere co-ordination to prevail by contrast with the spirit of subordination that dominates the rational systems. In Bayle there is no hierarchy of concepts, no deductive derivation of one concept from another, but rather a simple aggregation of materials, each of which is as significant as any other and shares with it an equal claim to complete and exhaustive treatment. Nor is Bayle ever discriminating in his acquisition of materials. In this matter he entertains scarcely any scruples and doubts whatever; he never follows a definite plan assigning limits to the various types of material and distinguishing the important from the unimportant, the relevant from the irrelevant. Frequently the most insignificant subjects, or even completely nonsensical ones, are treated in the *Dictionary* elaborately and conscientiously, while most important matters are neglected. It is not the importance of the things themselves which is decisive in the selection of materials, but the accidental, particular preference and subjective interest of Bayle, the scholar, in the most remote facts, in antiquarian details, and in historical curiosities. Bayle was well aware of this characteristic of his, and he often mentions it in autobiographical remarks in his writings and in his personal letters. In a letter to his brother, for instance, he remarks: "I know very well that my insatiable love of novelties is one of those obstinate maladies against which all remedies fail. It is a genuine hydropsy. The more you give it, the more it wants."[3] Love of the factual for its own sake, devotion to detail, are highly developed traits of Bayle's nature. This conception of knowledge and of its goal is deliberately opposed to the ideal of exact logical knowledge. However much the latter may surpass merely empirical historical knowledge in exactness and rigor, it must always pay for this advantage by an essential shortcoming. Precisely its strictly logical character prevents it from direct contact with reality and excludes reality from its own sphere. The formal conclusiveness of mathematical demonstrations cannot compensate for the fact that their application to the concrete reality of things remains basically dubious. Historical knowledge belongs to another kind of certainty (*genre de certitude*) than mathematical knowledge, but within its own kind the certainty of historical knowledge is capable of constant improvement. Metaphysically, it is more certain that an individual named Cicero lived than that any object as defined by pure mathematics really exists in the nature of things.[4]

Such considerations as these give access to the world of fact, but no principle has as yet been developed for taking real possession of this world and for controlling it intellectually. For historical knowledge still represents a mere aggregate, an accumulation of unrelated details exhibiting no inner order. History lies before Bayle like an enormous heap of ruins, and there is no possibility of mastering this abundance of material. To keep

[3] The translators have been unable to identify the source of this quotation. The German edition gave the following reference: "Letter to his brother, February 27, 1773, in 'Lettres de Bayle a sa famille' in the appendix to his *Oeuvres diverses*, The Hague, 1737, vol. I." Since Bayle died in 1706 and the letters appeared in 1737, the year is obviously wrong. Nor is there any letter in this collection dated February 27.

[4] *Projet d'un Dictionnaire Critique* (Dissertation à du Rondel), Rotterdam, 1692; cf. Delvolvé, *Religion Critique et philosophie positive chez Pierre Bayle*, Paris, 1906, pp. 226 ff.

up with the rising tide of specialized knowledge would require the inexhaustible assimilative powers of Bayle himself. Even the external framework of the *Dictionary* proves insufficient for this task. The original core of articles is reinforced by an army of notes and elucidations which finally completely bury the original text. Bayle's real interest is seldom connected with the main articles and with the important points of these articles; it usually manifests itself rather in the apparently irrelevant material. Again and again he luxuriates in this material. For such, to his way of thinking, is the new task of the historian. He does not fear the objection that he is indulging in trifles, nor does he shun the title of "most minute explorer of most minute things" (*minutissimarum rerum minutissimus scrutator*). He declares that his mode of treatment of materials is not an indulgence of personal inclination but the result of deliberate intention.[5] For modern historiography surpasses its ancient predecessor in this very matter of investigating and critically weighing every feature of a historical phenomenon rather than being content to sketch the broad outline as the ancient historiographer did.[6] A philosophical approach to history or a teleological interpretation of historical phenomena is far from Bayle's intention. His profound pessimism prevents him from finding anywhere in history evidence of a uniform plan or of a rational purpose. A glance at the facts, at the real history of mankind, suffices to cure us of all such premature speculation and system-building, for the facts teach us that history was in reality never anything else but an accumulation of the crimes and misfortunes of the human race.[7] Obviously, the more sharply we scrutinize the parts, the farther we are from a clear comprehension of the whole. Knowledge of details does not add up to an understanding of the whole; on the contrary, it destroys all hope of ever attaining such understanding.

Yet from this dissolution and disintegration of the historical world Bayle brings forth, nevertheless, a new, positive, and highly fruitful general conception. The parts unite again and

---

[5] "Dissertation à du Rondel," *op.cit.*

[6] *Dictionnaire*, article "Archelaus"; cf. Delvolvé, *op.cit.*, p. 226.

[7] *Ibid.*, article "Manichéens," Remarque D.

crystallize around a firm nucleus. This nucleus arises in that
Bayle understands the nature of the "fact" not only in a material
but in a formal sense, and in that he looks upon this nature both
as a problem of method and of content. It is through this insight
that Bayle achieves originality and importance in the history of
thought. Hardly a single "fact" which Bayle's *Dictionary* culled
with truly heroic labor is of real interest to us today from the
point of view of its content. But what gives this work lasting
value, nevertheless, is the circumstance that the pure concept of
the factual is here grasped as a profound problem. Bayle no
longer looks upon individual facts as the solid bricks out of
which the historian constructs his edifice; he is fascinated rather
by the intellectual labor which goes toward the acquisition of
these bricks. With unsurpassed clarity, with the most subtle
analytical art, Bayle dissects the complex of conditions on which
every factual judgment as such is based. And with this knowledge he becomes a logician of history. For a "fact" is no longer
the beginning of historical knowledge, but in a certain sense its
end; it is the "point toward which" (*terminus ad quem*), not the
"point from which" (*terminus a quo*) such knowledge proceeds.
Bayle does not take the fact as a starting-point, but as his goal;
he seeks to prepare the way to a "truth of facts." One should not
imagine that this truth is tangible, that it can be grasped in
immediate sense experience; it can only be the result of an
operation no less complex, subtle, and precise than the most
difficult mathematical operation. For it is only by the finest
sifting, by the most painstaking examination and evaluation of
the bits of evidence that the kernel of an historical "fact" can be
isolated.

The essential value of Bayle's conception of history is that he
did not lay down this requirement in the abstract, but that he
illustrated it to the last detail in actual practice. Never before
had criticism of tradition been carried out with such severity
and such inexorable ardor and exactness. Bayle is indefatigable
in revealing the gaps, obscurities, and contradictions of history.
In this process his real genius manifests itself. Bayle's genius,
paradoxically enough, does not lie in the discovery of the true

but in the discovery of the false. The external plan of the *Dictionary* and its original literary conception illustrate this. His first idea was not to write an encyclopaedia of knowledge but rather a record of errors. "About the month of November 1690," Bayle states in a letter, "I formed a plan to compose a *Critical Dictionary* which would contain a collection of the mistakes which have been made by compilers of dictionaries as well as by other writers, and which would summarize under each name of a man or a city the mistakes concerning that man or city."[8] Bayle's intellectual superiority and his scholarly and literary virtuosity found their proper medium here. In this activity his eagerness for the chase celebrates its real triumphs; his delight is never greater than when he comes upon the track of some hidden error which had survived through the centuries. The magnitude of the error is an almost indifferent matter; its mere existence and quality are sufficient to fascinate Bayle. Error must be pursued to its last retreat whether its object is great or small, sublime or humble, important or trifling. Bayle's critical fanaticism concerns itself with the most indifferent matters; in fact, it is precisely these which inflame his enthusiasm over and over again. For here the specific form of historical error, irrespective of its content, can be observed. Here we see how the most insignificant error in the transmission and continuation of tradition can have the most fateful consequences, and how it can lead to the most radical falsification of the true situation. Every such mistake must therefore be ruthlessly exposed, and this purely negative work of the historian must not weaken at any point or shun any detail however unmeaningful it may appear. No alteration of a report escapes his scrutiny; no quotation is admitted which is inaccurate or based on mere memory without reference to the real source.[9] Requirements like these made Bayle the originator of the ideal of historical accuracy. But so far as his real philosophical achievement is

[8] Letter to Naudis, May 22, 1692, "Lettres de Bayle à sa famille," *Oeuvres diverses*, vol. I, appendix, p. 161.

[9] "It is not to be tolerated that a man who quotes should in the least alter the testimony of his witness." *Nouvelles de la République des Lettres, Oeuvres diverses*, vol. I, p. 530. Cf. *Dictionary*, article on Pericles, Remark E. See also Lacoste, *Bayle. Nouvelliste et critique littéraire*, Paris, 1929, pp. 27 ff.

concerned, such accuracy is a means, not an end in itself. If one wishes to understand the goal toward which Bayle's conception of history strives, one must compare his work with the last great attempt at a purely theological presentation of history, namely, with Bossuet's *Discourse on Universal History*. Here once more is a sublime plan of history, a religious interpretation of the universe. But this bold structure rests on feet of clay so far as its empirical foundations are concerned. For the truth of the facts on which Bossuet builds can only be assured by a logically vicious circle. The authority of all historical facts, according to Bossuet, is based on the authority of the Bible. The authority of the Bible in turn rests on that of the Church, whose authority rests on tradition. Thus tradition becomes the foundation of all historical certainty—but the content and value of tradition can only be proved on the basis of historical evidence. Bayle is the first modern thinker to reveal this circle with ruthless critical subtlety and to point untiringly to its fateful consequences. In this respect Bayle accomplished scarcely less for history than Galileo did for natural science. Just as Galileo demands complete independence of the Bible in the interpretation of natural phenomena, and as he realizes and justifies this demand by his method, so Bayle lays down this requirement in the field of history. It is he who carries out the "Copernican revolution" in the realm of historical science. For he no longer bases history on some dogmatically given objective content which he finds in the Bible or in the doctrine of the Church; he returns rather to the subjective origins and conditions of this truth. The criticism of historical sources, which was at first his sole purpose, expands as he proceeds until it finally becomes a sort of "Critique of Historical Reason." According to Bayle, nothing is more erroneous and harmful than the prejudice that historical truth can and must be accepted like a stamped coin on trust and faith. It is rather the function of reason to stamp its own coin and always to examine each individual product with the greatest care. "Do you think, then, that there is any honest gain from trafficking in hearsay? Tradition, O fool, is indeed a chimera! Judgment is required; reason alone can rescue you from the bondage of belief—reason which you have already renounced."[10] These lines from Goethe's *West-Eastern Divan* characterize perhaps most clearly and pregnantly the gist of Bayle's contribution and its real trend. His sharp and unsparing analytical mind freed history once and for all from the bonds of creed and placed it on an independent footing. Bayle begins with the criticism of theological tradition, but goes further and extends his investigation to include the whole body of secular history as well. In taking this step he becomes the forerunner of the eighteenth century which found in his *Historical and Critical Dictionary* not only an inexhaustible treasury of knowledge, but an incomparable intellectual and dialectical exercise. From Bayle the philosophy of the Enlightenment learned to formulate its own problems; in his *Dictionary* it found already forged the weapons required for the emancipation of historical thinking. Bayle became indeed not only the logician of the new historical science but also its ethical teacher. He is the promulgator and the living embodiment of all the virtues of the true historian. He repeatedly declares that history is to be touched only with unsoiled hands, that the presentation of historical phenomena must not be hindered by any prejudice or distorted by any religious or political bias.[11] "All those who know the laws of history, will agree that a historian who wishes to fulfill his tasks faithfully must free himself of the spirit of flattery and slander. He must, as far as possible, adopt the state of mind of the Stoic who is moved by no passion. Impervious to all else, he must heed solely the interests of the truth, to which he must sacrifice resentment aroused by an injustice as well as recollection of favors—and even his love of country. He must forget that he belongs to any particular country, that he was brought up in any particular faith, that he is indebted to this person or to

[10] "Glaubst du denn: von Mund zu Ohr
　　Sei ein redlicher Gewinnst?
　　Überliefrung, o du Thor,
　　Ist auch wohl ein Hirngespinst!
　　Nun geht erst das Urtheil an;
　　Dich vermag aus Glaubensketten
　　Der Verstand allein zu retten,
　　Dem du schon Verzicht gethan."—*West-östlicher Divan*, Rendsch Nameh. Buch des Unmuths, "Wanderers Gemüthsruhe."
[11] *Dictionnaire*, article "Usson," Remark F.

that, and that he has these or those parents and friends. A historian in these respects is like Melchizedech, without father, without mother, and without genealogy. If he is asked: 'Whence art thou?' he must reply: 'I am neither a Frenchman nor a German, neither an Englishman nor a Spaniard, etc.; I am a citizen of the world; I am not in the service of the Emperor, nor in that of the King of France, but only in the service of Truth. She is my queen; to her alone have I sworn the oath of obedience.' " Through these sentiments and the ethical imperative on which they are based Bayle became the spiritual leader of the Enlightenment. He anticipated its "idea of a general history with a cosmological design," and he gave this idea its first classical expression.

2

Bayle does not give us a philosophy of history in the strict sense; in fact, as we have seen, in the light of his general conception of history and his methodological premises, he could not even strive for such a philosophy. The first to point the way to a philosophy of history in the eighteenth century was Giambattista Vico, whose *Principles of a New Science of the Common Nature of Nations* is the first systematic delineation of this field of knowledge. But this work, which was conceived in deliberate opposition to Descartes and was destined to remove rationalism from historiography and which is based rather on the logic of phantasy than on the logic of clear and distinct ideas, exerted no influence on the philosophy of the Enlightenment. It remained in obscurity until Herder late in the century brought it to light again. Within the era of the Enlightenment the first decisive attempt at the foundation of a philosophy of history is made by Montesquieu in *The Spirit of the Laws*. This work ushers in a new epoch. It did not arise directly from historical interest; Bayle's interest and delight in factual detail is foreign to Montesquieu. The very title of Montesquieu's book shows that he is concerned with the spirit of the *laws*, not with that of the facts. The facts are sought, sifted, and tested by Montesquieu not for their own sake but for the sake of the laws which they illustrate and express. Laws are comprehensible only in concrete situations; only in such situations can they be described and demonstrated. On the other hand, these tangible situations take on real shape and meaning only when we employ them as examples, as paradigms, illustrating general connections. Like Bayle, Montesquieu shows a decided love of detail; by extensive studies and travel he tries to acquaint himself with the minutiae of his subject. His delight in particulars is so great that at times his illustrative anecdotes overshadow the main lines of thought and threaten to make them unrecognizable. But with respect to content all this material is dominated by a strictly logical principle. In the preface of his masterpiece Montesquieu writes: "I began to examine men and I believed that in the infinite variety of their laws and customs they were not guided solely by their whims. I formulated principles, and I then saw individual cases fitting these principles as if of themselves, the history of all nations being only the consequence of these principles and every special law bound to another law, or depending on another more general law."

Factuality as such is thus no longer the guiding star of Montesquieu's study. It is simply his medium for attaining an understanding of something else which he is seeking. One can say of Montesquieu that he is the first thinker to grasp and to express clearly the concept of "ideal types" in history. *The Spirit of the Laws* is a political and sociological doctrine of types. Montesquieu proposes to show that the forms of government which we call republic, aristocracy, monarchy, and despotism are not mere aggregates of accidentally acquired properties but that each of these forms is, as it were, pre-formed, the expression of a certain structure. This structure remains concealed from us as long as we merely observe political and social phenomena. For no configuration of phenomena resembles any other; they offer us complete heterogeneity and almost unlimited variety. But this illusion vanishes as soon as we learn to go back from appearances to principles, from the diversity of empirical shapes to the forming forces. Now we recognize among many instances of republics the type of the republic, and among the countless monarchies of history we find the type of the monarchy. In particular Montesquieu tries to show that the principle on which the republic rests and to which it owes its existence is civic virtue, while monarchy depends on the principle of honor, and despotism on fear. Here we see as the essential distinction between forms of government the difference in the spiritual and moral impulses which shape and motivate each commonwealth. Montesquieu states: "Between the nature of a government and its principle there is this difference that its nature makes it what it is, while its principle determines its behavior. The one consists in its special structure; the other in the human passions which set it in motion."[12] Montesquieu is fully aware of the peculiar logical nature of the basic concepts introduced in this manner. He considers them by no means simply as abstract concepts possessing a purely generic generality, which are only designed to single out and crystallize certain common features found among actual phenomena. Montesquieu attempts rather to establish by these concepts, beyond any such empirical generality, a universality of meaning which is expressed in the individual forms of government; he is endeavoring to elicit the inner rule by which these governments are guided. The fact that this rule is not perfectly expressed in any particular instance of government, and that it cannot be completely and exactly realized in any historical case, in no way lessens its importance. If Montesquieu assigns to each of the various forms of government its own principle, and if he has the nature of the republic depend on virtue, of the monarchy on honor, etc., this nature must never be confused with concrete empirical existence, for it expresses rather an ideal than an actuality.[13] Accordingly, the objections which can be raised against the application of Montesquieu's system are not necessarily valid objections to his fundamental ideas. However imperfect the empirical groundwork on which he seeks to base this system may appear today in the light of our broadened historical hori-

[12] *L'Esprit des Lois*, Book III, ch. 1; cf. also chs. II ff.

[13] Cf. *L'Esprit des Lois*, Book III, ch. 11: "Such are the principles of the three governments: which does not signify that in a certain republic one is virtuous, but that one ought to be so. This does not prove that in a certain monarchy one has a sense of honor, and that in a particular despotic state one has a sense of fear, but that one ought to have such: *without these qualities the government will be imperfect.*"

zon, this fact need not prevent us from recognizing that Montesquieu in fact grasped a new and fruitful principle and founded a new method in social science. The method of ideal types, which he introduces and first applies effectively, has never been abandoned; on the contrary, it reached its full development only in the sociology of the nineteenth and twentieth centuries. On this method Montesquieu founds the doctrine that all elements which constitute a certain commonwealth stand in a strictly correlative relationship to one another. They are not merely the elements of a sum, but interdependent forces whose reciprocal action depends on the form of the whole. This interaction and structural arrangement can be shown to exist in the minutest details. The kind of education and justice, the form of marriage and family, the whole structure of domestic and foreign politics, depend in a certain way on the fundamental form of the state; these aspects of the state cannot be arbitrarily altered without affecting the form of the state and finally destroying it. For corruption in a commonwealth does not begin in particular activities but with the destruction of its inner principle: "The corruption of every government begins almost always with the corruption of its principles."[14] As long as the principle of a form of government as such is preserved, as long as it is healthy in itself, it has nothing to fear; and the shortcomings of its individual institutions and laws are not injurious. On the other hand, if the principle deteriorates, if the inner moving force weakens, then the best laws can offer no protection. "Once the principles of a government are corrupt, the best laws become bad and turn against the state; when the principles are healthy, bad laws have the effect of good ones. The force of the principle carries everything with it. . . . Few laws are not good when the state has not lost its principles; and, as Epicurus says in speaking of riches, it is not the liquor which is corrupt, but the vase."[15]

The outlines of a philosophy of politics have now been sketched, but the foundation of a philosophy of history has not of course been laid. For the ideal types which Montesquieu de-

---

[14] *L'Esprit des Lois*, Book VIII, ch. I.
[15] *Ibid.*, Book VIII, ch. II.

picts are purely static forms; they offer a principle of explanation for the structure of the social body but they contain no means of revealing the functioning of this body. However, Montesquieu does not doubt that his method will also prove fruitful in explaining this problem too. For he is convinced that the functioning process, like the structure, is not an aggregate or a sequence of individual and unrelated events but that it will also reveal certain characteristic tendencies. What we term history, seen from without, may nowhere exhibit such tendencies; it may seem like a tangle of accidents. But the further one penetrates into the real depth of the phenomena, the more this illusion vanishes. In this way the chaos and conflict of individual events is resolved, and the phenomena can be reduced to a certain foundation by which they can be explained and understood. At the outset of his work Montesquieu asserts: "Those who have said that a blind fatality has produced all the effects we see in the world have uttered a great absurdity; for what greater absurdity could there be than a blind fatality which had brought forth intelligent beings? There is then a primitive reason, and laws are the relations which exist between this reason and individual beings and the relations which exist among the various individuals themselves."[16] It often seems indeed as if a mere accident decided the fate of a people and determined its rise or fall. But closer examination discloses a different picture. "It is not fortune which rules the world. . . . There are general, intellectual as well as physical causes active in every monarchy which bring about its rise, preservation, or fall. All accidents are subject to these causes, and whenever an accidental battle, that is, a particular cause, has destroyed a state, a general cause also existed which led to the fall of this state as a result of a single battle. In short, it is the general pace of things which draws all particular events along with it."[17] Physical circumstances also affect this general trend; and Montesquieu is one of the first to indicate the importance of this trend and to show the connection existing between the form of government and

---

[16] *Ibid.*, Book I, ch. I.

[17] *Considérations sur les Causes de la Grandeur des Romains et de leur décadence,* ch. XVIII.

laws of a country and its climate and soil. But here too he rejects a simple derivation from the purely physical factors and he subordinates the material to the spiritual causes. Not every soil and climate are suitable and possible for a given form of government; yet this form, on the other hand, is not merely the result of physical conditions. It is the business of the legislator to bring about a proper and wholesome adjustment between the form of government and the prevailing physical circumstances. Bad legislators submit to unfavorable climatic conditions; good legislators recognize these disadvantages and counteract them by spiritual and moral forces. "The more physical causes produce inertia in men, the more moral causes should wake them from this state."[18] Man is not simply subject to the forces of nature; he recognizes these forces and by his knowledge of them is able to guide them toward a goal of his own choosing and to bring about an equilibrium which assures the preservation of the community. "If it is true that mentalities and passions are extremely different in different climates, then the laws must correspond to the difference of passions and to the difference in mentality."[19] The general course and trend of the history of man shows, then, that there is a law in man comparable in rigor and certainty to the laws of nature. At our present stage of development, to be sure, the moral world lacks the order of the physical world. For although the moral world has definite and immutable laws, it does not seem to follow them as persistently as physical nature follows its laws. The reason is that individual creatures endowed with understanding are limited and hence subject to error, and that they also act according to their own ideas and wills. Thus they do not always obey their fundamental laws or the rules they have laid down for themselves.[20] But Montesquieu is a man of his time, a genuine thinker of the Enlightenment, in that he expects from the advancement of knowledge a new moral order and a new orientation of the political and social history of man. And this is what brings him to the philosophy of history. From a knowledge of the general principles and moving forces

[18] *L'Esprit des Lois*, Book XIV, ch. 15; cf. also XVI, 12.
[19] *Ibid.*, Book XIV, ch. 1.   [20] *Ibid.*, I, 1.

of history he looks for the possibility of their effective control in the future. Man is not simply subject to the necessity of nature; he can and should shape his own destiny as a free agent, and bring about his destined and proper future. But the mere wish remains powerless as long as it is not guided by sure insight. Such insight can result only from a concentration of all the energies of the mind; it requires the most painstaking observation of empirical and historical details, just as logical analysis does when it offers various possibilities and distinguishes clearly among these. Montesquieu is equally masterful in the solution of both problems. Of all the thinkers of his circle he has the most profound historical sense, the purest intuition of the manifold forms of historical phenomena. He once said of himself that when he came to speak of ancient history, he tried to assume the spirit of antiquity and to become an ancient himself.[21] His eye for the particular and his love of detail protected him, even in his purely theoretical works, from any one-sided doctrinairism. He always successfully resisted any merely schematic presentation, any reduction of the variety of forms to an absolutely rigid pattern. In the *Spirit of the Laws* Montesquieu gives a striking characterization of this danger. In his account of the English constitution, which he admires as a political model, he emphasizes, nevertheless, that he by no means desires to urge the adoption of the same form by other countries and to assert that it is the sole standard: "How should I say that, I who believe that the very excess of reason is not always desirable and that men almost always accommodate themselves better to the mean than to the extreme?"[22] Even in his theoretical writings Montesquieu tries to hit upon the proper middle course; he tries to preserve an equilibrium between experience and reason. It is thanks to this gift that his influence has extended far beyond the narrower circle of the Enlightenment. Montesquieu's great work not only became the model for the Encyclopaedists' conception of history, but it cast its spell on the most outspoken opponent and critic of this conception. Herder attacked Montesquieu's method and his premises, but

[21] Cf. Sorel, *Montesquieu*, Paris, 1887, pp. 151 ff.
[22] *L'Esprit des Lois*, XI, 6.

he also admired his "noble gigantic work" and endeavored to imitate it in his own writings.[23]

3

When Lessing in the year 1753 announces Voltaire's *Essay on Manners* in the *Vossische Zeitung*, he begins his review with the remark that the noblest study of mankind is man but that there are two approaches to this study. "Either one considers man in particular or in general. Of the first approach one can hardly say it is the noblest pursuit of man. What is it to know man in particular? It is to know fools and scoundrels. . . . The case is quite different with the study of man in general. Here he exhibits greatness and his divine origin. Consider what enterprises man accomplishes, how he daily extends the limits of his understanding, what wisdom prevails in his laws, what ambition inspires his monuments. . . . No writer yet has selected this subject as his special theme, so that the present author can rightly boast: 'I was the first to take free steps through empty space' (*libera per vacuum posui vestigia princeps*)."[24]

In these words Lessing, who was Voltaire's greatest opponent and sharpest critic in the eighteenth century, did full justice to the importance of Voltaire's historical work. He hit the mark in this critique and expressed the fundamental trend of Voltaire's historical writing. For it is Voltaire's intention to raise history above the "all-too-human," the accidental, and merely personal. His aim is not to depict unique incidents, but to express the "spirit of the times" and the "spirit of nations." It is not the sequence of events which interests Voltaire, but the progress of civilization and the inner relationship of its various elements. The first draft of the *Essay on Manners* was intended, as Voltaire states, for the Marquise de Châtelet, who had complained of the disconnected state of historical knowledge as compared with natural science. An analogue of Newtonian science, a reduction of facts to laws, should also be possible in history. But here, as in nature, there can be no thought of any

[23] Cf. Herder, "Auch eine Philosophie der Geschichte zur Bildung der Menschheit," *Werke*, ed. Suphan, vol. v, p. 565.
[24] Lessing, *Schriften*, ed. Lachmann-Muncker, vol. v, p. 143.

knowledge of law until a point of rest has been found in the flux of phenomena. This immutable and self-identical element is not to be found in the course of human destinies which are infinitely variable and changeable; if at all, it can be met with only in human nature. Historians should cease, then, to heed only political events, the rise and fall of great kingdoms, the crumbling of thrones. They should study the human race. The saying: "I am a man"—*homo sum*—should have been the motto of every writer of history. But instead, most historians have done little else than describe battles. The true object of history is the story of the mind, not the tale of facts which are forever being distorted. "My aim has been much less to accumulate a vast quantity of facts, which are always self-contradictory, than to select the most important and best documented facts in order to guide the reader so that he may judge for himself concerning the extinction, revival, and progress of the human spirit, and to enable him to recognize peoples by their customs."[25] As the real weaknesses of previous historiography Voltaire sees, on the one hand, the mythical conception and interpretation of events and on the other, the cult of heroes. These weaknesses are mutually interdependent, representing simply a twofold expression of the same fundamental deficiency. For the cult of heroes, leaders, rulers sprang from this mythologizing tendency of history writers, who still continue to satisfy this appetite. "I do not like heroes; they make too much noise in the world. I hate those conquerors, proud enemies of themselves, who have placed supreme happiness in the horrors of combat, seeking death everywhere and causing a hundred thousand men of their own kind to suffer it. The more radiant their glory, the more odious they are."[26] These are the lines Voltaire

[25] Cf. Voltaire, "Remarques pour Servir de Supplément à l'Essai sur les Moeurs," *Oeuvres*, ed. Lequien, Paris, 1820, vol. XVIII, pp. 429 ff.

[26] "J'aime peu les héros, ils font trop de fracas,
Je hais ces conquérants, fiers ennemis d'eux-mêmes,
Qui dans les horreurs des combats
Ont placé le bonheur suprême,
Cherchant partout la mort, et la faisant souffrir
À cent mille hommes leurs semblables.
Plus leur gloire a d'éclat, plus ils sont haïssables."—Letter of May 26, 1742, *Oeuvres*, ed. Lequien, LI, 119.

wrote to Frederick the Great after his victory at Chotusitz. The center of gravity now moves from political history to cultural history by conscious methodological intention. In this transition we have an underlying tendency which distinguishes Voltaire from Montesquieu. Voltaire's *Essay on Manners* and Montesquieu's masterpiece appeared almost simultaneously and they sprang from similar cultural conditions; yet they pursue different objectives. In Montesquieu political events still occupy the center of the historical world; the state is the main, in fact, the only subject of world history. The spirit of history coincides with the spirit of laws. In Voltaire, on the other hand, the concept of the mind has gained broader scope. It comprises the entire process of inner life, the sum total of the transformations through which humanity must pass before it can arrive at knowledge and consciousness of itself. The real purpose of the *Essay on Manners* is to reveal the gradual progress of mankind toward this goal and the obstacles which must be overcome before it can be reached. If political developments alone are considered, this purpose can never be realized. The progress of mankind can only be understood if one also takes into account the growth of religion, art, science, and philosophy, and in this way sketches a complete picture of the various phases through which the human spirit has had to evolve in order to reach its present state.[27]

But in offering this basic plan for the writing of history Voltaire poses a difficult question. If we consider the matter more closely and analyze its basic presuppositions, we are led to a strange dilemma. Voltaire is the enthusiastic herald of the idea of progress, and it is through this idea that his influence on his own time as well as on following generations has been greatest. Condorcet's *Sketch of a Historic Tableau of the Progress of the Human Spirit* is a direct continuation of Voltaire's ideas and principles. But how, one asks, does Voltaire reconcile his belief

---

[27] This expression of Voltaire's conception of history very closely resembles the author's own view as expressed, for instance, in the conclusion of his *Essay on Man: An Introduction to a Philosophy of Human Culture* (New Haven, Yale University Press, 1944, p. 228): "Human culture taken as a whole may be described as the process of man's progressive self-liberation. Language, art, religion, science, are various phases in this process."—Tr.

in the progress of mankind with his no less strong conviction that mankind has always been basically the same, that its true nature has never changed? If the presupposition of the immutability of the human spirit is correct, then the real substance of this spirit remains aloof from all historical events, and these do not affect its innermost being. Whoever is able to separate the shell from the kernel of historical phenomena, knows that the forces which control and guide history are always and everywhere the same. This view of history which is typical of the Renaissance and is represented by Machiavelli and Lodovico Vives,[28] is retained throughout by Voltaire. He states it expressly in various passages in his historical works. Summing up his total accomplishment at the end of his *Essay on Manners*, Voltaire declares: "As a result of this presentation of the subject, it is clear that everything which belongs intimately to human nature is the same from one end of the universe to the other; that everything that depends on custom is different, and it is accidental if it remains the same. The empire of custom is much more vast than that of nature; it extends over manners and all usages, it sheds variety on the scene of the universe; nature sheds unity there; she establishes everywhere a small number of invariable principles. Thus the basis is everywhere the same, and culture produces diverse fruits."[29] If this is the case, can there be a philosophical history in the strict sense? Does not the illusion of change and development vanish the moment one penetrates beneath the glittering surface of appearances and approaches the underlying principles which are always one and the same? Would not then philosophical insight put an end to history? Can the philosopher take delight in the striking variety of events even though he has recognized it as illusion and realized that it is not derived from nature, but merely from habit? Voltaire's philosophy of history gives us no satisfactory explicit answer to all these questions. The implicit solution which the *Essay on Manners* offers is that Voltaire is never content with an account of mere happenings, but that he connects his presentation directly with an intellectual analysis of phenomena by means of which the accidental is to be

[28] Cf. the author's *Erkenntnisproblem*, vol. I, pp. 164 ff.
[29] *Essai sur les moeurs*, ch. CXCVII, *Oeuvres*, vol. XVIII, p. 425.

separated from the necessary, the permanent from the ephemeral. In this respect Voltaire considers the work of the historian in the same light as that of the natural scientist. The natural scientist and the historian have the same task; amid the confusion and flux of phenomena they seek the hidden law. Neither in history nor in natural science is this law to be considered as a divine plan which assigns to every particular thing its place in the whole. In the knowledge of history as in that of nature we must forego a naive teleology. Such a teleology Voltaire finds in Bossuet's *Discourse on Universal History*, which he admires as a literary masterpiece; but Voltaire objects that Bossuet continually sets false gems in real gold.[30] Genuine critical historiography should perform the same service for history which mathematics has performed for natural science. It should free history from the domination of final causes and lead it back to the real empirical causes. As natural science was emancipated from theology by the knowledge of the mechanical laws of natural processes, the same service is to be performed by psychology for the historical world. And psychological analysis finally determines the real meaning of the idea of progress. It explains and justifies this idea, but it also indicates its limitations and keeps its application well within these bounds. Psychological analysis shows that humanity cannot exceed the limits of its "nature"; but its nature is not given all at once, for it has to evolve gradually and assert itself constantly against obstacles. "Reason" is of course given from the first as a fundamental endowment of man, and it is everywhere one and the same. But reason does not manifest itself externally in this stable and uniform aspect; it hides behind the profusion of customs and habits and succumbs to the weight of prejudice. History shows how reason gradually overcomes these obstacles, how it realizes its true destiny. Hence real progress does not concern humanity as such; it refers only to the objective, empirical manifestation of humanity. But the process by which reason emerges empirically and becomes comprehensible to itself, represents the fundamental meaning of history. History need not raise the metaphysical problem of the origin of

[30] Voltaire, *Le Pyrrhonisme de l'histoire* (1768), ch. II, *Oeuvres*, vol. XXVI, p. 163.

reason, nor can it solve this problem. For reason as such is super-temporal. It is something necessary and eternal; the question of its development is meaningless. History can only show this much: how this eternal entity manifests itself, nevertheless, in time; and how it enters the stream of time and reveals there in gradually increasing purity and perfection its basic and original form.

In this conception of historiography Voltaire has set up the program followed henceforth by all historians of the epoch of the Enlightenment. He himself, to be sure, was unable to carry out this program fully in his *Essay on Manners*; but one must not impute the deficiencies of execution which occur in this work to its underlying systematic conception. Only superficial criticism would point to these deficiencies to demonstrate the basically un-historical attitude of the Enlightenment. For the weaknesses with which Voltaire as a historian has so often been reproached are far less weaknesses of his system than those arising from his personality and temperament. Voltaire is not inclined to pursue the peaceful path of historical exposition through to the end. When he turns to the past, he does so not for the sake of the past but for the sake of the present and the future. History for him is not an end but a means; it is an instrument of self-educa-tion of the human mind. Voltaire does not try simply to reflect and investigate; he demands and passionately anticipates the substance of his demands. For he no longer believes he is merely on the way; he imagines himself very near his goal, and he revels in expectancy and triumph at having attained his goal after so many toils and perplexities. Such personal feelings break into his historical exposition again and again. And the exposition becomes more perfect in the degree that Voltaire rediscovers his own ideals in the past. It reaches its climax in the *Age of Louis XIV*. Voltaire can of course see clearly and distinguish sharply outside this sphere; but his eagerness to judge or to condemn is often too great to permit calm consideration. The philosopher's pride in reason forestalls sober historical judgment. Again and again Voltaire reflects how far superior in true insight and knowledge the classical age of reason is, not only to the Middle Ages but even to the great eras of antiquity. He falls prey here to that naive teleology which as a pure theorist he so strongly rejects and attacks. Just as Bossuet projects his theological ideal into history, so Voltaire projects his philosophical ideal; as the former applies to history the standard of the Bible, so the latter freely applies his rational standards to the past. There is no doubt that such deficiencies impeded the execution of Voltaire's great plan for a truly universal history which was to embrace all cultures, all epochs, and all peoples with equal love. On the other hand, it is undeniable that these deficiencies belong for the most part to the "defects of his virtues." For that which objectively considered appears to be a limitation of his viewpoint, constitutes on the other hand the personal charm of his exposition lending it that individuality and vitality which fascinated his contemporaries. Voltaire is the first thinker of the eighteenth century who recreated and embodied in a classical example the type of the great historical work of art. He lightened history of the ballast of mere antiquarianism and freed it from the form of the mere chronicle. He prides himself especially on this achievement on which he bases his self-esteem as a historian. When in 1740 the Swedish Chaplain Nordberg published his learned account of the reign of Charles XII and in the course of his petty criticism pointed to various errors in Voltaire's *History of Charles XII*, Voltaire countered with satirical magnanimity. In his letter to Nordberg he writes: "It is perhaps an important matter for Europe that one know that the chapel of the castle of Stockholm, which burned down fifty years ago, was situated in the new northern wing of the palace . . . and that on days when sermons were preached the seats were covered with blue tapestry, that some of the seats were of oak, others of walnut. . . . We are quite willing to believe that it is of the utmost importance to be thoroughly informed that there was no counterfeit gold in the dais under which Charles XII was crowned and to know the width of the canopy and whether it was decked with red or blue cloth provided by the church. . . . All this may have its value for those who desire to learn the interests of princes. . . . A historian has many duties. Allow me to remind you here of two which are of some importance. The first is not to slander; the second is not to bore. I can excuse you for neglect of the first because few will read your work; I cannot, however, forgive you for neglecting the second, for I was forced to read you."[31] This is more than mere sarcasm; it is the expression of a new stylistic ideal of historical writing which Voltaire realized in his work and established as a norm. Lord Chesterfield said of Voltaire's historical works that they contained the history of the human spirit written by a man of genius for the use of a man of spirit. But in this field Voltaire succumbed less than in any other to the danger of being merely witty. For he fortifies himself with extensive and thorough research, and he was no stranger to historical scrutiny. His attention is particularly attracted by sociological details. He would rather know and depict the condition of society in various periods, the forms of family life, the kind and progress of the arts and crafts than describe over and over the political and religious aberrations of nations, their wars and battles. He seeks the aid of etymology, declaring that frequently a single reliable derivation of a word can give us insight into the wanderings of peoples. The alphabet a people uses appears to Voltaire to be indisputable proof as to who the real teachers of the nation had been and as to the sources from which it drew its first knowledge.[32] The history of science itself could not escape these methodological demands, and d'Alembert became Voltaire's pupil in this matter. The decisive influence which d'Alembert's preface to the French *Encyclopaedia* has exerted in both philosophical and literary respects is largely due to the fact that here for the first time the development of science was approached from the new viewpoint. D'Alembert does not look upon this development as simply an accumulation of more and more new scholarly information, but as the methodological self-development of the idea of knowledge itself. He demands that histories of individual subjects be replaced by a philosophical science of principles, and that the history of science be treated according to such principles. In the encyclopaedic plan of knowledge which d'Alembert gave in his

[31] Voltaire, "Lettre à Mr. Nordberg," Preface to new edition of *Histoire de Charles XII* (1744), *Oeuvres*, vol. XXII, pp. 12 ff. See the account of Nordberg and his criticism of Voltaire in Georg Brandes, *Voltaire*, vol. I, pp. 107 ff.

[32] Introduction to *Essai sur les Moeurs*, *Oeuvres*, vol. XV, p. 110. Cf. also Gustave Lanson, *Voltaire*, sixth ed., ch. VI, pp. 107 ff.

Elements of Philosophy, he defines the task of history in the same sense. "The general and classified history of the arts and sciences comprises four great subjects: knowledge, opinion, disputes, and errors. The history of knowledge reveals to us our wealth—or rather, our real poverty. On the one hand, it humbles man by showing him how little he knows; on the other hand, it elates and encourages him, or at least consoles him, by showing the effective use which he has been able to make of a small number of clear and certain concepts. The history of opinion teaches us how men, now activated by necessity, now by impatience, have with varying success put probability in the place of truth; it teaches us how that which at first was only probable, later became true and, so to speak, purified by further and deeper investigation in the course of the continued labors of several centuries. It offers for our scrutiny and for that of our descendants facts to be verified, viewpoints to be pursued, conjectures to be examined, incomplete information to be perfected. . . . Finally, the history of our most notable errors . . . teaches us to mistrust both ourselves and others; it shows us, moreover, the ways which have led away from the truth, and it helps us to find the right pathway."[33]

The plan here outlined by d'Alembert, so far as the history of the exact sciences is concerned, was brilliantly executed by his most gifted pupil. Lagrange's *Analytical Mechanics* offers us a model history of science which to this day has scarcely been surpassed. Later works, as for instance Eugen Dühring's *Critical History of the General Principles of Mechanics*, have generally followed the methodological model established by Lagrange. But d'Alembert himself goes still further; he attributes to history not only a theoretical but also an ethical value and he expects from history the true completion of the knowledge of moral man. "The science of historical facts encounters philosophy in two places, that is, by means of the principles which constitute the foundation of historical certainty and by means of the utility which one can derive from history. Men who are placed on the stage of the world are considered by the wise man

[33] D'Alembert, *Éléments de Philosophie*, sect. II, in *Mélanges de Littérature*, vol. IV, pp. 9 ff.

either as spectators or as actors. Such a man contemplates the intellectual just as he does the physical world without prejudice; he follows writers' reports with the same caution as he applies to natural phenomena. He observes all the subtle distinctions by which the historically true is differentiated from the probable, and the probable from the fictitious. He understands the different languages spoken by honesty and flattery, by prejudice and hatred; and he determines accordingly the various degrees of credibility and the importance of testimony and of the authority of witnesses. Guided by these subtle and dependable rules he studies the past above all in order to become better acquainted with his contemporaries. For the average reader, history is only so much food for curiosity or it is simply a momentary escape from boredom; for the philosopher it is a collection of intellectual and moral experiments (*expériences morales*) on the human race. It is a collection which would be more complete if it had been assembled by the wise alone; yet, incomplete as it is, it still contains the greatest teachings, such for instance as the accumulation of medical observations of all times, which, though it is constantly being enlarged and always remains incomplete, constitutes nonetheless the main body of medical science."[34] So it is that the Enlightenment derives from history the idea of a philosophical study of man, the idea of a general anthropology as Kant systematically developed and discussed it in his lectures.[35] The first attempts at a critical philosophy of history are closely connected with these speculative adventures. Diderot's articles in the *Encyclopaedia* on the various philosophical systems show little historical originality, and his dependence on Bayle, von Brucker, and on Deslandes' *Critical and Philosophical History* (1756 ff.) is very noticeable throughout. Yet a new spirit permeates these articles, especially in the accounts of modern philosophy—of Hobbes, Spinoza, and Leibniz. The mere enumeration of opinions is now gradually superseded by historical and systematic analysis of the content of individual doctrines and of the historical conditions of their development.

[34] D'Alembert, *Éléments de Philosophie*, sect. III, in *Mélanges*, pp. 16 f.
[35] See Kant's lecture plan for the winter semester of 1765-1766 in *Werke*, ed. Cassirer, vol. II, pp. 319 ff.

The Conquest of the Historical World

The analytical spirit, which is characteristic of the eighteenth century, reigns supreme in this field as well. This spirit tends to stress uniformity and constancy rather than change and flux in the treatment of historical phenomena. Only one thinker of the eighteenth century preserves even here his own independent attitude despite prevailing tendencies. Hume agrees as little with the general type of philosophy of history of the Enlightenment as he does with its theory of knowledge or its philosophy of religion. In him the static approach to history, which is oriented to the knowledge of the permanent properties of human nature, begins to relax; he looks more to the historical process as such than to the solid substratum presupposed by the process. Hume criticizes the concept of substance not only as a logician but also as a philosopher of history. He does not indeed portray history as a steady development but he delights in its unceasing change, in the observation of process as such. He neither looks for nor believes in any "reason" implicit in this process; it is rather a psychological and aesthetic than a rational interest which leads him back again and again to the study of the flux of things. The "imagination," which he opposes to abstract reason in his theory of knowledge, and on whose importance he insists, takes on a decisive preponderance in history. Hume looks upon the imagination as one of the basic forces of all historical thought. "In reality, what more agreeable entertainment to the mind than to be transposed into the remotest ages of the world, and to observe human society, in its infancy, making the first faint essays toward the arts and sciences; to see the policy of government, and the civility of conversation refining by degrees, and every thing which is ornamental to human life advancing toward perfection."[36] In this general presentation Hume is not seeking to anticipate the final goal of history; he is absorbed in the sheer wealth of concrete material. History, little as we can know of its ultimate grounds, is to Hume the noblest and most beautiful occupation of the mind. "Shall those trifling pastimes, which engross so much of our time, be preferred as more satisfactory, and more fit to engage our attention? How perverse must that taste

---

[36] Hume, "Of the Study of History," *Essays Moral, Political and Literary*, ed. Green and Grose, new impression, London, 1898, vol. II, pp. 388 ff.

be which is capable of so wrong a choice of pleasures?" High as Hume exalts history and much as he praises it as the noblest adornment of human existence, he does not suppress his skepticism here either. If one compares his praise of the science of history with the expectations, demands, and ideals which the eighteenth century originally cherished for history, the contrast becomes quite evident. With respect to these ideals Hume's statements have a very hollow ring; they are in a key of resignation and renunciation. What a dramatically stirring life does history parade before our eyes! What a pleasure to observe the rise, progress, fall and final extinction of the most prosperous kingdoms, and to see the virtues which made them great and the vices which led to their ruin. "In short, to see all the human race, from the beginning of time, pass, as it were, in review before us; appearing in their true colours, without any of those disguises, which, during their life time, so much perplexed the judgement of the beholders. What spectacle can be imagined, so magnificent, so various, so interesting? What amusement, either of the senses or the imagination, can be compared with it?"[37] What a spectacle—but, alas, it is only a spectacle! For Hume no longer believes it possible to grasp the ultimate significance of natural processes and to reveal their plan. He discards the question of the innermost relations of things and contents himself with the mere spectacle, without trying to bring the ever changing scenes which history causes to pass before him in line with any particular idea. But here again we shall fail to do justice to Hume's skepticism if we consider only its negative side. In history too this skepticism fulfills an important function despite its apparently destructive tendency. For Hume's resistance to any kind of hasty generalization, his concern with the pure facts of history, implies not merely a methodological warning but also a new methodological orientation. Hume's doctrine advocates the uniqueness and specific status of the particular and opens the way for its acknowledgment. To bring about really philosophical recognition of this aspect of Hume's thought, required, however, a further step which he could not take. The particular had to be presented not only as a "matter of fact," but as a problem. It was not sufficient to summon up the realm of facts against the realm of reason; the precise position of the particular within this latter realm had to be determined. The deeper requirement, which is also systematically more difficult to fulfill, consisted in formulating a new concept of the individual human being and tracing its various meanings, its applications and modifications. Hume's skepticism and empiricism were not prepared for such a task. To this end the eighteenth century had to find a new way and to turn to a new leader. It had to attempt to unearth the methodological treasure which lay hidden in Leibniz's doctrine; for this doctrine in its principle of the monad had given the clearest expression to the problem of individuality, and had indeed assigned to individuality a firm central position in a comprehensive philosophical system.

4

Leibniz's concept of substance is also intended to show permanence in change; but it is distinguished by the fact that it conceives the relationship between unity and multiplicity, between duration and change, as a pure correlation. Leibniz no longer wishes to subordinate the many to the one, the mutable to the permanent; he proceeds from the assumption that the two terms of the correlation can only be explained by each other. Genuine knowledge, accordingly, cannot be knowledge of the enduring or of the mutable; it must exhibit the correlation and mutual interdependence of these two elements. The unity of law and of substance can only be exemplified in constant change. Indeed, its only possible expression is in change. Substance remains but its stability implies no standstill; on the contrary, this stability involves the constant rule of its progression. A dynamic conception of substance now takes the place of the static conception. Substance is only a subject or substratum in so far as it is force, as it proves to be directly active and reveals its own nature in the sequence of its activities. The nature of substance does not consist in its being self-inclusive but rather in being fruitful and in producing ever new varieties of things. Its stability lies in this capacity to emanate new content without cessation, in this constant production of phenomena. The totality of these phenomena is of course pre-formed in the nature of substance; there is no such thing as epigenesis, as a new formation conditioned wholly from without. Everything that seems to accrue to substance by the influence of external forces must nevertheless be rooted in its own nature, must be pre-formed and predetermined in this nature. But such determination is not to be conceived as a rigid stereotyped pattern. The perfection of substance is revealed rather in the completeness of its development; its middle and end are as essential and necessary as its beginning. Leibniz bases the nature of the monad on its identity but he includes in this identity the idea of continuity. Identity and continuity combined are the basis of the totality of the monad, and they constitute its completeness and characteristic wholeness.[38]

This fundamental conception of Leibniz's metaphysics signified a new and promising step toward the understanding and conquest of the historical world. But it was a long time before further steps were taken and before this conception could unfold freely. Wolff's system had not entirely excluded the historical; it had sought rather to establish a strict relationship between the historical and the rational. In Wolff's theory of knowledge every particular discipline is divided into an abstract-rational, a concrete-empirical, and a historical part. In the structure of this system full justice is to be done to experience; general cosmology is supplemented by empirical physics, and rational psychology by empirical psychology. But the equilibrium which Wolff is striving after cannot be maintained by method alone. For the very form of the system with its mathematical deduction and demonstration is an obstacle to such an equilibrium. Philosophy is and remains by the nature of its task the science of the rational, not of the historical; the science of the possible, not of the factual and real: "knowledge of possibilities as far as they can be" (*scientia possibilium quatenus esse possunt*). A philosophy of history in the strict sense, therefore, can find no acceptance in Wolff's system; it would involve a mixture of the modes of knowledge and an obliteration of their boundaries, a real "trans-

[38] Cf. above ch. 1, pp. 29 ff.

formation into another kind" (μετάβασις εἰς ἄλλο γένος). The object of philosophy is not the world of fact with which history is concerned but that of the grounds of being; and the law of sufficient reason is the guiding star and first axiom of philosophy even in its relationship with empirical facts. The generality and necessity of the ground, however, is in conflict with that contingency and uniqueness which characterizes and is inseparable from all historical existence. The ideal of mathematical and philosophical lucidity cannot be realized in this field; hence history cannot gain admittance to the inner sanctum of knowledge and philosophy.

But this inner sanctum now seemed to be accessible to history from another approach. Philosophy in its abstract purity remained aloof from the historical; it thought it could and was forced to defend itself against such knowledge. But theology first opened its frontiers and removed the rigid barrier between the dogmatic and the historical content of belief. We have seen how this development began and by what intellectual motives it was determined.[39] In German intellectual history it is Lessing who follows this development through to its logical conclusion and, with respect to method, to its culminating point. His *Education of Humanity* reconciles religious and historical knowledge and recognizes the latter as a necessary factor, an indispensable element, of religion. But Lessing does not extend his consideration to world history as such. He does not doubt that Providence "has had a hand in the matter" of world history, even to its last detail, but he does not presume to lift the veil of this mystery. Herder takes the final, decisive step. Considered in its totality, his achievement is incomparable and without any real preliminary stages. It seems to descend spontaneously from the Gods and to be born out of nothing; it is derived from an intuition of the historical hitherto unequaled in its purity and perfection. But this new conception of the historical world could not have been properly established and it could not have been systematically developed if Herder had not found the intellectual tools ready at hand. His metaphysics of history is based on Leibniz's

[39] See above ch. IV, pp. 182 ff.

central doctrine,[40] while his vital intuition of history protects him from the first against any merely schematic application of this doctrine. For he is not merely striving for an outline of historical development; he tries to see and to assimilate every individual form as such. Herder definitely broke the spell of analytical thinking and of the principle of identity. History dispels the illusion of identity; it knows nothing really identical, nothing that ever recurs in the same form. History brings forth new creatures in uninterrupted succession, and on each she bestows as its birthright a unique shape and an independent mode of existence. Every abstract generalization is, therefore, powerless with respect to history, and neither a generic nor any universal norm can comprehend its wealth. Every human condition has its peculiar value; every individual phase of history has its immanent validity and necessity. These phases are not separated from one another; they exist only in and by virtue of the whole. But each phase is equally indispensable. It is from such complete heterogeneity that real unity emerges, which is conceivable only as the unity of a process not as sameness among existing things. The first task of the historian is, then, to suit his standards to his subject and not, conversely, to make his subject fit into a uniform, stereotyped pattern. Of Egypt, Herder says: "It is silly to take a single Egyptian virtue out of the context of its country and time, out of the youth of the human spirit, and then to appraise it with a standard of a different time! Even if the Greek could . . . be so mistaken in his judgment of the Egyptian, and if the Oriental could hate the Egyptian; yet it seems to me, one's first thought should be to see him in his proper place. Otherwise one sees, especially from the European viewpoint, a most distorted caricature." History can and should give up all general characterization. "Let somebody portray an entire people, an age, a region. What has he portrayed? Let him give an account of peoples succeeding one another and of events in everlasting alternation like the waves of the sea. What has he portrayed? What did his powerful words characterize? . . . He who has

---

[40] For the connection between Herder's philosophy of history and Leibniz's fundamental concepts, see the author's treatment in *Freiheit und Form*, Studien zur deutschen Geistesgeschichte, third edition, Berlin, 1916, pp. 180 ff.

observed what an ineffable thing is the unique nature of a single human being with his ability to express his distinctive characteristics in a distinct manner, to say how he feels and lives, how different and unique all things become once his eye has seen them, his soul measured them, and his heart felt them; he who has noticed too what depth lies in the character of a single nation which, even though one has watched and admired it often enough, beggars all description and is rarely recognizable in historical accounts so that one can understand and feel its character as it really is—such a one knows that insight into these things is like trying to survey and grasp the whole expanse of nations, times, and countries in a single glance, a feeling, a word! What a pale, blurred reflection is conveyed by words! The whole vital portraiture of the mode of life, habits, needs, geographical and climatic qualities would have to be added to the words, or to have gone before by way of introduction; one would have to feel with a nation in order to sense the meaning of a single one of its desires or actions; one must feel all of a nation's desires and actions simultaneously in order to find words for them and to think them in their rich variety. Otherwise one reads merely—words."[41] In the finding of words which immediately conjure up imaginative forms of things, which not only analytically divide but synthetically put together, Herder is inexhaustible; and herein lies his real mastery. He describes and characterizes and he imaginatively transports himself into the various epochs and creates for each its proper and unique atmosphere. For he rejects the dream picture of an "absolute, independent, and unalterable happiness, as the philosopher defines it." Human nature is no receptacle of such happiness: "It enjoys at all times as much happiness as it can; it is a molding clay which assumes different forms in accordance with different situations, needs, and afflictions. ... As soon as the inner sense of happiness, the inclination, has changed, as soon as the external occasions and needs have formed and sustained another sense; who can compare the different satisfaction of different senses in different worlds? ... Every nation has its own core of happiness just as every sphere

[41] Herder, "Auch eine Philosophie der Geschichte zur Bildung der Menschheit," *Werke*, ed. Suphan, vol. v, pp. 489 f., 501 f.

has its center of gravity!" Providence did not seek monotony and uniformity; it sought rather to attain its goal through change, through the constant production of new forces and the extinction of others: "Philosopher in a northern valley, with the infant's scales of your century in your hand, do you know better than Providence?"[42] With these words Herder, under the influence of Hamann, parts company with his age. No such tone as this had hitherto been heard in the philosophy of history of the eighteenth century; it had been as foreign to Montesquieu as to Voltaire or Hume. And yet, much as he outgrows the intellectual world of the Enlightenment, Herder's break with his age was not abrupt. His progress and ascent were possible only by following the trails blazed by the Enlightenment. This age forged the weapons with which it was finally defeated; with its own clarity and consistency it established the premises on which Herder based his inference. The conquest of the Enlightenment by Herder is therefore a genuine self-conquest. It is one of those defeats which really denote a victory, and Herder's achievement is in fact one of the greatest intellectual triumphs of the philosophy of the Enlightenment.

[42] *Ibid.*, vol. v, pp. 507 ff.

CHAPTER VI

Law, State, and Society

I. LAW AND THE PRINCIPLE OF INALIENABLE RIGHTS

A FUNDAMENTAL feature of the philosophy of the Enlightenment appears in the fact that, despite its passionate desire for progress, despite its endeavors to break the old tables of the law and to arrive at a new outlook on life, it returns again and again to the persistent problems of philosophy. Descartes had answered the objection that he was trying to found an entirely new philosophy by declaring that his doctrine could lay claim to the prerogative of age since it was grounded in reason and constructed according to strictly rational principles. For reason possesses the true right of the first-born, and it is older than any opinion or prejudice which has obscured it in the course of the centuries. The philosophy of the Enlightenment adopts this motto. It opposes the power of convention, tradition, and authority in all the fields of knowledge. But it does not consider this opposition as merely a work of negation and destruction; it considers rather that it is removing the rubble of the ages in order to make visible the solid foundations of the structure of knowledge. These foundations are looked upon as immutable and unshakable; they are as old as mankind itself. The philosophy of the Enlightenment, accordingly, does not understand its task as an act of destruction but as an act of reconstruction. In its very boldest revolutions the Enlightenment aims only at "restitution to the whole" (*restitutio in integrum*), by which reason and humanity are to be reinstalled in their ancient rights. Historically, this twofold tendency appears in that the Enlightenment, despite its struggle with the existing order and the immediate past, constantly goes back to the trends of thought and problems of antiquity. In this respect it follows the example of the Renaissance whose intellectual possessions it inherits. But as a purely philosophical movement, the Enlightenment disposes much more freely of its heritage than Humanism within the sphere of mere scholarly research had ever done. It selects only certain basic features which suit its own way of thinking and leaves the rest alone. But in this very selection the Enlightenment often succeeds in penetrating to the real source of its problems. Such was the case with the problem of law. The thinkers of this era are never satisfied with the consideration of conventional historical law; they go back rather to "the laws we were born with." But in the justification and defense of this type of law they return to our most ancient legal heritage, to Plato's radical formulation of the question. The philosophy of the Enlightenment tackles once more Plato's fundamental question of the relationship between right and might, adapting the ancient problem to its own intellectual milieu. After more than two thousand years the eighteenth century establishes direct contact with the thinking of antiquity, a fact equally significant in its historical and in its systematic aspects. The two fundamental theses represented in Plato's *Republic* by Socrates and Thracymachus oppose each other again. We meet them now indeed in a different shape and formulated in an essentially different conceptual world. But this change of relations does not destroy the inner affinity and the objective connection between the two worlds. One and the same dialectic is revealed in the language of different times. Without loss of strength and precision, this dialectic ignores all previous attempts at a reconciliation of its opposing theses and strives for a clear and fundamental solution.

The question Plato raises of the nature and essence of justice is no isolated problem involving only one idea and its philosophical explanation. It cannot be separated from the broader problem of the meaning and nature of the concept in general, and it can only be solved through its relation to the broader problem. Do our logical and ethical concepts express definite objective content existing by itself; or are these concepts merely verbal symbols which we arbitrarily attach to contents? Are there such things as identity, beauty, and justice existing in themselves, or do we search in vain among our changing ideas and opinions for something truly identical which is not swept away in the stream of our "phantasmata"? Is there a fundamental and original form toward which these concepts strive and to which they correspond? Or does the very question of such a form involve a misunderstanding and self-deception? This universal decision is at stake in the profound arguments concerning the nature of the just in the *Gorgias* and the *Republic*. The question of the nature (*eidos*) of justice and the question of the nature of the *eidos* as such are to be decided through their mutual relationship. If, upon closer examination, the idea of justice vanishes revealing no stable unchangeable meaning but only a passing figment of the imagination, then the same lot falls to everything else which has pretended to the dignity of an idea. The idea exists then only in the mind ($\theta\acute{\epsilon}\sigma\epsilon\iota$), not in nature ($\phi\acute{\upsilon}\sigma\epsilon\iota$); it exists merely by definition and derives its relative content and duration from this source. In opposing the sophistic solution of this problem, in undertaking to preserve the basic content of law in its truest and deepest sense from all admixture of mere power and to free this content from any foundation in power, Plato raises the really crucial question of his philosophy. This is the "to be or not to be" of both ethics and logic. Further historical development tends toward a loosening of this strict bond between right and might. The methodological form of the Platonic question is less and less frequently understood in its precise significance, but its content lives on and in one way or another constitutes an element in every future theory of law and the state.

Not until the seventeenth and eighteenth centuries is this problem seen again in its universal scope. It is especially Hugo Grotius who bridges the gap. He is not only a politician and jurist but a learned humanist; and he is the most important and independent thinker of the humanistic movement. In every respect he strives to establish direct contact with the theories of antiquity. In his doctrine of the origin of society and of law Grotius goes back first to Aristotle and then to Plato. As in Plato the problem of law arises from a correlation between ethics and logic, so in Grotius the problem of law is correlated with that of mathematics. This synthesis is typical of the fundamental tendency of the seventeenth century. For mathematics in this century is the universal medium and instrument for the revival of the Platonic "idea." Both natural science and the abstract sciences move in the same direction. But the methodological connection thus established seems at first glance to imply a most paradoxical and hazardous consequence for jurisprudence. For what the concept of law now gains in ideality, it seems necessarily to lose in reality, in its empirical application. It moves from the side of the actual, the real and active, to that of the possible. Leibniz was merely drawing a clear and definite conclusion from an idea stemming from Grotius when he declared that jurisprudence belongs to those disciplines which do not depend on experience, but on definitions, not on facts, but on strictly logical proof. For experience could never reveal what law and justice are in themselves. Both concepts involve the concept of a correspondence, a harmony and proportion, which would remain valid even if it were never realized in a single concrete instance, if there were no one to exercise justice and no one toward whom it could be extended. Law is in this respect like pure arithmetic; for the teachings of arithmetic concerning the nature of numbers and their relations imply an eternal and necessary truth which would not be affected, even if the whole empirical world were destroyed and there were no one to count with numbers and no objects to be counted.[1] In the preface to his masterpiece Grotius's argument centers around the same comparison and analogy. He expressly declares that his deductions concerning the law of war and peace are by no means intended for the solution of specific concrete questions, for problems of current politics. In this exposition Grotius says he placed all such considerations in the background, just as the mathematician treats the figures he is studying as abstracted from all corporeal matter. The mathematical treatment of law becomes even more pronounced in the later development of the doctrine of natural law. Pufendorf emphasizes that, although the application of the principles of natural law to certain concrete cases could give rise to some doubts as to their validity, it does not follow that these principles as such

---

[1] Georg Mollat, *Mitteilungen aus Leibniz' ungedruckten Schriften*, Leipzig, 1893, p. 22. For fuller treatment see the author's book *Leibniz' System in seinen wissenschaftlichen Grundlagen*, Marburg, 1902, pp. 425 ff., 449 ff. The following pages are taken in part from the author's essay "Vom Wesen und Werden des Naturrechts," *Zeitschrift für Rechtsphilosophie in Lehre und Praxis*, vol. VI, pp. 1 ff.

are unsound; on the contrary, they are just as capable of demonstration as the axioms of pure mathematics. If natural law connects law and mathematics in this way, it is because it considers both as symbolizing the same fundamental energy. The doctrine of natural law looks upon law and mathematics as the best evidence of the autonomy and spontaneity of the intellect. Just as the mind is capable of constructing the realm of quantity and number entirely from within itself by virtue of its "innate ideas," so it has the same constructive ability in the field of law. Here too the intellect can and should begin with fundamental norms, which it creates from within itself, and then find its way to the formulation of the particular. For only so can it rise above the accidental, detached, and external nature of the merely factual and achieve a system of law in which everything is woven into the whole and every individual decision receives its sanction and confirmation from the nature of the whole.

Two obstacles had to be overcome and two mighty enemies defeated if this fundamental thesis of natural law was to gain acceptance. On the one hand, law had to assert its originality and its intellectual independence of theological dogma and extricate itself from the perilous embrace of theology; on the other, the pure sphere of law had to be clearly determined and separated from the sphere of the state, and its unique nature and specific value had to be protected from state absolutism. The controversy over the foundation of the modern law of nature is fought out on this double front. It must be carried on as well against the theocratic viewpoint as against the Leviathan state—that is, against the derivation of law from a completely irrational divine will which is impenetrable to human reason. In both cases the axiom that "will stands for reason" (*stat pro ratione voluntas*) must be overthrown. Calvin had appealed to this axiom to show that all law is in the last analysis rooted in divine omnipotence, and that the latter is absolutely unconditional and subject to no limiting rules and norms. The core of Calvinistic dogmatics, especially the central doctrine of predestination, lies in this view; salvation and damnation are implied in it. There is no asking for the grounds and justice of the divine decision concerning the salvation of the soul, for the very question would signify wanton presumption and exaltation of human reason above God Himself. It is the absolute power of God which condemns the greater part of mankind, while it spares and exalts a narrow circle of the elect; both salvation and damnation take place without any "grounds" in the human sense, "without any foresight of faith or good works." The philosophical problem of natural law sprang from this religious problem. Grotius was the real spiritual champion of the movement led by Bishop Arminius in the Netherlands which opposed the Calvinistic doctrine of predestination. His defense of the Arminians and "Remonstrants" not only had a profound effect on his personal fate, since Grotius was discharged from his offices and thrown into prison following the condemnation of the teachings of Arminius at the Synod of Dort; but it also affected the course of all of his scholarly and literary activity. He stands at exactly the same spot where Erasmus had stood; he defends the humanistic idea of freedom against the fundamental thesis of the bondage of the will revived by the reformers, by Calvin and Luther, in all its rigor. But he finds himself engaged with another opponent at the same time. Just as he has to combat the omnipotence of God, he also has to encounter the omnipotence of the state, that "mortal God," as Hobbes pregnantly and characteristically terms it.[2] Grotius now faces a distinctively modern standpoint which had been developing steadily since the Renaissance. Following the publication of Machiavelli's *Prince* and Bodin's *Republic*, the doctrine that the wielder of the highest political power is subject to no legal conditions and limitations had received increasing emphasis. Against both these tendencies the advocates of natural law argue their fundamental thesis that there is a law which antedates all human and divine power and is valid independently of such power. The concept of law as such is not founded in the sphere of mere power and will but in the sphere of pure reason. In that which this reason

[2] The same struggle, which Grotius carries on in the Netherlands against Calvinistic dogma and against the principle of state absolutism, is resumed later in England by the Cambridge School and fought out under similar methodological and historical conditions. It is not necessary to go into further detail here since this subject is treated fully in the author's monograph, *Die platonische Renaissance in England und die Schule von Cambridge.*

conceives as "being," in that which is given in the pure nature of reason, nothing can be altered or curtailed by any decree. Law in its primary and original sense, in the sense of "natural law" (*lex naturalis*), can never be resolved into a sum of merely arbitrary acts. Law is not simply the sum total of that which has been decreed and enacted; it is that which originally arranges things. It is "ordering order" (*ordo ordinans*), not "ordered order" (*ordo ordinatus*). The perfect concept of law presupposes without doubt a commandment affecting individual wills. But this commandment does not create the idea of law and justice, it is subject to this idea; it puts the idea into execution, though the execution must not be confused with the justification of the idea of law as such. In this foundation of his doctrine, as we find it in the prolegomena of his work *On the Law of War and Peace*, the Platonism of modern natural law is most perfectly expressed. Just as the Platonic demiurge is not the creator of ideas but shapes the world of the real after the ideas as everlasting, uncreated models, so the same thing holds, according to Grotius, for the form and order within the political and legal community. In enacting his various positive laws the legislator follows an absolutely universally valid norm which is exemplary and binding for his own as well as for every other will. It was in this sense that Grotius made his famous statement that the propositions of natural law would retain their validity even if one were to assume that there was no God or that the Deity was not concerned with human things.[3] This statement is not intended to open up a chasm between religion on the one hand and law and morality on the other. For Grotius in his whole personality is a deeply religious thinker; moral reformation does not concern him less than the intellectual foundation and deepening of the idea of law. The assertion that there can and must be a law even without the assumption of divine existence, is therefore not to be understood as a thesis but as a hypothesis. For, understood as a categorical statement, as Grotius immediately adds, this assertion would of course signify non-sense. As a pure hypothesis in the Platonic sense of the word, it serves however to define clearly the spheres of compe-

[3] *De jure belli ac pacis*, Prolegomena, sect. XI.

tence within the realm of morality and religion, which is still considered by Grotius as an integral whole—the separation of religion and morals which takes place in the eighteenth century is far from Grotius's mind. Law is not valid because there is a God, nor is it based on any existence whether empirical or absolute. It springs from the pure idea of the good, from the idea which Plato had said surpasses everything in force and age. This transcendence of the idea of law which raises the just and the good above all being, which does not permit us to base its meaning on any existing thing, is repeatedly stressed by Grotius. And this is his real contribution to philosophy and intellectual history rather than his "discovery" of natural law. The Christian Middle Ages too had clung to the idea of natural law, which it chiefly derived from the Stoic school of thought. Scholastic theory recognizes besides "divine law" (*lex divina*) a special, relatively independent sphere of "natural law" (*lex naturalis*). Law is not exclusively subordinated to and derived from revelation; but natural morality and a natural knowledge of law are advocated, which reason retained even after the fall, and which are looked upon as the necessary presupposition and starting-point for the supernatural restitution by divine grace of the perfect knowledge possessed by man in his original state. Yet the Middle Ages could no more admit the complete autonomy of natural law than it could admit the autonomy of natural reason. Reason remains the servant of revelation. Its task within the realm of the mind and soul is to lead to, and to help prepare the way for, revelation. Natural law is therefore subordinated to divine law even though it is granted a relatively large degree of recognition. Thomas Aquinas calls both natural and divine law radiations of the divine being: the one law destined for earthly ends, the other ordained by revelation for super-terrestrial ends.[4] Grotius advances beyond scholasticism less in content than in method. He achieves the same thing in

---

[4] For the relation between natural and divine law in the Middle Ages see Gierke, *Johannes Althusius und die Entwicklung der naturrechtlichen Staatstheorien* (1879), third ed., Breslau, 1913, pp. 272 ff. In Protestant theology too the medieval conception remains for a time in full force. See Troeltsch, *Vernunft und Offenbarung bei Johann Gerhard und Melanchthon*, Göttingen, 1891, especially pp. 98 ff. See above pp. 39 ff.

the realm of law as Galileo had done in the realm of natural science. A source of legal knowledge is designated which does not arise from divine revelation, but which proves itself by its own nature, and by virtue of this nature it avoids defilement and falsification. As Galileo asserts and defends the autonomy of mathematical physics, so Grotius contends for that of jurisprudence. Grotius himself seems clearly to have recognized this ideal connection with Galileo. He is filled with admiration for him, calling him in a letter the greatest genius of his century. The concept and the word "nature" in the thought of the seventeenth century embrace two groups of problems, which we today usually distinguish from one another, and include them in a single unit. In that century the natural sciences are never separated from the abstract disciplines, much less considered as opposed to them in their nature and validity. For the term "nature" does not predicate merely the sphere of physical being from which the being of the mind and soul is to be distinguished; it does not oppose the "material" to the "spiritual." "Nature" at that time does not refer to the existence of things but to the origin and foundation of truths. To nature belong, irrespective of their content, all truths which are capable of a purely immanent justification, and which require no transcendent revelation but are certain and evident in themselves. Such truths are now sought not only in the physical but also in the intellectual and moral world; for it takes these two worlds together to constitute a real world, a cosmos complete in itself.

This connection between the physical and spiritual worlds is also maintained in the eighteenth century. Montesquieu begins as an empirical scientist,[5] and through this occupation he is gradually led on to his real problem, to the analysis of legal and political institutions. As a jurist he asks the same question that Newton the physicist had raised. He is not content with the empirically known laws of the political world. He attempts to trace the variety of these laws back to a few definite principles. The existence of such an order, of such a systematic interdependence among the various normative legal forms constitutes the "spirit of the laws." He is thus enabled to begin his work

[5] See above p. 47.

with an explanation of the concept of law which formulates this concept in its most comprehensive and universal sense, not limiting it to any special field of factual data. Montesquieu declares: "Laws in their broadest sense are the necessary relations which are derived from the nature of things."[6] Such a "nature of things" exists in the realm of the possible as well as in that of the real, in the realm of the purely conceptual as well as in that of the factually existent, in the physical as well as in the moral world. A given heterogeneity must never prevent us from seeking the hidden uniformity; the accidental must never deceive us regarding the necessary and block our access to a knowledge of the necessary order of things. Inspired by this fundamental conception Montesquieu, even in his *Persian Letters*, expressly repeats the principle on which Grotius had founded the law of nature. Justice is a certain relation (*un rapport de convenance*); and this relation remains always the same, no matter what subject it embraces, and no matter whether it is conceived by God or by an angel or man. And since God's will is always in harmony with His knowledge, it is impossible that He should offend against the known eternal norms of the just. Therefore, even if no God existed, we should have to love justice, and do everything in our power to be like a being of whom we have so sublime an idea, and who, if He existed, would necessarily be just. Once free from the yoke of religion, we should still be subject to the rule of justice.[7] Law, like mathematics, has its objective structure which no arbitrary whim can alter. "Before there were any enacted laws, just relations were possible. To say that there is nothing just or unjust excepting that which positive laws command or forbid is like saying that before one has drawn a circle, all of its radii were not equal."[8]

The philosophy of the Enlightenment at first holds fast to this apriority of law, to this demand for absolutely universally valid and unalterable legal norms. Even the pure empiricists and the philosophical empiricists are no exception in this respect.

[6] Montesquieu, *L'Esprit des Lois*, Book I, ch. I.
[7] Montesquieu, *Lettres Persanes*, Lettre LXXXII.
[8] *L'Esprit des Lois*, Book I, chap. I.

Voltaire and Diderot scarcely differ from Grotius and Montesquieu, but they fall indeed into a difficult dilemma. For how can this view be reconciled with the fundamental tendency of their doctrine of knowledge? How does the necessity and immutability of the concept of law agree with the proposition that every idea is derived from the senses and that, accordingly, it can possess no other and no higher significance than the various sense experiences on which it is based? Voltaire clearly grasped this contradiction, and at times he seems to waver as to his decision. But in the end the ethical rationalist, the enthusiast for the original competence and the fundamental force of moral reason, triumphs over the empiricist and skeptic. On this point he even ventures to oppose his leader and master, Locke. Locke's proof that there are no innate ideas, Voltaire objects, by no means signifies that there can be no universal principle of morality. For the acceptance of such a principle does not imply that it is present and active from the first in every thinking being but that it can be found by everyone for himself. The act of finding this principle is confined to a certain time and a certain stage of development. However, the content, which is discovered and disclosed to consciousness in this act, does not spring from the act itself, but has always existed. "I agree with Locke that there is really no innate idea; it clearly follows that there is no proposition of morality innate in our soul; but from the fact that we were not born with beards, does it follow that we were not born, we inhabitants of this continent, to be bearded at a certain age? We are not born with the strength to walk, but whoever is born with two feet will some day walk. Similarly, no one is born with the idea that it is necessary to be just; but God has so formed the organs of man that all at a certain age agree to this truth."[9] Even though he is a historian of civilization who delights in unfolding before us the variety and conflict of human habits and customs, and in painting out their complete relativity, their dependence on changeable and accidental circumstances, yet Voltaire never deviates from this viewpoint. For time and again he believes he has found be-

[9] Voltaire, Letter to Crown Prince Frederick, October 1737, *Oeuvres*, vol. L, p. 138.

neath this mutability of opinions, prejudices, and customs, the immutable character of morality itself. "Even though that which in one region is called virtue, is precisely that which in another is called vice, even though most rules regarding good and bad are as variable as the languages one speaks and the clothing one wears; yet it seems to me, nevertheless, certain that there are natural laws with respect to which human beings in all parts of the world must agree. . . . To be sure, God did not say to man: 'Here you have laws from my lips according to which I desire you to govern yourselves'; but He did the same thing with man that He did with many other animals. He gave to bees a powerful instinct by virtue of which they work together and gain their sustenance, and He endowed man with certain inalienable feelings; and these are the eternal bonds and the first laws of human society."[10] And again, in proof of his fundamental conviction, Voltaire refers especially to the great analogy of the laws of nature. Should nature everywhere have aimed at unity, order, and complete regularity, and have missed only in the case of its highest creation, man? Should nature rule the physical world according to general and inviolable laws, only to abandon the moral world completely to chance and whim? Here then we must leave Locke and seek support in Newton and his great maxim: "Nature is always in harmony with itself" (*natura est semper sibi consona*). Just as the law of gravity, which we find on earth, is not confined to this planet, just as this law reveals a fundamental force of matter which extends throughout the cosmos and connects every particle of matter with every other, so the fundamental law of morality prevails in all the nations we know. In the interpretation of this law there are, according to the circumstances, thousands of variations, but the basis always remains the same and this basis is the idea of the just and the unjust. "In the fury of passion one commits innumerable injustices, as one loses his reason when intoxicated; but when the intoxication wears off, reason returns, and that is in my opinion the sole cause of the preservation of human society, a cause subservient to our need for one

[10] Voltaire, *Traité de Métaphysique*, chap. IX, *Oeuvres*, vol. XXXI, pp. 65 f.

another."[11] To prove God's existence and His goodness, one should not appeal to apparent physical miracles, to the interruption of the laws of nature, but to this one moral miracle: "Miracles are good; but to aid one's fellow, to free one's friend from the bosom of misery, to pardon the virtues of one's enemies, this is a greater miracle and one which is no longer performed."[12]

In Diderot, too, belief in the immutable moral nature of man and in a firm principle of justice arising from this nature remains unshakable. And this belief constitutes the fixed point in Diderot's absolutely flexible and dynamic philosophy.[13] When Helvetius in his book *On the Mind* attempted to undermine this belief, when he sought to expose all ostensibly moral impulses as veiled egotism, Diderot expressly raised objections to any such leveling process.[14] He upholds eternal and immutable morality but his justification of this demand, if one compares it with the doctrines of the pure law of nature, points in a new direction. For that drift of meaning, which we can also trace in the concept of "nature" in the eighteenth century, is now finding increasingly general acceptance. The center of gravity is shifting from the side of apriority to that of empiricism, from the side of reason to that of pure experience. Men are not ruled and united by an abstract command of reason but by the uniformity of their inclinations, instincts, and appetites. It is here that we must look for the true organic unity of man; and only here, not in mere religious or moral precepts, do we find the real basis of this unity. Every transcendental system of ethics and religion becomes a mere castle in the air the moment it leaves this basis and abandons the natural sense impulses which motivate human behavior. For no mere obligation can presume to annul or to alter fundamentally the empirical nature of man. This nature will continue to appear and it will continue to be stronger than any obligation. A moral system which is an acknowledged enemy of nature is condemned to

[11] Voltaire, *Le Philosophe ignorant*, ch. xxxvi, *Oeuvres*, xxxi, 130.

[12] Voltaire, *Discours en vers sur l'homme*, Septième discours, *Oeuvres*, xii, 92.

[13] Cf. especially the opinion of Groethuysen, "La Pensée de Diderot," *La Grande Revue*, lxxxii (1913), 337 f.

[14] See above pp. 25 ff.

impotence from the outset. And if it were effective, it could not but stifle every morally noble and great sentiment in man along with his sensibility and all the natural love and devotion of which he is capable.[15] Let nature rule, let her obey only herself without fetters or conventional hindrances, and by this self-realization she will also realize the true and only good, the happiness of man and the welfare of the community. Diderot thus traverses the whole way from an *a priori* to a purely utilitarian foundation of ethics. Originally he starts with an idea of law and justice which is valid and immutable in itself. But the more he studies this idea, and the more precisely he tries to define its content, the more convinced he is that this content is only to be found in its immediate and concrete performance. The pure moralism which he constantly stresses in his criticism of religion and of religious dogma gradually turns into a mere pragmatism. "But, doctor, both vice and virtue?" questions Mademoiselle de l'Espinasse in the *Dream of d'Alembert* in objection to the naturalistic ethics of the physician. "Virtue, that word which is so holy in all tongues, that idea which is so sacred among all nations!" "It is necessary to change it," the doctor replies, "into the idea of beneficence and its opposite into that of malfeasance. One is fortunately or unfortunately born; one is irresistibly swept along by the general torrent which carries the one to glory, the other to ignominy."[16] Thus Diderot finally has to found the superiority of natural law and natural morality over theological ethics principally in the nature of their effectiveness. To both theological ethics and revealed religion he objects that their influence on society has always been disastrous. They cut all natural bonds between man and man; they sow dissension and hatred among the closest friends and among

---

[15] Cf. Diderot's judgment concerning his brother, the Abbé Diderot, in his letter to Sophie Volland, Aug. 17, 1759 (ed. Babelon, Paris, no date, vol. I. p. 71): "He is upright, but severe. He would have been a good friend and a good father, if Christ had not commanded him to trample all those miseries under foot. He is a good Christian, which proves to me every moment that it would be better to be a good man, and that that which they call evangelic perfection is merely the art of stifling nature, which would perhaps have spoken as forcefully through him as through me."

[16] Diderot, "Rêve d'Alembert," *Oeuvres*, ed. Assézat, vol. II, p. 176. Cf. Diderot's dialogue: "Est-il bon, est-il méchant?"

blood relations; they debase natural duties by subordinating them to another order of purely chimerical duties.[17] Diderot's articles in the *Encyclopaedia* preserve throughout this line of reasoning, which in fact set the standard for the treatment of ethical problems for the whole *Encyclopaedia*.[18] D'Alembert too remains within the same methodological limits; for him likewise a purely philosophical ethics can have no other goal than to assign to the individual his place in human society, and to teach him to employ his powers for the welfare of society and for the common happiness of all. "That which belongs essentially and uniquely to reason and which consequently is uniform among all peoples, is our duty toward our own kind. Consciousness of this duty is what one calls morality. . . . Few sciences have a more extensive object and principles more susceptible of convincing proofs. All these principles meet in a common point, concerning which it is difficult to delude ourselves; they tend to procure for us the surest means of being happy by showing us the intimate connection between our true interest and the performance of our duty. . . . Societies owe their birth to purely human motives; religion had no part in their original formation. . . . The philosopher is responsible only for placing man in society and leading him there; it is the missionary's task then to bring him to the foot of the altar."[19]

On this foundation the doctrine of human and civil rights was built up as we know it in the eighteenth century. It forms the spiritual center at which all the various tendencies toward a moral renewal and toward a political and social reform meet and in which they find their ideal unity. In recent literature on constitutional law the attempt has been made to establish the idea of human rights historically on a much narrower basis. Georg Jellinek, in his work *The Declaration of Human and Civil Rights*,[20] defended the thesis that there is no direct historical connection between the Declaration of Human Rights given

---

[17] Cf. Diderot, "Entretien d'un Philosophe avec la Maréchale de. . . ."

[18] For details see Hubert, *Les Sciences sociales dans l'Encyclopédie*, Paris, 1923.

[19] D'Alembert, *Éléments de Philosophie*, sect. VII, *Mélanges de Littérature*, vol. IV, pp. 79 f.

[20] *Die Erklärung der Menschen- und Bürgerrechte*, second ed., Leipzig, 1904; third ed., ed. Walter Jellinek, 1919.

at the French Constituent Assembly on August 26, 1789 and the fundamental concept of seventeenth and eighteenth century philosophy. He sees the model for the French declaration rather in the American "bills of rights," especially in the declaration of rights issued by the State of Virginia on June 12, 1776. But even if one agrees with the positive part of Jellinek's thesis—and the dependence of the French declaration on American models is undeniable and demonstrable in detail—the negative conclusion which he draws does not follow. For the American declarations themselves are under the prevailing influence of the new spirit of natural law. They are not the roots from which arose the demand for human and civil rights. They are rather but a single branch, a development of the general ideas of natural law determined by particular motives and fostered by historical circumstances. Hence these declarations are by no means deducible from the principle of freedom of belief alone, and from the religious quarrels which were fought in seventeenth century England because of this principle. Recent careful studies of the Virginia declaration of rights have clearly shown that at the time of its origin the question of religious freedom played no role at all or only a very subordinate one.[21] The school of ideas, to which the declaration of the French Constituent Assembly belongs and out of which it organically developed like ripening fruit, is current and available long before there is any thought of influencing American declarations of rights. These ideas go back to the beginnings of modern natural law in Grotius, and they undergo further systematic justification and elaboration especially in the philosophy of law of German idealism in the works of Leibniz and Wolff.[22] In England it was Locke who declared in his *Treatise on Government* that the social contract entered into by individuals by no means constitutes the only

[21] For details see G. A. Salander, *Vom Werden der Menschenrechte. Ein Beitrag zur modernen Verfassungsgeschichte unter Zugrundelegung der virginischen Erklärung der Rechte vom 12. Juni 1776*, Leipzig, 1926, and also E. Voegelin, "Der Sinn der Erklärung der Menschen- und Bürgerrechte von 1789," *Zeitschrift für öffentliches Recht*, VIII (1928), 82 ff. Cf. further J. Hashagen, "Zur Entstehungsgeschichte der nordamerikanischen Erklärungen der Menschenrechte," *Zeitschrift für die gesamte Staatswissenschaft*, 78th Jahrgang (1924), pp. 482 ff.

[22] For details see the author's essay *Die Idee der republikanischen Verfassung*, Hamburg, 1929.

ground for all legal relations among men. All such contractual ties are rather preceded by original ties which can neither be created by a contract nor entirely annulled by it. There are natural rights of man which existed before all foundations of social and political organizations; and in view of these the real function and purpose of the state consists in admitting such rights into its order and in preserving and guaranteeing them thereby. Locke counts the right of personal freedom and the right of property among these fundamental rights. Hence French philosophy of the eighteenth century by no means discovered the idea of inalienable rights; but it was the first to make a real moral gospel of this idea and to embrace it passionately and proclaim it enthusiastically. By the manner in which French philosophy proclaimed the doctrine of inalienable rights, it introduced it into real political life and gave it the impetus and explosive power which it revealed in the days of the French Revolution. Judged by his individual temperament and personal objectives Voltaire is certainly no revolutionary; yet he too senses the emergence of a new age, of which he makes himself the herald. His utterances as a theoretical philosopher and metaphysician on the subject of freedom are insufficient, indefinite, and inconsistent. In his *Treatise on Metaphysics* (1734) he defends the doctrine of the freedom of the human will against all opposition. All purely conceptual and dialectic objections which have been raised against the freedom of the will, fall, Voltaire tries to show, before the simple testimony of self-consciousness. The feeling for freedom, which is alive and immediately present in each of us, cannot be simply deception. Hence the mere phenomenon of the will is sufficient to prove its freedom: "To wish and to act, this is precisely the same thing as to be free." How human freedom is reconcilable with divine foresight, is and remains indeed an insoluble dilemma. But this difficulty need not frighten us because we encounter a limit here which confronts us in all purely metaphysical questions, and which exists too for all special problems.[23] Voltaire later reversed this decision to a strict determinism. The feeling of freedom does not as such, he

---

[23] *Traité de Métaphysique*, ch. VII, *Oeuvres*, XXXI, 51, 57.

now points out, conflict with such a determinism; for to be free, as we recognize this feeling in our self-consciousness, does not imply that one may "will" as he pleases, but that one may "do" as he pleases. A will without sufficient motive is absurd because it would fall outside the order of nature and destroy it. "It would be very singular that all nature and all the stars should obey eternal laws, and that there should be one little animal five feet tall which, despite these laws, could always act as suited its own caprice. It would act by chance, and we know that chance is nothing. We have invented this word to express the known effect of any unknown cause."[24] But the uncertainty and inner vacillation which Voltaire shows toward the purely metaphysical problem of freedom is merely an expression of the fact that this side of the question does not interest him. For him this is not a matter of merely theoretical exposition and abstract definition but of the most urgent practical question of the time. His ideal of freedom arose from his concrete political observations, from a comparison and appraisal of the various forms of government. And in Europe at that time Voltaire found this ideal most nearly realized in the English constitution because it alone offered real protection for the property of every citizen and for his personal safety. Whoever has once understood these blessings and recognized their reasonable necessity, will of himself find the strength to preserve them. The essential concept of freedom for Voltaire is therefore synonymous with the concept of human rights. "In fact, what does it mean to be free? It means to know the rights of man, for to know them is to defend them."[25]

All of Voltaire's political writings are inspired by this view of freedom. He is convinced that it is sufficient to reveal the idea of freedom in its true form to men in order to call forth all the forces necessary to its realization. Accordingly, to Voltaire, as to Kant, the "freedom of the pen," the right to influence others by word and teachings, is the real "Palladium of the rights of the people." "In general, we have a natural right to use both our pen and our tongue at our own risk. I know many tedious

[24] *Le Philosophe ignorant* (1766), sect. XIII, *Oeuvres*, XXXI, 85 f.
[25] Cf. especially *Lettres sur les Anglais*, Lettre IX, and the article "Gouvernement" in Voltaire's *Dictionnaire Philosophique*, sect. VI, *Oeuvres*, XXVI, 40 ff.; XL, 101 ff.

books, but I do not know a single one that has done any real harm."[26] With the conquest and consolidation of real freedom of thought everything else is decided. Such is the maxim which Voltaire introduced into the philosophy of his century, and in so doing he released that current of thought which takes its course irresistibly in the literature of the French Revolution. On all sides it is now asserted that the first step toward freedom, that the real intellectual constitution of the new order of the state, can only consist in a declaration of inalienable rights, the right of personal security, of free enjoyment of property, of equality before the law, and of the participation of every citizen in the government. Condorcet maintains: "It is not in the positive knowledge of laws established among men that one ought to seek for knowledge which he may adopt; it is in reason alone. And the study of laws instituted among different peoples and in different centuries is useful only in order to give reason the benefit of observation and experience."[27] In his *Tableau of the Progress of the Human Mind*, which contains his philosophy of history and culture, Condorcet presents clearly and precisely the historical relationship among the various motives which led up to the idea of inalienable rights. He declares that all knowledge of human society can have but one purpose, namely, to guarantee to men the free exercise of their fundamental rights in perfect equality and in the fullest measure. This purpose, according to Condorcet, has been brought nearer to realization in the free states of America; these states, therefore, have the distinction of being the first to convert the great ideas of the century into action. Condorcet traces the origin of these ideas back to the philosophy of the seventeenth and eighteenth centuries, and he credits Rousseau especially with having placed the conception of the rights of man among those truths which will never again be forgotten or disputed.[28] In this final survey of the whole movement of the Enlightenment we see once more how conscious the

[26] *Dictionnaire Philosophique*, article "Liberté d'imprimer," *Oeuvres*, XLI, 23.

[27] Condorcet, *Essai sur les assemblées provinciales*, second part, art. VI; cf. Henri Sée, *Les idées politiques en France au XVIIIe siècle*, Paris, 1920, p. 210.

[28] Condorcet, *Tableau des progrès de l'esprit humain*, 9e époque, *Oeuvres*, 1804, vol. VIII, p. 233. Cf. "De l'influence de la révolution de l'Amérique," Introd., *Mélanges d'Économie politique*, XIV, Paris, 1847, pp. 544 ff.

leading minds of the French Revolution were of the connection between theory and practice. They never look upon thought as distinct from action; they believe they can and must turn the one immediately into the other and test the one by the other.

II. THE CONTRACT AND THE METHOD
OF THE SOCIAL SCIENCES

If one wishes to understand the trend of social science in the seventeenth and eighteenth centuries, and if one wishes to gain a perfectly clear idea of the new method which develops in this period, one must consider them in connection with the simultaneous growth of logic. Paradoxical as such a connection may appear, it exactly characterizes one of the fundamental tendencies of the epoch. Ever since the days of the Renaissance it has been possible to trace with increasing clarity the development of a new form of logic which is not content merely to order and classify the given body of knowledge but which seeks also to become the tool of research. Rationalists and empiricists agree in the new conception of logic and they vie with one another in furthering it. Bacon seeks to create an organon of knowledge through his philosophy. Leibniz likewise stresses repeatedly that logic must abandon its traditional paths and break away from its scholastic forms if it wants to achieve real fruitfulness and to become a "logic of invention" (*logica inventionis*). This intellectual impulse was most immediately and distinctly felt in the theory of definitions. The scholastic method of definition of a concept by means of *genus proximum* (next genus above) and *differentia specifica* (specific difference) is more and more commonly recognized as inadequate. The object of a definition in this sense is not merely to analyze and describe a given conceptual content; it is to be a means for constructing conceptual content and for establishing it by virtue of this constructive activity. Thus arises the theory of the genetic or causal definition, in whose development all the great logicians of the seventeenth century participated.[29] The genuine and really fruitful explana-

[29] For the details of this development see the author's account in his work, *Das Erkenntnisproblem*, third ed., vol. II, pp. 49 ff., 86 ff., 127 ff., and *passim*.

tions of concepts do not proceed by abstraction alone; they are not content to divide one element from a given complex of properties or characteristics and to define it in isolation. They observe rather the inner law according to which the whole either originated or at least can be conceived as originating. And they clarify within this law of becoming the real nature and behavior of this whole; they not only show *what* this whole is, but *why* it is. A genuine genetic definition permits us to understand the structure of a complex whole; it does not, however, stop with this structure as such, but goes back to its foundations. Hobbes is the first modern logician to grasp this significance of the "causal definition." He does not look upon his discovery simply as a logical reform; he sees nothing less than a transformation of the ideal of philosophical knowledge itself. His charge against scholasticism is that it thought it could understand being, while in reality it considered being merely as a passive something with static properties and characteristics. This resulted in failure to grasp the structure of corporeal nature as well as that of thought, for both nature and thought are comprehensible only in process. We understand only what we can cause to develop under our observation. The concept of not-being is beyond our knowledge; the eternal uncreated being of God or of the heavenly intelligences transcends all human understanding. If one wants to "know" something, he must constitute it himself; he must cause it to develop from its individual elements. All science, the science of the corporeal world as well as that of the intellectual world, must be centered around this act of producing the object of knowledge. And where we cannot bring about this act, there all comprehension is of no avail. Where there is no possibility of constructively producing the object, there is also no possibility of gaining rational, strictly philosophical knowledge: "Where there is no generation . . . there no philosophy is perceived" (*ubi generatio nulla . . . ibi nulla philosophia intelligitur*)."[30]

With this preliminary and fundamental explanation of the task of philosophy we come to the very heart of Hobbes's philos-

[30] Hobbes, *De corpore*, part I, ch. I, sect. 8.

ophy of society. For him there is no separation and scarcely even a transition. His doctrine of the state is philosophy only in so far as it conforms to the universal method of knowledge; it is not intended as anything more than an application of this method to a particular object. For the state too is "body" (*corpus*), and therefore it can only be understood by analysis into its ultimate components and reconstruction from these. For the attainment of a real science of the state nothing else is necessary than to carry over into the field of politics the synthetic and analytic method which Galileo applied in physics.[81] Here too an understanding of the whole can be gained only by going back to the parts, to the forces which originally held these parts together and which continue to hold them together. And this analysis must not break off arbitrarily at any point; it must not stop until it has penetrated to the real elements, to the absolute indivisible units. Political and social structures must be broken up into their ultimate parts if we wish to understand them. Hobbes knows perfectly well that this ideal is not empirically realizable, but this objection does not keep him from a radical application of his general rational principle. He could not deny that wherever we encounter man in nature or in history, we always find him in some form of society, not as an isolated individual. But Hobbes deliberately transcends this barrier. The actual bond of the primitive forms of society as, for instance, the ties existing among members of a family, must be dissolved if we are to understand the nature of society and to derive it from its basic elements. Here again the statement holds that philosophy is not knowledge *that* something is, but *why* it is. All thinking, according to Hobbes, is computation, and all computation consists of addition and subtraction. The force of this subtraction, of conceptual abstraction, must be exerted to the utmost if the correct addition, the intellectual integration of a whole, is to succeed. True knowledge of the structure of a complex whole can only arise from the interplay of these two methods. Thus at first Hobbes proceeds by analytically isolating the elements of his problem; in order to use individual wills as counters in his calculation, he treats them as abstract units without any particular quality. Each will

[81] See above pp. 15 ff.

wants the same thing as every other, and each wants it only for itself. The problem of political theory consists in explaining how a connection can arise from this absolute isolation—a connection which not only joins individuals loosely together but which eventually welds them into a single whole. Hobbes's doctrines of the state of nature and of the social covenant attempt to solve this problem. Rule and submission are the only forces which can transform politically into one body that which by nature is divided, and which can keep this body in existence. Accordingly, the social contract, as Hobbes conceives it, can be nothing but a negotiation of surrender. To attenuate submission in any way, to admit any reservations, would be to destroy the state's reason for existence, to precipitate political cosmos back into chaos. Thus Hobbes's political radicalism springs from a logical radicalism, and the former in turn acts upon the latter. To limit authority in any sense is to assail its intellectual roots, to negate it logically. The act by which individuals renounce their own wills, each one submitting his will to that of the ruler upon the condition that the others do the same, does not take place within an already existing community; it is rather the beginning of community life, for it is this act which constitutes the community. The relationship between the two basic forms of the contract, between the "covenant of society" (*pactum societatis*) and the "covenant of submission" (*pactum subjectionis*), is so conceived by Hobbes that the dualism is dissolved which had existed between the two forms, that the covenant of submission is the only remaining form of social bond by virtue of which any sort of social life may arise.[32] Before individuals enter into the contract with the ruler, they are merely a disordered mass, an aggregate without any sign of integration. Only the authority of the ruler can found the political whole, and only through unlimited sovereignty can it be held together. The state contract as a covenant of subjection is therefore the first step leading from the "natural state" to the "civil state," and it remains the indispensable condition for the preservation and continuance of the latter.

[32] For the significance of this step for the general development of the theory of the state, see especially Gierke, *Johannes Althusius*, third ed., pp. 86 ff., 101 ff.

But this conception of political power as "authority unfettered by laws" (*potestas legibus soluta*) is now challenged by the principle of natural law. Wherever this principle was upheld, the concept of the social contract had to be formulated and defended in another way. Grotius does not look upon society as a mere organization of individuals for the attainment of a certain purpose; for him society is founded on an ineradicable instinct of human nature, a "social appetite" (*appetitus societatis*), by virtue of which man first really becomes a human being. The abstract individual man, on whom Hobbes bases his theory, would therefore in the opinion of Grotius fall outside the species, outside of the pure form of humanity. Nor could such a man enter into a contract; for the contract, the promise as such, contains a fundamental feature of human nature as a humanly sociable nature. Society then does not depend on a contract by means of which alone it comes into being. On the contrary, the contract is only possible and understandable under the presupposition of, and only upon the assumption of, an original "sociability." This sociability, which is founded in reason, cannot be replaced by any arbitrary act or by any mere convention. Accordingly, Grotius rejects any merely utilitarian justification and derivation of the state as well as of law. He too considers the preservation of society as the fundamental task of both these institutions, but he adds significantly and characteristically that this protection should be so constituted that it corresponds to the nature of the human intellect. "This protection of society, appropriate to the human intellect, is the source of its authority, and is therefore properly referred to by such a name."[33] The statement that utility is almost the mother of the just and the equitable[34] cannot then be accepted in this form, for man would not cease to seek and to further right for right's sake even if no use or profit were connected with it.[35] The capacity to rise to the pure idea of the right, of juridical obligation, and to become conscious of that element of this idea which is already contained in the community

[33] *De jure belli ac pacis*, Prolegomena, sect. 8: "Haec societatis custodia, humano intellectui conveniens, fons est eius juris, quod proprie tali nomine appelatur."

[34] Horace, *Satires*, Book I, No. 3: "Utilitas justi prope mater et aequi."

[35] Grotius, *op.cit.*, Prolegomena, sect. 16.

instinct is the privilege of man and the basis of all specifically human society. In this deduction one finds once more that union of the juridical and humanistic spirit which is characteristic of Grotius. He considers law not as an accidental human creation but as a genuine and necessary characteristic of man. For Grotius law is the source from which humanity itself springs and in which it is most perfectly reflected. According to him, the fundamental concept of the contract also receives its definite meaning and its complete justification from this source. The principle of unconditional fidelity to contract, which constitutes one of the highest axioms of natural law, is based on the view that the state is not to be conceived merely as a sum total of power and physical coercion. It is to be looked upon rather as an ideal entity whose nature is to be interpreted from its task, its meaning, and its ideal purpose. And this meaning is included in the concept of the covenant as a promise freely given, not as an obligation based on coercion. The validity of the original contract is thus inviolable for the political authority because the contract is the theoretical justification of authority; hence the power which abolished the contract would annul its own prerogative. The state can create and justify law only in so far as it bears within itself and realizes an original law. All the binding power of "civil law" (*lex civilis*) is anchored in this fundamental power of "natural law" (*lex naturalis*). Law as such is before and above the state, and it can provide an unshakable foundation for the life of the state only on the basis of its autonomy and independence.

In Rousseau we have another type of social covenant. Not infrequently Rousseau's social contract has been considered as belonging to pure natural law and interpreted on that basis. But such an interpretation ignores the systematic core and the real historical originality of Rousseau's fundamental idea. Rousseau has adopted and woven into his doctrine elements which he takes from Hobbes and Grotius, yet he freely criticizes both. In his *Discourse on the Origin of Inequality* he raises strong objections to certain of Grotius's assertions. Neither can Rousseau's *Social Contract* be considered simply as a continuation of thought on natural law. For Rousseau rejects natural law, especially in his social psychology, even though his view of social teleology has many points in common with the concept of natural law. He expressly repudiated the doctrine of an original social instinct (*appetitus societatis*) which drives men together. At this point he does not hesitate to go back to Hobbes.[36] He does not indeed describe the state of nature as a war of all against all but as a condition in which everyone is isolated from, and completely indifferent to, everyone else. Neither a moral nor a sentimental bond, neither a sense of duty nor a feeling of sympathy exists among individuals in this state. Each man lives only for himself and he seeks only that which is necessary to self-preservation. The only thing wrong with Hobbes's psychology, according to Rousseau, is that it assumes an active egotism within the state of nature instead of a merely passive one. The lust for robbery and for domination by violence are unknown to the man of nature as such. It can only appear and strike roots after man has entered society and become acquainted with all the "artificial" desires which society fosters. Not violent subjection of others, but indifference to them, the impulse toward separation and withdrawal, characterize the mentality of the man of nature. To be sure, according to Rousseau, natural man is also capable of sympathy; but this feeling is not rooted in an "innate" social instinct but simply in a gift of imagination. Man has by nature the ability to place himself in the position of others and to sense their feelings, and this faculty of "empathy" enables him to a certain degree to feel the sorrows of others as his own.[37] But it is still a long way from this ability, which is based on mere sense impressions, to an active interest, to activity with and for others. One is guilty of a strange hysteron proteron if he attributes the origin of society to any such interest. This form of fellow feeling, when it gains ascendancy over mere egotism, can indeed be the goal of society but it cannot constitute its point of departure. In the state of nature there can be no harmony be-

[36] The following passage is taken in part from the author's essay on Rousseau referred to above p. 147, note 17.

[37] Concerning Rousseau's psychology of natural man and his criticism of Hobbes, see especially the *Discourse on Inequality*, Part One.

tween self-interest and the general interest. Individual interest by no means coincides with the common interest; on the contrary, these interests are mutually exclusive. In the beginnings of society then—which are not deliberately shaped by the will but are the result of the blind rule of forces of which man is the slave not the master—social laws are simply a yoke which everyone wants to put upon others without thinking of yielding to it himself. Rousseau felt the whole burden of these traditional and conventional forms of society, and he protested bitterly against them. "You need me, for I am rich and you are poor. Let us therefore make a contract with one another. I will do you the honor to permit you to serve me under the condition that you give me what little you still have left for the trouble I shall take in commanding you."[38] Such, according to Rousseau, is the social contract which had prevailed in society hitherto, a contract involving a purely juridical obligation, but the opposite of any genuine moral obligation.

At this point Rousseau's protest begins and his will to reform is incited to action. The social contract—he now replies vigorously to Hobbes—is nothing in itself; it is absurd and unreasonable if, instead of uniting inwardly the individual wills, it compels them to unite by the use of external physical coercive measures. Such a bond is actually unstable and ethically worthless. For authority has moral value only when the individual is not simply subject to it but subjects himself to it. Rousseau's *Social Contract* seeks to establish the form and fundamental laws of this authority. No real unity results where the partners to the contract continue to act as individual wills despite this obligation, where only one person makes a covenant with another or individuals as such choose a ruler and subject themselves to him as private persons. For social unity cannot be attained by force; it must be founded in liberty. Such liberty does not exclude submission; it in no sense asserts arbitrariness, but rather the strict necessity of action. This submission, however, is no longer that of an individual will or of an individual person to other individuals. It means rather that the particular will as such

[38] See Rousseau's article, "Économie Politique," *Encyclopédie*, Paris, 1755, vol. V, p. 347.

ceases to be, that it no longer demands and desires for itself, but that it exists and wills only within the framework of the "general will" (*volonté générale*). This kind of contract, according to Rousseau, has the only force which is not physically compulsory but objectively obligatory. From this connection results the strict correlation which Rousseau conceives as existing between the genuine concept of liberty and the genuine concept of law. Liberty implies an obligation to an inviolable law which every individual enacts for himself. Not in license, but in the free acknowledgment of law, lies the true character of liberty. Rousseau's problem, then, is not to emancipate the individual in the sense of releasing him from the form of society altogether; his problem is to find a form of society in which the person of every member is protected by the whole united power of the political organization, in which the individual, while uniting with all other individuals, nevertheless obeys only himself within this union. "In short, each giving himself to all, gives himself to nobody; and as there is not one associate over whom we do not acquire the same rights which we concede to him over ourselves, we gain the equivalent of all that we lose, and more power to preserve what we have."[39] "So long as the subjects submit only to such conventions, they obey no one, but simply their own will."[40] To be sure, they have renounced once and for all that "natural independence" which they enjoyed in the state of nature but they have exchanged it for something better and more secure. For now for the first time they have become individuals in the higher sense; they have become subjects governed by the will, whereas heretofore they had been motivated by their appetites and sense passions. The autonomous personality comes into being only as a result of being bound by the "general will." Rousseau does not hesitate to place the goal of society, as he presents it in the *Social Contract*, far beyond the mere state of nature, which he at first seemed to glorify.[41] Al-

[39] *Social Contract*, Book I, ch. VI, tr. Henry J. Tozer, London, Allen and Unwin, 1924, p. 110.
[40] *Ibid.*, Book II, ch. IV, p. 127.
[41] That this does not constitute an inconsistency in Rousseau's development and that there is no systematic contradiction between the thesis of the *Discourse on Inequality* and that of the *Social Contract*, I have endeavored to show in the essay on

though man foregoes when he enters society various advantages
which he had enjoyed as an isolated being, yet he gains by this
transition such a development of his capacities, such an awakening of his ideas, and such an exaltation of his feelings that, were
it not for the corruption of this new order which often debases
him beneath the state of nature, he could but bless unceasingly
the happy moment which rescued him from that state, and which
"transformed him from a stupid and ignorant animal into an
intelligent being and a man."[42]

This enthusiasm for the force and dignity of law is characteristic of Rousseau's ethics and politics, and in this respect he
was the forerunner of Kant and Fichte.[43] In his ideal of society
and the state he leaves so little space for any personal decisions
of the individual that he seems to look upon such decisions as a
sin against the real spirit of all human society. On this issue his
thought shows no vacillation; for even in the first sketch of the
Social Contract law is called the most sublime of all human institutions and a real gift of heaven by virtue of which man has
learned to imitate in his earthly existence the inviolable com-
mandments of the Deity.[44] Historically speaking, the so-called
Storm and Stress period of German literature misunderstood
Rousseau's gospel of nature when it interpreted it to mean that
a return to nature would put an end to the dominion of law. If
Rousseau had pursued such a tendency, his *Social Contract* would
of course stand in flagrant, almost incomprehensible contradiction to the *Discourse on Inequality*. For the absolute rule, the
unconditional sovereignty, of law cannot be more rigorously
proclaimed than in the former work. Before the law the individual enjoys no reservation or qualification. Any clause inserted
into the social contract to the advantage of any individual rights
would destroy its real meaning and content. Real unity can only

Rousseau referred to above p. 147, note 17. See especially: "Das Problem Jean-
Jacques Rousseau," pp. 190 ff.

[42] *Social Contract*, Book I, ch. VIII, in *op.cit.*, p. 114.

[43] Cf. Gurvitch, "Kant und Fichte als Rousseau-Interpreten," *Kant-Studien*,
XXVII (1922), 138 ff. Cf. also Gurvitch's comprehensive treatment in his work
*L'Idée du Droit social. Notion et système du droit social. Histoire doctrinale depuis
le XVIIe siècle jusqu'à la fin du XIXe siècle*, Paris, 1932, pp. 260 ff.

[44] Cf. Schinz, *La Pensée de J. J. Rousseau*, Paris, 1929, pp. 354 ff.

prevail if the individual not merely gives himself up to the whole, but submits himself to it entirely: "the alienation being made without reserve, the union is as perfect as it can be and an individual associate can no longer claim anything."[45] Rousseau can abandon and silence all resistance of the individual on this point because he is convinced that where law prevails in its true purity and generality, the real moral requirements of the individual are immediately fulfilled. They are *aufgehoben*, that is, abolished and preserved, in the twofold sense of this word. On the one hand, they can no longer appear as independent requirements while, on the other hand, their real meaning has been taken up and preserved by the law. Where mere power rules, where an individual or a group of individuals reigns and forces its commands on the people, there it is of course requisite and necessary and sensible to set fixed limits to this usurped power. For all such power is subject to misuse, which must be prevented as far as possible. Yet all preventive measures are in fact ineffective; for when the will to remain within the law is lacking, no "fundamental laws," however carefully conceived, to whose execution the ruler is pledged, deter him from interpreting and applying them in his own sense. It is in vain to limit the extent of power if one does not change its nature, that is, its source and basis in law. Rousseau's legal and political doctrine concentrates upon this change. He proclaims the unconditional sovereignty of the will of the state but this sovereignty presupposes of course that the state has already been constituted so that in it no other source of law is recognized and active than that of the general will. Where this is the case, any limitation of sovereignty seems to be not only superfluous but also self-contradictory because here the question of the extent of power becomes meaningless. The question is simply one of the content and principle of power, concepts which admit no consideration of a "more" or a "less." In so far as the individual is no longer confronted with mere physical power, but with the pure idea of the constitutional state, he needs no more protection. From now on true protection for the individual is offered in and

<hr>

[45] *Social Contract*, Book I, ch. VI, in *op.cit.*, p. 110.

by the state and protection against the state becomes absurd. Accordingly, Rousseau does not relinquish the principle of inalienable rights. However, he never invokes it against the state because he looks upon it as embodied and firmly anchored therein. On the theoretical side this fundamental conception is realized when, following Hobbes's method as a model, Rousseau rejects the dualism which had prevailed heretofore in the theory of the social contract. He too no longer recognizes a twofold form of the contract, by the one form of which society constitutes itself out of individuals, and by the other sets up a ruler and subjects itself to his will. Just as Hobbes had reduced the whole process of the formation of the state to the covenant of subjection, so Rousseau reduces this process to the contract of association.[46] All legitimate power must be included in and derived from this contract. No authority which is derived from a given source can transcend its factual foundation and its original legal ground. Hence all governmental power, whether it is embodied in an individual or exercised by a majority, is never more than delegated power. It cannot abolish or infringe upon the sovereignty of the people as the adequate expression and the sole bearer and incumbent of the general will because governmental power is legitimate only in so far as it is derived from and confirmed by the people. The moment this mandate of the general will lapses, governmental power—which by its nature has merely administrative significance—relinquishes all claims to legality. For the law can of course limit itself in its execution and delegate to others some of the powers invested in it, but it cannot carry this process to the point of self-alienation and self-annihilation. The idea of inalienable rights, which in the theory of natural law was designed to draw a clear and precise line of demarcation between the sphere of the individual and that of the state and to preserve the independence of the former from the latter, is now asserted by Rousseau to belong to the sphere of the state. Not the individual, but the whole, the "general will," has certain fundamental rights which it cannot and must not give up or delegate to others, because in so doing it would destroy itself as a volitional subject and surrender its true nature.

[46] Cf. Gierke, *Johannes Althusius*, especially pp. 115 ff.

Law, State, and Society

We have already seen what revolutionary power lay in this new conception of the contract.[47] In one respect above all Rousseau went beyond his immediate historical environment, beyond the intellectual milieu of the French *Encyclopaedia*. In their determination to execute reforms and in the importance of their projects for this purpose Rousseau's contemporaries by no means lag behind him. The severe and incurable ailments of the "old regime" had been recognized long before this era. The criticism of the state and society which the *Encyclopaedia* epitomizes and systematizes had already been expressed in the seventeenth and in the early part of the eighteenth century. Men like Vauban, Boulainvilliers, and Boisguillebert pursued the line of thought which Fénelon had clearly expressed. In his *Examination of Conscience for a King* Fénelon brings to one intellectual focus all the objections that have ever been raised against an absolutist regime and its abuses. Nor did these objections remain abstract considerations; they went rather to the very root of the evil and looked for definite concrete preventive measures. In all fields a resolute will toward reform now develops. Radical changes are demanded in legislation and administration, in judicial proceedings, in taxation, and in the trial and punishment of criminals. It is not the philosophers who declare and wage this war on abuses; in almost all fields they had been anticipated by practical reformers.[48] In d'Argenson's work *Considerations on the Past and Present Government of France* (which was written in the year 1739 but circulated in manuscript form until it was printed in 1764), France is called a white sepulchre whose external splendor only poorly conceals the rottenness within. When d'Argenson was appointed to the French ministry in the year 1744, he was enthusiastically greeted by his philosophical friends, and by men of affairs and politicians he was wittily

[47] See above pp. 153 ff.

[48] Insight and perspective with regard to this development are now provided by a collection of the main texts in the works of Henri Sée, *Les idées politiques en France au XVIIe Siècle*, Paris, 1923, and *L'évolution de la pensée politique en France au XVIIIe Siècle*, Paris, 1925. Cf. also Henri Sée, "Les idées philosophiques et la littérature prérévolutionnaire," *Revue de Synthèse historique*, 1925. See furthermore Gustave Lanson, *Le Rôle d'Expérience dans la formation de la philosophie du XVIIe siècle en France*, Études d'Histoire Littéraire, Paris, 1930, pp. 164 ff.

characterized as "secretary of state of Plato's Republic."[49] Thus the soil for Rousseau's criticism of society was completely prepared both in practice and in theory when he appeared on the scene with his first two writings on the prize questions set by the Academy of Dijon. D'Argenson himself, as can be seen from his Diary, joyfully greeted Rousseau's *Discourse on Inequality* and considered it the work of a "true philosopher."[50] From this point on Rousseau remains in complete agreement with the general aspirations of the eighteenth century. It is therefore difficult to understand why not only Rousseau himself continued to believe that he had revolutionized the whole intellectual world of his century but why, after the leading minds of the epoch had tried in vain to bring Rousseau over to their way of thinking, they finally looked upon him as an intruder, as a thinker whose demonic power they felt but whom they had to reject unless they wanted to sacrifice the clarity and stability of their philosophical outlook.[51] The core of this discrepancy lies not so much in the content of Rousseau's thinking as in his method of reasoning. Rousseau differs from his century far less in his political ideals than in his deduction of his ideals, in their derivation and justification. However much this century was disturbed by existing political abuses, its criticism never went so far as to weigh the value of social existence as such. To this age such existence is looked upon rather as an end in itself, as a self-evident goal. None of the Encyclopaedists doubted that man can live otherwise than in fellowship and sociability, or that he could realize his destiny under other conditions. However, Rousseau's real originality consists in the fact that he even assails this premise, that he disputes the methodological presupposition which all previous projects for reform had implicitly acknowledged. Is it really true that the idea of community can be identified with the ideal of society which eighteenth century culture had up to now pursued blindly and credulously? Or is there not a radical dif-

[49] Cf. Voltaire's letter to the Duke de Richelieu on Feb. 4, 1757, *Oeuvres*, ed. Lequien, Paris, vol. LX, p. 238.

[50] Cf. Henri Sée, *L'évolution de la pensée politique*, p. 98.

[51] For a fuller account of Rousseau's relation to the Encyclopaedists see the author's essay, *Das Problem Jean-Jacques Rousseau*, pp. 201 ff. Cf. above p. 147, note 17.

ference between them? Or is not the true community only attainable and clearly justifiable when one has rigorously distinguished it from the idols of society and protected it from them? The controversy between Rousseau and the Encyclopaedists broke out over this question, and we must trace its development if we want to see in their proper perspective the divergent views which are thus called forth.

Taine's objection, expressed in his *Origins of Contemporary France*, that the Encyclopaedists were Utopian doctrinaires who constructed purely synthetic political and social systems which they proclaimed dogmatically without regard to concrete historical reality, has long been recognized as untenable. Their craving for reality and their flexible sense of the real are indisputable. They all want to set to work immediately, for they are aware that the road from theory to practice is long and toilsome. Even such a fanatical theorizer as Holbach (in his *System of Nature* for instance) does not attempt as a political thinker to transplant his speculations directly into realities. In his *Social System* he rejects all revolutionary solutions of political problems, declaring that such cures are always worse than the disease. The voice of reason is neither mutinous nor bloodthirsty; the reforms it proposes are gradual but thereby all the more effective.[52] On the other hand, all these thinkers are convinced that reason must bear the torch on the way to political and social betterment. The ability to overcome the evils of the state and of society can only arise from a real "enlightenment," from clear insight into the grounds and origins of abuses. This faith in the power of rational insight exhibited by the leading minds of the eighteenth century is not a purely intellectual matter. Even though the charge of intellectualism might be brought against the calmly reflective d'Alembert with his mathematical spirit, Diderot presents an entirely different picture. He is far more a visionary than an intellectualist; even in his purely speculative writings he allows his ever active and versatile imagination to lead the way and to carry him beyond all limits of the strictly demonstrable. If one proceeds on the basis of the ambiguous and

[52] Holbach, *Système social*, vol. II, p. 2.

indistinct contrast between "rationalism" and "irrationalism," then, as compared with Diderot, Rousseau appears rather as a rationalist; for the rigor of rational deduction which Rousseau achieves in his *Social Contract* is neither equaled nor approached by Diderot in his articles in the *Encyclopaedia* on fundamental questions of politics and society. Yet the really decisive contrast between the two men lies elsewhere. Diderot and the Encyclopaedists are convinced that one can entrust himself to the progress of culture because such progress, simply by virtue of its immanent tendency and law, will of itself bring about a better form of the social order. The refinement of manners and the growth and extension of knowledge will and must finally transform morality and give it a firmer foundation. This faith is so strong that for most of these thinkers the concept of the community which they are endeavoring to formulate and justify becomes synonymous not only with the concept of society but even with that of sociability. In the French expression *société* these two meanings constantly overlap. A sociable philosophy and a sociable science are here in request. Not only political, but also theoretical, ethical and aesthetic ideals are formed by and for the salons. Urbanity becomes a criterion of real insight in science. Only that which can be expressed in the language of such urbanity has stood the test of clarity and distinctness. Fontenelle in the seventeenth century attempts in his *Conversations on the Plurality of Worlds* to subject the teachings of Descartes to this test, and in the eighteenth century Voltaire undertakes to do the same thing for Newton's mathematical principles of natural philosophy. This movement also invades Germany and is excellently typified in Euler's *Letters to a German Princess*. Diderot epitomizes this trend when he asserts that the demand for popular expression is in fact a moral requirement. True humanity needs such expression for its realization. "Let us hasten to make philosophy popular. If we want the philosophers to march on before, let us approach the people at the point where the philosophers are. Will they say there are works which will never come within reach of everyone? If they say so, they only show that they are ignorant of what proper method and long practice can do."[53] Nor do the exact mathematical sciences want to do without the aid of the sociable spirit of the century any longer because the eminent representatives of these sciences are of the opinion that only in this form will their investigations really prosper and bear their ripest fruits. In his "Preliminary Discourse" in the *Encyclopaedia* d'Alembert declares that the essential advantage of the eighteenth century over the preceding era consists in the fact that it has brought forth more geniuses, more truly creative minds. Nature always remains the same; hence every age has great geniuses. But what can they achieve if they live in isolation and are left to their own thoughts? "The ideas which one acquires from reading and society are the germ of almost all discoveries. It is an air which one breathes without thinking about it and to which one owes his life." The vital and intellectual atmosphere of the *Encyclopaedia* finds perhaps its most precise and pregnant expression in these words. Society is the vital air in which alone true science, true philosophy, and true art can thrive. The *Encyclopaedia* endeavors to produce and establish this union. It conceives knowledge for the first time consciously as a social function, declaring that its development is possible only on the basis of a sound social organization. All political and social enterprise must stand on the same foundation, and a renaissance of political and moral life can be expected only from the growth and spread of intellectual and social culture.

Rousseau's criticism and radical opposition begin at this point. He ventures to sever the bond which is looked upon at large as indissoluble. The unity existing between the moral consciousness and the general cultural consciousness, which heretofore had been accepted naively and credulously, is treated by Rousseau as problematic and indeed as extremely questionable. And once the question as such has been understood and clearly formulated, the answer can no longer remain in doubt. The harmony between the ethical and theoretical ideals of the age collapses. Rousseau himself has given a most incisive account of the moment in which this collapse took place in his own case. It was when in preparing his prize essay for the Academy of Dijon he

---

[53] Diderot, *De l'interprétation de la Nature*, sect. XI, *Oeuvres*, ed. Assézat, vol. II, pp. 38 f.

faced the question whether or not the progress of the arts and sciences had contributed to the improvement of morals. In his famous letter to Malesherbes he writes: "If anything ever resembled a sudden inspiration, it was the emotion which surged up in me while perusing this question. All at once I felt myself dazzled by a thousand lights; a flood of ideas pressed in upon me with such force that I was thrown into an indescribable turmoil."[54] As if in a sudden vision Rousseau now sees the vast abyss before him which had remained veiled from the eyes of his contemporaries, and on whose edge they had moved with no idea of the threatening danger. The realm of will is separated from the realm of knowledge. They are distinguishable both as to their ends and as to their methods of approaching their ends. For in that very intellectual and sociable culture which the eighteenth century looks upon as the height of real humanity Rousseau sees the gravest peril. The content of this culture, its origins, and its present status are for him but so many unambiguous proofs that it lacks all moral motivation, and that it is founded on nothing but the lust for power and possession, ambition, and vanity. The social philosopher must here become the philosopher of history; he must attempt to trace the ways by which society arrived at its present form in order to bring to light the forces by which it was moved and which hold sway over it to this day. Nor is this part of his task conceived and carried out in a merely historical sense. When he contrasts the social state with the state of nature and when he describes the transition from one to the other, he is perfectly aware that he is not dealing with a mere question of facts which can be decided on historical grounds and within the framework of a historical presentation. In his description of the state of nature, as in his account of the social contract, the word and concept "development" is taken not so much in its empirical as in its logical and methodological sense. Rousseau offers us the picture of the development of middle-class society not as an epical narrative, but as arising from that "genetic definition" which is the fundamental method of the philosophy of law and of the state in the seventeenth and eighteenth centuries.[55] The

---

[54] Second letter to Malesherbes, Jan. 12, 1762.
[55] See above pp. 253 ff.

process of the formation of society is to be described because the secret of its structure can only be discovered in this way, and because the immanent forces of society can be made visible only through their action and effects. In his *Discourse on the Origin of Inequality* Rousseau had already expressed himself with precision on this basic viewpoint on method. Whoever talks of the "state of nature," he points out in the preface of this work, is referring to a state of things which no longer exists, *which perhaps never did exist and never will exist*, and of which one must, nevertheless, form an idea, in order to judge correctly concerning our present state. Rousseau, then, does not consider the state of nature as a mere fact or as an object of contemplation and nostalgic longing; he employs this concept rather as a standard and norm according to which he can show what in the present state of society is truth and what illusion, what is morally obligatory law and what is mere convention and caprice. In the mirror of the state of nature the present form of the state and contemporary society are to behold their own countenances and pass judgment on themselves.

If this judgment leads to the negation and overthrow of all order as it has existed heretofore, this by no means signifies that order in general is to be given up, that humanity is to be cast back into its original chaos. Rousseau as the enthusiastic herald of law and the general will is far from any such theoretical and practical anarchy. Nor did he ever draw any such conclusion with respect to the arts and sciences. On the contrary, he asserts again and again—and his assertion should have been believed rather than brushed aside as mere self-deception—that it never occurred to him in his attack on the arts and sciences to reject entirely their contribution to the social structure. "In these first writings," he says of his two prize essays, "it was my intention to dispel the illusion which fills us with such absurd admiration for the tools of our misfortune, to correct that fallacious valuation that has caused us to heap honors on pernicious talents, and to disdain virtues. But human nature does not move backward, and one can never turn back to the state of innocence and equality once he has forsaken it. The author of these writings has been persistently accused of a desire to destroy science and art, and to let humanity sink back into its original barbarism; yet, quite to the contrary, he always insisted on the preservation of existing institutions, declaring that their destruction would permit vice to survive and would merely do away with the means to its mitigation and moderation, and that such destruction would only replace corruption by unbridled power."[56] Such lawlessness, which is the opposite of real freedom, can, according to Rousseau, be avoided only if the present order, which is acknowledged to be corrupt and arbitrary, is abolished, if the whole political and social edifice is razed—and if in its stead another firmer structure is erected upon a really solid foundation. The purpose of the *Social Contract* is to erect this structure. Rousseau wants to transform the present improvised form of the state into a rational state; he wants to change society from a product of blind necessity to one of freedom. It was not an original moral inclination Rousseau had tried to show in his *Discourse on Inequality* that caused man to make the transition from the natural to the social state; nor is it original moral forces, or pure will and clear insight, which maintain him in this state. It is more likely that man fell a victim of society as a result of an inexorable fate, by the physical compulsion of external nature, and by the power of his emotions and passions, than that he chose society freely and shaped it according to his own needs and aspirations. This depraved condition is to be abolished. Man is to return to his original condition and to his original nature; not in order to remain there, but in order from this starting point to build up his social existence all over again. And this time he shall not succumb to the power of his appetites and passions but he shall himself choose and direct. He shall grasp the helm himself and determine both his course and his destination. He must know where he is going and why because only with this knowledge can he be sure of victory and the final realization of the idea of law. Obviously this is a perfectly rational demand, but an ethical rationalism has now gained the ascendancy over a merely theoretical rationalism. Once equilibrium among man's faculties has been safeguarded, there is no reason why knowledge should

---

[56] *Rousseau Juge de Jean-Jacques*, third dialogue.

not enjoy relative privileges and be protected in them. Following the *Social Contract* Rousseau persistently defends the thesis that knowledge is not dangerous so long as it is not entirely abstracted from life but supports the social order. It must not lay claim to absolute primacy, for in the realm of spiritual values it is the moral will which enjoys this position. Hence in the order of human society a sure and clear formation of the moral world must precede the construction of the scientific world. Man must first have found a firm law within himself before he seeks the laws of external objects. After this first and most urgent problem has been mastered and man has attained true freedom in the political and social order of the cosmos, he may then with confidence devote himself to the freedom of intellectual inquiry. Under these circumstances knowledge will not become a victim of mere "hair-splitting," nor will it render man effeminate and indolent. It was a false ethical order which led knowledge in this direction and caused it to become simply a kind of intellectual luxury. As soon as this obstacle has been removed, it will return to its proper path. Intellectual freedom profits man nothing without moral freedom; but this freedom is not to be had without such a transformation of the social order as would put an end to caprice and cause the inner necessity of law to triumph.

Thus in the clash of doctrines which we have just discussed, and in Rousseau's passionate quarrel with his epoch, the inner spiritual unity of the age appears once more in a new light. Rousseau is a true son of the Enlightenment, even when he attacks it and triumphs over it. Nor is his gospel of feeling irreconcilable with his era; for it is not merely emotional factors that we are dealing with here but genuine intellectual and moral convictions. Rousseau's sentimentalism is no mere "sensibility," but an ethical force and a new ethical will. By virtue of this fundamental tendency Rousseau's sentimentality was capable of arousing minds of an entirely different stamp and of casting its spell upon them—as, for instance, in the cases of such utterly unsentimental thinkers as Lessing and Kant in Germany. The strength of the Enlightenment and the systematic unity of its thought are perhaps never so clearly observable as in the circumstance that this movement withstood the attack of its most dangerous antagonist and succeeded in defending against him the treasure which belonged to it alone. Rousseau did not overthrow the world of the Enlightenment; he only transferred its center of gravity to another position. By this intellectual accomplishment he prepared the way for Kant as did no other thinker of the eighteenth century. Kant could find support in Rousseau when he came to build up his own systematic edifice—that edifice which overshadows the Enlightenment even while it represents its final glorification.

CHAPTER VII

Fundamental Problems of Aesthetics

I. THE "AGE OF CRITICISM"

THE eighteenth century is very fond of calling itself the "century of philosophy," but it is not less fond of calling itself the "century of criticism." The two phrases are only different expressions of the same situation, intended to characterize from diverse angles the fundamental intellectual energy which permeates the era and to which it owes its great trends of thought. The union of philosophy and literary and aesthetic criticism is evident in all the eminent minds of the century; in no case is it simply an accident; it is invariably based on a deep and intrinsically necessary union of the problems of the two fields of thought. There had always been a close relationship between the basic ·questions of systematic philosophy and those of literary criticism; and after the renewal of the philosophic spirit during the Renaissance, which professes to be a rebirth of the arts and sciences, this relationship develops into a direct and vital reciprocity between these disciplines. But the age of the Enlightenment goes one step further, interpreting the correlation between philosophy and criticism in another and stricter sense, that is, not only in a causal but in an original and substantial significance. The Enlightenment considers that the two bodies of knowledge are interdependent and in agreement in their indirect effects. It, as well, asserts and seeks for both a unity of nature. Systematic aesthetics sprang from this conception of the interdependence and unity of philosophy and criticism. It embraces two tendencies operating from different directions. There is, first the fundamental propensity of the century toward a clear and sure ordering of details, toward formal unification and strict logical concentration. The various threads which in the course of the centuries had been spun by literary criticism and aesthetic contemplation are to be woven together into one fabric. The material offered in

275

such abundance by poetics, rhetoric, and the theory of the fine arts is now to be ordered and arranged from unified points of view. But this demand for logical clarification and order forms only the preliminary step. From the problem of logical form a second and deeper problem of intellectual content evolves. A correlation is now sought between the content of philosophy and that of art; and an affinity is maintained which appears at first to be too dimly felt for expression in precise and definite concepts. The chief task of criticism seems now to consist in overcoming this obstacle. Criticism seeks to penetrate the chiaroscuro of sensation and taste with its ray; without tampering with their nature as such, criticism attempts to bring them both into the light of pure knowledge. For even where a limitation of the concept is admitted, where an irrational element is assumed and acknowledged, the eighteenth century wants, nevertheless, clear and sound knowledge of this limitation. It was the most profound thinker of the age who toward the end of the century declared that this demand was the really constitutive characteristic of philosophy in general, and who regarded philosophical reason itself as nothing else than an original and radical faculty for the determination of limits. The necessity for such a determination is most clearly seen where a conflict between two bodies of knowledge is concerned which are not only palpably different in structure, but in which this difference seems to amount to a diametrical opposition. From the consciousness of such an opposition arose that intellectual synthesis which led to the foundation of systematic aesthetics in the eighteenth century. But before this synthesis could be achieved, before it took on definite shape in the work of Kant, the philosophical idea had, so to speak, to go through a series of preliminary stages and exercises by means of which it strove to characterize the problematic unity of opposites from different angles and viewpoints. The controversy over the definition and relative order of the various basic concepts, in which eighteenth century aesthetics was engaged, reflects this universal tendency in all its phases. Whether it is the dispute between reason and imagination, the conflict between genius and the rules, the foundation of the sense of beauty in feeling or a certain form of knowledge: in all these syntheses the same fundamental problem recurs. It is as if logic and aesthetics, as if pure knowledge and artistic intuition, had to be tested in terms of one another before either of them could find its own inner standard and understand itself in the light of its own relational complex.

This process is recognizable in all efforts, however divergent, to found aesthetic systems in the eighteenth century, and it forms their latent center and intellectual focus. Individual thinkers participating in this movement are by no means aware from the start of the goal toward which they are steering; and in the clash of various tendencies a really consistent line of reasoning, a conscious orientation to a definitely conceived fundamental problem, is nowhere to be observed. The aesthetic problem remains in constant flux; and constant variations take place in the significance of the basic concepts depending on the choice of starting-point and on the predominance of the psychological, the logical, or the ethical interest. But in the end a new pattern crystallizes from all these various and apparently contradictory currents of thought. Logic and moral philosophy, natural science and psychology are confronted with a new complex of problems which have not yet been clearly distinguished from these disciplines. Indeed a thousand threads still hold these problems to the older bodies of knowledge; yet, loath as philosophical thought is to sever these connections, it begins, nevertheless, gradually to loosen them until finally it dissolves this bond, if not physically, at least logically. And from this dissolution, from this intellectual process of liberation, the new form of philosophical aesthetics results. Moreover, all those trends, which considered in themselves might resemble by-paths of eighteenth century aesthetics, contributed indirectly to the appearance and to the final attainment and determination of this form. The historian of aesthetics must not neglect or underestimate any of these unfinished, fluctuating, and ephemeral elements; for their very incompleteness shows perhaps most distinctly and immediately the growth of the philosophical consciousness of art and of the law governing the development of this consciousness.

But still another and deeper miracle marks the preliminary

history of systematic aesthetics. Not only is a new philosophical discipline worked out and mastered according to rigorous logical method but at the end of this development comes a new form of artistic creation as well. Kant's philosophy and Goethe's poetry form the intellectual goal toward which this movement prophetically beckons. And the inner relation existing between these two crowning achievements of the eighteenth century can be completely understood only in and through this historical connection. That such a "pre-established harmony" was possible in German intellectual history has always been regarded as a most remarkable coincidence. Windelband said of Kant's *Critique of Judgment* that it constructs, as it were, *a priori* the concept of Goethe's poetry, and that what the latter presents as achievement and act is founded and demanded in the former by the pure necessity of philosophical thought. This unity of demand and act, of artistic form and reflective contemplation, is not sought after or artificially induced in German intellectual history of the eighteenth century; it results directly from the dynamic interplay of its fundamental formative forces. These forces produce, as a necessary and immanent consequence, a radically new form of philosophy as well as a new mode, a new dimension, of the artistic creative process. This synthesis too, which marks the close and the climax of eighteenth century culture, is the product of the conscientious, painstaking, intellectual toil of the century. It is one of the imperishable titles to distinction of the epoch of the Enlightenment that it accomplished this task, that it joined, to a degree scarcely ever achieved before, the critical with the productive function and converted the one directly into the other.

II. CLASSICAL AESTHETICS AND THE OBJECTIVITY OF THE BEAUTIFUL

The new ideal of knowledge with which Descartes begins his philosophy professes to embrace all parts of knowledge, all sides and aspects of ability. Not only will the sciences in the stricter sense of the word—logic, mathematics, physics, and psychology—receive a new direction and definition through this ideal but art too is now subjected to the same rigorous demand. Art likewise is to be measured and tested by the rules of reason, for only such an examination can show whether or not it contains something genuine, lasting, and essential. Such content cannot be attributed to the momentary emotions of pleasure awakened in us by works of art. In so far as such content can be maintained and defended, it must be based on a different, firmer foundation; it must be freed from the unlimited variability of mere pleasure or displeasure and conceived as a necessary and stable element. Descartes did not include a systematic aesthetics in his philosophy but the broad outlines of an aesthetic theory are implied in his system as a whole. The absolute unity in which, according to him, the nature of knowledge consists, and which is to overcome all its arbitrary and conventional divisions, is extended in the Cartesian system to include also the realm of art. Descartes does not hesitate to expand his conception of "universal wisdom" (*sapientia universalis*) so that it also includes, as a universally valid postulate, art as a whole and in all its particular forms. When in his "rules for the direction of the understanding" (*regulae ad directionem ingenii*) he first describes with clarity and precision his ideal of "universal knowledge" (*mathesis universalis*), he includes under this ideal, according to medieval tradition, not only geometry and arithmetic, not only optics and astronomy, but also music. And the further the spirit of Cartesianism spread, and the more decisively and confidently it asserted itself, the more forcefully the new law is proclaimed in the realm of aesthetic theory. For if this theory wants to assert and justify itself, if it wants to be more than a mere conglomerate of empirical observations and haphazardly accumulated rules, it must realize the pure character and basic principle of theory as such. It must not permit itself to be led astray by the diversity of its objects. It must grasp the nature of the artistic process and of aesthetic judgment in its unity and in its characteristic entirety. We arrive at such an entirety in the sphere of the arts only when we succeed in reducing the various and apparently heterogeneous forms in which the arts manifest themselves to a single principle, and when we determine them by and derive them from that principle. The course of seventeenth and eighteenth century aesthetics was thus indicated once and for all. It is based on the idea that, as nature in all its manifestations is governed by certain principles, and as it is the highest task of the knowledge of nature to formulate these principles clearly and precisely, so also art, the rival of nature, is under the same obligation. As there are universal and inviolable laws of nature, so there must be laws of the same kind and of the same importance for the imitation of nature. And finally all these partial laws must fit into and be subordinate to one simple principle, an axiom of imitation in general. Batteux expressed this basic conviction in the title of his chief work, *The Fine Arts Reduced to a Single Principle*. This title seems to proclaim the fulfillment of the whole methodological trend in aesthetic criticism in the seventeenth and eighteenth centuries. The great example of Newton exerts its influence here too. The order which he achieved in the physical universe should be sought also in the intellectual, the ethical, and the aesthetic universe. As Kant saw in Rousseau the Newton of the moral world, eighteenth century aesthetics called for a Newton of art. And this demand no longer seemed incongruous after Boileau had been recognized as the "law-giver of Parnassus." His work seemed finally to elevate aesthetics to the rank of an exact science in that it introduced in the place of merely abstract postulates concrete application and special investigation. The parallelism of the arts and sciences, which is one of the fundamental theses of French classicism, now appeared to have been tested and verified in fact. Even prior to Boileau this parallelism had been explained on the grounds of the common derivation of the arts and sciences from the absolutely homogeneous and sovereign power of "reason." This power knows no compromise and tolerates no qualification. Not to acknowledge the power of reason as an integral and undivided whole and not to entrust oneself to this power without reserve, is to deny and destroy its real nature. "In all matters which depend on reason and common sense, such as the rules of the theater," says d'Aubignac in his work *Theatrical Practice* which appeared in 1669, five years before the appearance of Boileau's *Poetic Art*, "license is a crime which is never permitted." Thus poetic license is rejected and condemned just as scientific license is. "The arts have this in common with the sciences," Le Bossu writes at the beginning of his treatise on the epic, "that the former like the latter are founded on reason and that in the arts one should allow himself to be guided by the lights which nature has given us."[1] In this passage the concept of nature of classical aesthetics appears for the first time in its proper light. For as in "natural morality" and "natural religion," so too in aesthetic theory, the concept of nature has less a physically substantial than a functional significance. The norm and model which it offers is not immediately exemplified in a certain field of objects but rather in the free exercise of certain intellectual forces. Here also "nature" can be a synonym for "reason."[2] Everything springs from and belongs to nature which is not the product of a momentary impulse or a mere whim but is based on eternal great laws. The foundation is the same for both beauty and truth. If we go back to the origins of the formation of law in general, then all appearance of an exceptional and unique place for the beautiful vanishes. The exception, as a negation of the law, can be no more beautiful than true: "Nothing is beautiful but the true" (*rien n'est beau que le vrai*). Truth and beauty, reason and nature, are now but different expressions for the same thing, for one and the same inviolable order of being, different aspects of which are revealed in natural science and in art. The artist cannot compete with the creations of nature, he cannot breathe real life into his forms unless he knows the laws of this order, and unless he is completely imbued with these laws. The fundamental conviction of classical criticism is summed up and brought to a focus in a didactic poem by M. J. Chénier: "It is good sense, reason, which achieves all: virtue, genius, spirit, talent, taste. What is virtue? It is reason put in practice. And talent? Reason

---

[1] Le Bossu, *Traité du poème épique*, 1675. Concerning the aesthetic theory of d'Aubignac and Le Bossu see Heinrich von Stein, *Die Entstehung der neueren Ästhetik*, Stuttgart, 1886, pp. 25 ff., 64 ff.

[2] Cf. above pp. 241 ff.

brilliantly set forth. Spirit? Reason well expressed. Taste is simply refined good sense, and genius is reason sublime."[3]

But this reduction of genius and taste to "good sense" must not be understood merely as a glorification of "common sense." For the theory of French classicism has nothing to do with any philosophy of common sense; it does not concern itself with the everyday and trivial use of the understanding but with the highest powers of scientific reason. Like mathematics and physics, critical theory too recognizes the rigorous ideal of exactness, which constitutes the necessary correlate and presupposition for its requirement of universality. Here again we find complete harmony between the scientific and artistic ideals of the epoch. For aesthetic theory seeks only to follow the same way that mathematics and physics had taken and pursued to the end. Descartes had based all knowledge of nature on pure geometry, and in so doing he seemed to have achieved another victory for purely intuitive knowledge. For, according to his doctrine, all being, in order to be clearly and distinctly conceived and to be understood in pure concepts, must first be reduced to the laws of spatial intuition; it must be converted into geometrical figures. This mode of figurative representation is expressly taught by Descartes in his *Rules for the Direction of the Understanding* as a fundamental method of all knowledge. But the primacy of intuition[4] over pure thinking is only apparently asserted and justified in this method. Descartes immediately adds that a purely intuitive character belongs indeed to geometrical figures but that it by no means belongs to geometrical method. With respect to this method Descartes exerts himself to the utmost to

---

[3] "C'est le bons sens, la raison qui fait tout:
   Vertu, génie, esprit, talent et goût.
   Qu'est-ce vertu? raison mise en pratique:
   Talent? raison produite avec éclat:
   Esprit? raison qui finement s'exprime;
   Le goût n'est rien qu'un bon sens délicat;
   Et le génie est la raison sublime."—Marie Joseph Chénier, "La Raison," lines 8-14; *Poésies*, Brussels, 1842, p. 81.

[4] The German words *Anschauung* and *anschaulich* have been rendered in this passage by "intuition" and "intuitive" respectively. The sense is therefore "direct perception" and "directly perceived," and should not be confused with mystic "intuition" or with the common use of "intuitive" as a synonym for "instinctive."—Tr.

free it from the limitations of intuition and to make it independent of the obstacles which beset the "imagination." The result of this philosophical exertion was analytical geometry, whose essential accomplishment consists in its discovery of a method by which all intuitive relations among figures can be represented and exhaustively determined in exact numerical relationships. Thus Descartes reduces "matter" to "extension" and physical body to pure space; however, space in Cartesian epistemology is not subject to the conditions of sensory experience and of the "imagination" but to the conditions of pure reason, to the conditions of logic and arithmetic.[5] This criticism of the faculties of sense and imagination, which is introduced by Descartes, is taken up and extended by Malebranche. The entire first part of his chief work *Inquiry concerning Truth* (*Recherche de la vérité*) is devoted to this task. Here again the imagination appears not as a way to the truth but as the source of all the delusions to which the human mind is exposed, in the realm of natural science and in that of moral and metaphysical knowledge. To keep the imagination in check and to regulate it deliberately, is the highest goal of all philosophical criticism. To be sure, the aid of this faculty cannot be dispensed with entirely because it constitutes the first stimulus to knowledge. But the gravest mistake and the most dangerous error of knowledge, from which criticism must protect it, lies in the confusion of this beginning with the end, with the real meaning and goal of knowledge. This goal can be attained only by leaving the initial phase behind and proceeding in a clear, logical manner. Pure intuition itself is capable of and requires such transcendence of the imaginative phase; for here too the path of perceptual extension, as exemplified by physical objects, leads to that "intelligible extension" which alone can serve as the foundation for an exact science of mathematics.[6] We must also contemplate the

[5] Cf. Descartes' letter to Mersenne, July 1641: "All that knowledge which one could perhaps believe most subject to our imagination, because it is concerned only with magnitudes, figures, and movement, is not at all based on the phantasms of that faculty, but solely on the clear and distinct notions of our mind, as they know who have examined the matter ever so little." *Oeuvres*, ed. Adam-Tannery, vol. III, p. 395.
[6] Cf. above pp. 96 ff.

corporeal world in the medium of intelligible extension if we are to make it accessible to knowledge and to penetrate it with the light of reason. Seen in this light all sense properties and qualities are sifted out and relegated from the realm of truth to that of subjective illusion. What then remains as the real nature of the object is not that which the object presented to direct perception but certain pure relations which can be expressed in terms of exact and universal rules. These rules, which apply to general relations and proportions, are therefore the fundamental framework of all being. They are the norm from which being cannot deviate and which it cannot abandon without sacrificing its real character as being, that is, as objective truth.

Classical aesthetics was modeled after this theory of nature and after this mathematical theory point by point. In the development of its fundamental idea it was indeed faced with a new and difficult task; for despite all the limitations and restrictions which were placed upon the imagination in the realm of pure knowledge, it could not but seem a dubious and paradoxical beginning to turn the imagination entirely away from the threshold of the theory of art. For does not such a rejection amount to an actual negation of art? Will not such a transformation in the mode of contemplation nullify the object considered and rob it of its real meaning? As a matter of fact, the theory of classicism, strongly as it objected to founding a doctrine of art on the imagination, was by no means blind to the real nature of the imagination, and by no means impervious to its charm: tradition and veneration for antiquity would not have allowed classicism to be otherwise. According to tradition the execution of a perfect work of art required both a rigorous technique and innate talent (ingenium) which cannot be acquired but, as a gift of nature, must be present and active from the first. "I cannot see how study profits without a vein of genius, or skill without training. Thus each gift needs the other's aid and joins in friendly union."[7] Boileau begins his *Art of Poetry* with a paraphrase of these lines: "It is in vain that a rash author thinks to climb Parnassus by dint of his versifying art. If he does not feel the

[7] Horace, *Art of Poetry*, tr. T. A. Moxon, in *Aristotle's Poetics*, Everyman's Library, New York, E. P. Dutton, 1934, p. 74.

secret influence of heaven, if the star which presided at his birth did not make him a poet, then he will always remain the victim of his meagre genius. For him Phoebus is deaf and Pegasus stubborn."[8] Thus Boileau reasserts the maxim that the true poet is born, not made. But what is true of the poet is not entirely true of poetry. For the impulse which inspires and constantly sustains the process of creation is one thing, while the work that results from this process is another matter. If the work of art is to be worthy of its name, if it is to be independent form possessing objective truth and perfection, then it must purge itself of the subjective forces which were indispensable during its development. The work of art should burn behind it all bridges leading back to the world of mere fancy. For the law governing art as such is not derived from and produced by the imagination; it is rather a purely objective law which the artist does not have to invent but only to discover in the nature of things. Boileau considers reason as the epitome of such objective laws, and in this sense he commands the poet to love reason. The poet is not to seek external pomp and false embellishment; he should be content with what his subject itself offers. If he portrays it in its simple truth, he may be sure that he has satisfied the highest standard of beauty. For beauty can be approached only along the path of truth; and this path requires that we should not stop at the mere surface of things, at their impression on our senses and feelings, but that we should distinguish most sharply between reality and appearance. Just as the natural object cannot be known as that which it is unless we make a careful selection among the phenomena constantly obtruding themselves upon us, unless we distinguish between the changeable and the lasting, between the accidental and the necessary, between that which is valid only for us and that which has its ground in the object itself—so it is with the object of art. This

[8] *L'Art Poétique:*
> C'est en vain qu'au Parnasse un téméraire auteur
> Pense de l'art des vers atteindre la hauteur:
> S'il ne sent point du ciel l'influence secrète,
> Si son astre en naissant ne l'a formé poète,
> Dans son génie étroit il est toujours captif,
> Pour lui Phébus est sourd, et Pégase est rétif.

object is not simply given and known; it too must be determined and controlled by such a process of selection. By its second-rate imitators, not by its real originators, classical aesthetics was led into the error of attempting to establish definite rules for the production of works of art; it does, however, demand control of this process of selection, the right to establish its norms and to guide it by fixed standards. It does not pretend to be able to teach artistic truth directly but it believes it can protect the artist from error and establish criteria for determining error. In this respect also classical aesthetics shows its kinship with the Cartesian theory of knowledge which was guided by the methodological principle that we can attain to philosophical certainty only by an indirect path, namely, by insight into the various sources of error and by its conquest and elimination. According to Boileau, the beauty of poetic expression coincides with its propriety, and propriety becomes a central concept of his whole aesthetics. He opposes the burlesque as well as the *précieux* and pungent style because they both deviate in different directions from this ideal. And the highest, in fact the only, praise that he has for his own poetic work is that it always remains faithful to this fundamental norm, that it does not affect the reader merely by external charm but by the simple clarity of its thought and the economy and careful choice of its means of expression: "Nothing is beautiful but the true, the true alone is agreeable. It should reign everywhere, even in fable; the cunning artifice of all fiction tends only to make the truth shine forth more brilliantly. Do you know why my verses are read in the provinces? Why they are sought after by the people and well received by princes? It is not because their sounds are agreeable and varied and always pleasing to the ear; nor is it because the sense never distorts the meter and a word never defies the caesura. It is rather because the true, victorious over the false, is evident in them on every hand, and touches the heart; it is because good and evil are portrayed in proper proportion, because a scoundrel never rises to a dignified position in my verses, and my heart, always leading my mind, says nothing to the readers that it has not already said to itself. My thought always comes out clearly, and my verse, good or bad, always says something."[9]

The basic and central question of classical aesthetics, the problem of the relationship between the general and the particular, between the rule and the exception now appears in its true light. The objection has been raised on countless occasions that classical aesthetics lacked all sense of the individual, that it sought all truth and beauty in the general, dissolving both into mere abstractions. Taine, who adopts this view, takes it as the starting-point of criticism which is not merely directed against the aesthetics of the seventeenth and eighteenth centuries, but against the whole spirit of classicism—which attempts to rob this spirit of its borrowed splendor and to expose its impotence. Unbiased historical investigation, however, will have to proceed rather in the opposite direction. Instead of utilizing classical aesthetics to demonstrate the shortcomings and inner weakness of the "classical spirit," such investigation will seek out the strongest points of this spirit and endeavor to understand and interpret it in the light of its highest and really important achievements. Here again the parallelism between the development of aesthetics and that of mathematics in the seventeenth and eighteenth centuries is conspicuous. Descartes sees his real progress beyond the geometrical method of the ancients in the fact that he was the first to raise geometry to a position of real

[9] Rien n'est beau que le vrai, le vrai seul est aimable.
Il doit régner par-tout, et même dans la fable;
De toute fiction l'adroite fausseté
Ne tend qu'à faire aux yeux briller la vérité.

Sais-tu pourquoi mes vers sont ius dans les provinces?
Sont recherchés du peuple, et reçus chez les princes?
Ce n'est pas que leurs sons, agréables, nombreux,
Soient toujours à l'oreille également heureux;
Qu'en plus d'un lieu le sens n'y gêne la mesure
Et qu'un mot quelquefois n'y brave la césure:
Mais c'est qu'en eux le vrai, du mensonge vainqueur,
Par-tout se montre aux yeux, et va saisir le coeur;
Que le bien et le mal y sont prisés au juste;
Que jamais un faquin n'y tint un rang auguste;
Et que mon coeur, toujours conduisant mon esprit,
Ne dit rien aux lecteurs, qu'à soi-meme il n'ait dit.
Ma pensée au grand jour par-tout s'offre et s'expose
Et mon vers, bien ou mal, dit toujours quelque chose."—Boileau, "Épitre IX," *Oeuvres*, commentary by Saint-Surin, Paris, 1821, vol. II, pp. III ff.

logical independence and self-sufficiency. Ancient geometry is of course an incomparable school for the mind; but, as is pointed out in the *Discourse on Method*, it cannot sharpen the mind without at the same time constantly occupying the imagination and finally exhausting it with the most varied shapes and problems. Time and again inquiry in this subject matter loses itself in the study of special cases, and for each group of special cases it must find the proper demonstration. The new analytical method of Descartes seeks to put an end to this difficulty; it offers general rules and absolutely universal procedures in which the treatment of every special case is implied and determined *a priori*. And further decisive progress was achieved when mathematics advanced from Descartes' analytical geometry to Leibniz's infinitesimal calculus and Newton's method of fluxions. For now the rule of the general over the particular was established and affirmed from a new angle. The differential quotient of a given function represents the "nature" of this function; it gives us the whole course of the curve of the function with the greatest conceivable precision. All the details of this curve which any observation could discover are concentrated into one conceptual expression and brought to a logical focus. From the formula with which the analysis of the infinite supplies us we can directly determine all the properties of the curve and derive all its characteristics in a strictly deductive manner. Observation as such cannot achieve this form of unity. If observation wants to imagine a certain geometrical concept, as, for instance, an ellipse, it has no alternative but to review and compare with one another the whole scope of its possible forms. From such a comparison a certain "picture" of an ellipse finally results, which is, however, far from a truly homogeneous and simple figure. For to direct perception the various classes of ellipses exhibit outstanding differences. There are ellipses which approach the form of a circle; there are others elongated and narrow which are far from circular, and which from the viewpoint cf the figure directly perceived contrast sharply with the former type. Yet the geometric concept of analytical geometry treats all these differences as irrelevant, as not belonging to the "nature" of the ellipse. For, so far as this concept is concerned, this nature is not given in the diverse and countless observable differentiations of the ellipse but in a universal formative law; and it is this law that the equation of the ellipse exemplifies in exact form. Here mathematics grasps true "unity in multiplicity." It does not seek to deny multiplicity as such but to understand it and to deduce it from a general law. The formula of the function in its general form contains indeed only the universal rule according to which the dependence of the variables on one another is determined; but it is always possible to go back from the formula to any particular form of the figure which is characterized by certain quantities, that is, by its particular constants. Every determination of these quantities—for example, every length we assign to the major and minor axis—produces a new special case; yet all these special cases are the same in the sense that they mean precisely the same thing to the geometer. The same geometrical meaning, the identical being and truth of the ellipse in general, is concealed in the multitude of special shapes; and it is characterized and, as it were, revealed in its real essence by the analytical formula.

The aesthetic "unity in multiplicity" of classical theory is modeled after this mathematical unity in multiplicity. It is a mistake to think that the principle of unity in multiplicity as such is contrary to the spirit of classicism and that the opposite pole of classicism is most effectively expressed in this principle.[10] In the realm of art the spirit of classicism is not interested in the negation of multiplicity, but in shaping it, in controlling and restricting it. Boileau in his *Poetic Art* attempts to arrive at a general theory of the genres of poetry, just as the geometer attempts to arrive at a general theory of curves. In the wealth

[10] This is the view, for instance, of Alfred Baeumler, *Kants Kritik der Urteilskraft, ihre Geschichte und Systematik*, Halle, 1923, vol. I, p. 43. It is also an error to assert, as Baeumler does, that Crouzaz in his *Treatise on the Beautiful* (*Traité du beau*) in 1715 was the first to use the formula, "variety reduced to some unity" (*variété réduite à quelque unité*), in an aesthetic context. The philosophical meaning of this formula was systematic and thoroughly developed by Leibniz with express reference to the problems of aesthetics. Cf. Leibniz's work *On Wisdom* (*Von der Weisheit*), above pp. 121 f.

of actually given forms he seeks to discover the "possible" form, just as the mathematician wants to know the circle, the ellipse, the parabola, in their "possibility," that is, in the constructive law from which they can be derived. Tragedy, comedy, elegy, epic, satire, and epigram all have their definite laws of form which no individual creation can neglect, and from which it cannot deviate without offending against "nature" itself and without losing its claim to artistic truth. Boileau endeavors to develop into clarity and distinctness these implicit laws which are based on the nature of the various poetic genres, and which the actual practice of art has always followed without being aware of the fact. He seeks to express and formulate these laws explicitly, just as mathematical analysis makes possible for the various classes of figures such a formulation, such an expression of their real content and fundamental structure. Accordingly, the genre itself is not something for the artist to produce, nor is it a medium and instrument of creation for the artist to take up and use as he pleases. It is rather something given as such and self-contained. The genres and types of art correspond to the genera and species of natural objects; the former like the latter have their immutable and constant forms, their specific shape and function, to which nothing can be added and nothing taken away. The aesthetician is not therefore the lawgiver of art any more than the mathematician or physicist is the lawgiver of nature. Neither the artist nor the natural scientist creates order; they merely ascertain what "is." To be bound to these existing forms and to be obliged, as it were, to follow their laws, is no obstacle for genius; for it is only in this way that genius is protected against arbitrariness and enabled to attain the only possible form of artistic freedom. Even for genius there exist certain insuperable barriers both with respect to the objects of art and to the genres. For it is not possible to treat any object in any genre; the form of the genre in itself constitutes a certain selection. This form restricts the field of material just as it requires a certain mode of treatment. Freedom of movement must therefore be sought elsewhere; it is not concerned with content as such, which to a great extent is determined in advance, but with expression and representation. It is expression which shows what one commonly calls "originality."[11] Here the artist is to exhibit his real powers; and of all the different expressions of one and the same object the genuine artist will always prefer that expression which surpasses all others in technical mastery and faithfulness to its object, and in clarity and richness. But not even in expression will the artist strive for novelty at any price and for its own sake; he will seek only such novelty as will do justice to the demands of simplicity, conciseness, and cogent brevity of expression in a measure not previously attained. A new thought, according to Boileau, is by no means one that was never conceived before: "On the contrary, it is a thought which should have occurred to everyone and which some one took it into his head to express for the first time." But there is at once a further limitation. For once this complete adjustment has been reached between content and form and between object and expression, art has arrived at a goal beyond which it need not and cannot go. Progress in art does not mean indefinite advancement; art stops at a certain stage of completion. All artistic perfection signifies a *non plus ultra*, an ultimate limit. In his work *The Age of Louis XIV* Voltaire repeats once more the classical equation of the perfection of works of art and the temporal end of certain genres. Here again the analogy is realized which theory assumes to exist between artistic and scientific problems, and which it seeks to carry out in detail. Condillac saw the connection between art and science in their common relation to language. He looks upon both as different stages of one and the same intellectual function which is expressed in the creation and use of symbols. Both art and science substitute for objects symbols of objects, and they differ only in the use which they make of their symbols.[12] But the advantage of scientific symbols over linguistic ones, over mere words, is that the former are more definite than the latter, and that they strive for perfect, unam-

---

[11] Regarding this restriction of "originality" to novelty of expression in classical aesthetics, see, for instance, Gustave Lanson, *Boileau*, Paris, 1892, especially pp. 131 ff.: "The artist always has to create a form, the most true, the most expressive, the most beautiful that can be."

[12] Cf. Condillac, *Essai sur l'origine des connaissances humaines* and his *La Langue des Calculs*.

biguous expression. This is the real purpose of scientific symbols, but this purpose also sets up an immanent limit. Scientific theory can designate the same object by the use of different symbols; the geometer, for instance, can express the equation of a curve either in Cartesian or in polar co-ordinates. But one of these expressions will finally be relatively superior because it affords the simplest formula for the function in question. Classical aesthetics makes an ideal of "simplicity." It is looked upon as a corollary of true beauty just as it is the corollary and criterion of truth.

The weak points of this theory are obvious, and yet further historical development did not proceed from its systematic deficiencies. Here the deficiencies of execution weighed more heavily, which appeared when classical principles were applied to the consideration of the various genres and works of art. Paradoxical as it may seem, it can be said that in this respect one of the main shortcomings of classical doctrine was not that it went too far with abstraction but that it did not maintain its abstractions with sufficient consistency. For on every hand in the foundation and defense of the theory, intellectual factors enter which can by no means be strictly derived from its general principles and premises, but which have their origin in the particular situation of the problem, in the intellectual and historical structure of the seventeenth century. Inadvertently these factors influence the work of the leading theorists and cause them to deviate from their purely systematic goal. We find the clearest illustration of this situation in a controversy that has not infrequently been considered as the real core of all classical aesthetics. With the doctrine of the three unities this aesthetics seems to have faced a concrete test, and its philosophical and theoretical destiny seems indissolubly bound up with the unities. Yet the doctrine of the unities was not created by classical aesthetics; it lay ready at hand and was simply woven into its system.[13] Nor is a really convincing justification of the acceptance of the unities ever given. Even when Boileau proclaims the doctrine of the unities he speaks as the lawgiver of reason and

[13] For the historical development of the theory of the three unities see Lanson, *Histoire de la littérature française*, 22nd ed., Paris, 1930, pp. 420 ff.

in the name of reason. "But we whom reason pledges to its rules, we wish the action to suit the art, and that a single act accomplished in one day and in one place should keep the theater full to the end."[14] And yet this application of the doctrine contains a clear misrepresentation if measured by purely logical standards. For the ideal of reason, which Boileau otherwise always tries to uphold, is here supplanted by a merely empirical standard. At this point classical aesthetics clearly departs from its scientific concept of "universal reason" to take on characteristics of the philosophy of "common sense." Instead of seeking its support in truth, it appeals to probability, and probability itself is understood in a narrow, purely factual sense. But such an evaluation of the factual is basically contrary to the deeper principles of classical theory. It is obviously insufficient to resort to the spectator for proof of the absolute necessity of the unities of place and time on the grounds that it would be absurd for him to see in the course of a few hours an action embracing years or decades. For it had always been the aesthetics of classicism which had in accordance with its basic trend warned against confusion of what is true and valid "according to the nature of things" with what appears valid to an individual from his particular viewpoint. It had demanded of the individual as an aesthetic subject that he forget his idiosyncrasies in order to allow only the objective law, only the pure necessity of the object, to prevail. Is it not an offense against this requirement, is not the strictly impersonal character of reason as asserted by all theorists of classicism destroyed, if the accidental conditions of the spectator are made the standard for drama and the norm of its composition? And this is not the only instance of deviation from strict rational standards; it is simply the most conspicuous symptom of that strange inconsistency which we find generally among the advocates of strict classicism. They all strive for simplicity, propriety, and "naturalness" of expression, but they derive the standard of the natural without doubts or scruples

---

[14] Mais nous, que la raison à ses règles engage,
Nous voulons qu'avec art l'action se ménage;
Qu'en un lieu, qu'en un jour, un seul fait accompli
Tienne jusqu'à la fin le théâtre rempli.—Boileau, *Art poétique*, chant III.

from the world in which they live; they base this standard on their immediate environment, on habit and tradition. At this point the power of abstraction, with which the founders of classical doctrine are endowed, begins to fail; critical reflection is supplanted by naive credulity, by a veneration for all those things which were empirically given in the intellectual and artistic culture of the seventeenth century. The less this spell is recognized, the stronger its hold on individual thinkers. Boileau not only treats "nature" and "reason" as equivalents, but he also equates nature with a certain state of civilization. This state, in his view, can be attained only through the cultivation of all the forms which life in society has created and brought to their highest stage of refinement. Thus court and capital are now elevated to the status of aesthetic models and patterns, just as previously reason and nature had been. "Study the court and know the city; both have ever been fertile in models." Unnoticed, decorum has superseded nature, and convention truth. The theater especially, which represents the form and flowering of the noblest sociability, must adhere to this framework. Nowhere is the rule of reason as severe as here, but nowhere must it be guarded so closely and anxiously if the poet is to avoid offenses against the real purpose of the theater. Hence Boileau makes the exactness of the rule to which dramatic poetry must submit correspond to its narrowness, so that he can almost treat exactness and narrowness as synonyms: "Anything is easily excused in a shallow romance; it is enough if fiction amuses momentarily, and too much rigor would be out of place. But the stage calls for exact reason; its strict decorum must be safeguarded."[15] With this identification of reason with decorum the theory of classicism finally transformed its aesthetic ideals into sociological ones. Goethe remarks in the notes to his translation of *Rameau's Nephew*: "Different genres of poetry were treated like different societies, in which various modes of be-

---

[15] Dans un roman frivole aisément tout s'excuse;
   C'est assez qu'en courant la fiction amuse;
   Trop de rigueur alors seroit hors de saison:
   Mais la scène demande une exacte raison,
   L'étroite bienséance y veut être gardée.—Boileau, *Art poétique*, chant III.

havior are becoming. . . . A Frenchman by no means hesitates, in passing judgment on products of the intellect, to speak of the 'proprieties'—a word which in reality refers only to social behavior."[16]

The development which now takes place leads finally to the dissolution and decline of classical theory. During the first half of the eighteenth century the authority of this doctrine is scarcely disputed. Voltaire is too incisive and critical not to notice certain weaknesses; but he is, on the other hand, too great an admirer of the age of Louis XIV, of which he is the first historian, to escape its severe requirements in the field of taste. Moreover, in his skeptical and pessimistic moments Voltaire criticizes the culture of his time, and in his narrative *The Candid Man* (*L'Ingénu*) he seeks to hold up to this depraved culture the mirror of nature, simplicity, candor of thought, and innocence of manners. But in the very way he presents his hero he reveals most clearly how much he is indebted to his age for his ideal of nature; for the pure child of nature that he wishes to portray shows no trace of crudeness or ill-breeding. He not only is characterized by the greatest tenderness and consideration, but he knows the language of gallantry. As an aesthetician also, Voltaire holds that genuine and refined taste is the result of man's instinct of sociability and, as he explains in his *Essay on Taste*, the development of this sense is possible only in society. Before Rousseau came upon the scene the questions of nature and society had not yet been sharply distinguished in French culture of the eighteenth century. Nature is worshiped enthusiastically, but into the picture of "beautiful nature" (*belle nature*) come all the trappings of convention. In France, Diderot is the first to find fault with this convention, and his writings show the beginnings of a new revolutionary spirit. But in his immediate activity as a critic and writer, especially in his work as a playwright, not even he dares to cast off his shackles. The final step here was taken by Lessing in his *Hamburg Dramaturgy*. He exposes the untenable and baneful confusion which had existed in French drama and dramatic theory regarding

[16] Goethe, *Werke*, ed. Weimar, vol. XLV, p. 174.

the difference between the demands of pure aesthetic "reason" and merely conventional and temporally restricted demands. He distinguishes ruthlessly between the two elements. He eliminates from aesthetic principles all those things which owe their origin not to truth and nature but to that illusory existence of which every epoch boasts, however brilliant it may actually be. This existence can produce no real artistic shapes and no genuine dramatic characters. Only the magic wand of the poetic genius, not the rules of propriety of an aesthetic school, can succeed in producing such shapes: "If pomp and etiquette make machines out of men, it is the task of the poet to make men again out of these machines."

Eighteenth century aesthetics had thus prepared the way for Lessing. For the confusion of social and aesthetic standards, of which classical theory had been guilty, was bound to lead to a joint historical destiny for them both. From the moment when the social standards could no longer resist the rising tide of criticism, when their weak and questionable points began to appear, the aesthetic standards also could not help being loosened and finally resolved altogether. This event ushered in another important era for eighteenth century aesthetics. It clarified for aesthetics, in a concrete historical case of immediate concern, the connection between art and the spirit of the times. Boileau's poetics was profoundly influenced—as it were, saturated—with the spirit of his epoch; but this fact could not be represented and acknowledged in the theory as such. The rules which Boileau establishes, with respect to their purpose and systematic tendency, are conceived as universal, eternal rules. For only unreason, not reason, has a "history"; reason is and remains what it was from the beginning to the end of time. But now this premise of classical aesthetics also begins to waver along with the conclusions which had been drawn from it. With the advent of new scientific and philosophical ideas and of new political and social demands, one *experiences* the change of aesthetic standards. More and more emphatically the new era calls for a new art. To the pathos and hero worship of classical drama Diderot opposes a new social and aesthetic attitude, and for the expression of this attitude he requires a new poetic genre, namely, "domestic tragedy." Aesthetic criticism in the eighteenth century was prepared to assimilate such developments and to recognize and interpret them in theory. Dubos in his *Critical Reflections on Poetry, Painting and Music* had already done so. He is one of the first to understand and to be interested in the development of the individual arts, and to trace the causes of this development. Among the causes he is not only interested in the intellectual, but also in the natural ones, and even in climatic and geographic causes; besides "moral causes" he attributes a great deal of influence to "physical causes." He thus anticipates in the field of aesthetics the fundamental viewpoint which is later maintained by Montesquieu in sociology and political theory. Not every soil and not every age can bring forth the same art: "The whole earth cannot produce everything" (*non omnis fert omnia tellus*).[17] This insight meant the fall of the classical scheme. A theory is now required which suits the variety and changeability of aesthetic phenomena. The trend is from the mere formula to a knowledge of the real form of the artistic. This form, however, as becomes increasingly evident, is not derivable from works of art as such, but only from theory which participates directly in the process of creation and seeks to reproduce it in thought.

III. TASTE AND THE TREND TOWARD SUBJECTIVISM

The inner transition by which the domination of classical theory in the realm of aesthetics is broken corresponds exactly from the point of view of method with the change which takes place in the theory of natural science between Descartes and Newton. Both transitions, in different ways and with entirely different intellectual means, pursue the same goal. Their purpose is to free the mind from the absolute predominance of deduction; it is to make way for the facts, for the phenomena, for direct observation—not to the exclusion of deduction but side by side with it. Basic principles are not to be abandoned but

[17] Dubos, *Réflections critiques sur la poésie, la peinture et la musique*, Paris, 1719, part II, sect. XIX; see also part II, sect. XII ff.

are to be adapted to the phenomena, whereas previously the phenomena had been subordinated to certain principles possessing *a priori* validity. The method of explanation and deduction gradually approaches that of pure description.[18] But description does not begin directly with the works of art; it attempts first to characterize and ascertain the mode of aesthetic contemplation. It is no longer primarily a matter of artistic genres, but of artistic behavior, that is, of the impression which the work of art makes on the spectator and of the judgment he passes on his impression for himself and for others. This tendency of aesthetics sets up nature as the model for the artist to emulate in every respect. But the concept "nature" has now undergone a characteristic change of meaning. For the "nature of things" (*natura rerum*), to which aesthetic objectivism had been oriented, is no longer the guiding star; it has now been superseded by the nature of man. In this nature contemporary psychology and epistemology also seek their goal and the key to those problems for which metaphysics had always promised, but never found, a solution. If this approach to the problem is to be effective anywhere, then it should be so in the field of aesthetics, for by its very nature the aesthetic is a purely human phenomenon. In this field, it would seem, all transcendence is precluded from the outset; there can be no logical or metaphysical, only an anthropological, solution. Psychology and aesthetics now enter into so intimate an alliance that for a time they appear to be completely amalgamated. In no other field was the transition from the psychological to the transcendental approach, by which Kant finally resolved this alliance, so hard to realize and burdened with so many systematic difficulties as in that of the fundamental problems of aesthetics.

The psychological approach, which finds the origin and basis of the beautiful in human nature, by no means intends to give way to an unlimited relativism, or to recognize the individual subject as the absolute judge concerning works of art. This approach considers taste as a sort of "sense" shared by all, and it begins its formulation of the problem with the question of the nature and possibility of such a "common sense" (*sensus*

[18] See above pp. 51 ff.

communis). Even if the previous form of aesthetic principles is rejected, this does not signify the rejection of all rules and the complete abandonment of the aesthetic to chance and whim. The avoidance of arbitrariness and the discovery of a specific law of the aesthetic consciousness are now regarded as the goal of aesthetics as a science. In clear and emphatic language Diderot formulated this fundamental tendency in the beginning of his *Essay on Painting*. If taste is merely a matter of passing fancy, then where do all those delightful feelings come from, which arise so suddenly, so involuntarily, and so vehemently from the depths of the soul—those emotions which agitate our whole being, causing it to expand or contract, and which draw tears of joy or pain. Effects like these, which everyone observes in himself, cannot be explained away by abstract theories or discounted by skeptical arguments. "Begone sophist! (*apage sophista*)," cries Diderot, "you will never persuade my heart that it should not palpitate or my bosom that it should not be moved."[19]

This new approach, then, considerably limits or gives up entirely the claim to rational justification of aesthetic judgments; but it does not relinquish its claim to universality. The question now is merely that of a more exact determination of the nature of this universality and of the manner in which it can be asserted. Deduction and reasoning prove powerless here because correctness of taste cannot be demonstrated in the same way as the necessity of a logical or mathematical conclusion. Other forces must be brought into play here; another psychological wager must, so to speak, be risked. This conviction gradually gains currency even within the framework of classical theory. Bouhours' treatise *The Art of Thinking in Works of the Intellect* (*La manière de bien penser dans les ouvrages de l'esprit*, 1687) is only separated from Boileau's *Poetic Art* by a little more than a decade, and Bouhours seeks merely to supplement Boileau's work, not to overthrow his basic presuppositions. As the title indicates, this work attempts to give an aesthetic "doctrine of thinking," which appears as a companion piece to the *Art of Thinking* published by Port Royal. But the form of aes-

---

[19] Diderot, *Essai sur la peinture*, ch. VII, *Oeuvres*, ed. Assézat, X, 517 f.

thetic thinking and judging is distinguished more sharply than ever before from any form of merely discursive reasoning. In the latter form of thinking the highest goal is the goal of precision. Every concept employed must be strictly defined and determined in all its characteristics, and this defined meaning must be adhered to throughout the whole series of logical operations. All that is unclear and ambiguous is the death of the logical mathematical concept, which acquires its real meaning and value only through its exactness, and which is more perfect the more it succeeds in realizing this ideal. In aesthetics, on the other hand, another norm prevails. Here a whole group of phenomena can easily be found which are accessible to any unbiased observation and which, nevertheless, are so far from any precision that the application of the method of logical concepts would utterly destroy them. The value and charm of aesthetic appreciation do not lie in precision and distinctness but in the wealth of associations which such appreciation comprises; and this charm is not lost if one does not succeed in surveying the whole extent of this wealth and in analyzing its diversity into its individual elements. The significance of a given instance of aesthetic appreciation is not diminished, in fact it is more often really constituted, by the diverse and often conflicting associations which such appreciation gives rise to, by the manner in which it radiates a thousand hues, and by its fleeting and evanescent qualities. As Pascal had distinguished the "subtle spirit" (*esprit fin*) from the "geometric spirit" (*esprit géométrique*) and contrasted them in a sharply drawn antithesis, so Bouhours opposes the spirit of "correctness," which Boileau had made the principle of art, to the spirit of sensitivity (*délicatesse*). The concept of "délicatesse," as used by Bouhours, amounts, as it were, to a new organ. The aim of this organ is not, as with mathematical thinking, consolidation, stabilization, and fixation of concepts; on the contrary, it is expressed in lightness and flexibility of thought, in the ability to grasp the finest shades and the quickest transitions of meaning. For these transitions and nuances give thought its aesthetic coloring. Strange and objectionable as it may at first seem, one can nevertheless say that in addition to the aesthetic ideal of correctness and precision there is the other, diametrically opposed ideal of *inexactness*. To strict classicism everything inexact had been characterized as untrue and rejected. But aesthetic "reason," as Bouhours points out, is not tied to this limit of the "clear and distinct." It not only enjoys a certain amount of inexactness, but demands it; for the aesthetic imagination is inspired and fostered by the indeterminate and unfinished thought. It is not a matter of the mere content of thought and of its objective truth but of the process of thinking, of the subtlety, lightness and swiftness with which it operates. The decisive factor is not the mere result but the manner in which it is achieved. Aesthetically, a thought is more valuable the more it reflects process and the emergence of unexpected forms. If logic calls for constancy, aesthetics demands abruptness; if logic has to establish all presuppositions of a thought, to survey all the intermediate stages leading up to it, art, on the other hand, finds an inexhaustible source in the underived. That strictly "linear" thought which classical aesthetics established as its norm is insufficient here, for the straight line is the shortest distance between two points only in geometry, not in aesthetics. Bouhours' aesthetics, which is based on the principle of "*délicatesse*," seeks rather to teach the art of indirection and to maintain its validity and fruitfulness. An aesthetically valuable thought almost always makes use of this art in arriving at its goal, which is to startle the mind, and so to imbue it with a new impulse and new energy. Some poetic genres, as for instance the epigram, depend entirely on this condition. Truth alone by no means makes an epigram in the aesthetic sense, for if this were true a mere logical proposition lacking artistic life and motion could be an epigram. Life and motion accrue to the epigram less through the force of truth than of falsehood. "Thoughts are sometimes trivial because they are true"; and this danger of triviality can only be avoided by the manner in which the thought is introduced and presented, that is by some sudden turn of expression. The real emphasis now falls more and more on the expression rather than the content of the thought. Seen in this connection, it is not surprising or paradoxical that Bouhours demands for all works of artistic value not merely truth, but especially an admixture of falsehood, and that for this reason he defends the ambiguous because in it the true and the false are combined to form a unity.[20] It is only by means of the expression of the "false" that Bouhours, who still for the most part speaks the language of classicism, succeeds in casting off the fetters of the classical concepts of truth and reality and moving freely into the region of aesthetic illusion. The aesthetic as such does not originate and flourish in the pure and colorless light of thought; it requires a contrast, a distribution of light and shade. These two qualities are equally important; for art does not pretend to be a second, equally objective world of nature, but an image of this nature. The purely logical ideal of the "equality of the thing and the intellect" (*adaequatio rei et intellectus*) cannot then be realized in the same sense in aesthetics as in science. Classical aesthetics had clung to this ideal, and in doing so it was led to place the main stress on the "natural" and "correct." The representation is more perfect according to its degree of success in reflecting the object itself unencumbered with the cloudy spots and distortions resulting from the nature of the subject. But now this norm begins to change. The stress now falls not on proximity to, but on distance from, the object; not on that in which art resembles nature, but on the specific mode of artistic expression and representation. The logical inadequacy of the media of expression, their indirect and metaphorical character, are expressly admitted; but their value is not affected by this fact. For the image which art draws, since it never resembles or coincides with the object, is not condemned as untrue; it possesses rather its own immanent truth: "The figurative is not false and metaphor has its truth, just as fiction does."[21]

The new motif discernible in Bouhours' work reaches full development only in Dubos. What had merely been suggested by the former becomes the basic systematic idea investigated in all its phases in Dubos' *Critical Reflections on Poetry and Painting*. The phenomena which Bouhours had, so to speak, dis-

---

[20] For details see H. von Stein, *Die Entstehung der neueren Ästhetik*, pp. 87 ff.
[21] Bouhours, *Manière de bien penser dans les ouvrages de l'esprit*, p. 12. Cf. Baeumler, *Kants Kritik der Urteilskraft*, vol. I, pp. 36 f.

covered on the periphery of aesthetics, now move into the center of aesthetic theory. The problem is no longer that of gaining a place for imagination and feeling along with the forces of reason, but of asserting them as the real fundamental forces. If for this reason Dubos' work has been called the "first aesthetic of sentimentalism,"[22] this is true only with historical reservations; for none of those "sentimental" features, as they are later found in the epoch of "sensibility," are present in Dubos. He does not use the word "feeling" (*sentiment*) to mean introspection as a subjective tendency. He no longer proceeds simply from the contemplation and analysis of works of art; he pays attention particularly to their effect, from which he tries to determine the real nature of art. But in this analysis of the aesthetic impression subject and object are treated as equally necessary factors. The more exact character of this causal relation and the participation in it of subject and object cannot be determined in advance by abstract considerations, but only by experience. Dubos is the first to establish introspection as the specific principle of aesthetics and to defend it against all other merely logical methods as the real source of all sound knowledge. The nature of the aesthetic cannot be known by mere concepts, and the theorist in this field has no other means of communicating his insight to others and of convincing them of its truth than to appeal to their own inner experience. The immediate impression, with which all formulation of aesthetic concepts must start and to which it must constantly refer, cannot be replaced by any deductions. "I should not hope to be commended," says Dubos at the beginning of his work, "if I do not succeed in my book in making the reader acquainted with what goes on within himself, in a word, with the most intimate inclinations of his own heart. One hardly hesitates to throw away as unreliable the mirror in which he does not recognize himself."[23] The aesthetician no longer approaches the artist with a law book in his hand, nor does he attempt to lay down inflexible general rules for the spectator. Aesthetics has become simply the mirror in which both artist and spectator find them-

[22] Cf. Baeumler, *op.cit.*, p. 53.
[23] Dubos, *Réflexions critiques sur la Poésie et la Peinture*, part I, sect. I.

selves reflected, and in which they are to recognize themselves
and their fundamental experiences. All education and sharpen-
ing of aesthetic judgment can, in the last analysis, consist in
nothing but learning to see these experiences, these original
impressions, more and more clearly and to distinguish them
from the arbitrary and accidental elements added by reflection.
All doctrine and all consideration of aesthetic concepts which
do not serve this end are to be rejected. Everything which
does not contain the pure immediacy of the impression and
strengthen our faith in it misses the cardinal aim of aesthetics.
Taste in its real sense can neither be learned, nor can it be incul-
cated by merely theoretical considerations; for sense perception
has no need of any such training. "The heart is agitated of itself,
by a motion previous to all deliberation. . . . Our heart is made
and organized for this very purpose: Its operation therefore
runs before our reasoning, as the action of the eye and ear precedes it in their sensations. 'Tis as rare to see men born without
the sense here mentioned, as 'tis to meet with people born blind.
'But it can be no more communicated by art,' says Quintilian, 'to
those that have it not from nature, than the sense of taste, or
smelling.'. . . We weep at a tragedy, before we have discussed
whether the object which the poet presents us, be naturally
capable of moving, or whether it be well imitated. Our sense
tells us its nature, before ever we have thought of inquiring
into it. . . . If the chief merit of poems and pictures were to
consist in being conformable to written rules, one might then
say that the best method of judging their excellency . . . would
be certainly that of discussion and analysis. But the principal
merit of poems and pictures is to please us. . . . For, as Cicero
says, 'All men are capable of judging by the help of an inward
sense, tho' unacquainted with rules, whether the productions of
art are good or bad.' "[24]

Thus taste is no longer classified with the logical processes of
inference and conclusion but placed on a par with the immediacy
of the pure acts of perception—with seeing and hearing, tasting
and smelling. This transition has now brought us to the way

[24] Dubos, *Critical Reflections on Poetry and Painting*, tr. by Thomas Nugent,
fifth edition, London, 1748, vol. II, pp. 239 ff.

which Hume follows through to its logical conclusion. Explicitly Hume's philosophy is far less concerned with aesthetic than with epistemological and psychological, ethical and religious questions. Yet this philosophy occupies an important position in the field of aesthetics too, and its contribution from the viewpoint of method is entirely original. In Hume the whole battlefront of aesthetic controversy is reformed. However far the proponents of the aesthetics of feeling went in their defense of independent nature and immediacy of feeling, they were never able to attack reasoning as such and dispute its peculiar basic function. They endeavored to separate the powers of reason, but not to discredit or diminish the force of reason itself. Reason still remained unchallenged as the force underlying logical thought and causal inference on which depends all knowledge of reality. At just this point Hume takes a further and decisive step. He risks a struggle in the territory of his opponent by seeking to show that what had been looked upon as the pride and real strength of rationalism is in reality the weakest point of its position. Feeling no longer needs to justify itself before the tribunal of reason; on the contrary, reason is summoned before the forum of sensation, of pure "impression," and questioned regarding its claims. And the verdict is that all authority which pure reason had wielded had been unjust and unnatural, in short, had been usurped authority. Reason not only loses its position of dominance; even in its own field, in the domain of knowledge, it has to surrender its leadership to the imagination. Thus reason and the imagination have now changed sides in the controversy surrounding the foundation of aesthetics. Whereas formerly imagination had to fight for recognition and equal rights, it is now treated as the fundamental power of the soul, as the leader and ruler to whom all other faculties of the mind must submit. The conclusions regarding the structure of aesthetics which are implied in this change are obvious, and they were expressly drawn in Hume's essay "Of the Standard of Taste." Even aesthetics must be surrendered to skepticism, if by the latter one understands the rejection of universal and necessary norms which are valid for all times and for all judging subjects. Nowhere can the claim to such a norm of truth and necessity be so easily refuted as in the aesthetic field; for everyday experience teaches us that there is no fixed scale of aesthetic values and that there never has been one. The fundamental standard by which we measure beauty varies from one epoch to another and from one individual to another. It is hopeless to single out from this flood of opinions any particular ones and to make them the model, marking them with the stamp of truth and validity. But if, on the one hand, we must acknowledge the variability or relativity of the judgment of taste, this still does not imply the same dangers for aesthetics as it seems to contain for logic and the purely rational sciences. For these sciences neither want to nor can do without some objective standard derived from the nature of things. They require knowledge of the object itself and its essential properties; and if skepticism raises permanent barriers to any such knowledge, they consider themselves as deprived of their real fruits and purpose. To rational science, therefore, skepticism is always a purely negative and destructive principle. But it is quite otherwise the moment we turn to the sphere of feeling and of pure value judgments. For all value judgments as such are concerned not with the thing itself and its absolute nature but rather with a certain relation existing between the objects and ourselves as perceiving, feeling, and judging subjects. This relation can be "true" in every individual case without ever being exactly the same in any two instances. For the nature, and hence the truth, of a given relation never depends on just one term of the relation, but always results from the manner in which the two terms mutually determine each other. The judging and willing subject is not therefore something external to the content and meaning of the value judgment; on the contrary, it is a co-determinant and constituent of this content and meaning. Once this has been understood the aesthetic judgment gains a special primacy and advantage over the logical judgment. This advantage does not consist in the fact that the aesthetic judgment achieves more than the logical, but that it demands less. For in resisting all false generalizations and in making assertions not about objects as such, but about our relations to them, the aesthetic judgment is enabled to achieve that conformity for which the sciences of the objective world strive in vain. The individual subject can of course never presume to be a judge of things, but he is the only possible and the only qualified judge of his own states of being. Yet the aesthetic judgment is intended precisely as an expression of these states. Hence it can accomplish more because it attempts less. Reason can err; for its standard is not within itself but in the nature of the things to which it refers. However, feeling is not exposed to such aberrations; its content and standard are not outside, but within itself. "All sentiment is right; because sentiment has a reference to nothing beyond itself, and is always real, wherever a man is conscious of it. But all determinations of the understanding are not right; because they have a reference to something beyond themselves, to wit, real matter of fact; and are not always conformable to that standard." Among a thousand different judgments concerning the same objective situation, one and one only is correct and true. The only difficulty consists in determining this one true judgment. On the other hand, a thousand different feelings and evaluations referring to the same object can all be right. For no feeling seeks to grasp and describe anything objective; it merely expresses a certain conformity between the object and the organs and capacities of our minds. We can, therefore, in a certain sense judge "objectively" concerning beauty for the very reason that it is not an object but a condition within ourselves. "Beauty is no quality in things themselves: it exists merely in the mind which contemplates them, and each mind perceives a different beauty."[25]

The last remnant of universal validity now seems to have been eradicated from aesthetic judgment. But if Hume here, as in the field of pure logic, rejects any theoretical generality, this does not mean that he gives up all practical generality as well. Regarding the concepts involved, it must however be said that aesthetic feeling and judgment, since they make predications only concerning the nature of the subject, possess validity only with respect to the subject. But even though it is impossible here to speak of real equality or of real identity, in

[25] Hume, "Of the Standard of Taste," *Essays Moral, Political and Literary*, ed. Green and Grose, London, 1898, p. 268.

the logical sense of the terms, there exists nevertheless an empirical uniformity; and it is this uniformity which prevents the ever present and inevitable differences of feeling and taste from defying all standards of measurement. Such a standard is not of course given *a priori* by the nature of the beautiful, but it is in fact to be found in the nature of man. Man's nature prevents these diversities from becoming indefinitely great, holding them within the bounds established by humanity, not as a universal logical concept or as an ethical and aesthetic ideal, but as a biological species. If every individual differs from every other, yet it also agrees with others; variation itself has its own margin and law. Hence arises that relative agreement among aesthetic judgments which is observable everywhere as a mere matter of fact. Impossible as it is to set up absolute norms, yet there appears nevertheless an empirical regularity and, as it were, an empirical average. Difference remains, abstractly speaking, possible; but in the concrete it becomes meaningless. Whoever attempted to equate the genius and style of Ogilby and Milton, and Bunyan and Addison, could not on purely rational grounds be refuted; but his judgment would be considered no less extravagant than if he were to compare a molehill with the height of Teneriffe or a pond with the ocean.[26] The agreement which taste as a "common sense" asserts can indeed neither be deduced nor demonstrated; yet it occurs as a matter of fact, and in fact it finds a sounder basis than mere speculation ever could have given it. From the empirical viewpoint factual sameness of judgment can be established more quickly and reliably in the field of taste than in that of rational, philosophical knowledge. So far as philosophical systems are concerned, each generally holds sway in its own time; but its splendor rapidly wanes until it is totally eclipsed by a newly risen star. The great classical works of art, however, stand the test of time much better. Much as they are bound to their own epoch and much as an understanding of them seems to depend on conditions peculiar to the time of their origin, these conditions do not set limits to their effectiveness. It would be more correct to say that they bridge the centuries and become the best

[26] Hume, *op.cit.*, p. 269.

evidence that if human thinking changes, then at least human feeling and capacity for aesthetic impressions remain basically the same. The apparently objective truth, which was supposed to be conveyed in the works of ancient thinkers, has vanished for us; but the spell which ancient poetry exercises upon us is still unbroken and the intensity of its effect upon us as sentient subjects has not diminished. "Aristotle, and Plato, and Epicurus, and Descartes, may successively yield to each other: but Terence and Virgil maintain an universal, undisputed empire over the minds of men. The abstract philosophy of Cicero has lost its credit: the vehemence of his oratory is still the object of our admiration."[27]

A certain minimum of general validity in aesthetics is thus conceded, which did not however entirely satisfy the empirically minded thinkers of the eighteenth century. Even if these thinkers recognize experience as the source of aesthetic judgment, yet they undertake, nevertheless, to give experience a firmer foundation and to derive a certain "objective" significance from it. This is of course a reformulation of the problem; for consideration can no longer be content now with a mere description of aesthetic phenomena as such, but it must go back to their sources and attempt to establish their basis in fact. Where else could one look for this basis and how could it be more firmly established than by anchoring truth in purposiveness and by showing that it is only a veiled expression of such purposiveness? It is Diderot who reasserts this view in his aesthetic theory. Taste, according to Diderot, is both subjective and objective; it is subjective because it has no other basis than individual feeling, and objective because this feeling is simply the result of hundreds of individual experiences. In its factual appearance, in its immediate presence, taste is not capable of further definition or explanation; it is an "I know not what" (*je ne sais quoi*). But indirect knowledge of this "unknowable" is possible if one refers the immediate phenomenon to its past. In every judgment involving taste innumerable former experiences are brought to bear. It is no more attributable to speculative considerations than to a mere "instinct"; for an instinct

[27] *Ibid.*, p. 280.

for the beautiful would be nothing but an occult quality (*qualitas occulta*), whose assumption is as fruitless and forbidden in psychology as it is in natural science. We escape both these perils if we can find a purely empirical explanation of this supposed instinct, if we can show that it is derived rather than original. Since first we opened our eyes we have absorbed innumerable impressions, each accompanied by a certain feeling or value judgment of approval or disapproval. Our feeling for the beautiful results from the accumulation of all these observations and experiences in our memory and from their fusion into a new general impression. This feeling is "irrational" in the sense that in the pure experience of the beautiful, all recollection of those former experiences has vanished, and the actual process of this experience cannot therefore give us any knowledge of its development, of its genetic origin.[28] For Diderot this origin is, if not a directly demonstrable phenomenon, at least a postulate which he derives from the general premises of empiricism. "What then is taste? It is a facility acquired by reiterated experiences for grasping the true or the good along with the circumstances which render it beautiful, and for being readily and vitally moved by this perception."[29] The very wording of this declaration shows that Diderot, in his attempt to give a purely empirical explanation of the beautiful, runs the risk of obliterating its specific character and of confusing the beautiful with the physically or morally perfect, that is, with objective purposiveness. "Michelangelo gives St. Peter's Cathedral in Rome the most beautiful form he can imagine. The geometer La Hire, captivated by the beauty of this form, sketches its outline and finds that it forms the curve of greatest resistance. What was the source of Michelangelo's inspiration to choose this curve among innumerable others which he might have employed? Nothing but everyday experience. This is what teaches the simple carpenter as well as the sublime Euler the angle required for the beam used to buttress a wall which threatens to

---

[28] Cf. Diderot's letters to Sophie Volland of Sept. 2, 1762 and Oct. 4, 1767. On Diderot's aesthetics see especially the new detailed account in Folkierski, *Entre le Classicisme et le Romantisme, Étude sur l'Esthétique et les Esthéticiens du XVIIIe siècle*, Paris, 1925, pp. 355 ff.

[29] Diderot, *Essai sur la peinture*, ch. VII, *Oeuvres*, X, 519.

collapse; it has taught him the proper pitch for the wings of a windmill; it often introduces elements into his subtle calculation which no academic geometer could improve on."[30] In such an empirical and practical explanation the beautiful is exposed to the danger of being reduced to everyday experience, to the ordinary and useful both as regards its origin and its immediate form, just as Diderot considers the beauty of the human body to consist in its being so formed that it best fulfills its vital functions. "The handsome man is he whom nature has formed to fulfill as easily as possible the two great functions: preservation of the individual which consists of many things, and propagation of the species which consists of one thing."[31] Thus it appears that Diderot's empiricism has not eluded the danger which it tried to overcome, and that it did not escape the rock which threatened to wreck rationalistic aesthetics. Wherever Diderot seeks not only to describe but also to explain the beautiful, he finds this possible only if he considers the beautiful as dependent on the "true" and merely as a disguised form of the latter. Only now the norm of truth has changed; its content is no longer based on *a priori* propositions, on general and necessary principles, but on practical experience, on daily routine and utility. Both types of explanation fail, however, to account for the peculiar meaning and value of the beautiful; for the standard employed in both cases is on a different plane from that occupied by the pure phenomenon of beauty. As "reason" triumphs in classical aesthetics, so the "understanding" finally prevails in empirical aesthetics. The imagination is theoretically looked upon as an independent faculty, as a special power of the mind; the attempt is even made to show that it is the central faculty and one of the psychological roots of all theoretical activity. But this apparent elevation of the status of the imagination threatens this faculty with a process of leveling; for in entering the theoretical sphere in this manner and in being subordinated to it, the imagination is subject to incorporation with theory. Real autonomy of the beautiful and self-sufficiency of the imagination were attainable only along different lines. The

---

[30] *Ibid.*

[31] For details of Diderot's aesthetic "utilitarianism" see Folkierski, *op.cit.*, pp. 383 ff.

intellectual impulse which was requisite to the accomplishment
of this purpose existed neither in rationalistic nor in empirical
aesthetics. This impulse could come only from a thinker who
neither attempted to analyze beauty theoretically and to reduce it to rules, nor to describe it psychologically and explain
it genetically, but who is completely immersed in the contemplation of the beautiful. Such a thinker first appeared in the eighteenth century in Shaftesbury. His doctrine was destined to
found the first really comprehensive and independent philosophy of the beautiful.

IV. INTUITIONAL AESTHETICS AND THE
PROBLEM OF GENIUS

English aesthetics in the eighteenth century followed neither
the path of French classicism nor that of Hume. The constant
influence of both trends of thought is unmistakable in this
aesthetics both in its approach to the problem and in its development. Both the literature and the aesthetics of England in this
century look up to the great model offered by French classical
tragedy and show the marks of this influence in many respects.
And as for empiricism, it was all the more difficult to escape its
influence in as much as its essential elements were already contained in the first formulation of the aesthetic problem. For this
problem was generally approached from psychological points of
view. In eighteenth century English psychology no more hesitation seemed possible regarding the true and only "natural"
method of treatment. Locke, Berkeley, and Hume seemed to
have won the battle of strict empiricism for all time. Its principles henceforth were not to be discussed; they were to be applied
as extensively as possible to all the new spheres and to more and
more complex phenomena of the operations of the mind.

If, nevertheless, English aesthetics succeeded in breaking the
spell of empiricism and in extricating itself step by step from
the empirical approach, this is because English aestheticians
could appeal directly to and draw inspiration from a philosophical doctrine which had not been formed under the general
predominance of empirical thinking. The real leaders of Eng-

lish aesthetics in the eighteenth century draw their sustenance from Shaftesbury and consider themselves as his pupils and successors. Shaftesbury himself, however, did not pattern his philosophy after any models which he could find immediately in his own age. Locke was his teacher both in his childhood and youth; yet only certain elements of Shaftesbury's thought are traceable to this influence, while the form of his mind and teaching are his alone. He feels no kinship with contemporary philosophy but seeks other intellectual and historical models. It is only necessary to open Shaftesbury's philosophical diary to become aware of this aloofness toward his own time. There is scarcely an echo here of the problems affecting his era, or of the intellectual and practical decisions with which this era is confronted. Its concern lies beyond these urgent questions of the present; hence rather than to them, it looks back to the thought of the Renaissance and of antiquity. In his diary Shaftesbury communes directly with antiquity, with Plato and Aristotle, with Plotinus, with Seneca, and with Marcus Aurelius and Epictetus. To his way of thinking nothing is so repugnant as the reduction of philosophy to a system of logical concepts or to a disintegrated collection of scientific doctrines. He wants to revive and realize the original ideal of philosophy, namely, the ideal of a pure doctrine of wisdom. And in this way, not by way of abstract speculation or of empirical observation, Shaftesbury first approached the problems of aesthetics. These were his own personal problems long before they became purely theoretical problems. Shaftesbury does not consider aesthetics exclusively, nor even predominantly, from the viewpoint of the work of art; on the contrary, he seeks and needs a theory of beauty in order to answer the question of the true fashioning of character, of the law governing the structure of the inward personal world. Philosophy, conceived as a pure doctrine of wisdom, remains incomplete in so far as it does not culminate in a doctrine of the beautiful and find here its concrete fulfillment. For real truth can no more exist without beauty than beauty can without truth. The fundamental thesis of Shaftesbury's philosophy and aesthetics: "All beauty is truth," is understandable only in this context.

Fundamental Problems of Aesthetics

Taken literally, this statement is indistinguishable from the demand for objectivity represented by French classical aesthetics; and it would almost seem as if this were no more than a translation or paraphrase of Boileau's thesis: "Nothing but the beautiful is true" (*rien n'est beau que le vrai*). Yet this resemblance is only apparent, for in these two instances similar words express entirely different thoughts. When Shaftesbury declares that beauty is truth, he does not mean by truth a sum total of theoretical knowledge, of propositions and judgments which can be reduced to definite logical rules, to fundamental concepts and principles. To him "truth" signifies rather the inner intellectual structure of the universe, which cannot be known in terms of concepts alone or grasped inductively by means of an accumulation of individual experiences, but which can only be immediately experienced and intuitively understood. This form of experience and of intuitive understanding is available in the phenomenon of the beautiful. Here the barrier between the world within and the world without disappears; both worlds are governed by the same all-inclusive law, which each expresses in its own manner. The "interior numbers" which we discover in every instance of the beautiful reveal both the mystery of nature and of the physical world. For the latter too is only in appearance an "external" world, that is, a materially present, derived world. The deeper truth of this world also consists in the fact that an operative principle obtains in it, which is embodied in and reflected by all its creatures in varying degrees and force. It is this kind of "reflection," purified of all logically derived elements and showing the inner and outer worlds as indissolubly woven together, which we enjoy in the contemplation of the beautiful. All beauty springs from truth but the full, concrete meaning of truth can only be revealed in beauty. Shaftesbury takes from ethics the Stoic demand for "life according to nature" and applies it to aesthetics. The purest harmony between man and the world is attainable only through the medium of the beautiful. For here man not only understands, but experiences and knows that all order and regularity, all unity and law, depend on one and the same original form, on one and the same whole, which is immediately present in man as in every other creature. The truth of the universe speaks, as it were, through the phenomenon of beauty; it is no longer inaccessible, but acquires a means of expression, a language, in which the meaning of this truth, its real logos, is first completely revealed.

Shaftesbury transplants aesthetics from the classical system and from empirical theories to entirely new soil. We have now arrived at a really critical point in the development of aesthetics, a point at which minds and problems had to part. To be sure, this separation does not appear immediately, nor is it strictly adhered to once it has taken place. Shaftesbury's successors—Hutcheson, Ferguson, and Home, for instance—do not preserve the original doctrine in all its purity; they often unconsciously adopt ideas derived from other sources. But there was one theme which retained its force even in this eclectic dilution. The systematic focus of the whole aesthetic problem is transposed by Shaftesbury's doctrine. Classical aesthetics is oriented primarily to the work of art, which this aesthetics attempted to treat like a natural object and to study with analogous means. It sought a definition of the work of art comparable to a logical definition, which, like the logical definition, was to determine any particular given content by its class, by its genus (*genus proximum*) and its specific difference (*differentia specifica*). The doctrine of the invariability of the genres and of the strictly objective rules governing each genre originated in these efforts to arrive at such a definition. Empirical aesthetics is distinguished from this mode of investigation not only in its method but also in its object. For it is not directly interested in the works of art, in their classification and subsumption. This school of aesthetics is interested rather in the subject enjoying art and it endeavors to gain a knowledge of his inner state and to describe it with the instruments of empiricism. The main concern here is not with the creation, the mere form, of the work of art as such, but with the totality of the psychological processes by which the work of art is experienced and inwardly assimilated. These processes are to be analyzed into their ultimate components. In Shaftesbury, on the other hand, questions of this sort, although he by no means avoids them, never occupy the center of his philosophical interest. He is interested neither in the classification of works of art nor in an explanation of the psychological processes that take place in the spectator; his purpose is neither logical concepts nor psychological description. For him the beautiful signifies a revelation of quite a different sort; it springs from a different source and tends toward a basically different goal. In the contemplation of the beautiful, man turns from the world of created things to the world of the creative process, from the universe as a receptacle of the objectively real to the operative forces which have shaped this universe and constitute its inner coherence. This insight is not to be gained from the mere analysis of the work of art, nor from absorption in that reproductive process which takes place in the receptive subject during the contemplation and enjoyment of art. Rational analysis and psychological introspection, according to Shaftesbury, leave us on the periphery of the beautiful, not at its center. This center is not to be found in the process of enjoyment, but in that of forming and creating. The receptive act of enjoyment is insufficient and powerless since it does not lead us back to spontaneity, to the real source of the beautiful. But once this source has been discovered, the true and the only possible synthesis has been accomplished not only between subject and object, between the ego and the world, but also between man and God. For the difference between man and God disappears when we consider man not simply with respect to his original immanent forming powers, not as something created, but as a creator. The true significance of the creation of man in God's image does not appear so long as man still remains in the sphere of created things, of the empirically real, and tries to copy the order and outline of this world; it is revealed only in that original inspiration which precedes every genuine work of art. Here man's real Promethean nature comes to light; he becomes "a second maker, a just Prometheus under Jove."[32] The way to the contemplation and comprehension of the Divine Being must

[32] Cf. above pp. 84 f.

necessarily traverse this intermediate stage. Only the artist who constantly brings forth from within himself worlds in miniature giving them definite shape will be able to understand the universe as the creation of the same forces of which he is aware in his own creative processes. For him all being is but the symbol and hieroglyph of the Divine; he reads the soul of the artist in his Apollo.[33]

Now, beside reason and experience, a third force has been placed which, according to Shaftesbury, is superior to all others, and which first reveals to us the real depth of the aesthetic world. Neither the discursive form of thinking which feels its way slowly from one concept to another, nor the acute and patient observation of particular phenomena, can penetrate this depth. It is accessible only to an intuitive understanding which does not proceed from the parts to the whole, but from the whole to the parts. The idea and the ideal of such an intuitive understanding (*intellectus archetypus*) Shaftesbury derived from his principal philosophical model, from Plotinus's doctrine of "intelligible beauty." But he applies this idea in a fresh sense and imbues it with a tendency which it does not possess either in Plato or Plotinus. For with its aid he wants to invalidate the objection which Plato raised against art and on the basis of which Plato disfranchised art in the philosophical sense. Art is not imitation in the sense that it is content with the surface of things and with their mere appearance, and that it attempts to copy these aspects as faithfully as possible. Artistic "imitation" belongs to another sphere and, so to speak, to another dimension; it imitates not merely the product, but the act of producing, not that which has become, but the process of becoming. The ability to immerse itself in this process and to contemplate it from this standpoint is, according to Shaftesbury, the real nature and mystery of genius. As a result of this doctrine the problem of genius assumes a central position in aesthetic theory. Neither logical analysis nor empirical observation could lead up to this problem; only an intuitional aesthetics could give it content and substance. But we must be cautious here about

[33] Cf. the presentation of Shaftesbury's basic ideas in Schiller's *Philosophische Briefe, Werke*, ed. Cottasche Sekularausgabe, vol. XI, p. 118.

attempting to interpret the development of thoughts and ideas simply on the basis of the history of a word. Shaftesbury did not coin the word "genius"; he adopted it from common aesthetic terminology. He is the first to rescue the term from the confusion and ambiguity which had previously attached to it and to give it a fruitful and specifically philosophical meaning. In classical aesthetics the kinship of this term with the Latin *"ingenium"* ("genius," "natural disposition") is felt and stressed, and *"ingenium"* is treated as equivalent to "reason" as the predominant power of all operations of the mind. Genius is the highest sublimation of reason, the quintessence of all its faculties and abilities: "Genius is sublime reason" (*le génie est la raison sublime*).[34] The further development of this theory in Bouhours, which leads to a new basic trend in aesthetics, to the aesthetics of *"délicatesse,"* tries to overcome this one-sidedness. Bouhours no longer looks upon genius simply as the intensification and linear continuation of "good sense" (*bon sens*), but he assigns to this concept a considerably more complicated function. The power of genius is to consist not so much in grasping the simple truth of things and in expressing this truth as pregnantly and concisely as possible, as rather in its capacity to sense subtle and hidden connections. The "genial" thought is one which departs from the ordinary and leads to a new and surprising view of things, which delights in the unexpected expression, and in the metaphorical and figurative.[35] But here too genius is limited to the realm of pure intellect, in fact, of mere wit; it is the subtlety, precision, and agility of the mind which are now stressed, and which find collective expression in the concept of *"délicatesse."* Shaftesbury is equally far from both views of genius; for he deliberately raises the concept of genius above the realm of mere sensation and evaluation, above the sphere of propriety, sentiment, delicacy (*justesse, sentiment, délicatesse*), and reserves it entirely for the productive, formative, creative forces. Shaftesbury thus created for the first time a firm philosophical center for the future development of the problem of genius. He gave this problem a definite fundamental direction

[34] Cf. above p. 282.   [35] Cf. above pp. 300 ff.

which is henceforth pursued unswervingly by the real founders of systematic aesthetics, despite all the deviations to be observed among popular philosophical and psychological studies. From now on a direct path leads to the basic problems of German intellectual history in the eighteenth century—to Lessing's *Hamburg Dramaturgy* and to Kant's *Critique of Judgment*.[36]

[36] Strangely enough, Alfred Baeumler's thorough investigation of the historical background of the *Critique of Judgment* has almost entirely overlooked this derivation of the concept of genius. Shaftesbury's doctrine remains wholly in the background in Baeumler's account, and its importance is nowhere acknowledged. This has produced a curious distortion of historical perspectives and of systematic evaluations in this book. Baeumler not only defends in general the thesis that German aesthetics of the eighteenth century is oriented rather to France than to England, but he also endeavors to apply this thesis to the intellectual movement which culminates in Lessing's and Kant's concepts of genius. "Long before the English influence was more pronounced in Germany," Baeumler writes, "the genius concept was popular in the school of Wolff. If there is any foreign influence, it is from France, not from England. Helvetius's book *On the Mind* (1759) was one of the most read and most often quoted works of the second half of the century. It contained the definition: 'The mind is the faculty of the creative production of our thoughts,' and the axiom: 'Genius always presupposes invention.'" (*Op.cit.*, p. 162). But if Helvetius's book really exerted this historical influence, this fact would have to be looked upon as almost a miracle from the systematic viewpoint. For if we do not take Helvetius's explanation of the concept of genius literally, but consider it in the context of his work as a whole, then it becomes evident that Helvetius's doctrine of "mind" runs absolutely counter to the basic idea and to the logical and historical premises of the genius cult. Helvetius's work is oriented throughout to sensationalism; he carries the sensationalist thesis so far as to declare that the assumption of any higher spiritual powers which transcend sensation depends on mere illusion, on self-deception of the understanding. All these supposedly higher powers are radically leveled and reduced to simple sensation as the basic element of psychology. No writer in the eighteenth century went as far as Helvetius in this leveling movement of sensationalism, which negates all real spontaneity of thought and all freedom of the will; and this is the very point on which Helvetius was attacked even in France within the circle of his own friends. Hence it would be all the more incomprehensible that this work should have influenced the cult of genius in Germany and affected it more strongly than the English models did. For the growth of this movement was possible only because it broke away from all the theoretical principles on which Helvetius's work is based. Helvetius of course explains genius as invention. But he emphasizes again and again that there is no such thing as a truly spontaneous and original gift for invention in man, but that whatever we call invention consists merely in a combination, in a selection and skillful connection among given elements. Such a connection produces the appearance of novelty but nothing really new can arise from it since everything which develops in this manner is only a disguise, a metamorphosis, of that which is given in sensation. (Cf. above pp. 25 ff.) Obviously, then, Helvetius's doctrine of genius is the exact opposite of all the thoughts represented by the genius advocates in Germany. There is no path leading from Helvetius to the idea of the autonomy of the beautiful. Shaftesbury's doctrines of "enthusiasm," of "disinterested pleasure," of genius in man which is akin to and not inferior to the

But Shaftesbury's doctrine of the spontaneity of artistic creation would not have been able to exert the influence it actually did, had not the purely theoretical development of ideas, which culminates in this doctrine, received constant support from another intellectual movement. Wherever the problem of genius is treated in English literature of the eighteenth century and the attempt is made to define the relationship between genius and the rules, abstract reasoning soon turns to concrete cases. Two names, Shakespeare and Milton, confront us again and again. They form, so to speak, the fixed axis about which all theoretical investigation of the problem of genius rotates. By these two great examples writers endeavor to grasp the deepest essence of genius; all that theory had described as possible for genius, is realized in Shakespeare and Milton. Intellectual orientation to these men is most conspicuous in Young's *Conjectures on Original Composition*. From a consideration of Shakespeare's tragedies and Milton's *Paradise Lost*, Young reached the conviction that the creativity of the poetic genius cannot be described by the usual merely intellectual standards, by the standards of the discursive understanding; much less can such creative activity be exhaustively explained in this fashion. The genius is as far removed from such understanding as the magician from the builder. In this analogy Young sums up his whole doctrine of genius. He has an intense and profound feeling for the magic which underlies every great work of art, and his theory is an attempt to clothe this feeling in words and to transform it into conceptual knowledge. The magic of poetry neither requires nor tolerates the mediation of the intellect, for the real power of this magic lies in its immediacy. Shakespeare had no scholarly education, but there were two books which were always open before him and in which he could read as no other. These were the book of nature and the book of man.[37] The elemental power from which Shakespeare's tragedies are

---

"Genius of the World," contain the first seeds of this new fundamental conception whose development and systematic justification took place at the hands of Lessing, Herder, and Kant.

[37] Young, *Conjectures on Original Composition*. For an account of Young's doctrine see H. von Stein, *Die Entstehung der neueren Ästhetik*, pp. 136 ff.

derived seemed to have been long extinct in eighteenth century drama, and the vital breath with which he inspired playwriting appeared dead. Yet theory still seeks to conjure up that great shade and to speak with it because it is convinced that the true nature of the beautiful can be discovered only through the contemplation of the real "original compositions," and that it cannot be learned from imitators. For the genius alone possesses real magic power; he not only speaks to our understanding and taste but arouses and soothes the tempest of passion in our souls.

The elaboration and the patient and thorough exposition and clarification of the fundamental ideas of aesthetics which Shaftesbury had touched on in his rhapsodic, hymnic style are accomplished in Hutcheson's *Inquiry into the Original of Our Ideas of Beauty and Virtue* (1726). The widespread vogue of Shaftesbury's ideas in learned circles dates from Hutcheson's work, but they do not of course retain all of their original significance in this interpretation. In Hutcheson the boundaries between "receptivity" and "spontaneity," between "sensation" and "intuition," which Shaftesbury had drawn so sharply, begin to fade. The expression he chose to designate the nature of the beautiful is characteristic. He can think of no better analogy for the immediacy with which we grasp the beautiful than that of sense perception. There is a special sense of beauty, which is not further definable or reducible, just as the eye is the specific sense for the perception of colors, the ear for sounds. Whoever does not possess this sense cannot learn its use indirectly any more than the existence of colors and sounds can be known otherwise than by actual perception.[38] The fact that Hutcheson connects the feeling for beauty, for harmony and regularity, with an "inward sense" which is different from and independent of the external senses, cannot delude us regarding the leveling and blunting process which Shaftesbury's thoughts suffer at the hands of Hutcheson. For genius can again be described here as merely the gift of receptivity and equated with "fine taste." But since Hutcheson upholds Shaftesbury's basic presuppositions, he finds himself faced with a difficult dilemma in his

[38] Cf. Hutcheson, *op.cit.*, sect. 12 and *passim*.

doctrine of a sixth sense. Heinrich von Stein in his *Development of Modern Aesthetics* says of Hutcheson's doctrine that it suffers from the contradiction of a sort of *a priori* sense; for, while rejecting all the consequences of empiricism, he founds beauty on perception whose general validity he maintains. But the objection raised by von Stein applies rather to the phraseology of Hutcheson's fundamental idea than to the content of the idea itself. This expression is insufficient and ambiguous in as much as it attempts to clothe in the language of empiricism a conception which originates in Shaftesbury's intuitional aesthetics. It is characteristic of Shaftesbury's concept of aesthetic intuition that he does not recognize the alternative between reason and experience and between *a priori* and *a posteriori*. The contemplation of beauty is to show how to overcome the schematic conflict which dominates all eighteenth century epistemology; it is to place the mind on a new vantage point from which it sees beyond this conflict. Shaftesbury considers the beautiful neither as an "innate idea" in Descartes' sense nor as a concept derived and abstracted from experience in Locke's sense. The beautiful is independent and original, and innate and necessary, in the sense that it is no mere accident but belongs to the substance of the spirit and expresses this substance in an entirely original way. The beautiful is not a content gained from experience or an idea present in the mind from the first as a stamped coin; it is rather a specific basic direction, a pure energy, and an original function of the spirit.

Thus in his conception of art as in his view of nature Shaftesbury represents a purely dynamic standpoint. But this "dynamism" has to be sharply distinguished from other, apparently related views. At first glance there would seem to be the closest agreement between Shaftesbury and Dubos; for Dubos' *Critical Reflections on Poetry, Painting, and Music* develops the thesis that the value and charm of the beautiful consists in the stimulation and intensification of the powers of the soul. Since Dubos, however, treats aesthetic experience simply from the standpoint of the spectator, not from that of the artist, since he considers the activity of the observer, not that of the creator, his standards and scale of values differ widely from those of Shaftesbury. They agree only in the negative, not in the positive points of their theory; they reject the same things, but they assert different things. They are opposed to all attempts to confine the beautiful to strict immutable rules; they admit that genius has the right and power to break the tablets of the law and to establish new rules by virtue of its own authority. They also turn against all attempts to comprehend the nature of the beautiful by mere reasoning, by means of discursive definitions and analytical distinctions. They advocate an "immediate" knowledge of the beautiful but the sources of immediacy are different in Shaftesbury and Dubos. For the former it lies in the process of pure creation, while for the latter it is sought in the region of certain modes of reception and conception which admit of no further derivation. All aesthetic enjoyment owes its existence to certain reactions called forth in the spectator by the presence of the work of art. He feels himself overwhelmed by the work of art and enraptured by its movement. The stronger this movement, the more intensely we feel it and the more perfectly the artist's aim is accomplished. Since Dubos seeks movement for its own sake, he makes the intensity of the emotion aroused by the work of art almost the only standard of aesthetic value. The quality and peculiar character of the work of art become definitely a secondary matter; at times indeed he treats them as if they were quite meaningless. At the very beginning of his work, when he is justifying his thesis that the mind has its needs as well as the body does and that the greatest need of the mind is to be in perpetual motion, Dubos characteristically does not interpret his thesis primarily in terms of aesthetic phenomena but rather in a different and broader sense. He does not hesitate to place the impression we gain from the contemplation of a painting or from listening to a tragedy immediately alongside of those other emotions which we feel, for instance, at the execution of a criminal or at gladiatorial combats and bullfights. In all these instances man obeys the same motive; he not only can endure the sight of extreme suffering but he even seeks such sights because they free him from the burden of inactivity. "The boredom which soon follows inactivity of the soul is so grievous an evil for man that he often undertakes the most painful labors in order to spare himself the torments of inactivity. . . . Thus we instinctively pursue objects which can excite our passions, even though these objects make impressions on us which often cost us unquiet nights and sorrowful days. But in general men suffer still more from living without passions than the passions cause them to suffer."[39]

Thus the dynamism by means of which Dubos seeks to understand the nature and effects of a work of art is not, as in Shaftesbury, the dynamism of the pure process of forming and creating, but that of pain and passion. He does not, like Shaftesbury, develop an intuitive aesthetics which takes its stand in the midst of the artistic process and strives to show the unique nature of this process; he gives us an aesthetics of "pathos." Dubos seeks to examine and survey the reactions, the pure feelings, which are occasioned in man by works of poetry and fine art. The highest requirement which we can make of the artist, the highest and only rule to which we can subject genius, is not that genius must follow certain objective norms in its productions but that it, as subject, must always be present in all its creations, and that it can communicate and force upon the spectator its own profound emotions. "Always be passionate (pathétique) and never allow either your spectators or your listeners to languish." Such, according to Dubos, is the first maxim which the aesthetician has to urge upon the artist. The value of a scene in painting or in poetry lies in the pathos of its images, not in its verisimilitude. By going back to the original force of passion Dubos undoubtedly exerted a vitalizing influence on aesthetics, yet the limitation of his method is recognizable from the outset. For a theory of art so exclusively oriented to the observer, as is the case with the Dubos theory, runs the constant risk of measuring the aesthetic content of a work of art simply by spectator reaction and finally of completely confusing these two terms of the aesthetic relation. The work of art threatens to become a mere spectacle. If it satisfies the desire to see something, if it arouses

[39] Dubos, *op.cit.*, part II, sect. I.

the inner concern of the auditor and constantly entertains and intensifies his emotion, then it makes no difference with what means this effect is achieved. The mere intensity of the effect is looked upon as its valid aesthetic standard, and the degree of emotion decides its value. Poetry and painting aim only to please and to move, and know no higher goal; and herein lies their real sublimity: "The sublime in poetry and painting is that which moves and pleases."[40] Kant argued against the ethics of eudemonism that it reduced all moral values to one level and in the end even eliminated that. For whoever judges the ethical value of an action according to the quantity of pleasure it produces, does not ask about the kind and source of the pleasure any more than someone who wants gold asks whether it was dug from a mountain or washed from the sand. A similar objection can be raised against Dubos' aesthetics, which resolves all aesthetic content into feeling, and then resolves feeling into states of stimulation and emotion. The fact of this emotion finally becomes the only reliable criterion of the value of a work of art: "The true means of knowing the merit of a poem will always be to consult the impression it makes."[41]

In Dubos' theory of taste, if we compare it with Shaftesbury's, the same characteristic difference appears. At first he seems to be in complete agreement with Shaftesbury when he stresses the immediacy of taste and declares that the work of art must be judged not by way of discussion, but by way of feeling.[42] But here again he gives another meaning to immediacy and justifies it in an entirely different manner. If Shaftesbury seeks it in the principle of pure aesthetic intuition, Dubos does not go beyond sensation. Aesthetic taste thus approximates the physical sense of taste. Feeling judges the value of a work of art just as the tongue judges the quality and excellence of a ragout, Dubos asserts. This approach lacks any sure principle for distinguishing between feeling and mere sensation, between the beautiful and the agreeable. In Shaftesbury, on the other hand, this distinction occupies the focal point of consideration and serves as the basis of his doctrine of "disinterested pleasure"—Shaftesbury's

[40] Dubos, *op.cit.*, part II, sect. I.   [41] *Ibid.*, part II, sect. 24.
[42] *Ibid.*, part II, sect. 22; see above pp. 303 f.

most important individual contribution to aesthetics. For, according to him, the nature and value of beauty do not lie in the mere emotional effect they produce on man, but in the fact that they reveal the realm of form. The animal, which is irrevocably subject to the power of its emotional response, is therefore excluded from the world of pure forms. For form can never be understood and assimilated unless it is distinguished from its mere effect and made an independent object of aesthetic contemplation.[43] The intuition of the beautiful, which is to be distinguished carefully from the mere sensation of the beautiful, arises only from such contemplation, which is not simply a passive condition of the soul but the purest sort of activity, namely, the activity peculiar to the soul.

The relation between beauty and truth, between art and nature, now undergoes a change of meaning. Shaftesbury not only insists on complete agreement between these terms of the relation but he seems to want to push this agreement to the extent of eliminating all distinctions. Yet it would indicate a complete misunderstanding of his thesis: "All beauty is truth" if one were to consider it as an attack on the immanence and autonomy of the beautiful. For the harmony which Shaftesbury asserts as existing between truth and beauty does not signify the dependence of the one on the other; it is supposed to prevent any assumption of such a one-sided dependence. The relation is substantial, not causal; it involves the essence of nature and art, not their temporal creations. Art, according to Shaftesbury, is strictly confined to nature; it can achieve nothing and should attempt nothing which goes beyond nature. But the inner agreement with nature which is demanded of art does not mean that art is caught in the world of empirical objects and must be content to copy them but that in artistic creation the "truth" of nature is attained. For nature itself in its deeper sense is not the sum total of created things but the creative power from which the form and order of the universe are derived. In this sense only should beauty compete with truth and the artist with

---

[43] Shaftesbury, *The Moralists*, part III, sect. 2, *Characteristics*, second edition, London, 1714, vol. II, p. 424.

nature. The genuine artist does not laboriously collect the elements of his creation from nature; he copies rather a model which stands before him as an original and indivisible whole. And this imaginative model is no mere illusion; on the contrary, it is sure to agree with the essential truth of things, if not with their factual reality. The creation of the artist is no mere product of his subjective imagination, no empty phantasm; it is an expression of true being in the sense of an inner necessity and law. Genius does not receive its law from without, but from within itself; it produces this law in its original form. And now it appears that this form which was not borrowed from nature is, nevertheless, in complete harmony with it, that it does not contradict the fundamental form of nature but rather discovers and confirms this form. "Nature is forever in league with genius; what the one promises, the other is sure to perform." In these words Schiller has perhaps given the most brief and striking characterization of Shaftesbury's fundamental view of the relation between art and nature. Genius has no need to go in quest of nature or truth; it bears them within itself and can rest assured that if it remains true to itself, it will meet them again and again. The principle of subjectivity in aesthetics is thus maintained in opposition to that form of imitation of nature which had been demanded by the classical schools. Yet in the systems of psychological empiricism this subjectivity means something entirely different. For, if here the ego finally resolves itself into a mere bundle of perceptions, it is in Shaftesbury's theory a primary whole and an indivisible unity. It is that unity through which we have immediate insight into the fundamental form and meaning of the cosmos, in which we comprehend the "universal Genius" through intuition and sympathy. Shaftesbury's conception of truth implies this "nature in the subject" rather than the mere objectivity of facts and things, and makes it the norm of beauty. When Kant in his *Critique of Judgment* defines genius as that talent (natural gift) which gives to art its rule, he follows his own path in his transcendental exposition of this proposition; but with respect to content alone Kant's definition is in complete agreement with Shaftesbury and the principles and presuppositions of the latter's "intuitional aesthetics."

A further step toward a new and more profound conception of aesthetic subjectivity consists in the increasing breadth of the field of aesthetic problems. After the middle of the eighteenth century, for example, the problem of the sublime rises to the same level as the problem of the beautiful. This did not indeed contribute to aesthetic content, for the theme of the sublime can be traced back to the very beginnings of philosophical aesthetics. Classical doctrine had also borrowed this *motif* from ancient tradition. In the year 1674 Boileau published his paraphrase and commentary on Longinus's treatise *On the Sublime*.[44] But in this commentary there are no signs of that new direction which the question of the sublime takes in eighteenth century aesthetics or of the systematic significance which it acquires. Burke's *Philosophical Inquiry into the Origin of Our Ideas of the Sublime and the Beautiful* (1756) constitutes the first important presentation of this problem. Burke's essay is not primarily philosophical but rather psychological; it sets forth no unified aesthetic doctrine but seeks instead to distinguish sharply and to describe faithfully and fully certain aesthetic phenomena. Yet this very description brings him upon an error in traditional aesthetic systems. Order, proportion, definite delimitation, and simple structure are customarily taken as the characteristics of beautiful objects; yet these characteristics are obviously insufficient to comprehend all the elements which make up the aesthetically significant and effective. This definition fails to cover a whole class of phenomena whose reality cannot be disregarded by any observation unless it is dimmed by theoretical prejudice. The contemplation of beauty as harmonious proportion and strict unity of form does not awaken in us the deepest emotions of the soul or the most intense artistic experiences. A different and stronger emotional effect appears when, instead of unity of form, we are confronted with its disintegration, or even with its complete dissolution. Not only form in the classical sense, but distortion, has aesthetic value and a rightful place in aesthetics.

[44] For an account of this paraphrase, see H. von Stein, *op. cit.*, pp. 4 ff.

Fundamental Problems of Aesthetics

Not only that which is governed by rules, but that which is not subject to rules, not only that which can be measured by certain standards, but that which is incommensurable by any standards whatever, can please. This phenomenon, which shatters the conceptual framework of previous aesthetic systems, is called by Burke the sublime. The sublime defies the aesthetic demand for proportionality; for transcendence of all mere proportionality constitutes its real character. The sublime consists precisely in this transcendence and derives its effectiveness from it. Not only what we form and shape within in pure intuition affects us, but also that which eludes any such attempt, which overwhelms us instead of being formed and controlled by us. We are never more powerfully moved than by this incomprehensible element of experience; never do we feel the power of nature and of art so much as when we are confronted with the terrible. That we do not succumb to the terrible, but that we maintain ourselves against it and that we actually feel an exaltation and intensification of our powers in its presence—these are the elements of the phenomenon of the sublime and the basis of its deepest aesthetic effect. The sublime removes the boundaries of the finite. The ego, however, does not experience this removal as a destruction, but as a kind of exaltation and liberation. For in the sense of the infinite which the ego now discovers in itself, it enjoys a new experience of its own boundlessness. This conception and explanation of the sublime not only goes beyond the limits of classical aesthetics but beyond Shaftesbury as well. For although in the apostrophes to nature in the *Moralists* Shaftesbury shows a profound sensitivity to all the charms of the sublime, yet he always treats the idea of form as the fundamental principle of aesthetics. Subjectivity in aesthetics thus takes on new meaning and raises new claims. The significance of the doctrine of the sublime consists in the fact that from the direction of art it indicates the limitations of eudemonism and overcomes its narrowness. A result for which eighteenth century ethics had striven in vain now falls with the aid of aesthetics like ripe fruit into its lap. In order to develop his doctrine of the sublime Burke has to introduce a sharp distinction in the concept of aesthetic pleasure. He recognizes and describes a kind of pleasure which has nothing in common with mere sense enjoyment or with that delight which we feel in the contemplation of the beautiful, but is of an entirely different type. The sense of the sublime is not the intensification of that enjoyment and delight but the opposite of them both. It cannot be described simply as pleasure; it is the expression of a quite different emotion, namely, of a peculiar sort of delight that does not exclude the terrible and the fearful but rather involves and depends upon these emotions. There is then a source of pure aesthetic enjoyment which is strictly distinguished from the mere desire for happiness, from the striving for enjoyment, and from the satisfaction of finite ends: "a sort of delight full of horror, a sort of tranquillity tinged with terror."[45] And there is still another exaltation and liberation which results from the problem of the sublime. Not only the inner freedom of man from the objects of nature and from the power of destiny is expressed in the sense of the sublime but this sense releases the individual from a thousand ties to which he is subject as a member of the community and of the social and civil order. In the experience of the sublime all these barriers vanish; the individual must stand entirely on his own feet and assert himself in his independence and originality against the universe, both physical and social. Burke expressly points out that there are two basic impulses in man: the one urges him to preserve his own being, the other to live in society. The sense of the sublime is based on the former; the sense of the beautiful on the latter. The beautiful unites, the sublime isolates; the one civilizes by teaching the proper forms of social intercourse and by refining morals, the other penetrates to the depths of our being and reveals these depths to us for the first time. There is no other aesthetic experience of man that gives him so much self-confidence and courage to be original as the impression of the sublime. A barrier is thus overcome which, as we have seen, had

[45] Cf. Burke, *A Philosophical Inquiry into the Origin of Our Ideas of the Sublime and Beautiful*, London, 1756, especially pp. 208 ff. For Burke's distinction between "pleasure" and "delight" see Folkierski, *Entre le Classicisme et le Romantisme*, pp. 59 ff.

been felt repeatedly in the development of classical aesthetics. This system was convinced that in its rules it expressed only the strict and simple truth of the work of art and that it subjected art to no other laws than those deriving from the nature of the various artistic genres. But in practice classical aesthetics never completely realized its theoretical ideal. Instead of the "truth of nature" a relative and accidental truth appeared; instead of universally valid laws of reason came certain social conventions.[46] This danger is recognized in the theory of the sublime. With more rigor than heretofore this theory distinguishes essence from appearance, nature from custom, the substance and true depth of the ego from its merely accidental properties and relations. The problem of genius and the problem of the sublime are now moving in the same direction, and they become the twin bases upon which a new and deeper conception of individuality gradually evolves.

V. REASON AND THE IMAGINATION: GOTTSCHED AND THE SWISS CRITICS

If one compares the development of German aesthetics in the eighteenth century with the course of French and English aesthetics, a characteristic difference in tendency and temper appear at once. To be sure, if one considers simply the content of the various problems and the analysis and explanation of the various basic concepts, it is impossible to draw a sharp line of demarcation along national cultural barriers. As in all other fields in the eighteenth century, so in aesthetics there is an uninterrupted exchange of ideas. The threads become so intertwined that they can scarcely be distinguished in the finished fabric and traced back to their various origins. The special position of German aesthetics does not rest on individual concepts or principles. Hardly a concept or principle of German aesthetics could be mentioned which could not be paralleled in French and English literature. And yet all these influences constantly streaming in are employed in a new sense and directed toward a new goal. In Germany for the first time the problem of aes-

[46] See above pp. 293 ff.

thetics is placed under the guidance and care of systematic philosophy. No leading German aesthetician wants merely to observe and describe; none wishes to confine himself to aesthetic phenomena alone. The question of the relationship between art and the other spheres of intellectual life is constantly investigated, and a clear and sharp distinction is sought between the specific nature of the aesthetic faculty and the other faculties of understanding, reason, and will. By virtue of this distinction aestheticians attempt to formulate a general view of the intellect in its inner unity and in its various aspects and gradations. Such was the systematic spirit which had been implanted in German philosophy by Leibniz, and which received its strict schooling in the doctrine of Christian Wolff. No such exacting theoretical discipline of aesthetics existed either in France or in England. In France after the beginning of the eighteenth century and following the influence of the writings of Bouhours and Dubos, the strict rational spirit of Cartesian philosophy retreats more and more into the background. In the course of subsequent developments the close connection between philosophy and aesthetic and literary criticism remains but philosophy itself now expressly rejects the form of the system. Following Condillac's *Treatise on Systems* the battle against the system-building spirit is joined from all sides.[47] Lessing said of Diderot that, since Aristotle, no other philosopher had devoted himself to the theater; but Diderot's philosophy of drama, as he expresses it in his dialogues on dramatic art, is anything but systematic. It is not logically constructed and does not follow a direct line of inference and conclusion. It consists rather of a series of disconnected ideas and is erratic and eclectic. Similarly, in England it was the most profound and fruitful thinker in the field of aesthetics and the real originator and instigator of all future developments in this field who scorned the constraint of the philosophical system. Shaftesbury coined the expression: "The most ingenious way of becoming foolish is by a system."[48] In Germany meantime, even where aesthetics was waging war

---

[47] Cf. above pp. 8 ff.

[48] *Soliloquy or Advice to an Author*, part III, sect. I, *Characteristics*, vol. I, p. 290.

for the autonomy and originality of the imagination, it never revolted against the dominion of logic but remained in an intimate alliance with this discipline. Aestheticians did not attempt to free the imagination from the predominance of logic; they wanted to discover a logic of the imagination. When the Swiss thinkers, the protagonists of the imagination in its struggle with reason, turn against Gottsched, they have no intention of rejecting the logical rigor of Wolff. Bodmer's treatise *Of the Influence and Use of the Imagination for the Improvement of Taste* (1727) is dedicated to Wolff and thus placed directly under his patronage; Wolff's "demonstrative manner of philosophizing," declares Bodmer, will make it possible for the first time to construct the system of the arts according to certain principles. The Swiss philosophers go back from Wolff to Leibniz, and again it is Leibniz the logician to whom they primarily appeal. They assert that the chief service which Leibniz performed for the foundation of a philosophy of art consists in the fact that by his system of pre-established harmony he "struck a mortal blow at sensation . . . he deposed it from the judgeship which it had usurped for so long and made it simply a ministering and occasional cause of a judgment of the soul."[49] It is clear from the central position which the Swiss school gives to judgment that it in no sense intended to sever the bond between logic and aesthetics. These thinkers represent a phase of the development toward a synthesis of and a firmer connection between logic and aesthetics—of the development which reaches its climax in Kant's *Critique of Judgment*.

If one considers the historical position of the Swiss critics, it becomes all the more difficult to say just what the subject of their quarrel with Gottsched was. The quarrel itself deeply moved German thinkers in the eighteenth century. Goethe's mention of it in his *Poetry and Truth* is evidence of how deeply the controversy penetrated the general intellectual life of Germany, and of how strongly it influenced the inner growth of German poetry. But even contemporaries had trouble finding

---

[49] Bodmer, *Briefwechsel von der Natur des Poetischen Geschmacks* (1736). For the relations of the Swiss critics to the Leibniz-Wolffian philosophy, see H. von Stein, *op.cit.*, pp. 279 ff., 295.

the kernel of the matter amid the abundance of polemical writings. "It seems to us," write Mylius and Cramer, in the preface to their work entitled *Halle Efforts to Promote Criticism and Good Taste*, "that the Swiss writings on poetry could have occupied the same desk drawer with Gottsched's poetics without causing a quarrel, as Swift has said of the books of the ancients. We cannot give an adequate answer to those who ask for the real causes of this critical dispute. The poet who some day will sing of this war will need inspiration as much as Homer did when he wanted to describe the quarrel between Achilles and Agamemnon."[50] And it would almost seem as though all subsequent analyses of the controversy have lacked this inspiration, for judgments concerning the real motives and forces involved are still diametrically opposed. Hettner declares that the decisive thought which thrived beneath the surface of personal antagonisms is easily perceived. He sees the quarrel as "the first serious conflict between French and English influences." Gottsched was the eager and passionately one-sided partisan of French classicism, and in this fact lies his historical worth or worthlessness. But the roles in this quarrel are by no means so simply distributed. For, on the one hand, Gottsched did not reject the influences of English literature. He quotes Shaftesbury and Addison, and imitated the form of Addison's periodicals. On the other hand, the critical theory of the Swiss school of thought is subject to constant influences derived from French aesthetics. In the preface to Breitinger's *Critical Poetics* Bodmer appeals directly to Dubos in order to prove "that the best writings were not the result of the rules, but, on the contrary, the rules are derived from the writings." The real point at issue between Gottsched and the Swiss school cannot be described in terms merely of external influences to which both sides of the controversy were exposed, but only in terms of the different approach to their systematic problem. And this difference appears clearly only if we look beyond the merely literary and aesthetic problems, if we recognize that this conflict is but one phase in a much more comprehensive intellectual struggle. The

[50] Quoted from Hettner, *Literaturgeschichte des achtzehnten Jahrhunderts*, third edition, part III, Book I, p. 359.

thesis which Gottsched and the Swiss scholars are to establish within the realm of poetics can only be understood in relation to the whole intellectual picture in the eighteenth century. Curious as it may at first appear, a clear historical view of this conflict involves not only an examination of the logical problem but also of the problem of natural science. For within natural science and through its influence a new form of logic had begun to develop in the eighteenth century. The ideal of a purely deductive logic, which proceeds from the general to the particular, deducing the latter from the former, was gradually supplanted by the ideal of empirical analysis. This analysis does not of course reject axioms and general principles; but it does not assert them as irrefutable *a priori* postulates. It seeks rather to evolve its postulates from the phenomena, and it sees the validity of the postulates as resting on the phenomena. The correlation between phenomenon and principle remains, but the emphasis in this relation has changed. The phenomena are not to be deduced from certain principles established prior to experience; the principles themselves are to be formulated and constantly tested on the basis of the observation of phenomena.[51] In the interpretation of nature this change of method is most clearly seen in the advance from Descartes to Newton, while in aesthetics it appears most strikingly in the controversy between Gottsched and the Swiss critics. The surprising affinity existing between two remote districts which is evidenced by this dispute, proves once more how widespread the unity of thought was in the eighteenth century. Descartes' outline of physics, as he sketches it in his treatise *The World*, illustrates the motto: "Give me matter, and I will build you a world." The physicist and natural philosopher can risk such a construction, for the plan of the universe lies clearly before him in the general laws of motion. He does not have to take these laws from experience; they are of a mathematical nature and, accordingly, are contained in the fundamental rules of "universal knowledge" (*mathesis universalis*) whose necessary truth the mind recognizes within itself. Gottsched, as a pupil of Descartes and Wolff, believes he can apply the same requirement to poetry and thus

[51] Cf. above pp. 50 ff.

subject this realm too to the domination of reason. "Give me any matter you please, any definite theme, and I will show you how, according to the general rules of poetics, a perfect poem can be made of it"—such could be an expression of the content and underlying tendency of Gottsched's *Critical Poetics*. He wrote: "First of all, one should choose an instructive moral thesis suitable to the nature of the purposes one desires to fulfill; then one should think of a general event involving an action which concretely illustrates the chosen moral." The "theorem," the theoretical or moral truth, thus comes first; the poetic action follows simply to exemplify this truth in a concrete case. The Swiss critics, on the other hand, look at the matter exactly in reverse; they maintain the primacy of the event over the "theorem." To be sure, they have by no means renounced a moral intention; they stress such an intention repeatedly. But this poetic moral is now to be realized not by way of reason but by way of the imagination. The task of poetry—on this point the Swiss critics agree with Dubos—is to stir the emotions, but the "pathetic" is not of course their only and highest goal. Stimulation of the imagination is rather to prepare the way for rational insight and to predispose the mind of the listener to such insight. What the mere concept and the abstract doctrine cannot achieve is to be accomplished by the proper choice of metaphor and poetic imagery. For this reason poetic imagery now assumes decisive importance and comes to occupy the central position in poetics. Breitinger wrote a special *Critical Treatise on the Nature, the Purposes, and the Use of Imagery*[52] in which he seeks to explain this use on the basis of examples from the writings of famous authors of ancient and modern times. But here again the image has no independent meaning and value; it is only a preparation for something else and the garment in which this other element is clothed. "Just as a skillful physician gilds or sugarcoats his bitter pills, so must they also proceed who wish to utilize truth to the furtherance of human happiness." Aesop's Fables, therefore, are declared by Breitinger in his *Critical Poetics* to be the most perfect poetic

[52] *Critische Abhandlung von der Natur, den Absichten und dem Gebrauch der Gleichnisse,* Zurich, 1740.

genre because they best perform this double task. The fable was invented in order, by means of a charming artistic disguise, to achieve for the driest and bitterest truths so sure an access to the human heart that it cannot refuse its assent.[53] Swiss poetics also clearly formulates for the first time the concept of the "wonderful." Nor does the value of the wonderful consist in the fact that it is derived from the free play of the imagination or that it transcends all the laws of reason. The most wonderful invention is not of course bound to a given reality, but to the laws of the possible; yet, if it is to be truly poetic, it is nevertheless limited by its purpose. Such invention seeks to move the soul by the novel and the surprising in order to guide this emotion to the goal desired by the poet, namely, to a moral purpose. The same conflict as to the direction of investigation, by no means an absolute conflict, is visible in the controversy over the relationship between genius and the rules. Both Gottsched and the Swiss school are far from that view of genius which appeared in Shaftesbury's "intuitional aesthetics." Bodmer and Breitinger have no intention of freeing genius from the strict discipline of the rules; they too want to establish norms. But they try to discover these norms in the phenomena, in the available works of poetry, instead of forcing them on poetry from without. They start with poetic contemplation in order to reduce this to concepts and to "speculative principles." Their essential advantage over Gottsched lies in the fact that, to an incomparably higher degree and in a far deeper sense than he, the Swiss critics are capable of such contemplation. To them Homer, Dante, and Milton are real poetic experiences. But for the critic these experiences can only serve as the beginning, not as the end. The rules which are implicitly contained in them must be raised to the level of clear consciousness. What nature has performed through poetic genius, the art of criticism must extract from the works of poets and transform into a secure possession. Here again the force of empirical analysis proves its worth in finding the general in the particular and in discovering the concealed rule in the concrete shape and phenomenon. Bodmer declares

[53] Breitinger, *Critische Dichtkunst*, Zurich, 1740, p. 166. Cf. Hettner, *op.cit.*, p. 382.

in his preface to Breitinger's *Critical Poetics* that rules are no mere product of willfulness or of blind chance; they are derived from an observation of the truly constant elements in the aesthetic impression and of that which exercises a certain invariable influence on the mind. As natural science in the eighteenth century combines experience with geometry, constantly referring the one to the other, as it starts with experiment and sense observation in order to seek mathematical determinability within the realm of the observable itself, so the Swiss thinkers demand of the genuine art critic that he do justice to both requirements. He should expose himself to the great works of art and permit himself to be guided by his experience of them, but this guidance does not imply absolute subjection. As the physicist finds mathematical precision amid sense data, so the art critic seeks in the creations of the imagination that which is necessary and above all caprice. He begins with direct contemplation and remains faithful to this method; but in it he discovers the specific form of determination and that "demonstrative certainty" of which such contemplation is capable.

VI. THE FOUNDATION OF SYSTEMATIC AESTHETICS—BAUMGARTEN

When Kant speaks of Alexander Baumgarten, whom he esteems very highly among contemporary German thinkers, he usually calls him the "excellent analyst." And this is indeed a brief and apt characterization of a fundamental feature of Baumgarten's intellect and of his scientific performance. In his works the art of definition and analysis is developed to a high degree of perfection. Among all of Wolff's pupils Baumgarten is the one who really mastered the logical technique which Wolff taught and by which he first gave German philosophy a definite shape of its own. Because of the precision of its formulations of concepts, because of the painstaking quality of its definitions and the conclusiveness of its proofs, Baumgarten's *Metaphysics* long remains an admired model. Kant recurred to this work constantly and he always used it as the basis for his lectures on metaphysics. Yet Baumgarten's decisive historical merit lies elsewhere. He was not only the outstanding scholastic logician who was master of all aspects of this discipline, and who developed it to its highest degree of formal perfection, but his real intellectual accomplishment consists in the fact that through his mastery of the subject he became especially conscious of both the intrinsic and the systematic limitations of formal logic. As a result of his consciousness of these limitations, Baumgarten was able to make his original contribution to the history of thought, which lay in the philosophical foundation of aesthetics. As Baumgarten the logician surveys his special field, he becomes aware of a new task. And as he undertakes this task according to his logical premises, the limitations of these premises become apparent. Thus aesthetics evolves from logic, but this evolution discloses the immanent weakness of traditional scholastic logic. Baumgarten does not remain a mere "artist of reason"; in him that ideal of philosophy is realized which Kant called the ideal of the "self-knowledge of reason." He is a master of analysis; yet this mastery does not lead him to overestimate its value but rather to define clearly, and to distinguish sharply between, the means and the ends of analysis. The highest development of analysis stirs it into productivity again, bringing it to the point where, as if by itself, a new starting-point appears and a new intellectual synthesis opens up.

It is this ideal synthesis which gives force and significance to Baumgarten's first definition of aesthetics as a science. Aesthetics would not be a science and could never become one if it confined its activity to giving technical rules for the production of works of art or to making psychological observations concerning its effect on the spectator. Such activities belong to that kind of empiricism which is the exact opposite of real philosophical insight, and from the viewpoint of method they form the sharpest conceivable contrast to such insight. The philosophical content and significance of every science is derived from the understanding of its meaning within the whole body of human knowledge, and from the position it occupies in this whole. Every science must fit into the general genus of knowledge; but within this genus it must claim a special task, and it must fulfill this task in a manner characteristic of the given science.

The genus of science is designated by the concept of knowledge; this concept must therefore come first, and it alone can form the genus for a definition of aesthetics. But more important than this *genus proximum*, which is to create only the framework of the definition, is the content within, and the determination of the specific difference. Baumgarten signifies this specific difference in his definition of aesthetics as the doctrine of sensibility, of "sensitive knowledge." Judging from the standpoint of formal logic and its traditional standards, he seems to have created a logical hybrid; what he gives aesthetics with one hand he seems to take away with the other. For is not sense knowledge, according to a terminology which Baumgarten adopts, the realm of the confused and indistinct, in other words, of the opposite of pure knowledge, since this realm is impenetrable to knowledge? And can aesthetics maintain its rank and dignity as a science if it is confined to this humble sphere? Doubts of this kind were in fact the main obstacle to the reception of Baumgarten's aesthetics, and they delayed its effect for a long time. Bodmer reacts to Baumgarten's definition with surprise and displeasure, and with a scarcely concealed personal bad temper. "It seems," he writes in his review of Baumgarten's work,[54] "that the opinion is getting out of hand that taste is a lower form of judgment whereby we can have only confused and dark knowledge. In this sense it will be no great praise to have a taste which is so uncertain, and it is scarcely worth striving for." But this judgment expresses the exact opposite of Baumgarten's real purpose. The "excellent analyst" Baumgarten has no intention of maintaining the logical contradiction of confused and dark knowledge; he is seeking and demanding rather a knowledge of the "dark" and the "indistinct." The predicate indicates the theme and the objective field, not the kind of insight and the mode of treatment. Science is not to be dragged down to the region of sensibility, but the sensible is to be lifted to the dignity of knowledge and impregnated with a special form of knowledge, and in this way subjected to rational treatment. What if the sensible world as such with respect to its

[54] This review appeared in *Freymüthige Nachrichten*; cf. H. von Stein, *op.cit.*, p. 281.

mere matter is dark; must therefore the form in which we know
and assimilate it remain dark and indistinct too? Or does not this
form offer a new and most insistent mode of understanding the
content of the sensible world? Such is the question with which
Baumgarten begins his aesthetics, and which he unreservedly
answers in the affirmative. He erects a new standard of sensibility whose function is not to destroy but to preserve the value
of this mode of experience. He attributes new perfection to
sensibility; but this perfection bears with it the condition that
it be understood as an immanent advantage, as a "phenomenal
perfection" (*perfectio phaenomenon*). Such perfection, however, in no sense corresponds to that perfection for which logic
and mathematics strive in the development of their "distinct
concepts." It asserts itself side by side with the perfection of
logic and remains an irreducible and independent element. It
still costs Baumgarten considerable pains to establish this coordi-
nation; and in the expression of his thought, in the terminology
which he does not create but adopts largely from the schools,
he relapses again and again into the language of subordination
and mere subsumption. This terminology forces him to set up
a definite scale, an arrangement according to rank and value;
and on this scale aesthetics, as the knowledge of the sensible
world, is assigned to the lowest place. It stands at the beginning,
but the beginning seems to be a mere preliminary: "Only
through the morning gates of the beautiful didst thou enter the
land of truth."[55] But it would seem that this dawn of the beautiful will and must sometime pale before the full splendor of the
day. In the face of the strict and pure truth which is no longer
confined to appearances of things, but gives us their deepest
being, beauty, which exists only as a property of appearances,
must fade away. The metaphysician Baumgarten never completely abandoned this fundamental view; but as an analyst, as
a pure phenomenologist, he goes beyond it. This casting off of
traditional logical and metaphysical fetters was the historical
and systematic condition which permitted aesthetics to find its

[55] "Nur durch das Morgentor des Schönen
Drangst du in der Erkenntnis Land."—Schiller, "Die Künstler."

place in the sun and to constitute itself as a philosophical discipline in its own right.[56]

Leibniz's doctrine of the degrees of knowledge, as developed in his *Meditations on Truth, Cognition, and Ideas*, forms the point of departure and framework for all of Baumgarten's inquiries. But it is not sufficient to recall the words of this doctrine if one wishes to do justice to Baumgarten's intention. Leibniz distinguishes between a clear and a distinct idea, and he assigns a special meaning and purpose to each. That idea is "clear" which suffices and is suitable for the needs of daily life, which enables us to orient ourselves to our sense environment. For this orientation all that is necessary is that we distinguish carefully among the various objects we encounter and that we pattern our behavior toward these objects after our distinctions. Whoever sees in gold merely an object for use is satisfied if he can tell genuine gold from impure or false gold. In its color, its hardness, its malleability, etc., in all these purely empirical specifications, he can find enough criteria to protect him against confusing true with false gold. But such truth, according to Leibniz, is still not the real, complete truth for which scientific knowledge strives and which it must demand. For the highest knowledge is not "that" something is, but "why" it is. Science does not want to collect mere facts, nor is it satisfied to distinguish objects by their sensory properties and to classify them according to these distinctions. Science endeavors to proceed from the variety of attributes to the unity of substance; and it can only discover this substance by going back to the ultimate ground of this plurality and variety. Hence the law of sufficient reason, along with the law of identity and contradiction, be-

[56] Lotze's statement, which is often quoted and not infrequently accepted uncritically, "that German aesthetics began with a definite disregard for its object" (*Geschichte der Ästhetik in Deutschland*, p. 12), misses the main point of Baumgarten's doctrine. In his very first publication, *Philosophical Meditations on Matters Pertaining to Poetry* (Halle, 1735), Baumgarten assails the prejudice that preoccupation with questions of art is unworthy of the philosopher: "Now, however . . . I have chosen this material which will be regarded by many as thin and far removed from the keen thought of philosophers; for to me it seems important enough. So that, indeed, for this very reason I would think of philosophy and knowledge of poetic composition as often joined together in most compatible wedlock [up to section 11]; in working out the idea of poetry and its allied fields I am constrained, etc. . . . ."

comes the real norm of all exact science. To understand things is not to grasp them as phenomena *a posteriori* but to comprehend them *a priori* in terms of their causes. Knowledge *a priori* and knowledge based on a determination of the foundation of things mean the same thing for Leibniz; the causal definition is the only satisfactory type of definition. The procedure of "distinct knowledge" can then be no other than that of resolving every complex phenomenon into the various elements which determine and condition it. So long as this resolution has not been finished, so long as any unanalyzed complex remains in any of these elements, the real goal of "adequate" comprehension has not been attained. Our concept is commensurable with its object only when it succeeds not merely in reflecting this object but in causing it to develop before us, in tracing it back to its original elements and in reconstructing it from them.

Baumgarten recognized this ideal in its full scope and he never questioned it within the realm of scientific knowledge. He holds fast to Leibniz's demand for a "thought alphabet," especially since meanwhile this ideal had progressed considerably owing to the steadfast pioneering led by Wolff and his school and seemed decidedly nearer realization. Yet there is, according to Baumgarten, a field of knowledge where the reduction of phenomena to their basic substance is subject to a limitation. If, in accordance with the method of exact science, we explain the phenomenon of color by resolving it into a pure process of motion, then we have not only destroyed its sense impression but we have also robbed it of its aesthetic significance. The reduction of color to its physical concept annihilates, as it were with one blow, its whole significance as an artistic means of expression, its whole function in the art of painting. With the loss of this concept all recollection of the sense experience of color and all evidence of its aesthetic function vanish likewise. But is this function really meaningless and absolutely indifferent? Or does it not possess its specific value; is it not justified in refusing to be pushed aside and in demanding recognition for what it really is? The new science of aesthetics strives for such recognition. It abandons itself to sensory appearance without attempting to go beyond it to something entirely different, to the grounds of all appearance. For such a step forward would not explain the aesthetic content of appearance, but destroy it. If somebody attempted to communicate his impression of a landscape by dividing its appearance into its various components and by finding for each component a clear concept by describing the landscape in geological language, he would have gained new scientific insight, but in this insight not the slightest trace of the beauty of the landscape would be preserved. This beauty can be perceived only by undivided observation, by pure contemplation of the landscape as a whole. Only the artist, the painter or the poet can reflect this totality and put life into every feature of his representation. A perfect painting or poetic description of a landscape conjures up its pure image, and the spectacle and enjoyment of this image causes us to forget all scientific questions regarding its basic substance. We must yield to the pure effect of the phenomenon as such, or else it will slip from our hands. The effects of appearance do not, to be sure, constitute its metaphysical nature, but they include its purely aesthetic aspect.[57] The observation of an object under the microscope may reveal to the naturalist its composition and thereby its real objective nature, but its aesthetic impression becomes a total loss. Goethe gave poetic expression to this thought in a poem of his *Leipzig Song Book*:

> Fluttering the fountain nigh
> The iridescent dragonfly
> An hour mine eye has dwelt upon;
> Now dark, now light alternately
> Like the chameleon;
> Now red, now blue,
> Now blue, now green:
> How would its hues appear
> If one could but come near!

[57] Cf., for instance, Baumgarten, *Aesthetica*, § 588: "Nor is it ordinarily the function of the analogue of reason to examine too deeply into the first causes of the universe, its elements, and primal energies, so long as this analogue inheres in the actual phenomena" (*Nec est analogi rationis ordinario primas universi causas, elementa et stamina prima penitius examinare, dum haeret in effectis phaenomenis*).

It flits and hovers, resting not—
Hush! on a willow bough it lights;
I have it in my fingers caught,
And now I seek its colors true,
And find a melancholy blue—

Such is thy lot, dissector of delights![58]

Here Goethe has transformed the essential content of his
own philosophy, which is in complete agreement with what
Baumgarten as an aesthetic theorist teaches, into a pure image
and given it concrete expression. We are now entering a region
where the law of sufficient reason, that principle and condition
of all "distinct" knowledge, has no jurisdiction. This law is the
thread of Ariadne put into our hands to lead us out of the labyrinth of phenomenal reality and to guide us to the intelligible
world, to the realm of noumena. But no such transcendence
takes place in art, nor could it take place in this sphere. Art has
no desire to go beyond appearance, but only to remain in its
midst; art does not want to go back to the beginnings of appearance, but to grasp its immediate content and to represent the
specific nature of this content. And we need not fear lest the
renunciation of this guiding thread in the form of the law of
sufficient reason will plunge our intellectual world back into
chaos. For not even purely intuitional reality is complete confusion, it possesses its peculiar standard within itself. Every
genuine work of art presents us with such a standard; it not
only displays a wealth of observations but it masters this wealth;

[58] Es flattert um die Quelle
Die wechselnde Libelle,
Mich freut sie lange schon;
Bald dunkel und bald helle,
Wie der Chamaeleon:
Bald rot, bald blau,
Bald blau, bald grün;
O dass ich in der Nähe
Doch ihre Farben sähe!

Sie schwirrt und schwebet, rastet nie!
Doch still, sie setzt sich an die Weiden.
Da hab' ich sie! Da hab' ich sie!
Und nun betracht' ich sie genau
Und seh' ein traurig dunkles Blau—

So geht es dir, Zergliedrer deiner Freuden!

it molds it and causes its inner unity to appear in the form which results. All genuinely aesthetic intuition exhibits variety and diversity, but these qualities in turn show a certain order and rule. If the realm of aesthetics can be characterized by the expression "confused perception," this can only be done on the condition that we understand this expression in its strictly etymological sense. This would mean that in all aesthetic intuition a confluence, a fusing together, of elements takes place, and that we cannot isolate the individual elements from the totality of the intuition. But such a confluence creates no disorder; for this complex presents itself to direct perception as a definite and harmonious whole. According to the fundamental thesis of Baumgarten's aesthetics, no such organization is attainable solely by means of concepts. It must be attributed to that preconceptual sphere which pure logic as such need not know or take into account since from the logical standpoint such organization is looked upon as belonging to the inferior powers of the soul and of knowledge. Yet these "inferior" cognitive forces also have their rational principle, and for them too a special epistemology, an "inferior knowledge" (*gnoseologia inferior*), is requisite. Baumgarten remains completely subservient to the strict rule of reason; he permits no exception, for he does not want to see the slightest relaxation of the rigor of the pure logical norms. However, he defends the cause of pure aesthetic intuition before the tribunal of reason itself. He seeks to rescue intuition by showing that it too is ruled by an inner law. Even though this law does not coincide with the law of reason, it constitutes an analogue of reason.[59] This analogue indicates that the sphere of the law of aesthetic intuition is not synonymous with that of the logical concept, but much more comprehensive, and that there is a law which is above all willfulness and which excludes all subjective whims. This law cannot be expressed in the form of mere concepts. Reason as a whole embraces both the aesthetic law and the logical concept. It does not confine itself to the merely conceptual but is concerned with order and law in general, no matter in what medium it finds its representa-

[59] Baumgarten calls aesthetics the "art of the analogue of reason" (*ars analogi rationis*) at the very beginning of his work on the subject. Cf. Prolegomena, § 1.

tion and embodiment.[60] Reason remains queen of this realm as a whole; but her rule never becomes harsh and she never resorts to external coercion. It was Baumgarten who made the pregnant and happy statement that dominion over all inferior powers belongs to reason but that this rule must never degenerate into tyranny.[61] The subject shall not be deprived of its own nature, nor shall it renounce its peculiar character; it is rather to be understood and protected in both these aspects. The legitimation of the inferior powers of the soul, not their suppression and extinction, is the aim of Baumgarten's aesthetics.[62]

All the elements of Baumgarten's doctrine are included in this beginning; all the peculiarities of the work of art which he indicates, especially all aspects of the poetic mode of presentation and of the poetic means of expression, can be developed from his beginning. With his penchant for thoroughness and completeness Baumgarten loves to amass terms for those qualities in which the difference between the poetical and the logical presentation is expressed. Of the former he requires light and clarity, abundance and truthfulness, wealth of content and lucidity; he insists that all ideas used by the poet should contain inner significance, persuasive power, and vivacity. But all these specifications of abundance (*ubertas*) and magnitude (*magnitudo*), truth (*veritas*) and clarity (*claritas*), and light (*lux*) and certainty (*certitudo*) can be reduced to one requirement, for which Baumgarten chose the characteristic expression: "life of knowledge" (*vita cognitionis*). He has no intention of separating poetry from the source of thought, as appears when he defines aesthetics at the very outset as the art of thinking beautifully (*ars pulcre cogitandi*).[63] But he demands of poetic thought

[60] Cf. *Aesthetica*, § 18: "The beauty of sensory cognition will be the universal agreement of the thoughts as long as we abstract from their order and signs down to the last one, which is the phenomenon" (Pulcritudo cognitionis sensitivae erit universalis consensus cogitationum, quatenus adhuc ab earum ordine et signis abstrahimus, inter se ad unum, qui phaenomenon sit).

[61] *Ibid.*: "Rule over the lower faculties is required, but not tyranny" (Imperium in facultates inferiores poscitur, non tyrannis), § 12.

[62] This fundamental tendency of the new science appears especially in Georg Friedrich Meier's work entitled *Anfangsgründe aller schönen Wissenschaften*, Part I, Halle, 1748, pp. 5, 13, 16 ff.

[63] *Aesthetica*, §1: "Aesthetics (the theory of the liberal arts, inferior knowledge, the art of thinking beautifully, the art of the analogue of reason) is the

that it convey not only form but color; not only objective truth but sensitive force; and not only correct but vital insight. Such insight requires that we proceed not simply, according to the rules of the formation of logical concepts, from the particular to the general, but that we apprehend the general in the particular and the particular in the general. Abstraction, which shows us the way to the higher classes of things, always means impoverishment and depletion so far as direct perception is concerned. The process of abstraction is also a process of subtraction. Generality is attained only by disregarding particularity. Hence generality is attainable here only at the expense of definiteness; generality and definiteness lie in opposite directions.[64] Aesthetics bridges this chasm; for its "truth" cannot be found beyond or in opposition to concrete qualities, but it can be realized only amid and by virtue of such qualities. Beauty requires not only intensive clarity, as do scientific concepts; it possesses also extensive clarity. Intensive clarity is achieved when we succeed in condensing the manifold of perception to a few fundamental definitions in which the essential nature of this manifold is recognizable. Aesthetic extensive clarity, however, does not tolerate any such conceptual reduction and concentration. For the artist seeks to portray the full scope of intuitively perceived reality; he seeks to encompass both center and periphery in a single glance.[65] According to Baumgarten, the artistic genius must possess not only great sensory receptivity and imaginative power but also a "natural disposition to perspicacity" (*dispositio naturalis ad perspicaciam*).[66] But artistic acumen differs from the analytical penetration of the scientific thinker in that it does not look away from the phenomena, but dwells upon them; in that it does not seek the causes of appearance, but appearance itself. The artist endeavors to comprehend

---

science of sensory cognition" [Aesthetica (theoria liberalium artium, gnoseologia inferior, ars pulcre cogitandi, ars analogi rationis) est scientia cognitionis sensitivae].

[64] For the difference between Baumgarten's "individualizing concept formation" and Wolff's "abstracting concept formation" see Baeumler, *op.cit.*, pp. 198 ff.

[65] For the distinction between "intensive" and "extensive" clarity see especially Baumgarten: *Meditationes de nonnullis ad poema pertinentibus*, § 13 ff.

[66] *Aesthetica*, § 32.

phenomena in their totality and in their purely immanent mode of existence and to fuse them into one lucid picture.

Baumgarten was able to describe this contrast between the artistic and scientific mind and to express it for the first time in a strictly philosophical formula because he could base his description on vital personal experience. In his *Development of Modern Aesthetics*, H. von Stein has shown how false and misleading is the view that Baumgarten discovered and founded systematic aesthetics as a result of an exclusively epistemological interest and of a sort of logical pedantry. Baumgarten approaches aesthetics from immediate experience of works of literature, and he tried his own hand at poetic composition. In the preface to his *Meditations on Poetry* he declares that he had let scarcely a day go by without composing a poem. Slight as was his real poetic talent, he at least learned from this preoccupation what a poetic theme is and how it differs from a merely scientific theme. He needed only to consider his own activity in order to observe this difference directly. It is a step of equal importance for the philosophy of language and for aesthetics that, in order to formulate this difference, Baumgarten went back primarily to the form and special character of the language of poetry. Language is the common medium of scientific and artistic representation. The thoughts which the logician and the scientist develop, like the sensations and ideas which the poet seeks to stimulate in us, stand in equal need of the instrumentality of the word. But in the two cases the same means serves an entirely different end. In the scientific treatment of a topic the word functions simply as a symbol for a concept; its whole content lies in its abstract significance. Words are used here simply as "counters" of the mind, as Hobbes expressed it; and in the highest development of scientific language we find that every trace of concrete content which still inevitably clung to the word has been eliminated. We are no longer in the realm of words but in that of symbols; and we attempt to give unambiguous expression to every operation of thought in terms of these symbols. "General science" (*scientia generalis*), as Leibniz had repeatedly emphasized, is complete only with the development of a "general characteristic" (*characteristica gene-*

ralis). But that which for science constitutes the highest stage of development would, if applied to art, amount to a death penalty; it would deprive art of all phenomenal content. The new science of aesthetics seeks to prevent such impoverishment; it does not strive for the perfection of knowledge in general but for the perfection of sensory, of intuitively experienced, knowledge. "The goal of aesthetics is the perfection of sensory cognition as such. And this is beauty" (*Aesthetices finis est perfectio cognitionis sensitivae, qua talia. Haec autem est pulcritudo*).[67] The power and greatness of the artist, of the true poet, consists in his ability to endow the "cold symbols" of the language of daily life and of the language of science with the breath of life, with the "life of knowledge" (*vita cognitionis*). No word used by the artist remains dead or empty; it is inwardly alive and saturated with immediate sensory content. Everything of the nature of an abstract formula vanishes from the language of poetry; it is supplanted by metaphorical expression. Thus Baumgarten still subsumes the poem under the general concept of language, but this does not mean that he forsakes his fundamental aesthetic idea; he is not misled by the spell of mere rhetoric. His more exact definition of language immediately precludes such a danger. "The perfect language of sense is poetry" (*Oratio sensitiva perfecta est poema*).[68] Only that language which possesses the power of perfect sense expression, which conjures up before us and crystallizes a vivid intuition, can be called a poem.

In such terms Baumgarten has characterized in strictly systematic form a problem which had constantly occupied the attention of eighteenth century aestheticians. Since the time of Dubos and the Swiss critics, aesthetic theory had consistently stressed the intuitive character of everything genuinely poetic. But it was able to give definite form to this view only by appealing to the art of painting for aid. This is the reason for the widespread currency of the slogan "A poem is like a picture" (*ut pictura poesis*) before the publication of Lessing's *Laokoon*. Bodmer writes his critical reflections on the "poetic paintings" of poets,

[67] *Aesthetica*, § 14.
[68] *Meditationes de nonnullis ad poema pertinentibus*, § 9.

and Breitinger's *Critical Poetics* expressly sets out "to investigate thoroughly poetic painting with regard to the function of invention" and to illustrate his investigation with examples from the ancients and the moderns. But a new question now arises. Is it really possible for the poet to compete with the painter and to give us the same thing with his "artificial symbols" that the painter represents with his "natural symbols"? Or does not any such competition amount to an arbitrary confusion of the arts and to a repudiation of the specifically poetic instrument of style? Baumgarten anticipated such confusion by recognizing the demand for pictorial expression as the fallacy of mistaking a part for the whole. This requirement is not philosophical and systematic, but metaphorical. Instead of the true general concept of sensory cognition it posits only one form of such cognition, namely, pictorial description. The poet cannot and should not paint in words; he can and should employ words to awake in his auditors clear and vivid sensuous ideas. Such is his fundamental gift, the gift of the "capacity to please" (*ingenium venustum*), as Baumgarten puts it. From the standpoint of intellectual history this reads like a prophecy; four decades before the *Critique of Judgment* and before Karl Philipp Moritz's work *On the Plastic Imitation of the Beautiful*[69] it suggests Goethe's objective thinking. The "capacity to please" attempts not only to understand objects according to genus and species but it thrives on the contemplation of objects. It possesses that "beautiful plenitude" (*venusta plenitudo*) which can never result from a mere combination, and which cannot be resolved into separate components. This kind of "disposition" (*ingenium*) expresses rather a spiritual attitude which imparts its own hue to everything it grasps and assimilates. It is this attitude of the mind as a whole which characterizes the artistic spirit as such and gives it that character which cannot be acquired or learned, but with which the artist is born. "For the general character of the successful aesthetician a connate natural aesthetics (nature, good constitution) is required, that is, a natural disposition of

---

[69] *Über die bildende Nachahmung des Schönen* (1788).

the whole soul to beautiful thinking, with which the soul is born."[70]

Again Baumgarten's aesthetics goes beyond the sphere of mere logic. It seeks to be a logic of the "lower cognitive forces"; by means of this logic it strives, however, to serve not only the system of philosophy, but above all the doctrine of man. It is no accident that Herder follows Baumgarten and calls him the "real Aristotle of our time."[71] For he found in Baumgarten's works that new ideal of humanity to which all his writings are devoted. At the very beginning of Baumgarten's *Aesthetics* we encounter this new humanistic imperative which he offers to philosophy as a doctrine of wisdom. "The philosopher is a man among men; nor does he rightly think so great a part of human knowledge alien to himself."[72] The development of particular talents, especially the talent of the analysis of concepts, may be becoming to the scholar and laudable in the specialist; but the task of philosophy can never be realized in this way. This task requires that no field of knowledge lie fallow and that no gift of the mind go unnourished. The philosophical mind must not think itself above the gifts of intuition and imagination; it must be fully endowed with these gifts, and it must balance them with the gift of judgment and inference. The comprehensiveness and inner unity of the philosophic system can only arise from such harmony, and only from it can the highest individual embodiment of the philosophical spirit develop. The highest and purest development of this spirit is not attainable by the mere cultivation of the powers of the understanding.[73] The philosopher is and remains akin to the artist in a fundamental feature of his thinking, in his striving for totality;[74] and, if he cannot

[70] *Aesthetica*, § 28: "Ad characteram felicis aesthetici generalem requiritur Aesthetica naturalis connata (φύσις, natura, εὐφυΐα), dispositio naturalis animae totius ad pulcre cogitandum, quacum nascitur."

[71] Herder, "Fragment über die Ode," *Werke*, ed. Suphan, vol. XXXII, p. 83. Cf. especially "Von Baumgartens Denkart in seinen Schriften," *Werke*, XXXII, 178 ff. and "Entwurf zu einer Denkschrift auf A. G. Baumgarten, J. D. Heilmann und Th. Abbt," *Werke*, XXXII, 175 ff.

[72] *Aesthetica*, § 6.

[73] Cf. especially *Aesthetica*, § 41 ff.

[74] Cf. Baumgarten's characteristic remark in his *Meditations on Poetry* (*Meditationes de nonnullis ad poema pertinentibus*), § XIV: "If anyone . . . excels in both branches of the cognitive faculty and has learned to set each in its proper

compete with the artist in the creation of the beautiful, yet he can seek a knowledge of the beautiful and by this knowledge, by means of systematic aesthetics, he can bring to completion his own world picture. The new discipline of aesthetics is thus not only logically validated, but so to speak ethically postulated and justified. For the "beautiful sciences" now form no longer simply a relatively independent province of knowledge; they "activate the whole man" and are indispensable to man's realization of his true destiny.[75]

The problem of the beautiful thus leads not only to the foundation of systematic aesthetics but to the foundation of a new "philosophical anthropology," and an idea which is characteristic of the entire culture of the eighteenth century gains credence and confirmation. We now see from a new angle that a radical transformation of previous standards is beginning to take place in eighteenth century thought. A change becomes increasingly apparent in the relation between human and divine understanding, between "ectypal mind" (*intellectus ectypus*) and "archetypal mind" (*intellectus archetypus*). It is no longer a matter, as it had been in the great metaphysical systems of the seventeenth century—for instance in Malebranche and Spinoza—of resolving the finite into the infinite and thus, so to speak, of eliminating it. What is required is that the finite assert itself in its own character even in the presence of this highest standard; that it preserve its specific nature even while it recognizes this nature as finite. While the foundation of systematic aesthetics sustains the autonomy of reason, it also maintains implicitly the fundamental prerogative of finite nature to an independent form of existence. For one of the principal points which German school philosophy took over from the teachings of Leibniz is that divine being as such lies beyond the sphere of

---

place, surely in this matter he will make every effort to improve the one without detriment to the other, and he will realize that Aristotle and Leibniz, along with six hundred others who join the pallium with the laurel, were prodigies, not miracles." (Si quis . . . in utraque facultatis cognoscitivae parte excellat et quamlibet suo adhibere loco didiscerit, nae, illi sine alterius detrimento ad alteram exasciandam incumbet, et Aristotelem, Leibnitium cum sexcentis aliis pallium lauro jungentibus fuisse sentiet prodigia, non miracula.)

[75] Cf. G. F. Meier, *Anfangsgründe aller schönen Wissenschaften*, vol. I, §§ 5, 13, 15, 20, and *passim*.

the phenomenon of beauty and is essentially above that sphere. It is of the nature of divine knowledge, according to Leibniz, that it does not move in the realm of sensory ideas but that it is wholly concerned with "adequate" ideas; that is to say, it completely penetrates every complex whole and resolves it into its ultimate constituent elements.[76] The result of such a mode of knowledge can only be the complete extinction of the phenomenon of beauty. "We must not," says Mendelssohn in his *Letters on Sensation*, "confuse the 'heavenly Venus' which consists in perfection, in the perfect adequacy of all concepts, with the 'earthly Venus,' that is, with beauty. From the metaphysical viewpoint, therefore, the idea of the beautiful lies not so much in a faculty of the human soul as in the lack of such a faculty; a more perfect cognitive power would not have access to the experience of the beautiful and thus would not participate in beauty."[77] Mendelssohn can refer to Baumgarten for this sharp contrast between sensuous beauty and purely intellectual perfection, but for the latter this contrast serves another intellectual tendency and exhibits a different emphasis. For in marking off the limits of the beautiful, Baumgarten seeks to keep man, nevertheless, within these limits. Man should not transcend the finite, but explore it in all directions. In so far as, in so doing, he falls short of the ideal of divine, adequate knowledge, he realizes by this very deficiency his own nature and destiny. Thus, in the severe discipline of German school philosophy the same thought emerges which we have already found operative in the philosophy of morals and religion, and of law and politics, in the age of the Enlightenment. The Enlightenment gradually learned to do without the "absolute" in the strictly metaphysical sense, without the ideal of "God-like knowledge." Instead appears a purely human ideal which the age seeks to define and to realize with increasing precision and rigor.

With the "humanization" of sensibility a further question which had constantly excited discussion in the eighteenth century found a solution. The philosophy of the eighteenth century

[76] Cf. Leibniz, *Meditationes de cognitione, veritate et ideis, Philosophische Schriften*, ed. *Gerhardt*, vol. IV, p. 423.

[77] Mendelssohn, *Briefe über die Empfindungen* (1755), fifth letter.

maintains not only the place of the imagination in human knowledge, but of the senses and the passions as well. The Cartesian doctrine, according to which the passions are supposed to be nothing but "perturbations of the soul" (*perturbationes animi*), is gradually supplanted; the passions now become the vital impulses, the real motivating forces which stimulate the mind as a whole and keep it in operation.[78] From all sides, especially in French psychology and ethics, the cry for the emancipation of sensibility is raised and grows louder and louder. The Stoicism of the seventeenth century, which had not remained simply a philosophical doctrine but had exerted an influence on classical tragedy, is now challenged by a purely Epicurean attitude. Epicureanism now assumes the most varied forms and nuances. It can advocate, as, for instance, in Lamettrie's *The Art of Enjoyment*, plain sense pleasure, or it can constitute a subtle technique of intellectual refinement and sublimation of the joys of existence. The "libertines" of the seventeenth century, who met in the "Temple" or in the salons of Ninon de l'Enclos in Paris and of Madame de Mazarin in London, tried to carry this art to perfection, and in St. Évremond it found its finest and most important representative.[79] A whole series of treatises published by this circle profess to be the work of a real school of the art of enjoyment, and even in a theoretical sense attempt to make pleasure accessible and to teach ways and means of constantly intensifying and thoroughly exploiting the possibilities of enjoyment.[80] The refinement of pleasure taught by these works is without doubt aesthetically significant, but the aesthetics which developed on this basis remains an aesthetics of the stimulus-reaction situation. It sharpens to the utmost receptivity and impressionability for

[78] See above pp. 105 ff.

[79] For details concerning this circle of libertines, see Mornet, *La pensée française au XVIIIe siècle*, Paris, 1929, p. 28.

[80] Cf. Saint Évremond, *Oeuvres meslées*, Amsterdam, 1706; Rémond le Grec, *Agathon ou Dialogue de la volupté* (1702), printed in *Recueil de divers écrits*, published by Saint-Hyacinthe; Baudot de Juilly, *Dialogue entre M. M. Patru et d'Ablancourt sur les plaisirs* (1700). A penetrating analysis of these writings is contained in G. Lanson's essay: "Le rôle de l'expérience dans la formation de la philosophie du XVIIIe siècle en France," *Études d'histoire littéraire*, Paris, 1930, pp. 164 ff.

sense stimuli, but it lacks any relationship with the real source of the artistic and spontaneous. Baumgarten's aesthetics overcomes precisely this deficiency. Baumgarten too upholds the validity of sensibility; he does not, however, merely seek to release sensibility from all restraint but rather to lead it to its spiritual perfection. This perfection cannot lie in enjoyment but only in beauty. Beauty is pleasure, but this pleasure is specifically different from that other kind which is derived from mere sense impulses. It is not swayed by the power of mere desire but by a longing for pure contemplation and pure knowledge. Thus only through the pleasure which beauty affords do we experience the inner vitality and the pure spontaneity which also dwells in the sensuous, in other words, the "life of sensory cognition" (*vita cognitionis sensitivae*). As Baumgarten's aesthetics has already reminded us of Herder's humanism, so now we are reminded of Schiller's *Letters on Aesthetic Education*. Baumgarten was one of the first thinkers to overcome the antagonism between "sensationalism" and "rationalism" and to achieve a new productive synthesis of "reason" and "sensibility."

But Baumgarten himself did not indeed fully realize the ideal goal that he set for himself; he did not follow to the end the path which he saw clearly marked out before him. At the beginning of his aesthetic system he states that his work seeks merely to clear the road for the new science, but that he does not intend to complete the systematic development of this science.[81] Moreover, he was from the first handicapped in this enterprise by certain subjective limitations, for his work was written in the style of school philosophy. Hence the new conception which Baumgarten advocates does not find adequate expression; it must submit to being laced up in the Spanish boots of formal paragraphs until this confinement sometimes seems to rob it of all its flexibility. Those who know how to read Baumgarten correctly will of course discover, even beneath this thick shell, the pure kernel of his thought and an original mode of expression. In one of his so-called "school speeches" Herder discussed the subject of the "concept of grace in the schools";

[81] Cf. *Aesthetica*, § 5.

and, in order to illustrate the idea of grace, he referred especially to Baumgarten. It was grace which produced the aesthetics of its favorite, the immortal Baumgarten, "in his subtle simplicity and full of the charming little points that escape ordinary eyes and to the completely uninitiated appear as blemishes."[82] Baumgarten influenced only a narrow circle and his effect on German creative literature is almost negligible. Lessing first broke the spell. He was destined to synthesize thought and action, theory and practice, and so to realize fully Baumgarten's requirement of the life of sensory cognition. All that Baumgarten considers as belonging to the character of the genuine aesthetician (*ad characterem felicis aesthetici pertinens*) is illustrated in Lessing's mind. In this one individual are embodied all the elements of richness, magnitude, truth, clarity, assurance, abundance, and nobility which Baumgarten demanded of the aesthetician; in him too are most happily wedded the "disposition to feel acutely" (*dispositio acute sentiendi*) with a "natural disposition to imagine" (*dispositio naturalis ad imaginandum*), with a "disposition to uncommon, nay, delicate taste" (*dispositio ad saporem non publicum, immo delicatum*), and the "natural disposition to perspicacity" (*dispositio naturalis ad perspicaciam*). It is this union of characteristics which constitutes the incomparable originality of Lessing's work, and which assured its place in the history of thought. If one considers merely the content of the various aesthetic concepts in Lessing's work, one does not find a sufficient explanation for the recognition accorded him. For he did not create this content but found it almost entirely ready at hand. There is scarcely a single aesthetic concept and scarcely a single principle in Lessing which did not have its exact parallel in contemporary literature, which could not have been documented in the writings of Baumgarten, the Swiss critics, Shaftesbury, Dubos, or Diderot. But it is a complete mistake to seek to raise objections to the originality of Lessing's basic thoughts on the grounds of any such documentation of his sources. Lessing's originality does not manifest itself in the invention of new ideas, but in the order and connection, in the logical arrangement and selection, which he accomplished

[82] Herder, *Werke*, XXX, 32 f.

with the materials already available. In these respects Lessing is primarily a logician, but his mode of arrangement and selection, his criticism and systematization, are to be sure far more than the mere execution of an operation in formal logic. For his interest is never exclusively, or even primarily, concerned with the logical relations of concepts as such; he possesses a gift for penetrating to the heart of every concept and for understanding and interpreting it in this perspective. This is what he accomplished with all the major concepts of contemporary aesthetics. In his treatment these concepts lose every trace of abstraction, and they are filled to saturation with a definite, concretely experienced content. By virtue of this content they are able to participate directly in the artistic process of creation and to influence this process. The decisive aspect of Lessing's achievement does not lie in the matter of his concepts themselves, but in their form, not in what they are in the sense of a logical definition, but in their intellectual transformation. In the melting pot of his mind this metamorphosis and metempsychosis goes on and on. Lessing disclaimed the title of poet in the highest and most rigid sense of the word because he was aware that he did not possess that elemental creative magic by which the poet not only invents or conceives his forms but by means of which he endows them with "a local habitation and a name." He knew that he did not command the creative power he saw in the highest epic and dramatic performances, in Homer and Shakespeare. But if Lessing did not possess the profound genius of the great poet, he had in its stead a power of thought such as scarcely ever existed either before or after his time. Every concept that enters the magic circle of his thinking begins at once to undergo a transformation. Instead of remaining mere end products, they again become original creative forces and directly moving impulses. We no longer perceive them as ready-made forms, as a sum total of definitely specifiable properties; we see them develop and, in the character of this process, in the mode of their application and in the remote and still unknown goal toward which they move, we recognize their real value and meaning. Lessing's doctrines of the relation between genius and rule, of the limits of painting and poetry, of "mixed sensations," of the significance of symbols for the classification of the arts, can as abstract doctrines all be paralleled point by point in the basic works on aesthetics in the eighteenth century. But it is only in him that mere doctrine really comes to life again, that its energy is implanted into and assimilated by the life of art. Lessing's criticism not only seeks to be productive, to foster and inspire artistic creation by acting as an external influence, it is also an immanent factor of the creative process. It is called "productive" criticism because it participates in the process of production and exists through this process. Lessing thus leads the aesthetics of the Enlightenment beyond its previous goals and frontiers, even though he seems merely to inherit its intellectual possessions. He alone was able to accomplish what Gottsched and the Swiss critics, Voltaire and Diderot, and Shaftesbury and his followers, could not achieve. He not only brings the aesthetic thought of an epoch to its climax but, reaching beyond all given realities of art, he discovers new possibilities for poetry. His chief merit in German literature lies in the fact that he saw the place for these possibilities and cleared the way for them. This merit is vastly underestimated and deprived of its real meaning in intellectual history if, as was again the case in a recent account of Lessing's aesthetic theory,[83] one finds in his criticism only a national, not a European achievement. The relation between Lessing's general concepts and the specific state and the problems of German literature in the eighteenth century is undeniable; but as a result of this relation Lessing discovered a new horizon of artistic creation in general. Goethe said of Herder that his significance as a historian and philosopher of history consists in the fact that he concentrates with all his might on the factual, the unique, and the particular without succumbing to the sheer material power of the factual, to mere "matter of fact." He commends as Herder's fundamental ability his gift to "transform the rubbish of history into a living plant."[84] The same thing can be said of Lessing and of the originality of his critical and aesthetic achievement. He

[83] Cf. Folkierski, *Entre le Classicisme et le Romanticisme*, p. 578: "The merit of Lessing is national, and not European."

[84] Goethe's letter to Herder, May 1775.

possesses the same capacity with respect to concepts and theorems that Herder has with respect to the world of historical reality. Whenever he approaches aesthetic ideas, whether to criticize, to arrange, to sift, or simply to report them, he breathes new life into this logical process and the ideas undergo a characteristic regeneration. Lessing does not seek novelty; he never strives for originality for its own sake. Instead he firmly upholds tradition, which he knows by heart, and which he loves to pursue along its most dark and difficult pathways. But here too he prefers the process of acquisition to possession. And for this reason he possesses a creative power unrivaled in his epoch —which does not spring from any opposition to the prevailing order but which feels within itself the power and the impulse to transform things so that they will not become entrenched in rigidity. Lessing delivered the concepts and doctrines of eighteenth century aesthetics from the peril of such rigidity, a service for which the younger generation was especially grateful to him. In *Poetry and Truth* Goethe depicts the effect of Lessing's *Laocoon* thus: he found himself transported by the majesty of Lessing's "principal and fundamental concepts" from the "region of servile observation to the open spaces of thought." Lessing not only possessed this magic power in the sphere of poetry, but in the whole realm of eighteenth century philosophy. It is above all because of him that the century of the Enlightenment, to a very great extent dominated by its gift of criticism, did not fall prey to the merely negative critical function—that it was able to reconvert criticism to creative activity and shape it and use it as an indispensable instrument of life and of the constant renewal of the spirit.

INDEX

Index

Index

Index

Index

Index

BEACON PAPERBACKS